Latest Research in Bioinformatics

Volume II

Latest Research in Bioinformatics Volume II

Edited by **Christina Marshall**

New York

Published by Callisto Reference,
106 Park Avenue, Suite 200,
New York, NY 10016, USA
www.callistoreference.com

Latest Research in Bioinformatics: Volume II
Edited by Christina Marshall

International Standard Book Number: 978-1-63239-446-0 (Hardback)

Printed in the United States of America.

Contents

Preface

In order to study the impactful alterations in cellular functions in different diseases, the advanced data collected must be processed to give a comprehensive understanding of the pictures obtained. It should be collaborated in such a manner that it can be later re-used for further research or comparisons. The primary function of bioinformatics is to develop software tools to produce advanced biological results. Advanced researches in the field of biology raised a considerable amount of data to be stored categorically and arranged in a certain fashion so as to be helpful in further derivations. Thus, came into existence the science of bioinformatics.

The current scenario of science is transforming it from being an exclusively laboratory based science to a more informational field of study. This transformation will revolutionize the science of biology. One of the major steps in this drastic reformation will be to train a new generation of scientists who are well-versed with both computational science and the mainstream laboratory practices. The future of biology will only prefer computational biologists. Thus, bioinformatics plays a vital role in today's world of biology.

This book provides an overview of the most important aspects of bioinformatics along with their evolution and application. We hope that this book facilitates the fruitful development of science. I would like to thank all the people associated with this book at every stage. This book would not have been accomplished without your rigorous efforts.

Editor

Producing High-Accuracy Lattice Models from Protein Atomic Coordinates Including Side Chains

Martin Mann,[1,2] **Rhodri Saunders,**[3] **Cameron Smith,**[1]
Rolf Backofen,[1] **and Charlotte M. Deane**[3]

[1] *Bioinformatics, University of Freiburg, Georges-Köhler Allee 106, 79110 Freiburg im Breisgau, Germany*
[2] *Theoretical Biochemistry, University of Vienna, Währingerstraße 17, 1090 Vienna, Austria*
[3] *Department of Statistics, Oxford University, 1 South Parks Road, Oxford OX1 3TG, UK*

Correspondence should be addressed to Charlotte M. Deane, deane@stats.ox.ac.uk

Academic Editor: Shandar Ahmad

Lattice models are a common abstraction used in the study of protein structure, folding, and refinement. They are advantageous because the discretisation of space can make extensive protein evaluations computationally feasible. Various approaches to the protein chain lattice fitting problem have been suggested but only a single backbone-only tool is available currently. We introduce `LatFit`, a new tool to produce high-accuracy lattice protein models. It generates both backbone-only and backbone-side-chain models in any user defined lattice. `LatFit` implements a new distance RMSD-optimisation fitting procedure in addition to the known coordinate RMSD method. We tested `LatFit`'s accuracy and speed using a large nonredundant set of high resolution proteins (SCOP database) on three commonly used lattices: 3D cubic, face-centred cubic, and knight's walk. Fitting speed compared favourably to other methods and both backbone-only and backbone-side-chain models show low deviation from the original data (~1.5 Å RMSD in the FCC lattice). To our knowledge this represents the first comprehensive study of lattice quality for on-lattice protein models including side chains while `LatFit` is the only available tool for such models.

1. Introduction

It is not always computationally feasible to undertake protein structure studies using full atom representations. The challenge is to reduce complexity while maintaining detail [1–3]. Lattice protein models are often used to achieve this but in general only the protein backbone or the amino acid centre of mass is represented [4–12]. A huge variety of lattices and energy functions have previously been developed and applied [4, 13, 14].

In order to evaluate the applicability of different lattices and to enable the transformation of real protein structures into lattice models, a representative lattice protein structure has to be calculated. Mañuch and Gaur have shown the NP completeness of this problem for backbone-only models in the 3D-cubic lattice and named it the *protein chain lattice fitting (PCLF) problem* [15].

The PCLF problem has been widely studied for backbone-only models [13, 16–24]. The most important aspects in producing lattice protein models with a low root mean squared deviation (RMSD) are the lattice coordination number and the neighbourhood vector angles [18, 23]. Lattices with intermediate coordination numbers, such as the face-centred cubic (FCC) lattice, can produce high resolution backbone models [18] and have been used in many protein structure studies (e.g., [3, 25, 26]). However, the use of backbone models is limited since they do not account for the space required for side chain packing.

To overcome this restriction lattice protein models that include side chains have been introduced [27–33]. Reva et al. [32] have, to our knowledge, developed the only previous approach to solve the PCLF problem including side chains. They apply dynamic programming to find an optimal solution according to their error function. Unfortunately, the

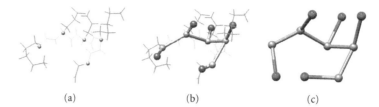

(a)   (b)   (c)

FIGURE 1: The diagram depicts the fitting process of LatFit for side chain models. (a) Original full atom data is given. The five C_α atoms of the segment are highlighted as balls while the backbone and side chain parts are given in light and dark green, respectively. (b) The coordinates for each amino acid to fit are extracted, that is, for side chain models the C_α position (light blue) and the centroid of the side chain (dark blue). (c) These positions are fitted to derive an according lattice protein model in the underlying lattice (here 3D knight's walk lattice).

approach is shown to often yield no solution in the 3D cubic lattice. The CABS tools by Kolinski and coworkers utilize a hybrid on-lattice (backbone) and off-lattice (side chain) protein representation to study folding dynamics but do not attempt to answer the PCLF problem [31, 34].

In this paper we use the side chain model definition of Bromberg and Dill [28], where each amino acid is represented by two on-lattice monomers: one represents the side chain and one the C_α atom. This explicit representation of side chains prevents unnatural collapse during structural studies [35] and enables the reconstruction of full atom protein data [36]. Full on-lattice protein models are constrained in their possible side chain placement but enable exhaustive studies of folding kinetics and structure space [11, 37, 38] not applicable within off-lattice side chain models like the CABS approach.

To the best of our knowledge, there is only one other publicly available implemented approach, namely, LocalMove, to derive lattice protein models from real proteins despite a large number of published methods. LocalMove is a web interface introduced by Ponty et al. [22] for backbone-only models in 3D-cubic and FCC lattice and applies a Monte-Carlo search in order to find lattice protein models.

We present our tool LatFit to tackle this lack of available implementations. The program is freely available for academic download and as a webserver: http://cpsp.informatik.uni-freiburg.de/LatFit/. LatFit solves the PCLF problem, that is, transforms a protein from full atom coordinate data to a lattice model, and is available as both a stand-alone tool for high-throughput pipelines and a web interface for *ad hoc* usage. A new fitting procedure that optimises distance RMSD enables rotation-independent lattice model creation of protein structures. The method is applicable to arbitrary lattices and handles both backbone and side chain representations with equivalent accuracy. A depiction of the workflow is given in Figure 1.

Utilising LatFit we present the first comprehensive study of lattice quality for protein models including side chains. In our test, LatFit fitted the majority of models on an FCC lattice within 1.5 Å RMSD.

2. Material and Methods

In order to enable a precise formulation of the method we introduce some preliminary definitions. A lattice L is a set

of 3D coordinates x defined by a set of neighboring vectors $v \in N$. The neighboring vectors are of equal length ($\forall_{v,v' \in N} : |v| = |v'|$), each with a reverse within the neighborhood ($\forall_{v \in N} : -v \in N$), such that each coordinate in L can be expressed by a linear combination of the neighboring vectors, that is, $L = \{ x \mid x = \sum_{v \in N} d \cdot v \wedge d \in \mathbb{Z}_0^+ \}$. $|N|$ gives the coordinate number of the lattice, for example, 6 for 3D-cubic or 12 for the FCC lattice.

A lattice protein structure with side chains of length l is defined by a sequence of lattice nodes $M^b = (M_1^b, \ldots, M_l^b) \in L^l$ representing the backbone monomers of the protein (one for each amino acid) and the according sequence $M^s = (M_1^s, \ldots, M_l^s) \in L^l$ for the side chain positions. A valid structure ensures backbone connectivity ($\forall_{i<l} : M_i^b - M_{i+1}^b \in N$), side chain connectivity ($\forall_i : M_i^b - M_i^s \in N$), as well as self-avoidance ($\forall_{i \neq j} : M_i^b \neq M_j^b \wedge M_i^s \neq M_j^s$ and $\forall_{i,j} : M_i^b \neq M_j^s$). The two sets together define the lattice protein structure $M = (M^b, M^s)$.

2.1. Fitting Procedure. Given a protein structure of length l in Protein Database (PDB) format [39], LatFit builds up the lattice protein sequentially, one amino acid at a time, starting from the amino terminus.

First, all neighboring vectors $v \in N$ of the used lattice L are scaled to a length of 3.8 Å, which is the mean distance between consecutive C_α atoms and close to the mean distance between a C_α atom and the associated side chain centroid. The latter distance was found to be on average ≈ 3.6 Å within available PDB structures (data not shown). While this ignores the shorter CIS-PRO C_α linkage and the nonexistence of a side chain for Glycine, this scaling enables a reasonable mapping of proteins into the lattice, where each amino acid will be represented by two monomers and all covalent bonds are scaled to $|v| = 3.8$ Å. Therefore, all resulting measures will be directly interpretable in Å units.

The positions for each amino acid i to be fitted, that is, the C_α position of the backbone P_i^b, and the centroid P_i^s (geometric center) of all nonhydrogen atom coordinates of the side chain, are extracted from the PDB file. They form the data to fit $P = (P^b, P^s)$.

The lattice model is derived by one of the following procedures optimising either a distance or coordinate RMSD. Both methods are introduced for lattice proteins including side chains but can be used to derive backbone-only lattice models as well. A sketch of the fitting workflow is given in Figure 1.

2.2. dRMSD Optimisation.

The fitting follows a greedy iterative chain-growth procedure. The initial lattice model's backbone and side chain position (M_1^b and M_1^s) are placed arbitrarily but adjacent ($M_1^b - M_1^s \in N$). For each iteration $1 < i \leq l$, all valid placements of the next M_i^b and M_i^s on the lattice are calculated. A distance RMSD (dRMSD, Eqn. 1) evaluation is used to identify the best n_{keep} structures of length i for the next extension iteration. Since dRMSD is a rotation/reflection-independent measure, symmetric structures must be filtered.

To calculate the final fit of the initial protein P, a superpositioning of the dRMSD-optimised structure M and a reflected version M' is done using the method by Kabsch [40]. The superpositioning translates and rotates M/M' in order to achieve the best mapping onto P. The superpositioning with lowest coordinate RMSD (cRMSD, (2)) is selected and finally returned.

$$\text{dRMSD} = \sqrt{\frac{\sum_{i<j} \left(\left| P_i - P_j \right| - \left| M_i - M_j \right| \right)^2}{l \cdot ((2 \cdot l) - 1)}}$$

with $P = P^s \cup P^b$, and $M = M^s \cup M^b$.

$$(1)$$

$$\text{cRMSD} = \sqrt{\frac{\sum_{i=1}^{l} \left(\left| P_i^b - M_i^b \right| \right)^2 + \left(\left| P_i^s - M_i^s \right| \right)^2}{2 \cdot l}}.$$

$$(2)$$

2.3. cRMSD Optimisation.

A cRMSD evaluation according to (2) depends on the superpositioning of the protein and its model. Thus, the best relative lattice orientation has to be identified in addition to the best model. Once the orientation is fixed, a cRMSD evaluation allows for a fast, additive RMSD update along the chain extension.

We implement a cRMSD-optimising method following [6, 18] as an alternative fitting strategy. In general a user defined number of rotation intervals r are performed for each of the XYZ rotation axes. For each rotation, we transform P^b and P^s into $\hat{P}^b$ and $\hat{P}^s$, respectively, to obtain the rotated current target structure.

The fitting procedure follows a chain-growth approach: P_1^b is placed onto an arbitrary lattice node M_1^b. The according side chain monomer M_1^b is placed to the adjacent node closest to the position P_1^s to be represented. Now, all valid placements of the next M_i^b and M_i^s on the lattice are calculated. Using the coordinate RMSD (cRMSD, (2)) we evaluate all derived models and keep the best n_{keep} for the next extension following [18] until all amino acids have been placed.

By applying the above cRMSD-based fitting procedure we obtain the best fit for the current rotation. An iterative application of this procedure then results in the overall best fit for all screened rotations. Since our screen

of XYZ rotations was discretised, the current rotation might be refineable. Therefore, another rotational refinement can be applied that investigates r^{ref} small rotation intervals around the best rotation from the first screen [6].

The run time of the cRMSD-method scales with respect to the lattice coordination number, n_{keep}, and most importantly the number of rotation intervals r and r^{ref} considered.

2.4. Further Features.

Coordinate data in the PDB is often incomplete. For example flexible loop structures are hard to resolve by current methods [41]. This results in missing coordinate data for certain substructures within PDB files. LatFit enables a structural fitting of even such fragmented PDB structures and produces a lattice protein fragment for each fragment of the original protein.

Currently, LatFit supports the 2D-square, 3D-cubic (CUB, 100), 3D-face centered cubic (FCC, 110), and 3D knights walk (210) lattice. The modular software design of our open source program enables an easy and straight forward implementation of other lattices via a specification of the according neighboring vectors N.

The implementation is open source and freely available for academic use at http://www.bioinf.uni-freiburg.de/Software/LatPack/.

2.5. Webserver.

The web interface of LatFit, integrated into the CPSP web tools [42], enables *ad hoc* usage of the tool. Either a protein structure in PDB format can be uploaded or a valid identifier from the PDB database given. In the latter case, the full atom data is automatically retrieved from the database.

Our default parameters enable a direct application of LatFit resulting in a balanced tradeoff between runtime and fitting quality. The computations are done remotely on a computation cluster while the user can trace the processing status via the provided job identifier and according link. Results are available and stored for 30 days after production.

Supported output formats of LatFit are the PDB format, the Chemical Markup Language (CML) format, as well as a simple XYZ coordinate output. The output files are available for download. In addition, a highly compact string representation of the lattice protein is also given in absolute move strings that encode the series of neighboring vectors $v \in N$ along the structure.

The generated absolute move string can be directly used to apply other lattice protein tools onto the resulting structures, for example, from the CPSP package for HP-type lattice protein models [10, 42] or from the LatPack tools for arbitrary lattice models [11, 38].

Results are visualised using Jmol [43] for an interactive presentation of the final protein structure. The final dRMSD and cRMSD values of the lattice protein compared to the original protein are given as well as the absolute move string encoding of the resulting structure. For an example of the LatFit web interface see Figure 2.

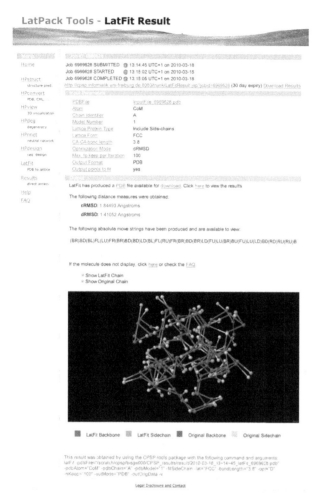

FIGURE 2: A screenshot of the `LatFit` web interface result visualisation.

Further details regarding the methods implemented, the output formats supported and the applicable parameterisation are located in the `LatFit` manual distributed with the source code. We provide an extensive help page and a frequently asked questions (FAQ) section within the web interface. Note, the web server is based on JavaServer Pages (JSP) technology and requires a connection via the JSP standard port 8080. A web interface for *ad hoc* usage is available at http://cpsp.informatik.uni-freiburg.de/LatFit/ and http://cpsp.informatik.uni-freiburg.de:8080/.

3. Results and Discussion

In the following, we evaluate the average fitting quality of our new LatFit tool to results known from literature [6, 8, 13]. Furthermore, we investigate the performance of the new dRMSD-based fitting procedure implemented in `LatFit`. To this end, we compare its results to the cRMSD-optimizing approach that follows [6, 18], both implemented within `LatFit`.

We use `LatFit` to derive protein models on the commonly used 3D cubic, FCC, and knights walk lattices

[18] using the dRMSD-based approach, parameterised with $n_{keep} = 1000$. Our test set was taken from the PISCES web server [44]. We enforced 40% sequence identity cutoff, chain length 50–300, R-factor ≤ 0.3, and resolution ≤ 1.5 Å to derive a high-quality set of proteins to model. Given our requirement for side chains, C_α-only chains were ignored. The resulting benchmark set contains 1198 proteins exhibiting a mean length of 160 ($\sigma = 64$).

In accordance with previous studies [18], cRMSD and dRMSD are used to assess model quality. cRMSD measures the similarity in according coordinate position of two structures whereas dRMSD measures the similarity of intramolecular distances. Due to the scaling of our lattice, RMSD results are in Å rather than the scaled values provided by Ponty et al. [22].

Our backbone model RMSD values presented in Table 1 are competitive or superior to known fitting results known from the literature [6, 13, 18]. Both the new dRMSD- as well as the reimplemented cRMSD-optimisation method reproduce the high quality previously achieved by other methods using the FCC and 210 lattices. The slightly higher mean cRMSD values for the dRMSD method are due to the nonoptimisation of that measure. Note, `LatFit` outperforms the results reported for `LocalMove` by Ponty et al. [22]. We found the `LocalMove` webserver currently not working for the proteins tested. Therefore, only results reported in [22] for the 3D cubic lattice and no FCC results are available.

`LatFit` is designed for side chain models and results here are strong (see Table I(b)). In general, side chain models produce slightly larger RMSD values than the equivalent backbone-only model. This is due to the fact that the variation in distance between consecutive C_α atoms (fitted in both models) is lower than that between C_α atoms and their side chain centroid (fitted only in side chain models). In lattice models every distance is fixed at 3.8 Å which results in a higher mean displacement of the side chain. Nevertheless, high accuracy fits are still attained. Results in our test set have mean dRMSDs of about 1.2 Å and 1.5 Å in the 210 and FCC lattice, respectively, for both optimisation strategies. When comparing the dRMSD optimisation with the cRMSD-optimising version, we observe very similar results. This is in accordance to our observations from the backbone-only models.

The strength of `LatFit` is its ability to produce both side chain and backbone-only lattice protein models. High accuracy models can be produced on the FCC lattice within seconds to minutes depending on the parameterisation. Fits on the 210 lattice take orders of magnitude longer for relatively little gain in model accuracy. For this reason we recommend using the FCC lattice for detailed high-throughput protein structure studies in both backbone-only and side chain representing lattice models.

4. Concluding Remarks

LatFit enables the automated high resolution fitting of both backbone and side chain lattice protein models from

TABLE 1: (a) compares the RMSD mean values for *backbone-only* models for approaches from literature to the results from our `LatFit` dRMSD-optimisation method on three different lattices. (b) gives according results for side chain including models. *Some reported values had to be rescaled to Å.

(a) Backbone-only models

| | Park and Levitt [18] | | Reva et al. [14, 22] | Ponty et al. [22] | LatFit | |
	cRMSD	dRMSD	cRMSD*	cRMSD*	cRMSD	dRMSD
CUB	2.84	2.34	2.84 (0.748·3.8)	3.46 (0.911·3.8)	2.97	**2.08**
FCC	1.78	1.46	—	—	1.89	**1.34**
210	1.24	1.02	—	—	1.29	**0.92**

(b) Side chain models

| | LatFit | |
	cRMSD	dRMSD
CUB	4.16	2.78
FCC	2.10	1.50
210	1.60	1.13

full atomic data in PDB format. We demonstrate its high accuracy on three widely used lattices using a large, nonredundant protein data set of high resolution. Side chain fits show on average a higher deviation than backbone models, but both produce high quality fits with results generally less than 1.5 Å on the face-centred cubic lattice. To our knowledge, this is the first study and publicly available implementation for side chain models in this field. Available via web interface and as a stand-alone tool, `LatFit` addresses the lack of available programs and is well placed to enable further, more detailed investigation of protein structure in a reduced complexity environment. Even now the `LatFit` webserver is in daily use worldwide (monitored via Google Analytics, http://www.google.com/analytics/), which shows the need for efficient implementations such as `LatFit`.

Conflict of Interests

The authors have declared no conflict of interest.

Authors' Contribution

M. Mann and R. Saunders contributed equally to this work.

References

[1] L. Mirny and E. Shakhnovich, "Protein folding theory: from lattice to all-atom models," *Annual Review of Biophysics and Biomolecular Structure*, vol. 30, pp. 361–396, 2001.

[2] K. A. Dill, S. B. Ozkan, M. S. Shell, and T. R. Weikl, "The protein folding problem," *Annual Review of Biophysics*, vol. 37, pp. 289–316, 2008.

[3] S. Istrail and F. Lam, "Combinatorial algorithms for protein folding in lattice models: a survey of mathematical results," *Communications in Information and Systems*, vol. 9, no. 4, pp. 303–346, 2009.

[4] K. A. Dill, "Theory for the folding and stability of globular proteins," *Biochemistry*, vol. 24, no. 6, pp. 1501–1509, 1985.

[5] A. Renner and E. Bornberg-Bauer, "Exploring the fitness landscapes of lattice proteins," *Pacific Symposium on Biocomputing*, pp. 361–372, 1997.

[6] J. Miao, J. Klein-Seetharaman, and H. Meirovitch, "The optimal fraction of hydrophobic residues required to ensure protein collapse," *Journal of Molecular Biology*, vol. 344, no. 3, pp. 797–811, 2004.

[7] R. Backofen and S. Will, "A constraint-based approach to fast and exact structure prediction in three-dimensional protein models," *Constraints*, vol. 11, no. 1, pp. 5–30, 2006.

[8] F. P. E. Huard, C. M. Deane, and G. R. Wood, "Modelling sequential protein folding under kinetic control," *Bioinformatics*, vol. 22, no. 14, pp. e203–e210, 2006.

[9] C. M. Deane, M. Dong, F. P. E. Huard, B. K. Lance, and G. R. Wood, "Cotranslational protein folding—fact or fiction?" *Bioinformatics*, vol. 23, no. 13, pp. i142–i148, 2007.

[10] M. Mann, S. Will, and R. Backofen, "CPSP-tools—exact and complete algorithms for high-throughput 3D lattice protein studies," *BMC Bioinformatics*, vol. 9, article 230, 2008.

[11] M. Mann, D. Maticzka, R. Saunders, and R. Backofen, "Classifying proteinlike sequences in arbitrary lattice protein models using LatPack," *HFSP Journal*, vol. 2, no. 6, pp. 396–404, 2008.

[12] R. Saunders, M. Mann, and C. M. Deane, "Signatures of cotranslational folding," *Biotechnology Journal*, vol. 6, no. 6, pp. 742–751, 2011.

[13] A.] Godzik, A. Kolinski, and J. Skolnick, "Lattice representations of globular proteins: how good are they?" *Journal of Computational Chemistry*, vol. 14, no. 10, pp. 1194–1202, 1993.

[14] B. A. Reva, M. F. Sanner, A. J. Olson, and A. V. Finkelstein, "Lattice modeling: accuracy of energy calculations," *Journal of Computational Chemistry*, vol. 17, no. 8, pp. 1025–1032, 1996.

[15] J. Mañuch; and D. R. Gaur, "Fitting protein chains to cubic lattice is NP-complete," *Journal of Bioinformatics and Computational Biology*, vol. 6, no. 1, pp. 93–106, 2008.

[16] D. G. Covell and R. L. Jernigan, "Conformations of folded proteins in restricted spaces," *Biochemistry*, vol. 29, no. 13, pp. 3287–3294, 1990.

[17] D. A. Hinds and M. Levitt, "A lattice model for protein structure prediction at low resolution," *Proceedings of the*

National Academy of Sciences of the United States of America, vol. 89, no. 7, pp. 2536–2540, 1992.

[18] B. H. Park and M. Levitt, "The complexity and accuracy of discrete state models of protein structure," *Journal of Molecular Biology*, vol. 249, no. 2, pp. 493–507, 1995.

[19] D. S. Rykunov, B. A. Reva, and A. V. Finkelstein, "Accurate general method for lattice approximation of three-dimensional structure of a chain molecule," *Proteins*, vol. 22, no. 2, pp. 100–109, 1995.

[20] B. A. Reva, D. S. Rykunov, A. V. Finkelstein, and J. Skolnick, "Optimization of protein structure on lattices using a self-consistent field approach," *Journal of Computational Biology*, vol. 5, no. 3, pp. 531–538, 1998.

[21] P. Koehl and M. Delarue, "Building protein lattice models using self-consistent mean field theory," *Journal of Chemical Physics*, vol. 108, no. 22, pp. 9540–9549, 1998.

[22] Y. Ponty, R. Istrate, E. Porcelli, and P. Clote, "LocalMove: computing on-lattice fits for biopolymers," *Nucleic Acids Research*, vol. 36, pp. W216–W222, 2008.

[23] C. L. Pierri, A. De Grassi, and A. Turi, "Lattices for ab initio protein structure prediction," *Proteins*, vol. 73, no. 2, pp. 351–361, 2008.

[24] M. Mann and A. Dal Palu, "Lattice model refinement of protein structures," in *Proceedings of the Workshop on Constraint Based Methods for Bioinformatics (WCB '10)*, p. 7, 2010.

[25] E. Jacob and R. Unger, "A tale of two tails: why are terminal residues of proteins exposed?" *Bioinformatics*, vol. 23, no. 2, pp. e225–e230, 2007.

[26] A. D. Ullah, L. Kapsokalivas, M. Mann, and K. Steinhöfel, "Protein folding simulation by two-stage optimization," in *Proceedings of the International Symposium on Intelligence Computation and Applications (ISICA '09)*, vol. 51 of *Communications in Computer and Information Science*, pp. 138–145, 2009.

[27] S. Sun, "Reduced representation model of protein structure prediction: statistical potential and genetic algorithms," *Protein Science*, vol. 2, no. 5, pp. 762–785, 1993.

[28] S. Bromberg and K. A. Dill, "Side-chain entropy and packing in proteins," *Protein Science*, vol. 3, no. 7, pp. 997–1009, 1994.

[29] W. E. Hart, "Lattice and off-lattice side chain models of protein folding: linear time structure prediction better than 86% of optimal," *Journal of Computational Biology*, vol. 4, no. 3, pp. 241–259, 1997.

[30] V. Heun, "Approximate protein folding in the HP side chain model on extended cubic lattices," *Discrete Applied Mathematics*, vol. 127, no. 1, pp. 163–177, 2003.

[31] A. Kolinski and J. Skolnick, "Reduced models of proteins and their applications," *Polymer*, vol. 45, no. 2, pp. 511–524, 2004.

[32] B. A. Reva, D. S. Rykunov, A. J. Olson, and A. V. Finkelstein, "Constructing lattice models of protein chains with side groups," *Journal of Computational Biology*, vol. 2, no. 4, pp. 527–535, 1995.

[33] Y. Zhang, A. K. Arakaki, and J. Skolnick, "TASSER: an automated method for the prediction of protein tertiary structures in CASP6," *Proteins*, vol. 61, no. 7, pp. 91–98, 2005.

[34] A. Kolinski, "Protein modeling and structure prediction with a reduced representation," *Acta Biochimica Polonica*, vol. 51, no. 2, pp. 349–371, 2004.

[35] V. A. Eyrich, D. M. Standley, and R. A. Friesner, "Prediction of protein tertiauy structure to low resolution: performance for a large and structurally diverse test set," *Journal of Molecular Biology*, vol. 288, no. 4, pp. 725–742, 1999.

[36] M. Feig, P. Rotkiewicz, A. Kolinski, J. Skolnick, and C. L. Brooks III, "Accurate reconstruction of all-atom protein representations from side-chain-based low-resolution models," *Proteins*, vol. 41, no. 1, pp. 86–97, 2000.

[37] M. T. Wolfinger, S. Will, I. L. Hofacker, R. Backofen, and P. F. Stadler, "Exploring the lower part of discrete polymer model energy landscapes," *Europhysics Letters*, vol. 74, no. 4, pp. 726–732, 2006.

[38] M. Mann, M. Abou Hamra, K. Steinhöfel, and R. Backofen, "Constraint-based local move definitions for lattice protein models including side chains," in *Proceedings of the Fifth Workshop on Constraint Based Methods for Bioinformatics (WCB '09)*, 2009.

[39] H. M. Berman, J. Westbrook, Z. Feng et al., "The protein data bank," *Nucleic Acids Research*, vol. 28, no. 1, pp. 235–242, 2000.

[40] W. Kabsch, "A discussion of the solution for the best rotation to relate two sets of vectors," *Acta Crystallographica*, vol. A34, pp. 827–828, 1978.

[41] Y. Choi and C. M. Deane, "FREAD revisited: accurate loop structure prediction using a database search algorithm," *Proteins*, vol. 78, no. 6, pp. 1431–1440, 2010.

[42] M. Mann, C. Smith, M. Rabbath, M. Edwards, S. Will, and R. Backofen, "CPSP-web-tools: a server for 3D lattice protein studies," *Bioinformatics*, vol. 25, no. 5, pp. 676–677, 2009.

[43] A. Herráez, "Biomolecules in the computer: jmol to the rescue," *Biochemistry and Molecular Biology Education*, vol. 34, no. 4, pp. 256–261, 2006.

[44] G. Wang and R. L. Dunbrack, "PISCES: recent improvements to a PDB sequence culling server," *Nucleic Acids Research*, vol. 33, no. 2, pp. W94–W98, 2005.

2

Correction of Spatial Bias in Oligonucleotide Array Data

Philippe Serhal[1] and Sébastien Lemieux[1,2]

[1] *Institute for Research in Immunology and Cancer (IRIC), Université de Montréal, C.P. 6128, Succursale Centre-Ville, Montréal, QC, Canada H3C 3J7*
[2] *Department of Computer Science and Operations Research, Université de Montréal, C.P. 6128, Succursale Centre-Ville, Montréal, QC, Canada H3C 3J7*

Correspondence should be addressed to Sébastien Lemieux; s.lemieux@umontreal.ca

Academic Editor: Tatsuya Akutsu

Background. Oligonucleotide microarrays allow for high-throughput gene expression profiling assays. The technology relies on the fundamental assumption that observed hybridization signal intensities (HSIs) for each intended target, on average, correlate with their target's true concentration in the sample. However, systematic, nonbiological variation from several sources undermines this hypothesis. Background hybridization signal has been previously identified as one such important source, one manifestation of which appears in the form of spatial autocorrelation. *Results.* We propose an algorithm, *pyn*, for the elimination of spatial autocorrelation in HSIs, exploiting the duality of desirable mutual information shared by probes in a common probe set and undesirable mutual information shared by spatially proximate probes. We show that this correction procedure reduces spatial autocorrelation in HSIs; increases HSI reproducibility across replicate arrays; increases differentially expressed gene detection power; and performs better than previously published methods. *Conclusions.* The proposed algorithm increases both precision and accuracy, while requiring virtually no changes to users' current analysis pipelines: the correction consists merely of a transformation of raw HSIs (e.g., CEL files for Affymetrix arrays). A free, open-source implementation is provided as an R package, compatible with standard Bioconductor tools. The approach may also be tailored to other platform types and other sources of bias.

1. Background

Microarray technology, a fairly recent yet already well-established and extensively dissected method, allows for the simultaneous quantification of expression levels of entire genomes or subsets thereof [1]. *In situ* oligonucleotide arrays are by far the most popular type, representing at the time of writing 70% of all arrays deposited in the Gene Expression Omnibus (GEO), a public microarray database, in the last year; of these, 58% are Affymetrix GeneChips [2]. These are designed such that each gene is targeted by multiple perfectly complementary oligonucleotide probes at various locations along its sequence (forming a *probe set*); copies of each of these probes are covalently linked to a solid surface at a predetermined location on a grid; a labelled RNA sample is allowed to hybridize to each of these probes; and finally a hybridization signal intensity (HSI) is obtained for each probe [3]. The technology relies on the assumption that,

on average, HSIs observed in a given probe set correlate with the true concentration of the given mRNA species in the biological sample, that is, the true expression level of the targeted gene. Variations on this architecture exist; for example, tiling arrays, are designed such that probes target contiguous regions of a genome, usually without regard for transcript annotations [4].

Because the objective of such experiments is generally to assess gene expression differences between one or more biological samples, separating *biologically interesting* variation from all other sources of *obscuring* variation is of utmost importance [5]; consequently, this has been a major focus of microarray research in the last decade. Whereas random error (i.e., noise) can be estimated via sample variance and cancelled out by some form of averaging, systematic errors introduce biases in the data that cannot be estimated without an independent source of information and cannot be explicitly corrected for without being estimated [6]. As has been shown repeatedly, there are several important sources of systematic errors—notably arising from RNA sample preparation [7]; probe-target binding efficiency [8], specificity [9], and spatial uniformity [10–14]; secondary structure in probes [15] and transcripts [16], and other thermodynamic properties [17] such as GC content [18]; scanner calibration [19]; and algorithmic processing of raw image data [20]— and underestimating their effect on analyses leads to tangible consequences [21].

An initial attempt to address nonuniform "background intensity" was incorporated directly in the design of the GeneChip platform: for each "perfect match" (PM) probe, there is a corresponding "mismatch" (MM) probe which features a single different base [3]. The intention was twofold: to correct for specificity biases, by assuming each PM/MM pair would share nonspecific hybridization signal, while only the PM probe would exhibit specific signal, and to correct for spatial biases, by making each PM/MM pair physically adjacent on the array. In practice, MM probes contain significant specific signal and do not share common nonspecific background with their respective PM probes; in fact, early studies found that approximately one-third of MM intensities are greater than their PM counterpart [22, 23], which is evidently incompatible with their stated purpose. In recent years, MM intensities have largely been ignored, and recent array designs by Affymetrix do not include them [24]. Current popular methods make no attempt to correct for either of these biases.

In order to make data from multiple arrays directly comparable, normalization methods such as locally weighted scatterplot smoothing (LOWESS or loess) [25–28] and Bolstad et al.'s quantile normalization algorithm [27] have been proposed and are currently widely regarded as essential preprocessing steps. The former modifies the HSIs such that a log HSI ratio versus mean log HSI plot becomes locally linear, while the latter forces the HSIs from each array in the experiment to follow the same distribution. It is important to note, then, that neither of these methods attempts to correct for any specific source of obscuring variation, but rather they make a general attempt to craft the raw data from separate arrays such that they become more directly comparable, inevitably discarding information in the process.

It has been noted that the choice of background correction methodology has a significant impact on downstream analysis accuracy [29], which implies that nonspecific hybridization and spatial nonuniformity should not be ignored. We focus here exclusively on the latter; the reader is referred to [30–32] for treatments of the former. A few methods addressing spatial biases in spotted cDNA arrays have been proposed. Dudoit et al. proposed the only such method to gain wide acceptance in the community, which consists of applying the loess-based intensity-dependent bias correction method individually within each print-tip group [25, 26, 33]. Colantuoni et al. proposed to subtract a 2D loess fit of intensities on the array surface [34], while Workman et al. similarly subtract an estimate of local bias based on a 2D weighted moving average with a Gaussian kernel [35], and Wilson et al. fit a loess curve on the MA plot as in Dudoit et al.'s study, but then adjust it by smoothing residuals

spatially on the array [36]. Various other methods have also been published [37, 38]. Some methods have been proposed in the case of *in situ* oligonucleotide arrays as well, although none is commonly used. Reimers and Weinstein proposed to visualize spatial biases by computing the deviation of each probe intensity from a robust average of that probe's intensity across all arrays in the experiment and plotting these values on the array surface [10]; Suárez-Fariñas et al. used these to identify array regions to discard [11]. Upton and Lloyd propose to subtract the smallest intensity around each probe on the array surface [12]. Arteaga-Salas et al. essentially combine the ideas of Reimers and Weinstein and those of Upton and Lloyd to come up with an algorithm: subtract, from each probe intensity, the average local deviation from the average intensity across replicate arrays, that is, an estimate of locally induced, array-specific error [13]. Various other methods have also been published [14], some of which are applicable only to specific platforms, such as CGH arrays [39] and SNP arrays [40].

The currently advocated standard operating procedure with respect to the well-known issue of spatial bias in *in situ* oligonucleotide array data, when one is used at all, consists of performing quality control steps to identify arrays deemed to be beyond arbitrary acceptability thresholds, and discarding these while leaving others intact [10]. While this may appear to reduce noise on affected probes, it also silently increases noise globally by decreasing replication, and there is comparatively little information on any given gene to begin with [41]. Discarding array regions or even individual probes [10, 11, 42] may alleviate this issue somewhat, though this merely shifts the issue to a lower level. Several studies have concluded that most, if not all, arrays are affected by spatial bias, regardless of platform [14]. We believe that very few of these are likely to be truly unrecoverable; thus, we propose to correct all arrays without prejudice.

We posit that *a priori* information about sources of systematic variation, in the form of known relationships between probes, can be exploited to identify, quantify, visualize, and effectively correct probe-level systematic errors. Here, we present an algorithm, *pyn*, to correct for sources of obscuring variation dependent on spatial location of probes on the array. The algorithm works by leveraging the power of expected mutual information found in probe sets with that of unexpected mutual information found in spatially proximate probes.

2. Methods

2.1. Algorithm. Using notation inspired by [22], let Y_{ijn} be the $\log_2$-transformed HSI of probe $j = 1, \ldots, J_n$ belonging to probe set $n = 1, \ldots, N$, on array $i = 1, \ldots, I$. Error estimates for observed intensities can then be expressed as deviation from some given intensity estimator

$$R_{ijn} = Y_{ijn} - \widehat{Y}_{in}, \tag{1}$$

and we propose the following estimator:

$$\widehat{Y}_{in} = \frac{1}{J_n} \sum_j Y_{ijn}. \tag{2}$$

The probe residual, R_{ijn}, is thus simply the deviation of each HSI from the mean observed in its probe set on the same array.

In justifying the use of spike-in and dilution datasets for assessing accuracy, Cope et al. assert that "to estimate bias in measurements, we need truth, in an absolute or relative form, or at least a different, more accurate measurement of the same samples" [6]. We propose two extensions to this view: first, *a priori* information about relationships between probes provides a form of relative truth; and second, this bias estimate is better used as a correction term than as an accuracy assessment.

Although a given probe residual merely quantifies one HSI's deviation from an estimate and thus contains contributions from many probe-specific biases (e.g., binding efficiency and specificity) and random noise, a sufficiently large pool of probe residuals with similar locations on the array provides a summary of the average bias induced by such a location. Noting that residuals (and accordingly means of residuals) share units and scale with HSIs, we thus simply propose to subtract this estimate of location-induced bias from each HSI to obtain corrected signals:

$$Y_{ijn}^* = Y_{ijn} - \widehat{R}_{ijn}, \tag{3}$$

where

$$\widehat{R}_{ijn} = \frac{1}{k} \sum_{j'n' \in kNN(jn)} R_{ij'n'}, \tag{4}$$

and $kNN(jn)$ returns the k nearest neighbours of probe jn, physically on the array, in terms of Euclidian distance.

It is of theoretical interest to note that, as k increases, the computed estimates of local bias tend to approach a constant as they become less local and approach a global measure on the entire array; in the limiting case, where $k \rightarrow \sum_n J_n$, the correction factor is almost exactly zero. Of practical interest is that this is also the expected behaviour in the case of an ideal array (lacking spatial bias) with a reasonable k.

The optimal choice of k, the only free parameter of our algorithm, is explored in the *Results* section. When a value is not given in the text, $k = 20$ is to be assumed.

2.2. Data. In this paper, three typical Affymetrix Human Genome U133A datasets are used to evaluate the proposed algorithm: two datasets obtained from the public microarray repository GEO [2] and a well-known benchmark dataset; these are referred to in the text as "GSE1400," "GSE2189," and "spike-in," respectively. The GSE1400 experiment compares two samples, with three replicates each: RNA associated with membrane-bound polysomes and RNA associated with free polysomes [44]. The GSE2189 experiment assesses the impact of the chemotherapeutic drug motexafin gadolinium relative to an untreated control sample, at three time points, with

three replicates for each of these six samples [45]. In the spike-in experiment, 42 transcripts are spiked in at 14 different concentrations, arranged in a Latin Square design across 14 arrays, such that each transcript is spiked in once at each concentration, with three replicates for each array [46]. For practical reasons, some results present data for only one array per dataset; in these cases, the arrays in question are GSM23121, GSM39803, and Expt1_R1, respectively.

2.3. Implementation. An implementation of the proposed spatial correction procedure is provided as part of an R package ("pyn"), with critical parts written in C++ for efficiency. An "AffyBatch" object ("batch") can be replaced with a corrected version by running the following command within an R session:

```
> batch <- normalize.pyn(batch)
```

The procedure runs for approximately one second per array (Intel Core 2 Duo 3.33 GHz) and accepts any valid AffyBatch object, independent of array platform. The user can then proceed with his usual analysis pipeline, for example, "rma" and "limma." The package also contains some utility functions for generating assessment figures similar to those found in this paper; users are referred to the package's internal documentation for instructions. The package is released under a BSD license and is available at http://lemieux.iric.ca/pyn/.

2.4. Alternative Methods. In this paper, "CPP" and "LPE" refer to the two algorithms proposed by Arteaga-Salas et al. in [13]; implementations provided by Dr. Arteaga-Salas were used as they are, with default parameters. "Upton-Lloyd" refers to the method proposed in [12]; as code was not made available by its authors, we used our own implementation, which is provided for convenience in the R package made available with this paper, as the function "upton.lloyd.2005." We now briefly describe these three algorithms.

2.4.1. LPE. For each probe on each array in a batch, a value similar to our residual is computed, relating the deviation of the probe's intensity from its median intensity across all arrays. A "code" is then computed for each probe, which identifies the array where this value is the largest and whether it is positive or negative. Then, to determine whether a given location in a batch of arrays is affected by spatial bias, PM and MM probes in a 5×5 window are inspected; if an "unusual" number of these exhibit the same code, the location on the array identified by this code is flagged for correction. Finally, for each flagged location, a standardized average of the previously defined deviations within its window is subtracted.

2.4.2. CPP. Residuals are computed for each probe on each array as in LPE, but the authors require in this case for all arrays to be replicates of one another. Each PM intensity is corrected by subtracting its MM counterpart's residual and vice versa. Residuals are scaled before subtraction to address differences in PM and MM distributions.

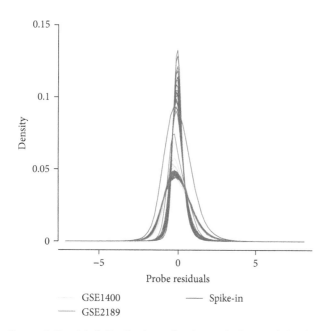

FIGURE 1: Empirical distributions of probe residuals R, as defined in the text, with one curve associated with each of the 66 arrays found in the three datasets. In each case, the mean residual is almost zero $(|\mu| < 10^{-17})$.

2.4.3. Upton-Lloyd. From each intensity at a given location on an array, the smallest intensity found in a $(2m + 1) \times (2m + 1)$ window is centred on it is subtracted; if the result is negative, it is replaced with zero. The authors find that $m = 1$ works best.

3. Results

Figure 1 shows the empirical distribution of probe residuals in each of the 66 arrays found in the three datasets described in the Data subsection. In all cases, the residuals appear to follow an approximately normal distribution with sample mean near zero $(|\mu| < 10^{-17})$. The parameters of this distribution vary from one array to another, based on their intensity distributions, which notably vary in offset ("background intensity") and scale ("dynamic range"); however, arrays in a common "batch" usually share these parameters. Thus, identifying outliers in residual distributions within a batch may be useful in identifying arrays significantly affected by spatial bias.

Under the assumption that probes are randomly located on the array, these residuals are expected to be randomly spatially distributed across the array; thus, any spatial patterns must be ascribable to some form of technical error. In practice, we frequently observe various manifestations of such patterns. Figure 2(a) plots the empirical spatial distribution of probe residuals for three arrays as heat maps, allowing for visual, qualitative assessment. GSE1400 is a typical case, in which the only noticeable regularities perceived are a few array-wide, horizontal stripes showing a greater density of either positive or negative residuals; GSE2189 presents a more problematic case, where a large region of the array (left side)

exhibits a large cluster of positive residuals; finally, the spike-in dataset reveals similar stripes as in GSE1400, in addition to a small localized artefact showing exclusively negative residuals (bottom right).

The spatial patterns identified in Figure 2 are reminiscent of those previously identified by plotting each probe intensity's deviation from an arbitrary reference array [47], from the average of that probe's intensity in replicate arrays [10], in all arrays in the experiment [11, 13], or in all arrays found in GEO [14], and by plotting the residuals (or some variation thereof) of a probe-level model-based method [48, 49]. However, previous work has been limited to qualitative and subjective quality control purposes, with few exceptions to the best of the authors' knowledge [12, 13]. We propose to exploit these values in a background correction algorithm. Moreover, our definition of probe residuals, not based on other arrays, allows for the indiscriminate identification of both systematic (e.g., batch effects, scanner effects) and array-specific spatial biases (e.g., sample spatial nonuniformity, smudges, scratches).

Figure 2(b) shows the spatial distribution of probe residuals on the three arrays after correction by *pyn*. Qualitatively, all three types of artefacts previously identified appear to have been eliminated or at least severely reduced, thereby marginalizing spatial dependence between residuals.

This "spatial dependence" can be defined quantitatively as *spatial autocorrelation*, the bidimensional extension to autocorrelation, which itself is a special case of correlation in which the two vectors under analysis u and v are such that $u_i = v_{i+1}$ for $i = 1, \ldots, |u|$. This additional dimensionality and directionality leads to multiple alternative formulations of a quantitative metric: Geary's C [50] and Moran's I [51] are widely used in geostatistics, while Reimers and Weinstein [10] and Wilson et al. [36] have proposed metrics specifically for microarrays. Though we have implemented all four of these metrics, results are only shown for Reimers-Weinstein as all results were found to be comparable (data not shown). Figure 3 assesses the impact of correcting each of the 66 arrays in our study with the four methods described in the Methods section. CPP and LPE leave all arrays largely unchanged, with the exception of GSM38903 (the selected array from GSE2189, with large blob in Figure 2(a)); in all cases, Upton-Lloyd results in the lowest spatial autocorrelation (near zero), while *pyn* results in the second lowest.

As effective correction of array-specific spatial biases should result in greater reproducibility, we evaluated the impact of each spatial correction method on variance across replicate arrays. Figure 4 shows the standard deviation across replicate arrays of gene expression values as obtained by RMA after pretreatment by each of the methods, as a function of mean log expression value. At low expression levels, *pyn* performs best, Upton-Lloyd critically inflates standard deviation, and CPP and LPE appear to have no effect whatsoever; at higher expression levels, all methods appear to have virtually no effect.

In order to assess the impact of the spatial correction methods on more tangible, biological results, we used the *affycomp* package [43] to assess differentially expressed gene (DEG) detection power in a dataset in which DEGs

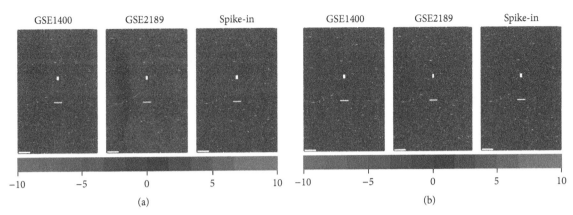

FIGURE 2: Empirical spatial distribution of probe residuals in original and corrected data. Mapping probe residuals back to their originating physical locations and displaying them as a heat map reveals a variety of spatial artefacts in (a) original data: horizontal stripes (all arrays), a large region of positive residuals (GSE2189, left), and a small region of negative residuals (spike-in, bottom right); (b) after correction ($k = 20$), all of these artefacts appear to have been eliminated or greatly attenuated. Non-PM locations (MM and control probes) are coloured in white.

are "known." The tool separates genes spiked in at low (Figure 5(a)), medium (Figure 5(b)), and high concentrations (Figure 5(c)); in each plot, the x-axis conveys 1 − specificity, while the y-axis conveys sensitivity (see [6, 43] for details). *pyn* significantly improves low- and medium-concentration DEG detection power, while Upton-Lloyd clearly deteriorates it, and CPP and LPE appear to have virtually no effect; at high concentrations, no method can improve DEG detection power, though Upton-Lloyd and CPP deteriorate it significantly.

Finally, we assessed the effect of parameter k, the number of neighbouring residuals pooled in (3). ROC curves are generated before correction and after correction with varying values of k, and the area under the curve (AUC) is computed for each ROC curve. Figure 6 shows the difference between the AUC in corrected data and the AUC in original data (ΔAUC), as a function of k, separately for low-, medium-, and high-concentration spike-in genes. Small values of k produce less robust (noisy) estimates, as they are more susceptible to contain contributions from other sources of probe-specific, but not location-dependent, variations; thus, as expected, small values of $k (< 6)$ perform badly. Conversely, as k increases, estimates of local bias, that is, the $\widehat{R}_{ijn}$'s, become increasingly robust; thus, low- and medium-concentration DEG detection power is increased significantly above this threshold, peaking around $k = 20$ then levelling off (not shown, convergence to ΔAUC = 0). Above the $k = 6$ threshold, high-concentration DEG detection power is unaffected. As explained in the Algorithm subsection, as k continues to increase, the correction gradually becomes a simple scaling of all intensities by a constant; thus, the curves in Figure 6 would approach zero as k continues to increase (data not shown).

4. Discussion

Systematic, nonbiological variations have been long known to obscure microarray data. In the case of spotted arrays, array- and print-tip-dependent biases were the first to be considered. Array bias could trivially be visualized by inspecting box plots of a batch of arrays or using more sophisticated approaches such as RLE and NUSE plots [33]; correction of such biases usually consisted of subtracting each array's mean or median intensity to impose a common average on each array's HSI distribution [33]. Print-tip bias could similarly be visualized by inspecting intensity distributions for each print tip, plotted side by side; a proposed correction consisted of subtracting a loess fit of this plot for each array [25, 26]. Intensity-dependent bias can be visualized and corrected for in the same manner, in which case the plots are known as MA plots and the correction is that first proposed in [25].

This strategy of addressing known sources of bias individually has been somewhat abandoned in the case of *in situ* oligonucleotide arrays, perhaps based on the assumption that streamlined commercial manufacturing of such high-density arrays is much less prone to significant systematic errors. For example, background correction and normalization steps in two of the most popular analysis packages, RMA [22] and GCRMA [52], do not take into account known sources of bias, but rather make global, sweeping transformations of the data, via a convolutional model [53] and quantile normalization [27], respectively.

We posit, as initially asserted by Dudoit et al. in 2002, that correcting for known biases using *a priori* information is preferable to global, blind, generic normalization, and/or reliance on unverified modelling assumptions [26]. We have thus proposed such a scheme for correcting spatial bias in Affymetrix GeneChip data, which can readily be applied on other platforms using multiple probes per gene.

We have shown that this method reduces spatial autocorrelation in HSIs, reduces variance in gene expression measures across replicate arrays, improves DEG detection power, and performs better than previously published methods in terms of replicate variance reduction and DEG detection power increase. As for spatial autocorrelation reduction, we conclude that Upton-Lloyd removes "too much" due to its working directly on HSIs as opposed to *pyn*'s working with

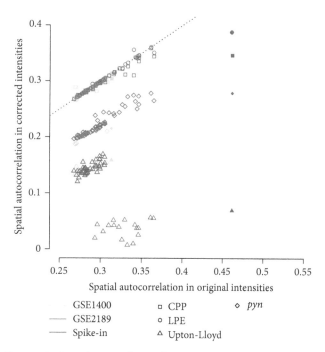

GSE1400   □ CPP   ◇ *pyn*

GSE2189   ○ LPE

Spike-in   △ Upton-Lloyd

FIGURE 3: Quantitative effects of correction on spatial autocorrelation. Reimers-Weinstein spatial autocorrelation metric computed in data corrected by various methods (*y*-axis) and in original data (*x*-axis) for each array in each dataset, with the "selected" array from each dataset being emphasized by a solid bullet. The Reimers-Weinstein metric is a Pearson correlation coefficient computed between each intensity and the average intensity among its four neighbours on the array [10]. An unchanged metric lies on the dotted unit line, while a value below (above) this line indicates a decrease (increase) in spatial autocorrelation. Upton-Lloyd consistently results in the greatest decrease, followed by *pyn*, while CPP and LPE have no effect in all but one case.

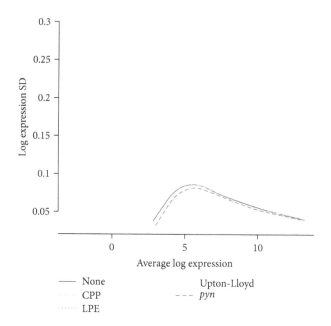

—— None   Upton-Lloyd

– – CPP   – – – *pyn*

······ LPE

FIGURE 4: Effect of correction on reproducibility across replicate arrays. Standard deviation of log expression index of probe sets across replicate arrays as a function of mean log expression, as computed in data obtained with RMA (all default parameters) after pretreatment with each of the spatial correction methods (or none). *pyn* performs best, resulting in an increase in reproducibility notably for low-expression genes, while Upton-Lloyd deteriorates data for low-expression genes, and CPP and LPE have virtually no effect.

residuals, which may avoid subtracting the "baseline" spatial autocorrelation inherent to each microarray platform.

Our analysis of parameter k, the number of neighbouring residuals pooled in (3), identified $k = 6$ as a minimum in order for correction to improve DEG detection power and $k = 19$ as the optimal value. As computational time is linearly proportional to k and values in the $12 \leq k \leq 30$ range all result in comparable performance, we propose to compromise with $k = 20$, and this is the default in the provided implementation.

An assessment based on a spike-in benchmark dataset indicated that DEG detection power is increased for low- and medium-concentration genes and is insignificantly affected for high-concentration genes. However, it should be noted that, by its very design, this central *affycomp* assessment does not take into account methods' ability to increase detection power *across replicate arrays*, that is, to take array-specific effects and so-called "batch effects" into consideration: a ROC curve is computed for each possible pair of arrays *within each of the three 14-array batches*, and the $3 \times C(14, 2) = 3 \times 91 = 273$ curves are averaged to generate plots such as Figure 5 [6, 43]. As the great majority of microarray experiments feature more than one replicate array per sample, this setup is highly

unrepresentative of real conditions. Additionally, it should be noted that the spike-in dataset is at the high end of the quality control spectrum; thus, if our correction method is able to improve biological results resulting from this data, it is to be expected that improvement will be even more significant for everyday datasets, such as GSE1400 and GSE2189.

Although the "random" spatial distribution of probes on the array surface was presented in this paper as a necessary assumption, this is an oversimplification and, thus, not strictly correct. In reality, the underlying assumption is that probe locations are independent of their targets, or—in more practical terms—of the locations of probes in the same probe set, such that any correlation between locations and residuals is always considered undesirable noise or bias; this can also be expressed as the assumption that probes are randomly spatially distributed on the array surface *within each probe set*. Thus, although recent studies have uncovered a significant dependence between probe locations and their sequences by observing spatial patterns when spatially mapping probe sequence GC content on the array [10, 14], our algorithm's assumptions are unaffected. This may also explain why, although Upton-Lloyd appears to reduce spatial autocorrelation further than our method, it performs much worse in replicate array variance and DEG detection power. In addition, these results imply that spatial bias correction procedures may unintentionally (likely only partially) correct sequence biases as well; conversely, it implies that sequence bias correction may somewhat correct spatial biases in the

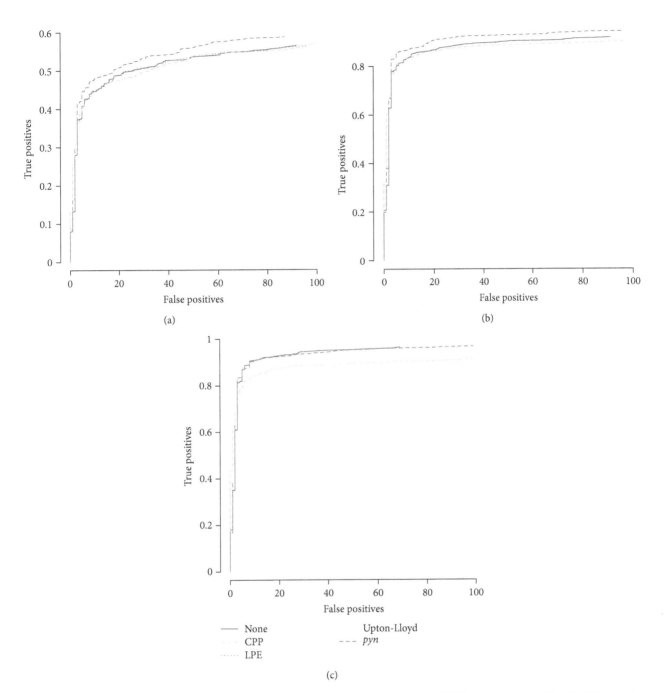

FIGURE 5: Effect of correction on DEG detection power. Receiver operating characteristic (ROC) curves generated by the R/bioconductor package *affycomp*, plotting *sensitivity* as a function of (1 – *specificity*), as computed in data obtained with RMA (all default parameters) after pretreatment with each of the spatial correction methods (or none) for (a) low-, (b) medium-, and (c) high-concentration spike-in genes. See [6, 43] for details. At low and medium concentrations, *pyn* performs the best; at all concentrations, Upton-Lloyd performs the worst by a large margin; CPP and LPE have virtually no effect, with the exception of CPP degrading results at high concentration.

process as well. This does not appear to be problematic *per se*, but is likely worthy of further investigation in order to fully understand its implications.

Finally, the framework established herein provides opportunity for implementing further types of microarray data pretreatments: correction of a specific source of bias which can be expressed as the presence of undesirable mutual information shared by "neighbouring" probes in some given coordinate space (e.g., physical location on the array) or based on some given distance metric, as opposed to expected, desirable mutual information shared by some other sets of probes (e.g., Affymetrix "probe sets"). This approach (which we dub *pyn: probe your neighbours*) should be applicable to other biases such as probe composition as well as to other microarray platforms such as tiling arrays, and preliminary results indicate that this is indeed the case.

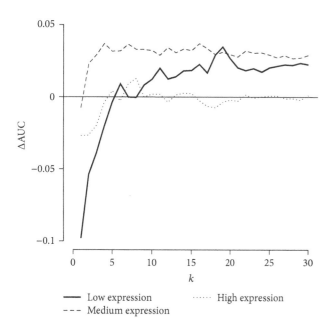

FIGURE 6: Effect of k on DEG detection power. Difference between area under the curve (AUC) of receiver operating characteristic (ROC) curves computed in corrected data and AUC computed in original data, as a function of the value used for k, separately for low-, medium, and high-concentration spike-in genes. *pyn* improves low- and medium-concentration DEG detection power with $k > 5$, with optimal performance at $k = 19$, and has virtually no effect on high-concentration DEG detection power above $k = 5$.

5. Conclusions

Oligonucleotide array data is invariably biased by a number of confounding factors, some of which can be effectively quantified and eliminated. We have proposed a method for correcting bias arising from a known source and show the efficacy of one case, namely, spatial bias in Affymetrix GeneChip data. An implementation is provided as a convenient R package, released under the BSD license, available at http://lemieux.iric.ca/pyn/.

Acknowledgments

The authors thank Dr. Jose Manuel Arteaga-Salas for providing implementations of CPP and LPE. This work was supported by the Canadian Institutes of Health Research (CTP-79843). IRIC is supported in part by the Canadian Centre of Excellence in Commercialization and Research; the Canada Foundation for Innovation; and the Fonds de Recherche en Santé du Québec.

References

[1] M. Schena, D. Shalon, R. W. Davis, and P. O. Brown, "Quantitative monitoring of gene expression patterns with a complementary DNA microarray," *Science*, vol. 270, no. 5235, pp. 467–470, 1995.

[2] R. Edgar, M. Domrachev, and A. E. Lash, "Gene Expression Omnibus: NCBI gene expression and hybridization array data repository," *Nucleic Acids Research*, vol. 30, no. 1, pp. 207–210, 2002.

[3] D. J. Lockhart, H. Dong, M. C. Byrne et al., "Expression monitoring by hybridization to high-density oligonucleotide arrays," *Nature Biotechnology*, vol. 14, no. 13, pp. 1675–1680, 1996.

[4] D. W. Selinger, K. J. Cheung, R. Mei et al., "RNA expression analysis using a 30 base pair resolution Escherichia coli genome array," *Nature Biotechnology*, vol. 18, no. 12, pp. 1262–1268, 2000.

[5] A. J. Hartemink, D. K. Gifford, T. S. Jaakkola, and R. A. Young, "Maximum likelihood estimation of optimal scaling factors for expression array normalization," *Microarrays: Optical Technologies and Informatics*, vol. 2, no. 23, pp. 132–140, 2001.

[6] L. M. Cope, R. A. Irizarry, H. A. Jaffee, Z. Wu, and T. P. Speed, "A benchmark for Affymetrix GeneChip expression measures," *Bioinformatics*, vol. 20, no. 3, pp. 323–331, 2004.

[7] R. Gentleman, *Bioinformatics and Computational Biology Solutions Using R and Bioconductor*, Springer Science and Business Media, New York, NY, USA, 2005.

[8] F. Naef and M. O. Magnasco, "Solving the riddle of the bright mismatches: labeling and effective binding in oligonucleotide arrays," *Physical Review E*, vol. 68, no. 1, part 1, Article ID 011906, 2003.

[9] Z. Wu and R. A. Irizarry, "Stochastic models inspired by hybridization theory for short oligonucleotide arrays," *Journal of Computational Biology*, vol. 12, no. 6, pp. 882–893, 2005.

[10] M. Reimers and J. N. Weinstein, "Quality assessment of microarrays: visualization of spatial artifacts and quantitation of regional biases," *BMC Bioinformatics*, vol. 6, article 166, 2005.

[11] M. Suárez-Fariñas, A. Haider, and K. M. Wittkowski, ""Harshlighting" small blemishes on microarrays," *BMC Bioinformatics*, vol. 6, article 65, 2005.

[12] G. J. G. Upton and J. C. Lloyd, "Oligonucleotide arrays: information from replication and spatial structure," *Bioinformatics*, vol. 21, no. 22, pp. 4162–4168, 2005.

[13] J. M. Arteaga-Salas, A. P. Harrison, and G. J. G. Upton, "Reducing spatial flaws in oligonucleotide arrays by using neighborhood information," *Statistical Applications in Genetics and Molecular Biology*, vol. 7, no. 1, article 29, 2008.

[14] W. B. Langdon, G. J. Upton, R. da Silva Camargo, and A. P. Harrison, "A survey of spatial defects in Homo Sapiens Affymetrix GeneChips," *IEEE/ACM Transactions on Computational Biology and Bioinformatics*, vol. 7, no. 4, pp. 647–653, 2010.

[15] R. Z. Gharaibeh, A. A. Fodor, and C. J. Gibas, "Software note: using probe secondary structure information to enhance Affymetrix GeneChip background estimates," *Computational Biology and Chemistry*, vol. 31, no. 2, pp. 92–98, 2007.

[16] V. G. Ratushna, J. W. Weller, and C. J. Gibas, "Secondary structure in the target as a confounding factor in synthetic oligomer microarray design," *BMC Genomics*, vol. 6, article 31, 2005.

[17] H. Wei, P. F. Kuan, S. Tian et al., "A study of the relationships between oligonucleotide properties and hybridization signal intensities from NimbleGen microarray datasets," *Nucleic Acids Research*, vol. 36, no. 9, pp. 2926–2938, 2008.

[18] M. P. Samanta, W. Tongprasit, H. Sethi, C. Chin, and V. Stolc, "Global identification of noncoding RNAs in Saccharomyces cerevisiae by modulating an essential RNA processing pathway," *Proceedings of the National Academy of Sciences of the United States of America*, vol. 103, no. 11, pp. 4192–4197, 2006.

[19] G. J. G. Upton, O. Sanchez-Graillet, J. Rowsell et al., "On the causes of outliers in Affymetrix GeneChip data," *Briefings in*

Functional Genomics and Proteomics, vol. 8, no. 3, pp. 199–212, 2009.

[20] A. A. Ahmed, M. Vias, N. G. Iyer, C. Caldas, and J. D. Brenton, "Microarray segmentation methods significantly influence data precision," *Nucleic Acids Research*, vol. 32, no. 5, article e50, 2004.

[21] J. T. Leek and J. D. Storey, "Capturing heterogeneity in gene expression studies by surrogate variable analysis," *PLoS Genetics*, vol. 3, no. 9, pp. 1724–1735, 2007.

[22] R. A. Irizarry, B. Hobbs, F. Collin et al., "Exploration, normalization, and summaries of high density oligonucleotide array probe level data," *Biostatistics*, vol. 4, no. 2, pp. 249–264, 2003.

[23] F. Naef, D. A. Lim, N. Patil, and M. Magnasco, "DNA hybridization to mismatched templates: a chip study," *Physical Review E*, vol. 65, no. 4, part 1, Article ID 040902, 2002.

[24] Affymetrix, "GeneChip Gene 1.0 ST Array System," Santa Clara, Calif, USA, 2007.

[25] Y. H. Yang, S. Dudoit, P. Luu, and T. P. Speed, "Normalization for cDNA microarray data," *Microarrays: Optical Technologies and Informatics*, vol. 2, no. 23, pp. 141–152, 2001.

[26] S. Dudoit, Y. H. Yang, M. J. Callow, and T. P. Speed, "Statistical methods for identifying differentially expressed genes in replicated cDNA microarray experiments," *Statistica Sinica*, vol. 12, no. 1, pp. 111–139, 2002.

[27] B. M. Bolstad, R. A. Irizarry, M. Astrand, and T. P. Speed, "A comparison of normalization methods for high density oligonucleotide array data based on variance and bias," *Bioinformatics*, vol. 19, no. 2, pp. 185–193, 2003.

[28] J. A. Berger, S. Hautaniemi, A. Järvinen, H. Edgren, S. K. Mitra, and J. Astola, "Optimized LOWESS normalization parameter selection for DNA microarray data," *BMC Bioinformatics*, vol. 5, article 194, 2004.

[29] M. E. Ritchie, J. Silver, A. Oshlack et al., "A comparison of background correction methods for two-colour microarrays," *Bioinformatics*, vol. 23, no. 20, pp. 2700–2707, 2007.

[30] S. L. Carter, A. C. Eklund, B. H. Mecham, I. S. Kohane, and Z. Szallasi, "Redefinition of Affymetrix probe sets by sequence overlap with cDNA microarray probes reduces cross-platform inconsistencies in cancer-associated gene expression measurements," *BMC Bioinformatics*, vol. 6, article 107, 2005.

[31] C. Wu, R. Carta, and Zhang, "Sequence dependence of cross-hybridization on short oligo microarrays," *Nucleic Acids Research*, vol. 33, no. 9, p. e84, 2005.

[32] H. Binder, J. Brücker, and C. J. Burden, "Nonspecific hybridization scaling of microarray expression estimates: a physico-chemical approach for chip-to-chip normalization," *Journal of Physical Chemistry B*, vol. 113, no. 9, pp. 2874–2895, 2009.

[33] Y. H. Yang, S. Dudoit, P. Luu et al., "Normalization for cDNA microarray data: a robust composite method addressing single and multiple slide systematic variation," *Nucleic Acids Research*, vol. 30, no. 4, p. e15, 2002.

[34] C. Workman, L. J. Jensen, H. Jarmer et al., "A new non-linear normalization method for reducing variability in DNA microarray experiments," *Genome Biology*, vol. 3, no. 9, research0048, 2002.

[35] C. Colantuoni, G. Henry, S. Zeger, and J. Pevsner, "Local mean normalization of microarray element signal intensities across an array surface: quality control and correction of spatially systematic artifacts," *BioTechniques*, vol. 32, no. 6, pp. 1316–1320, 2002.

[36] D. L. Wilson, M. J. Buckley, C. A. Helliwell, and I. W. Wilson, "New normalization methods for cDNA microarray data," *Bioinformatics*, vol. 19, no. 11, pp. 1325–1332, 2003.

[37] D. Baird, P. Johnstone, and T. Wilson, "Normalization of microarray data using a spatial mixed model analysis which includes splines," *Bioinformatics*, vol. 20, no. 17, pp. 3196–3205, 2004.

[38] A. L. Tarca, J. E. Cooke, and J. Mackay, "A robust neural networks approach for spatial and intensity-dependent normalization of cDNA microarray data," *Bioinformatics*, vol. 21, no. 11, pp. 2674–2683, 2005.

[39] P. Neuvial, P. Hupé, I. Brito et al., "Spatial normalization of array-CGH data," *BMC Bioinformatics*, vol. 7, article 264, 2006.

[40] H. S. Chai, T. M. Therneau, K. R. Bailey, and J. A. Kocher, "Spatial normalization improves the quality of genotype calling for Affymetrix SNP 6.0 arrays," *BMC Bioinformatics*, vol. 11, article 356, 2010.

[41] J. M. Arteaga-Salas, H. Zuzan, W. B. Langdon, G. J. G. Upton, and A. P. Harrison, "An overview of image-processing methods for affymetrix genechips," *Briefings in Bioinformatics*, vol. 9, no. 1, pp. 25–33, 2008.

[42] T. H. Stokes, R. A. Moffitt, J. H. Phan, and M. D. Wang, "Chip artifact CORRECTion (caCORRECT): a bioinformatics system for quality assurance of genomics and proteomics array data," *Annals of Biomedical Engineering*, vol. 35, no. 6, pp. 1068–1080, 2007.

[43] R. A. Irizarry, Z. Wu, and H. A. Jaffee, "Comparison of Affymetrix GeneChip expression measures," *Bioinformatics*, vol. 22, no. 7, pp. 789–794, 2006.

[44] N. O. Stitziel, B. G. Mar, J. Liang, and C. A. Westbrook, "Membrane-associated and secreted genes in breast cancer," *Cancer Research*, vol. 64, no. 23, pp. 8682–8687, 2004.

[45] D. Magda, P. Lecane, R. A. Miller et al., "Motexafin gadolinium disrupts zinc metabolism in human cancer cell lines," *Cancer Research*, vol. 65, no. 9, pp. 3837–3845, 2005.

[46] "Latin Square Data for Expression Algorithm Assessment," http://www.affymetrix.com/support/technical/sample_data/datasets.affx.

[47] C. Cheng and L. M. Li, "Sub-array normalization subject to differentiation," *Nucleic Acids Research*, vol. 33, no. 17, pp. 5565–5573, 2005.

[48] C. Li and W. H. Wong, "Model-based analysis of oligonucleotide arrays: expression index computation and outlier detection," *Proceedings of the National Academy of Sciences of the United States of America*, vol. 98, no. 1, pp. 31–36, 2001.

[49] B. Bolstad, J. Brettschneider, K. Simpson, L. Cope, R. Irizarry, and T. P. Speed, "Quality assessment of affymetrix GeneChip data," in *Bioinformatics and Computational Biology Using R and Bioconductor*, R. Gentleman, V. Carey, W. Huber, R. Irizarry, and S. Dudoit, Eds., Springer, 2005.

[50] R. C. Geary, "The contiguity ratio and statistical mapping," *The Incorporated Statistician*, vol. 5, no. 3, pp. 115–146, 1954.

[51] P. A. Moran, "Notes on continuous stochastic phenomena," *Biometrika*, vol. 37, no. 1-2, pp. 17–23, 1950.

[52] Z. Wu, R. A. Irizarry, R. Gentleman, F. Martinez-Murillo, and F. Spencer, "A model-based background adjustment for oligonucleotide expression arrays," *Journal of the American Statistical Association*, vol. 99, no. 468, pp. 909–917, 2004.

[53] B. M. Bolstad, *Low-level analysis of high-density oligonucleotide array data: background, normalization and summarization [Ph.D. thesis in biostatistics]*, University of California, Berkeley, 2004.

3

Using Protein Clusters from Whole Proteomes to Construct and Augment a Dendrogram

Yunyun Zhou,[1] **Douglas R. Call,**[1,2] **and Shira L. Broschat**[1,2,3]

[1] *School of Electrical Engineering and Computer Science, Washington State University, P.O. Box 642752, Pullman, WA 99164-2752, USA*

[2] *Paul G. Allen School for Global Animal Health, Washington State University, P.O. Box 642752, Pullman, WA 99164-2752, USA*

[3] *Department of Veterinary Microbiology and Pathology, Washington State University, P.O. Box 642752, Pullman, WA 99164-2752, USA*

Correspondence should be addressed to Shira L. Broschat; shira@eecs.wsu.edu

Academic Editor: Yves Van de Peer

In this paper we present a new ab initio approach for constructing an unrooted dendrogram using protein clusters, an approach that has the potential for estimating relationships among several thousands of species based on their putative proteomes. We employ an open-source software program called *pClust* that was developed for use in metagenomic studies. Sequence alignment is performed by *pClust* using the Smith-Waterman algorithm, which is known to give optimal alignment and, hence, greater accuracy than BLAST-based methods. Protein clusters generated by *pClust* are used to create protein profiles for each species in the dendrogram, these profiles forming a correlation filter library for use with a new taxon. To augment the dendrogram with a new taxon, a protein profile for the taxon is created using BLASTp, and this new taxon is placed into a position within the dendrogram corresponding to the highest correlation with profiles in the correlation filter library. This work was initiated because of our interest in plasmids, and each step is illustrated using proteomes from Gram-negative bacterial plasmids. Proteomes for 527 plasmids were used to generate the dendrogram, and to demonstrate the utility of the insertion algorithm twelve recently sequenced pAKD plasmids were used to augment the dendrogram.

1. Introduction

The availability of complete proteomes for hundreds of thousands of species provides an unprecedented opportunity to study genetic relationships among a large number of species. However, the necessary software tools for handling massive amounts of data must first be developed before we can exploit the availability of these proteomes. Currently the tools used for clustering either are restricted in terms of the number of proteomes that can be examined because of the time required to obtain results or else are restricted in terms of their sensitivity. For example, clustering by means of hidden markov models (HMM), multiple sequence alignment, and pairwise sequence alignment by means of the Smith-Waterman alignment algorithm are limited by their time complexity. The Smith-Waterman algorithm, a dynamic programming algorithm, is known to give optimal alignment between two protein sequences for a given similarity matrix [1], but alignment of two sequences of lengths m and n requires $O(mn)$ time. On the other hand, heuristic approximate alignment methods, frequently based on BLAST and its variants [2], reduce the computational time required; for example, in practice BLAST effectively reduces the time to $O(n)$, but this comes at the risk of losing sensitivity to homology detection. In fact, numerous articles—for example, see [3, 4]—have discussed this loss of sensitivity in BLAST-based results compared to those of the Smith-Waterman algorithm. To ensure that a maximum number of homologous sequences are identified, highly sensitive pairwise homology detection is required. Otherwise, the clusters of homologous sequences

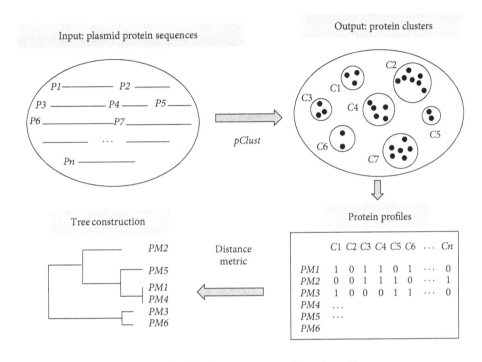

FIGURE 1: Flowchart for tree construction using *pClust*.

obtained by means of a given clustering method will not include all possible members and, ultimately, the final results will be less accurate.

In this work we use an alternative sequence comparison algorithm and clustering method called *pClust*. Rather than approximating Smith-Waterman, *pClust* systematically eliminates sequence pairs with little likelihood of having alignments and then only employs the Smith-Waterman algorithm on promising pairs [5]. Clustering is accomplished using a method based on a previously developed approach called shingling [6]. By filtering out unlikely sequences and using the Smith-Waterman algorithm judiciously, *pClust* remains highly sensitive to sequence homology without loss of speed. In an unpublished study of 6,602 proteins from four bacterial proteomes, *pClust* and BLAST results were compared, and BLASTp missed more than 69% of the aligned pairs identified by *pClust*. In a different study, a direct clusters-to-clusters comparison was performed with BLAST results used as the test and *pClust* results used as the benchmark [7]. The results showed that all the BLAST results were included within the *pClust* results but BLAST missed 14% of the clustered pairs obtained with *pClust*. In addition to its sensitivity and speed, *pClust* is readily parallelizable, and to cluster proteins from the proteomes of thousands of species will require high-performance computing platforms and the use of parallel algorithms.

This work was initiated by our interest in plasmids. We wanted a software tool that would allow us to obtain genetic relationships among 527 Gram-negative bacterial plasmids based on their putative proteome sequences. In addition, we wanted an efficient means of adding new plasmids to our initial dendrogram as their proteomes become available. Plasmids are typically circular DNA sequences that can transfer between and replicate within bacteria and that are generally classified as broad- or narrow-host range [8, 9]. Plasmid sequences are described as mosaic because they are composed of DNA arising from many sources [10]. Plasmids serve to shuttle important adaptive traits, such as antibiotic resistance, between organisms [11, 12]. Consequently, understanding the genetic relationships among plasmids is important, for example, in the study of microbial evolution, in medical epidemiology, and in assessing the dissemination of antibiotic resistance genes [13, 14]. There are a number of approaches to examine plasmid relationships. Some researchers focus on the identification of important plasmid backbone genes that are involved in horizontal gene transfer (HGT) or replication within bacterial hosts [15, 16]. Some approaches compare compositional features such as genomic signatures and codon usage [5, 17]. Some researchers use network-based representations to explore genetic relationships among plasmids [5, 18, 19]. In this work we use the whole proteomes of 527 Gram-negative (GN) bacterial plasmids to construct a dendrogram.

We use protein cluster information from *pClust* to construct our dendrogram and then to predict the relationship of new plasmids within the structure of this tree. A binary profile is created for each species, indicating the presence or absence of a protein in each cluster (Figure 1). The concatenation of all the profiles results in a binary matrix from which a distance matrix is calculated, and neighbor joining is then used to construct a dendrogram. The binary matrix also can be viewed as a library of individual profiles that can serve as correlation filters for a new taxon. A profile for a new taxon can be quickly correlated with the profiles in the library to filter out the profile with the highest correlation coefficient. This correlation coefficient is then evaluated based on known biological information and a decision is made as to whether

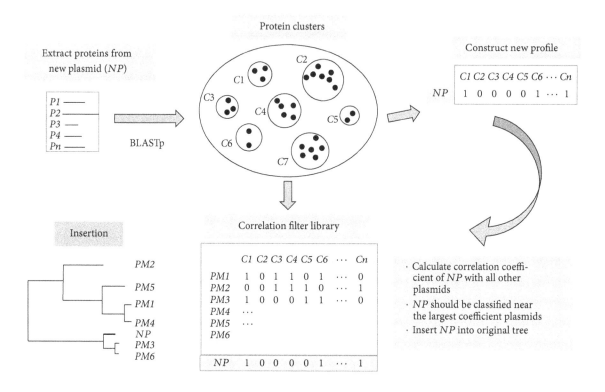

FIGURE 2: Flowchart for insertion of a new taxon into an existing tree using a correlation filter library.

the taxon should be added to the tree. If it is to be added, its binary profile is added to the binary matrix, a new distance matrix is calculated, and neighbor joining is again used to construct a new dendrogram with the additional taxon. To utilize the algorithm for new plasmids, we focus on sequences from twelve pAKD plasmids that were isolated from Norwegian soil [20]. These plasmids belong to incompatibility groups IncP-1(β) and IncP-1(ε). A phylogenetic tree constructed using multiple alignment of the relaxase gene *traI* is presented by Sen et al. [20] and serves as a basis of comparison for our augmentation results.

2. Materials and Methods

2.1. Data Preparation. Zhou et al. [21] presented a virtual hybridization method to construct a dendrogram for 527 GN bacterial plasmids with 50 or more putative coding genes. The same plasmids are used in this study to facilitate comparison. BLASTp with default parameters was used to remove duplicate proteins within plasmid sequences using a similarity score defined by the formula (length of matching sequence)*(BLAST identity score)/(length of reference protein + length of matching sequence) ≥0.45—that is, proteins with scores ≥0.45 were considered to be duplicates [22]. The maximum score 0.5 is obtained when two proteins are an exact match. Including the matching sequence length in the denominator of the formula insures that a large difference in sequence lengths does not bias the results. After removal

of duplicate proteins, more than 97,000 protein sequences remained.

2.2. Dendrogram Construction. The flowchart in Figure 1 shows the approach used to construct a dendrogram for the plasmids based on the >97,000 plasmid protein sequences. The protein sequences $P1, P2, \ldots, Pn$ are used as input into the *pClust* program [5], which employs the Smith-Waterman algorithm to perform pairwise comparison of a subset of the sequences. The output from *pClust* is composed of clusters $C1, C2, \ldots, Cm$ of homologous proteins. Protein profiles $PM1, PM2, \ldots, PMn$ are then created for all the plasmids from the *pClust* output files. Each profile consists of a binary sequence with 1 indicating the presence of a protein and 0 indicating absence (Figure 1). The *pClust* software was used with default settings in the configuration file except for Exact-MatchLen for which a value of 4 was used. A total of 6,618 clusters (defined as having at least two proteins) were identified by *pClust*. The resulting $527 \times 6{,}618$ binary matrix was used to construct the dendrogram for two different distance measures. The Jaccard distance metric was originally developed for computation with binary matrices and is given by

$$d_{ij} = \frac{(q+r)}{(p+q+r)}, \tag{1}$$

where q is the number of clusters $C1, C2, \ldots, Cn$ that are 1 for species i and 0 for species j, r is the number of clusters that are 0 for species i and 1 for species j, and p is the number of

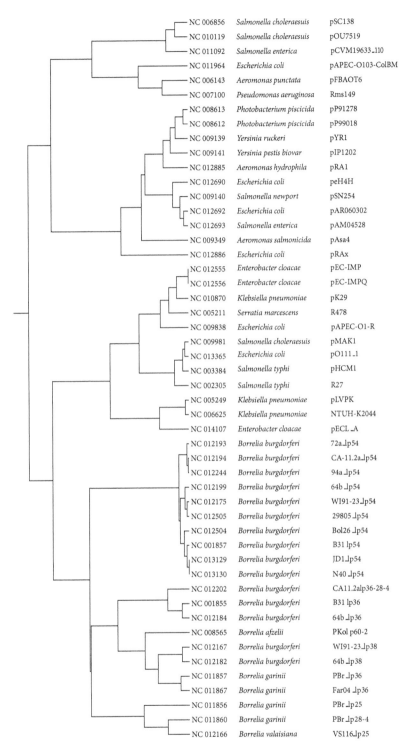

NC 006856	*Salmonella choleraesuis*	pSC138
NC 010119	*Salmonella choleraesuis*	pOU7519
NC 011092	*Salmonella enterica*	pCVM19633_110
NC 011964	*Escherichia coli*	pAPEC-O103-ColBM
NC 006143	*Aeromonas punctata*	pFBAOT6
NC 007100	*Pseudomonas aeruginosa*	Rms149
NC 008613	*Photobacterium piscicida*	pP91278
NC 008612	*Photobacterium piscicida*	pP99018
NC 009139	*Yersinia ruckeri*	pYR1
NC 009141	*Yersinia pestis biovar*	pIP1202
NC 012885	*Aeromonas hydrophila*	pRA1
NC 012690	*Escherichia coli*	peH4H
NC 009140	*Salmonella newport*	pSN254
NC 012692	*Escherichia coli*	pAR060302
NC 012693	*Salmonella enterica*	pAM04528
NC 009349	*Aeromonas salmonicida*	pAsa4
NC 012886	*Escherichia coli*	pRAx
NC 012555	*Enterobacter cloacae*	pEC-IMP
NC 012556	*Enterobacter cloacae*	pEC-IMPQ
NC 010870	*Klebsiella pneumoniae*	pK29
NC 005211	*Serratia marcescens*	R478
NC 009838	*Escherichia coli*	pAPEC-O1-R
NC 009981	*Salmonella choleraesuis*	pMAK1
NC 013365	*Escherichia coli*	pO111_1
NC 003384	*Salmonella typhi*	pHCM1
NC 002305	*Salmonella typhi*	R27
NC 005249	*Klebsiella pneumoniae*	pLVPK
NC 006625	*Klebsiella pneumoniae*	NTUH-K2044
NC 014107	*Enterobacter cloacae*	pECL_A
NC 012193	*Borrelia burgdorferi*	72a_lp54
NC 012194	*Borrelia burgdorferi*	CA-11.2a_lp54
NC 012244	*Borrelia burgdorferi*	94a_lp54
NC 012199	*Borrelia burgdorferi*	64b_lp54
NC 012175	*Borrelia burgdorferi*	WI91-23_lp54
NC 012505	*Borrelia burgdorferi*	29805_lp54
NC 012504	*Borrelia burgdorferi*	Bol26_lp54
NC 001857	*Borrelia burgdorferi*	B31 lp54
NC 013129	*Borrelia burgdorferi*	JD1_lp54
NC 013130	*Borrelia burgdorferi*	N40_lp54
NC 012202	*Borrelia burgdorferi*	CA11.2alp36-28-4
NC 001855	*Borrelia burgdorferi*	B31 lp36
NC 012184	*Borrelia burgdorferi*	64b_lp36
NC 008565	*Borrelia afzelii*	PKol p60-2
NC 012167	*Borrelia burgdorferi*	WI91-23_lp38
NC 012182	*Borrelia burgdorferi*	64b_lp38
NC 011857	*Borrelia garinii*	PBr_lp36
NC 011867	*Borrelia garinii*	Far04_lp36
NC 011856	*Borrelia garinii*	PBr_lp25
NC 011860	*Borrelia garinii*	PBr_lp28-4
NC 012166	*Borrelia valaisiana*	VS116_lp25

FIGURE 3: Jaccard distance tree for 50 Gram-negative plasmids.

clusters that are 1 for both species i and j. We also employ a conventional Euclidean distance metric. For both metrics, a neighbor-joining algorithm was used to obtain the final dendrogram.

2.3. Insertion of New Plasmids. As additional plasmid gene sequences become available, we can repeat the procedure described in the previous section to obtain a new dendrogram. The amount of computation and time required to accomplish this task, however, is excessive considering the incremental gain that may be achieved. For example, the original execution time for the 527-plasmid tree was 72 hours on an Intel Xeon CPU E5420 machine with 32 GB of memory. Instead it is preferable to have a means of inserting new

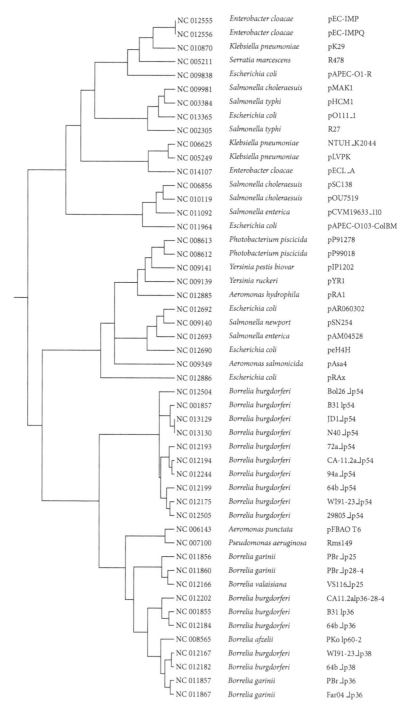

NC 012555	*Enterobacter cloacae*	pEC-IMP
NC 012556	*Enterobacter cloacae*	pEC-IMPQ
NC 010870	*Klebsiella pneumoniae*	pK29
NC 005211	*Serratia marcescens*	R478
NC 009838	*Escherichia coli*	pAPEC-O1-R
NC 009981	*Salmonella choleraesuis*	pMAK1
NC 003384	*Salmonella typhi*	pHCM1
NC 013365	*Escherichia coli*	pO111_1
NC 002305	*Salmonella typhi*	R27
NC 006625	*Klebsiella pneumoniae*	NTUH_K2044
NC 005249	*Klebsiella pneumoniae*	pLVPK
NC 014107	*Enterobacter cloacae*	pECL_A
NC 006856	*Salmonella choleraesuis*	pSC138
NC 010119	*Salmonella choleraesuis*	pOU7519
NC 011092	*Salmonella enterica*	pCVM19633_110
NC 011964	*Escherichia coli*	pAPEC-O103-ColBM
NC 008613	*Photobacterium piscicida*	pP91278
NC 008612	*Photobacterium piscicida*	pP99018
NC 009141	*Yersinia pestis biovar*	pIP1202
NC 009139	*Yersinia ruckeri*	pYR1
NC 012885	*Aeromonas hydrophila*	pRA1
NC 012692	*Escherichia coli*	pAR060302
NC 009140	*Salmonella newport*	pSN254
NC 012693	*Salmonella enterica*	pAM04528
NC 012690	*Escherichia coli*	peH4H
NC 009349	*Aeromonas salmonicida*	pAsa4
NC 012886	*Escherichia coli*	pRAx
NC 012504	*Borrelia burgdorferi*	Bol26_lp54
NC 001857	*Borrelia burgdorferi*	B31 lp54
NC 013129	*Borrelia burgdorferi*	JD1_lp54
NC 013130	*Borrelia burgdorferi*	N40_lp54
NC 012193	*Borrelia burgdorferi*	72a_lp54
NC 012194	*Borrelia burgdorferi*	CA-11.2a_lp54
NC 012244	*Borrelia burgdorferi*	94a_lp54
NC 012199	*Borrelia burgdorferi*	64b_lp54
NC 012175	*Borrelia burgdorferi*	WI91-23_lp54
NC 012505	*Borrelia burgdorferi*	29805_lp54
NC 006143	*Aeromonas punctata*	pFBAO T6
NC 007100	*Pseudomonas aeruginosa*	Rms149
NC 011856	*Borrelia garinii*	PBr_lp25
NC 011860	*Borrelia garinii*	PBr_lp28-4
NC 012166	*Borrelia valaisiana*	VS116_lp25
NC 012202	*Borrelia burgdorferi*	CA11.2alp36-28-4
NC 001855	*Borrelia burgdorferi*	B31 lp36
NC 012184	*Borrelia burgdorferi*	64b_lp36
NC 008565	*Borrelia afzelii*	PKo lp60-2
NC 012167	*Borrelia burgdorferi*	WI91-23_lp38
NC 012182	*Borrelia burgdorferi*	64b_lp38
NC 011857	*Borrelia garinii*	PBr_lp36
NC 011867	*Borrelia garinii*	Far04_lp36

FIGURE 4: Euclidean distance tree for 50 Gram-negative plasmids.

plasmids into the existing tree structure as described in this section, where execution of the insertion algorithm takes only a few minutes on a laptop computer.

To insert a new plasmid into an existing dendrogram, proteins $P1, P2, \ldots, Pn$ from a new plasmid are extracted from the plasmid proteome (Figure 2). BLASTp is performed with these proteins against all the proteins in the 6,618 clusters to determine the protein profile for the new plasmid. A protein is considered to be a member of a cluster when its similarity score is >0.2. The similarity score is given by (length of matching sequence)*(BLAST identity score)/(length of reference protein + length of matching sequence). The cutoff value of 0.2 is consistent with the 40% sequence similarity used as a parameter setting in *pClust*. Correlation filtering is then performed with the correlation filter library consisting of the protein profiles of the original 527 GN bacterial plasmids. The Pearson's product-moment correlation coefficient, whose absolute value is less than or equal to 1, is used to measure the correlation between two profiles [23, 24]. The larger the correlation value, the greater the similarity between

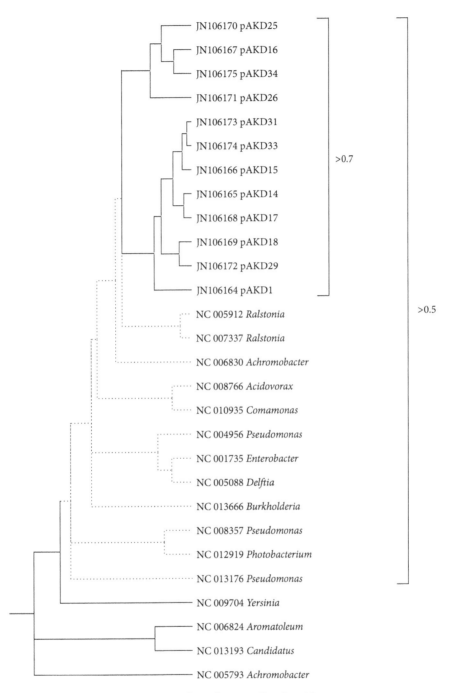

FIGURE 5: Subtree for 12 pAKD plasmids.

two profiles. This value is used to determine whether the plasmid fits into the dendrogram and, if so, where it should be located as explained in the discussion section. When appropriate, the new protein profile is added to the binary matrix, and a tree is constructed from the entire matrix as described in the previous section.

3. Results and Discussions

3.1. 527-Plasmid Dendrogram. Following the procedure described above, a dendrogram was constructed for 527 GN

bacterial plasmids. Because of its size, it is not shown, but it is available as supplementary information in Newick standard format (.nwk) for both Jaccard and Euclidean distance metrics and can be viewed using MEGA5 [25]. A tree constructed using the Jaccard distance metric for the same subset of 50 plasmids used in [21] is shown in Figure 3, and the Euclidean distance version is shown in Figure 4. These trees are very similar with only a slight difference in the clustering of the *Borrelia* plasmids. The tree constructed using the Euclidean distance metric is closer to the one shown in [21], but the Jaccard tree does a better job of clustering the

Borrelia plasmids [26, 27]. The Jaccard distance metric is commonly used for a binary matrix. Nevertheless, the results based on Euclidean distance compare favorably with those obtained for a nonbinary intensity matrix using a different approach [21]. It is not clear which distance method gives more accurate results so users should use both matrices and the decision as to which one is more accurate should be determined on the basis of the biology of the system.

3.2. Insertion of New Plasmids. We applied our correlation filter algorithm to twelve new plasmids from the pAKD family [20]. The twelve plasmids cluster together and are most closely grouped with genera typical of other soil bacteria. The correlation coefficient values among the pAKD plasmids were >0.7 and decreased relative to the other plasmids with distance to >0.5 (Figure 5). pAKD plasmids 16, 25, and 34 belong to the IncP-1(ε) compatibility group and form a discrete cluster: pAKD plasmids 1, 14, 15, 17, 18, 29, 31, and 33 cluster as the IncP-1(β) compatibility group. Although pAKD26 falls into the IncP-1(ε) clade, it should be in the IncP-1(β) group if compatibility grouping is considered the gold standard for comparison. Nevertheless, the placement is distal from the eight other plasmids in the β group, and pAKD26 was actually designated as IncP-1β-2 to differentiate it from the other eight plasmids as recently described in [28]. Our results are consistent with [20].

Importantly, the correlation coefficient is used to check the final dendrogram—that is, a new plasmid should be located near the plasmid with which it is most highly correlated. In addition, the correlation coefficient is used to determine whether a plasmid should even be inserted into a dendrogram. In other words, how does the magnitude of the correlation coefficient influence our confidence in the placement of a new plasmid within an existing dendrogram? Several works offer guidelines for the interpretation of a correlation coefficient [29, 30], but all criteria are in some way arbitrary and ultimately interpretation of a correlation coefficient depends on the purpose. In our case, we chose a value of 0.5, but we also require biological evidence—for example, that a plasmid is, in fact, from a GN bacterium.

To further examine the correlation coefficient, we randomly selected 10 Gram-positive bacterial plasmid proteomes from 10 different genera. The correlation coefficients were found to range from 0.112 to 0.234. GP bacterial plasmids do not belong in our GN bacterial plasmid dendrogram, and our minimum correlation value of 0.5 suffices to exclude these unrelated plasmids. While this level of discrimination is easy to identify, we should note that the 527 GN bacterial plasmids considered in this study do not represent the full diversity of GN plasmids. Thus, it is possible to obtain a small correlation coefficient value for a completely new and uncharacterized GN plasmid. If the new plasmid is able to meet an underlying correlation threshold, it can be placed within the dendrogram structure, and by incorporating the new plasmid sequence information into the correlation filter library, we can group future plasmids that may be closely related to it.

While the method of inserting new plasmids into an existing tree is fast and efficient, at some point, generation of a new dendrogram using all proteins from all the taxa will probably be required. We do not know at what point this will occur, but we assume it will be necessary eventually to insure that all possible protein clusters are included. Recall that a cluster must contain at least two proteins to be considered a cluster. Thus, any new plasmid containing a protein that would have formed a cluster with a single discarded protein represents incomplete information in the library. It is probable that the total number of clusters for all Gram-negative plasmids will ultimately be much greater than 6,818.

4. Conclusion

In this work we present a new ab initio method for constructing a dendrogram from whole proteomes that begins with output from *pClust*, a software program developed for homology detection for large-scale protein sequence analyses. We develop an efficient approach for insertion of a new species into the dendrogram based on the use of a correlation filter library. This is much more efficient than constructing an entirely new tree which is computationally costly. We illustrate our method by creating a dendrogram for 527 Gram-negative bacterial plasmids and augmenting this dendrogram with twelve pAKD plasmids isolated from Norwegian soil. For purposes of comparison, we also construct a smaller dendrogram consisting of 50 species and use two different distance metrics. The two resulting trees agree well with results shown in [21]. The classification results for the twelve plasmids agree with a phylogenetic tree constructed using multiple sequence alignment of the relaxase gene *traI* presented in [20].

Authors' Contribution

Y. Zhou and S. L. Broschat performed the research for this paper, and all three authors shared in the preparation of the paper.

Conflict of Interests

This work was not influenced by any commercial agency, and no conflict of interests exist.

Acknowledgments

The authors are grateful to Carl M. Hansen Foundation for partial support of Y. Zhou and the Washington State Agricultural Research Center and College of Veterinary Medicine Agricultural Animal Health program for support of D. R. Call.

References

[1] T. F. Smith and M. S. Waterman, "Identification of common molecular subsequences," *Journal of Molecular Biology*, vol. 147, no. 1, pp. 195–197, 1981.

[2] S. F. Altschul, T. L. Madden, A. A. Schäffer et al., "Gapped BLAST and PSI-BLAST: a new generation of protein database search programs," *Nucleic Acids Research*, vol. 25, no. 17, pp. 3389–3402, 1997.

D. L. Brutlag, J.-P. Dautricourt, R. Diaz, J. Fier, B. Moxon, and R. Stamm, "BLAZE: an implementation of the Smith-Waterman sequence comparison algorithm on a massively parallel computer," *Computers and Chemistry*, vol. 17, no. 2, pp. 203–207, 1993.

[4] E. G. Shpaer, M. Robinson, D. Yee, J. D. Candlin, R. Mines, and T. Hunkapiller, "Sensitivity and selectivity in protein similarity searches: a comparison of Smith-Waterman in hardware to BLAST and FASTA," *Genomics*, vol. 38, no. 2, pp. 179–191, 1996.

[5] C. Wu, A. Kalyanaraman, and W. R. Cannon, "PGraph: efficient parallel construction of large-scale protein sequence homology graphs," *IEEE Transactions on Parallel and Distributed Systems*, vol. 23, no. 10, Article ID 6127863, pp. 1923–1933, 2012.

[6] D. Gibson, R. Kumar, and A. Tomkins, "Discovering large dense subgraphs in massive graphs," in *Proceedings of the 31st International Conference on Very Large Data Bases*, pp. 721–732, September 2005.

[7] A. Kalyanaraman, S. Aluru, S. Kothari, and V. Brendel, "Efficient clustering of large EST data sets on parallel computers," *Nucleic Acids Research*, vol. 31, no. 11, pp. 2963–2974, 2003.

[8] E. Bapteste, Y. Boucher, J. Leigh, and W. F. Doolittle, "Phylogenetic reconstruction and lateral gene transfer," *Trends in Microbiology*, vol. 12, no. 9, pp. 406–411, 2004.

[9] E. Fidelma Boyd, C. W. Hill, S. M. Rich, and D. L. Hard, "Mosaic structure of plasmids from natural populations of *Escherichia coli*," *Genetics*, vol. 143, no. 3, pp. 1091–1100, 1996.

[10] H. Ochman, J. G. Lawrence, and E. A. Grolsman, "Lateral gene transfer and the nature of bacterial innovation," *Nature*, vol. 405, no. 6784, pp. 299–304, 2000.

[11] C. M. Thomas, "Paradigms of plasmid organization," *Molecular Microbiology*, vol. 37, no. 3, pp. 485–491, 2000.

[12] C. M. Thomas and K. M. Nielsen, "Mechanisms of, and barriers to, horizontal gene transfer between bacteria," *Nature Reviews Microbiology*, vol. 3, no. 9, pp. 711–721, 2005.

[13] M. Couturier, F. Bex, P. L. Bergquist, and W. K. Maas, "Identification and classification of bacterial plasmids," *Microbiological Reviews*, vol. 52, no. 3, pp. 375–395, 1988.

[14] J. J. Dennis, "The evolution of IncP catabolic plasmids," *Current Opinion in Biotechnology*, vol. 16, no. 3, pp. 291–298, 2005.

[15] J. Huang and J. P. Gogarten, "Ancient horizontal gene transfer can benefit phylogenetic reconstruction," *Trends in Genetics*, vol. 22, no. 7, pp. 361–366, 2006.

[16] S. Karlin and C. Burge, "Dinucleotide relative abundance extremes: a genomic signature," *Trends in Genetics*, vol. 11, no. 7, pp. 283–290, 1995.

[17] S. Karlin, "Detecting anomalous gene clusters and pathogenicity islands in diverse bacterial genomes," *Trends in Microbiology*, vol. 9, no. 7, pp. 335–343, 2001.

[18] M. Brilli, A. Mengoni, M. Fondi, M. Bazzicalupo, P. Liò, and R. Fani, "Analysis of plasmid genes by phylogenetic profiling and visualization of homology relationships using Blast2Network," *BMC Bioinformatics*, vol. 9, article 551, 2008.

[19] S. Halary, J. W. Leigh, B. Cheaib, P. Lopez, and E. Bapteste, "Network analyses structure genetic diversity in independent genetic worlds," *Proceedings of the National Academy of Sciences of the United States of America*, vol. 107, no. 1, pp. 127–132, 2010.

[20] D. Sen, G. A. Van der Auwera, L. M. Rogers, C. M. Thomas, C. J. Brown, and E. M. Top, "Broad-host-range plasmids from agricultural soils have IncP-1 backbones with diverse accessory genes," *Applied and Environmental Microbiology*, vol. 77, pp. 7975–7983, 2011.

[21] Y. Zhou, D. R. Call, and S. L. Broschat, "Genetic relationships among 527 Gram-negative bacterial plasmids," *Plasmid*, vol. 68, no. 2, pp. 133–141, 2012.

[22] D. R. Call, R. S. Singer, D. Meng et al., "blaCMY-2-positive IncA/C plasmids from *Escherichia coli* and *Salmonella enterica* are a distinct component of a larger lineage of plasmids," *Antimicrobial Agents and Chemotherapy*, vol. 54, no. 2, pp. 590–596, 2010.

[23] J. L. Rodgers and W. A. Nicewander, "Thirteen ways to look at the correlation coefficient," *The American Statistician*, vol. 42, pp. 59–66, 1988.

[24] M. S. Stigler, "Francis Galton's account of the invention of correlation," *Statistical Science*, vol. 4, pp. 73–79, 1989.

[25] K. Tamura, D. Peterson, N. Peterson, G. Stecher, M. Nei, and S. Kumar, "MEGA5: molecular evolutionary genetics analysis using maximum likelihood, evolutionary distance, and maximum parsimony methods," *Molecular Biology and Evolution*, vol. 28, no. 10, pp. 2731–2739, 2011.

[26] M. Lescot, S. Audic, C. Robert et al., "The genome of *Borrelia recurrentis*, the agent of deadly louse-borne relapsing fever, is a degraded subset of tick-borne *Borrelia duttonii*," *PLoS Genetics*, vol. 4, no. 9, Article ID e1000185, 2008.

[27] J. E. Purser and S. J. Norris, "Correlation between plasmid content and infectivity in *Borrelia burgdorferi*," *Proceedings of the National Academy of Sciences of the United States of America*, vol. 97, no. 25, pp. 13865–13870, 2000.

[28] P. Norberg, M. Bergstrom, V. Jethava, D. Dubhashi, and M. Hermansson, "The IncP-1 plasmid backbone adapts to different host bacterial species and evolves through homologous recombination," *Nature Communications*, vol. 2, article 268, 2011.

[29] A. Buda and A. Jarynowski, "Life-time of correlations and its applications," *Wydawnictwo Niezalezne*, vol. 1, pp. 5–21, 2010.

[30] J. Cohen, *Statistical Power Analysis For the Behavioral Sciences*, Law-rence Erlbaum Associates, Hillsdale, NJ, USA, 2nd edition, 1988.

4

Sequence Complexity of Chromosome 3 in *Caenorhabditis elegans*

Gaetano Pierro

System Biology, PhD School, University of Salerno, Via Ponte Don Melillo, 84084 Fisciano, Italy

Correspondence should be addressed to Gaetano Pierro, gaetanopierro@hotmail.it

Academic Editor: Ramana Davuluri

The nucleotide sequences complexity in chromosome 3 of *Caenorhabditis elegans* (*C. elegans*) is studied. The complexity of these sequences is compared with some random sequences. Moreover, by using some parameters related to complexity such as fractal dimension and frequency, indicator matrix is given a first classification of sequences of *C. elegans*. In particular, the sequences with highest and lowest fractal value are singled out. It is shown that the intrinsic nature of the low fractal dimension sequences has many common features with the random sequences.

1. Introduction

The *Caenorhabditis elegans* (*C. elegans*) is a 1 mm length transparent nematode. Thanks to its simple organic structure, it was taken as a model for research into genetic field. Early studies on *C. elegans* began in 1962 with some works on cell lineage and apoptosis [1, 2]. There are 2 distinct sexual types of the *C. elegans*, the hermaphrodite and the male. The second one is very rarely represented in nature (being approximately only the 0.05% of the population). We have 959 cells in the hermaphroditic species and 1031 cells for the male. The sexual difference at the chromosomal level provides: XX chromosomes for hermafrodite and X0 for the male. The sexual reproduction of *C. elegans* is realized by 2 distinct pathways: mating or, in case of the hermaphrodite, by a self-fertilization. The life cycle of *C. elegans* consists of 4 larval stages (from L1 to L4); however, if there exists some hard environment conditions, such as lacking of food, the *C. elegans* remains in the L3 larval stage, until the conditions improve.

The complete sequencing of *C. elegans* genome was completed in 2002. The *C. elegans* has 5 chromosomes autosomes plus the sex chromosome X. Totally, it is made up of nearly 100 million base pairs and 19000 genes [3–5]. Study on fractal analysis of multigenome of *C. elegans* has shown that chromosome 3 is the one with multifractal

characteristics higher than the others, the less multifractal appears to be the chromosome sexual X [6]. For the first time, in this work, we have analyzed the different types of sequences belonging to the genome of *C. elegans*, focusing our investigation on those that show fractal characteristics. Thus, chromosome 3 of *C. elegans* has been carefully studied because its unsymmetrical and inhomogeneous statistical characteristics. Through the analysis of this chromosome we can investigate what are the features that make it more "complex" from a biostatistical point of view and in particular with the use of statistical parameters such as the complexity, the fractal dimension, the matrix correlation, and the nucleotide frequency. The concept of fractality in biology is further clarified.

On the chromosome 3 of *C. elegans*, 2780 genes have been identified. In this paper, almost all nucleotide sequences that are located on chromosome 3 of *C. elegans* were analyzed and compared with random sequences. In particular, it will be shown that the nucleotide sequences with a low fractal value have common features with random sequence with low fractal dimension. Moreover, the highest fractal dimension corresponds to sequence close to random sequence with high fractal value, and in particular, it is shown a high frequency of cytosine.

From mathematical point of view, a fractal is a geometric object, characterized by the self-similarity; that is, it repeats

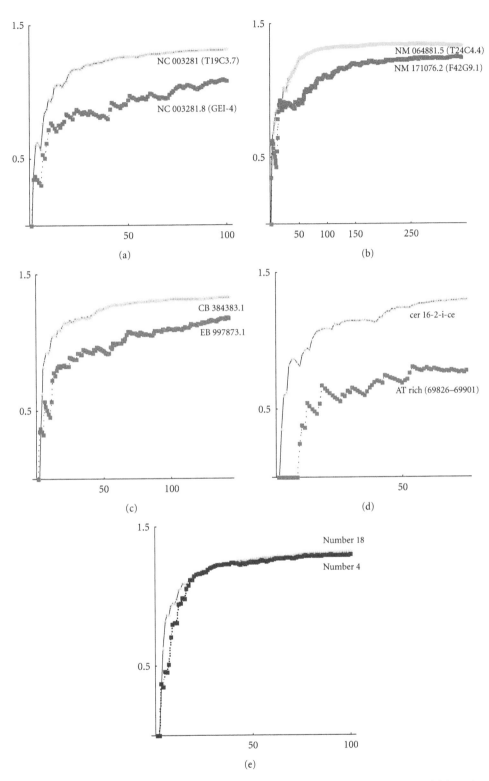

FIGURE 1: Curves of min-max complexity: (a) whole gene, (b) noncoding, (c) coding, (d) repeats, and (e) random sequences.

its structure cyclically in the same way at different scales. A more rigorous definition of a fractal is based on four properties: self-similarity, fine structure, irregularities, and noninteger dimension [7]. The fractal dimension is a parameter to compute the degree of complexity or disorder by measuring the unsmoothness of the object. This value enables to measure the amount of information contained in the sequence, the higher value corresponds to a higher information content. Generally, this value ranges between 1 and 2, so that the higher value corresponds to the higher

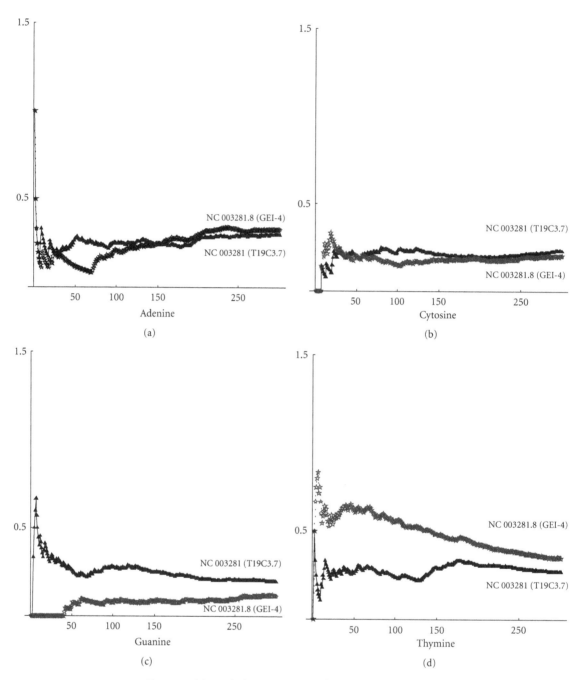

FIGURE 2: Max-min frequency curves for the whole sequence.

complexity. Fractality has been observed and measured in pathology and cancer models [8, 9], the study of branching blood vessels, or the irregularity of the contours of tumor cells [10, 11], the analysis of complete genomes [12], the correlation analysis of protein sequences [13] tissue pathology [14], in exons, introns [15], and nuclei [16], and it is involved in blood cancer [17, 18].

2. Materials and Methods

In the chromosome 3 of *C. elegans,* there have been singled out 2780 genes [19]. Some of them are very short,

less than about 50 nucleotides, thus being useless for any statistical analysis, and some of them are still under investigation, so that some nucleotides are not yet properly identified. For this reason, there have been selected only some sequences with significant length, the shortest being about 100 nucleotides. In particular, we investigated 100 genes (whole sequence), 85 repeats sequences, 71 noncoding sequences (introns), and 100 coding sequences (exons lacks of UTR). In order to make a comparison with random sequences, 100 random sequences of 100 nucleotides have been generated. In this work, all sequences were downloaded from the National Center for Biotechnology Information

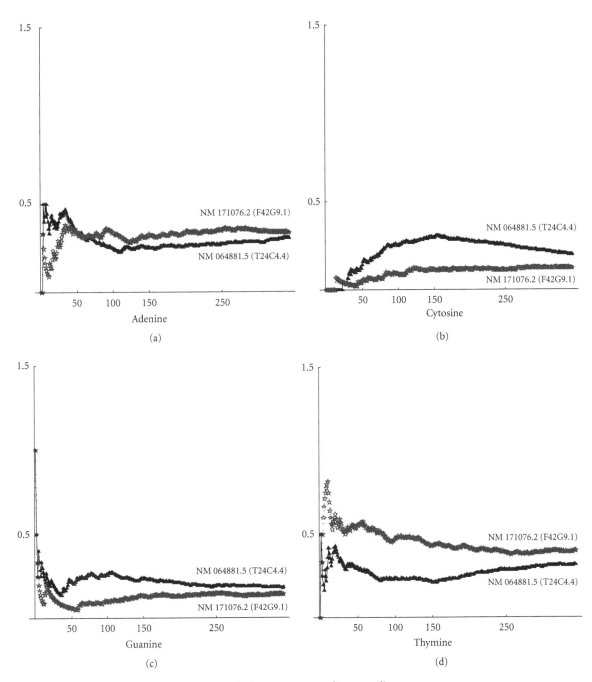

FIGURE 3: Max-min frequency curves for noncoding sequences.

[19]. A simple formula to estimate the fractal dimension has been given in [20, 21] and based on the correlation matrix, as follows. The fractal dimension is defined as the average of the number $p(n)$ of 1 in the randomly taken $n \times n$ minors of the $N \times N$ correlation matrix u_{hk} (see also [20–24]).

In particular, let

$$\aleph_4 = \{A, C, G, T\} \tag{1}$$

be the finite set (alphabet) of nucleotides and $x \in \aleph_4$ any member of the 4 symbols alphabet.

A DNA sequence is the finite symbolic sequence $\mathfrak{D}(N) = \yen \times \aleph_4$ so that

$$\mathfrak{D}(N) = \{x_h\}_{h=1,\dots,N}, \quad N < \infty \tag{2}$$

being

$$x_h = (h, x) = x(h), \quad (h = 1, 2, \dots, N; x \in \aleph_4) \tag{3}$$

the acid nucleic x at the position h.

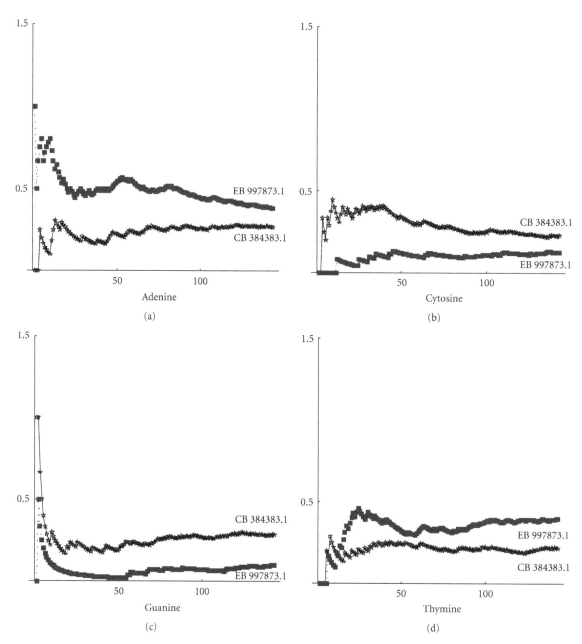

FIGURE 4: Max-min frequency curves for coding sequence.

Let $\mathfrak{D}_1(N)$, $\mathfrak{D}_2(N)$ be two DNA sequences, the indicator function [20, 22–26] is the map

$$u : \mathfrak{D}_1(N) \times \mathfrak{D}_2(N) \longrightarrow \{0, 1\} \qquad (4)$$

such that the correlation matrix

$$u_{hk} = u(x_h, x_k) = \begin{cases} 1, & \text{if } x_h = x_k, \\ 0, & \text{if } x_h \neq x_k, \end{cases} \qquad (5)$$

$$(x_h \in \mathfrak{D}_1(N), \ x_k \in \mathfrak{D}_2(N))$$

is a matrix of 0's and 1's showing the existence of correlation. When $\mathfrak{D}_1(N) \equiv \mathfrak{D}_2(N)$, the indicator function shows the existence of autocorrelation on the same sequence.

The probability distribution of nucleotides can be defined by the frequency

$$p_X(n) = \frac{1}{n} \sum_{i=1}^{n} u_{Xi}, \quad (X \in \aleph_4, \ x_i \in \mathfrak{D}(N); \ 1 \leq n \leq N) \qquad (6)$$

that the acid nucleic X can be found at the position n. This value can be approximated by the frequency count (on the indicator matrix) of the nucleotide distribution before n [20, 21, 23, 24]

$$D = \frac{1}{2} \frac{1}{N} \sum_{n=2}^{N} \frac{\log p(n)}{\log n}. \qquad (7)$$

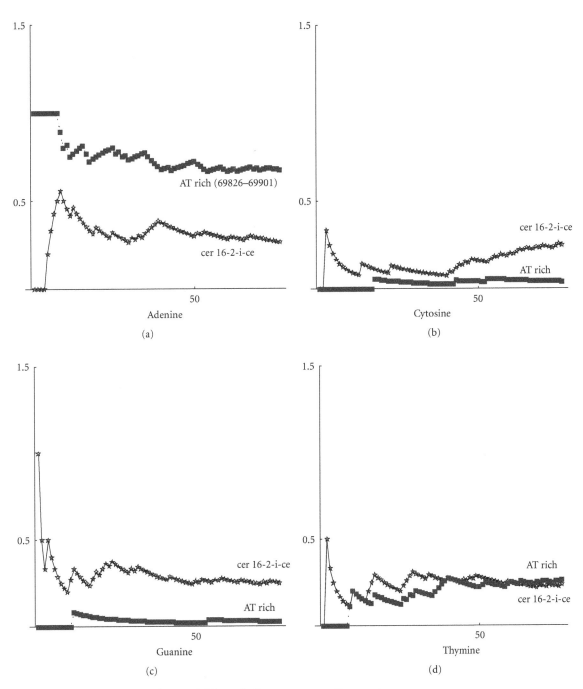

FIGURE 5: Max-min frequency curves for repeats sequence.

TABLE 1: Max value of fractal dimension of sequences.

Type of sequence	Max value of fractal dimension	Tag of genomic sequence
Whole sequence of gene	1.29850	NC 003281 (T19C3.7)
Noncoding	1.29808	NM 064881.5 (T24C4.4)
Coding	1.30639	CB 384383.1
Repeats	1.31280	CER 16-2-i-CE
Random sequence	1.28452	Number 18

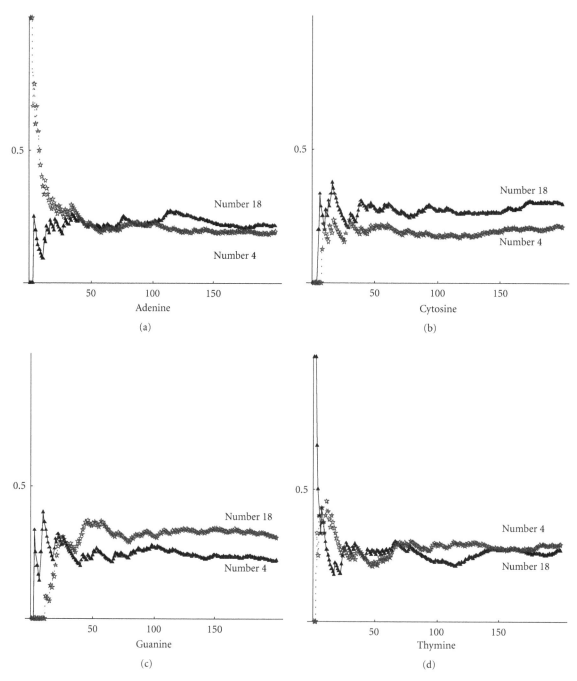

FIGURE 6: Max-min frequency curves for random sequences.

TABLE 2: Min value of fractal dimension of sequences.

Type of sequence	Min value of fractal dimension	Tag of genomic sequence
Whole sequence of gene	1.27016	NC 003281.8 gei-4
Noncoding	1.27494	NM 171076.2 (F42G9.1)
Coding	1.27846	EB 997873.1
Repeats	1.24155	AT rich (69826–69901)
Random sequence	1.28201	Number 4

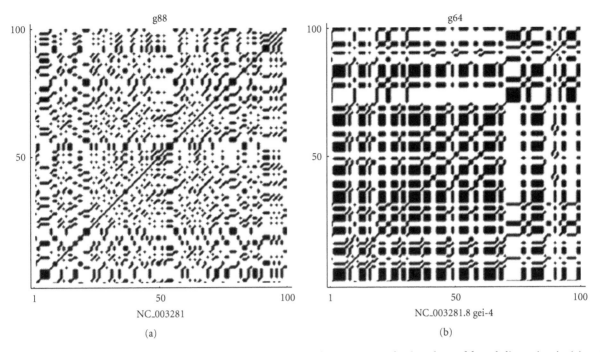

FIGURE 7: Autocorrelation plots on the whole sequence gene corresponding to max and min values of fractal dimension in (a) and (b), respectively.

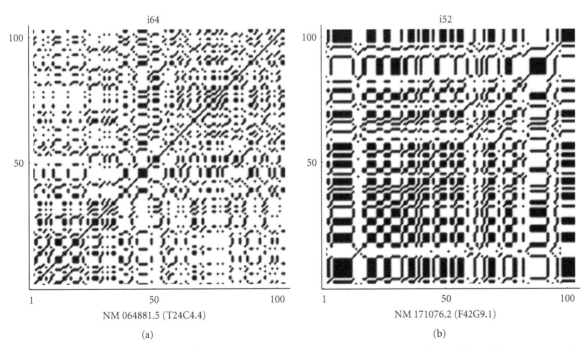

FIGURE 8: Autocorrelation plots on the noncoding sequences corresponding to max and min values of fractal dimension in (a) and (b), respectively.

In order to have a measure of complexity, for an n-length sequence, we use the following definition [20–24]:

$$K = \log \left(\frac{n!}{a_n! c_n! g_n! t_n!} \right)^{1/n} \qquad (8)$$

with

$$a_n = \sum_{h=1,\dots,n} u(A, x_h), \qquad c_n = \sum_{h=1,\dots,n} u(C, x_h),$$

$$g_n = \sum_{h=1,\dots,n} u(G, x_h), \qquad t_n = \sum_{h=1,\dots,n} u(T, x_h). \qquad (9)$$

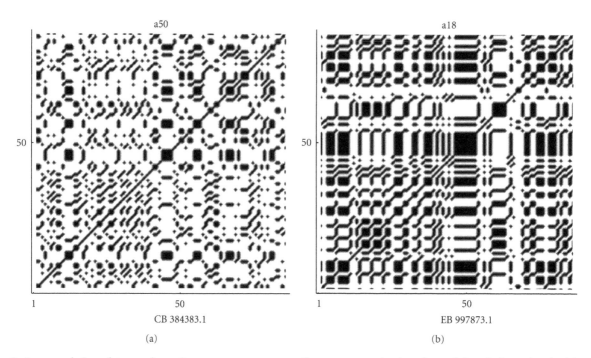

FIGURE 9: Autocorrelation plots on the coding sequences corresponding to max and min values of fractal dimension in (a) and (b), respectively.

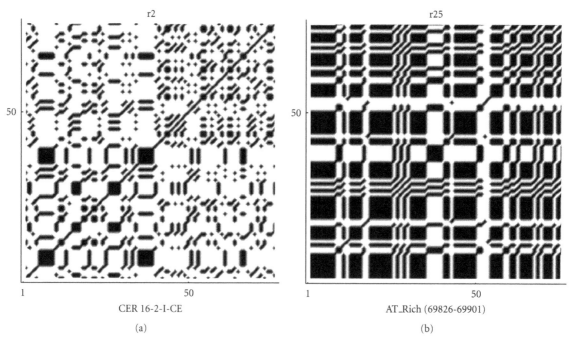

FIGURE 10: Autocorrelation plots on the repeats sequences corresponding to max and min values of fractal dimension in (a) and (b) respectively.

3. Results

By using formula (7), for each sequence of nucleotides, the corresponding fractal dimension has been computed, and obtained results are shown in Tables 1 and 2. In particular, the sequences with max/min values of fractal dimension

among the whole sequences, coding/noncoding sequences, repeat sequences, random sequences have been singled out.

From these computations, we can see that the repeats sequence AT rich (69826–69901) has the lowest fractal value 1.24155. This could be explained because we have a large number of only 2 nucleotides, so that the sequence is simple

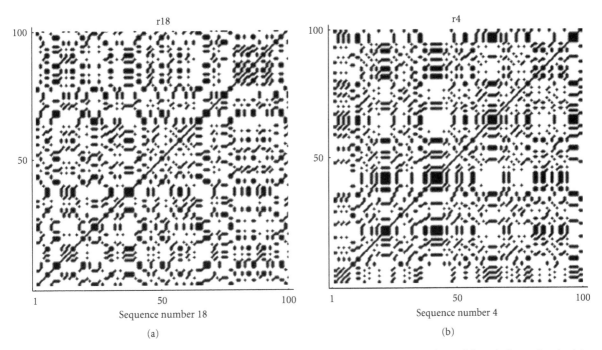

FIGURE 11: Autocorrelation plots on the random sequences corresponding to max and min values of fractal dimension in (a) and (b), respectively.

in the sense that there is a low variability and it shows a low complexity. Analogously, the sequence with the highest value of fractality is still a repeats sequence CER 16-2-i-CE with a fractal dimension 1.31280. Although there are some fluctuations, due to the fact that random generation, by a computer, is indeed a pseudorandom generation, the values of fractal dimension for random sequences are localized around 1.28, which appears to be the intermediate value between the maximum and minimum values obtained for all sequences examined. Further information about the heterogeneity of data is given by the complexity parameter (8). In Figure 1, the complexity curves corresponding to the sequences for maximum and minimum values of the fractal are plotted.

We investigated the complexity of the nucleotide sequences. In all cases, we obtained that the curve of higher complexity corresponds to the sequence with the highest fractal dimension. Thus, we can draw the conclusion that complexity and fractal dimension are equivalent parameters for studying the complexity. These results depend on the distribution of nucleotides. By using the definition (6), we can compute the frequency distribution on a sequence. Below are shown the frequencies for each nucleotide (adenine, cytosine, guanine, thymine). In particular, in Figure 2, the max-min curves for frequencies on the whole gene sequence are plotted. It can be seen that, in this case, adenine and cytosine tend to have the same value, while thymine and guanine maintain a significant distance between the max and min curves. Max-min frequency curves for noncoding sequences are shown in Figure 3. By taking into account the values of fractal dimensions, as given in Tables 1 and 2, we can observe that the higher frequency of cytosine corresponds to the higher fractal dimension.

Thymine, instead, is more present in sequences with low fractal dimension. In Figure 4, the curves for max-min frequency of coding sequences are drawn. It can be seen, also in this case, that adenine and thymine are more present in the sequence with lower fractal dimension. As before, cytosine is more present in sequences with higher fractal dimension. Repeats and random sequences are given in Figures 5 and 6, respectively. In the first case for adenine, we have more frequencies rate for the low fractal sequence, while for cytosine we have more frequencies rate for the high fractal sequence. For random sequences, we have that the cytosine is more frequent in the sequence that has the highest value of fractal.

By the frequency analysis and the results of Tables 1 and 2 on the fractal dimension we can see that there is a correspondence between the frequencies of nucleotides and the fractal dimension. So that, sequences that show a lower fractal dimension have always a higher frequency for the adenine and thymine (in most cases), while the cytosine is more frequent in high fractal sequences. Almost the same results are true also for random sequences, especially for the thymine and cytosine. According to (5), the indicator map of the N-length sequence can be easily represented by the $N \times N$ sparse matrix of binary values $\{0, 1\}$ and this matrix can be visualized by the following (autocorrelation) dot-plots [20, 22] of Figures 7, 8, 9, 10, and 11. Figure 11(a) shows the sequences (of Table 1) with max value of fractal dimension, while in Figure 11(a), there are the sequences of Table 2 with min value of fractal dimension. We can see that also in these plots the distribution of nucleotides gives rise to some typical patterns.

All sequences with low fractal dimension (Figure 11(b)) turn out to have an important presence of nucleotide correlation, this feature is less present in the sequences with higher fractal dimension, where we expect to have a more complex structure of the sequence.

4. Discussion

In this work, by means of statistical parameters such as indicator matrix, complexity, frequency, and fractal dimension, the different types of sequences (repeats, coding, noncoding, whole gene, random) of chromosome 3 (the one with the highest fractality) of the *C. elegans* have been analyzed. Our attempt was to give a statistical classification of these sequences and to understand the complexity of the sequences as a function of the nucleotides' distribution. By using (7) the values of the fractal dimension for all sequences are obtained. In detail, it was observed that the repeats sequences (which do not code for proteins) have a higher variability of values, since they assume the minimum and maximum on all sequences in the *C. elegans*. This leads us to analyze the role and the functional meaning of the repeats within the sequences of genes. Thereafter, we have verified the equivalence, with respect to the complexity, between the fractal dimension and complexity, since the sequences with highest fractality appear to have also a greater degree of complexity. Through the frequency distribution of nucleotide, it was noticed that the adenine is more present in sequences having a lower fractal dimension and, in particular, for the one being in absolute the lowest fractal (AT RICH). This result seems to be dependent on the fact that the sequence is made up of only 2 nucleotides, that is, adenine and thymine. Cytosine, instead, appears to be the most frequent nucleotide in the sequence with the highest fractal value and in particular for the sequence CER 16-2-i-CE. These results lead us to conjecture that there is a correlation between fractal dimension and the frequency of nucleotides such as adenine and cytosine. The information contents of a sequence of nucleotides depend on the different distribution of nucleotides, so that two sequences having the same nucleotides which are distributed according to two different permutations might have two different complexities (fractal dimension). In future work, this aspect of the different organization within the sequence will be further analyzed. Moreover, these results must be confirmed in other organisms which are evolutionarily distant from each other to better investigate the findings so far. At the moment, the obtained results were compared with some random sequences, which have a nucleotide random distribution, and in that case, we have obtained a significant correspondence with the complexity of the nucleotide sequences.

References

[1] S. Brenner, "The genetics of Caenorhabditis elegans," *Genetics*, vol. 77, no. 1, pp. 71–94, 1974.

[2] C. Kenyon, "The nematode Caenorhabditis elegans," *Science*, vol. 240, no. 4858, pp. 1448–1453, 1988.

[3] J. Hodgkin, H. R. Horvitz, B. R. Jasny, and J. Kimble, "C. elegans: sequence to biology," *Science*, vol. 282, no. 5396, p. 2011, 1998.

[4] A. F. Bird and J. Bird, *The Structure of Nematodes*, Academic Press, San Diego, Calif, USA, 1991.

[5] D. L. Riddle, T. Blumenthal, R. J. Meyer, and J. R. Priess, *C. elegans II*, Cold Spring Harbor Laboratory Press, New York, NY, USA, 1997.

[6] P. E. Velez, L. E. Garreta, E. Martinez et al., "The Caenorhabditis elegans genome: a multifractal analysis," *Genetics and Molecular Research*, vol. 9, no. 2, pp. 949–965, 2010.

[7] B. Mandelbrot, *The Fractal Geometry of Nature*, W. H. Freeman & Co, San Francisco, Calif, USA, 1982.

[8] S. S. Cross, "Fractals in pathology," *Journal of Pathology*, vol. 182, no. 1, pp. 1–8, 1997.

[9] J. W. Baish and R. K. Jain, "Fractals and cancer," *Cancer Research*, vol. 60, no. 14, pp. 3683–3688, 2000.

[10] S. S. Cross and D. W. K. Cotton, "The fractal dimension may be a useful morphometric discriminant in histopathology," *Journal of Pathology*, vol. 166, no. 4, pp. 409–411, 1992.

[11] A. L. Goldberger and B. J. West, "Fractals in physiology and medicine," *Yale Journal of Biology and Medicine*, vol. 60, no. 5, pp. 421–435, 1987.

[12] Z. G. Yu, V. Anh, and K. S. Lau, "Measure representation and multifractal analysis of complete genomes," *Physical Review E*, vol. 64, no. 3, Article ID 031903, pp. 319031–319039, 2001.

[13] Z. G. Yu, V. Anh, and K. S. Lau, "Multifractal and correlation analyses of protein sequences from complete genomes," *Physical Review E*, vol. 68, no. 2, Article ID 021913, pp. 021913-1–021913-10, 2003.

[14] G. A. Losa and T. F. Nonnenmacher, "Self-similarity and fractal irregularity in pathologic tissues," *Modern Pathology*, vol. 9, no. 3, pp. 174–182, 1996.

[15] Y. Xiao, R. Chen, R. Shen, J. Sun, and J. Xu, "Fractal dimension, of exon and intron sequences," *Journal of Theoretical Biology*, vol. 175, no. 1, pp. 23–26, 1995.

[16] J. G. McNally and D. Mazza, "Fractal geometry in the nucleus," *The EMBO journal*, vol. 29, no. 1, pp. 2–3, 2010.

[17] R. L. Adam, R. C. Silva, F. G. Pereira, N. J. Leite, I. Lorand-Metze, and K. Metze, "The fractal dimension of nuclear chromatin as a prognostic factor in acute precursor B lymphoblastic leukemia," *Cellular Oncology*, vol. 28, no. 1-2, pp. 55–59, 2006.

[18] D. P. Ferro, M. A. Falconi, R. L. Adam et al., "Fractal characteristics of May-Grünwald-Giemsa stained chromatin are independent prognostic factors for survival in multiple myeloma," *PLoS ONE*, vol. 6, no. 6, Article ID e20706, 2011.

[19] National Center for Biotechnology Information, http//www.ncbi.nlm.nih.gov/genbank/.

[20] C. Cattani, "Fractals and hidden symmetries in DNA?" *Mathematical Problems in Engineering*, vol. 2010, Article ID 507056, 31 pages, 2010.

[21] C. Cattani and G. Pierro, "Complexity on acute myeloid leukemia mRNA transcript variant," *Mathematical Problems in Engineering*, vol. 2011, Article ID 379873, 16 pages, 2011.

[22] C. Cattani, "Wavelet algorithms for DNA analysis," in *Algorithms in Computational Molecular Biology: Techniques, Approaches and Applications*, M. Elloumi and A. Y. Zomaya, Eds., Wiley Series in Bioinformatics, chapter 35, pp. 799–842, John Wiley & Sons, New York, NY, USA, 2010.

[23] C. Cattani, "On the existence of wavelet symmetries in archaea DNA," *Computational and Mathematical Methods in Medicine*, vol. 2012, Article ID 673934, 21 pages, 2012.

[24] C. Cattani, "Complexity and simmetries in DNA sequences," in *Handbook of Biological Discovery, (Wiley Series in Bioinformatics)*, M. Elloumi and A. Y. Zomaya, Eds., Chapter 5, pp. 700–742, John Wiley & Sons, New York, NY, USA, 2012.

[25] R. F. Voss, "Evolution of long-range fractal correlations and 1/f noise in DNA base sequences," *Physical Review Letters*, vol. 68, no. 25, pp. 3805–3808, 1992.

[26] R. F. Voss, "Long-range fractal correlations in DNA introns and exons," *Fractals*, vol. 2, no. 1, pp. 1–6, 1992.

5

BRASERO: A Resource for Benchmarking RNA Secondary Structure Comparison Algorithms

Julien Allali,[1, 2] Cédric Saule,[3] Cédric Chauve,[4] Yves d'Aubenton-Carafa,[5]
Alain Denise,[3, 6] Christine Drevet,[6] Pascal Ferraro,[1, 2] Daniel Gautheret,[6] Claire Herrbach,[3, 6]
Fabrice Leclerc,[7] Antoine de Monte,[8] Aida Ouangraoua,[8] Marie-France Sagot,[9]
Michel Termier,[6] Claude Thermes,[5] and Hélène Touzet[8]

[1] LaBRI, UMR 5800 CNRS, Université Bordeaux, 351, Cours de la Libération, 33405 Talence Cédex, France
[2] The Pacific Institute for the Mathematical Sciences, University of British Columbia, CNRS UMI 3069, 200-1933 West Mall Vancouver, BC, Canada V6T 1Z2
[3] LRI, UMR 8623 CNRS, Université Paris-Sud and INRIA Saclay, 91405 Orsay Cédex, France
[4] Department of Mathematics, Simon Fraser University, 8888 University drive, Burnaby, BC, Canada V5A 1S6
[5] Centre de Génétique Moléculaire, UPR 3404 CNRS, Avenue de la Terrasse, Bât. 26, 91198 Gif-Sur-Yvette, France
[6] IGM, CNRS UMR 8621, Université Paris-Sud, 91405 Orsay Cédex, France
[7] MAEM, CNRS UMR 7567, Université Henri Poincaré, 1 Boulevard des Aiguillettes, BP 239, 54506 Vandoeuvre-Les-Nancy Cédex, France
[8] LIFL, CNRS UMR 8022, Université Lille 1 and INRIA, 59655 Lille Cédex, France
[9] Inria Rhône-Alpes and LBBE, UMR 5558 CNRS, Université Claude Bernard, Bât. Grégor Mendel, 43 Boulevard du 11 Novembre 1918, 69622 Villeurbanne Cédex, France

Correspondence should be addressed to Julien Allali, allali@labri.fr

Academic Editor: Alejandro Schäffer

The pairwise comparison of RNA secondary structures is a fundamental problem, with direct application in mining databases for annotating putative noncoding RNA candidates in newly sequenced genomes. An increasing number of software tools are available for comparing RNA secondary structures, based on different models (such as ordered trees or forests, arc annotated sequences, and multilevel trees) and computational principles (edit distance, alignment). We describe here the website BRASERO that offers tools for evaluating such software tools on real and synthetic datasets.

1. Introduction

Motivated by the fundamental role of RNAs, and especially of small noncoding RNAs, several methods for high-throughput generation of noncoding RNA candidates have been developed recently [1–3]. A fundamental problem is then to infer functional annotation for such putative RNA genes [4, 5] which often involves RNA structure comparisons. Most approaches to compare RNA structures focus on the secondary structure, an intermediate level between the sequence and the full three-dimensional structure, which is both tractable from a computational point of view and relevant from a functional genomics point of view. The

problem we consider here is the following: given a new RNA secondary structure (*the query*) and a database of known and annotated RNA secondary structures which of these known structures display most structural features similar to the query? Databases such as RFAM [6] or RNA STRAND [7] come naturally to mind, but in-house collections of RNA structures resulting from high-throughput experiments can also be considered.

Fundamentally, mining a database of RNA secondary structures naturally reduces to pairwise comparisons between the query and the (or a subset of the) structures recorded in the database. The pairwise comparison of RNA secondary structures is a long-standing problem in computational biology, that is still being investigated, as shown by several recent papers, based on different RNA structure representations and computational principles (e.g., [8–12]).

We present here BRASERO, a website that contains several benchmark data sets and automatic software tools to compare the performances of RNA secondary structure comparison methods. The software tools available on BRASERO are flexible and can be used with alternative benchmarks data sets, for example designed by a user with some specific application in mind, with the purpose to assess which models/software tools/parameters are relevant for their own specific application. We describe below the main features of BRASERO and illustrate its use by presenting a short evaluation of several *pairwise comparison* programs based on computing an edit distance or alignment.

2. BRASERO Benchmarks and Tools

A BRASERO benchmark, either provided on BRASERO or designed by a user, aims at assessing the ability of several pairwise RNA secondary structures comparison software tools to properly classify the sequences into positive and negative sets with respect to a given reference set. This assessment is motivated by the practical problem of identifying similar structures (structural homologs) into a large RNA database (see Figure 1).

2.1. Structure of a Benchmark. A benchmark is composed of three sets of RNA (sequences and structures): the *reference*, *positive*, and *negative* sets. For the BRASERO benchmarks currently available, the reference is a set of RNA secondary structures which are all assumed to be members of a same RNA family and for which reliable secondary structures are known; the notion of family or reliable structure could be relaxed in an ad hoc way for specific new benchmarks.

The positive set contains RNA secondary structures that are assumed to belong to the same family as the reference set. The negative set is a set of RNA secondary structures that do not belong to the reference family. More precisely, let $\mathcal{F}$ be an RNA family. The reference set is denoted by R. A set P_s of RNA gene *sequences* that belong to $\mathcal{F}$ but not to R is folded into putative secondary structures using various programs such as mfold [13], RNAshapes [14], or RNAsubopt [15]. For each RNA folding method, both optimal and several suboptimal structures are kept. The set of secondary structures obtained from this folding is the *positive set* and denoted by P. Finally, we consider a set N_s of sequences randomly picked from a noise source that is supposed to be free of RNA from $\mathcal{F}$ and whose lengths have the same distribution as the RNA in R. Sequences of N_s are folded (using the same programs and parameters as for P_s) to form the *negative set N*.

BRASERO currently comes with data for 5 families: subunit 16S of ribosomal RNAs, microRNAs, small RNAs (sRNAs), Signal Recognition Particles (SRP), and transfer RNAs (tRNAs). The reference genes have been selected manually by the RNA biologists of our team to satisfy the following criteria: accuracy of the structures and inclusion of a large set of possible variations, both in terms of structure and length. To generate sequences of the negative set F, we use several sources: viral genomes (from the NCBI Viral Genome Resource) [16], ENCODE sequences [17], and GenRGenS, a generator of random structured sequences [18]. The BRASERO website contains also a documentation on the file formats of a benchmark and the required steps to design a benchmark.

2.2. Assessing RNA Comparison Methods Performances. To assess a pairwise RNA secondary structure comparison method, we compare each structure of R with each structure of T and F using this method. Then for each sequence of T and F the best score obtained over the comparison of its putative secondary structures and the elements of R is kept. Finally, sequences of T and F are sorted according to these scores. A receiver operating characteristic (ROC) curve is plotted to represent the capability of separating true events (sequences known to be from the $\mathcal{F}$ family) and false events (sequences not in $\mathcal{F}$). This curve shows the false-positive rate *versus* the true-positive rate. The ROC curve of a given benchmark is based on a single run. Indeed, the process of analyzing a benchmark is purely deterministic, the only random aspect lying in the design of the benchmark. For a given RNA family it is possible to design several benchmarks, with several sources (possibly random) of negative sequences.

To perform such experiment with several RNA comparison methods on the same benchmark, a *benchmarking engine* is available on the BRASERO website. It consists of a Java program, that takes as input a benchmark, the considered comparison software tools, and, for every comparison software, a parameters file and a Java class to interface it with the engine. The Java interfaces for several of the classical RNA secondary structure comparison software tools are provided on the website, and a documentation on the format of such interface is also available. For each integrated tool, a Java class indicates if the best score is the smallest (distance approach) or the largest (similarity approach). This information is used to sort the results. Additional Python and Java programs are available to analyze results, to compute ROC curves or to build new benchmarks.

We conclude this section with two important remarks. First the results of a benchmark depend on the method used to fold the positive and negative sets, so our approach can be seen as an evaluation of the combined folding + comparison process. Next, in order to perform a proper assessment of pairwise RNA secondary structure comparison method, the scripts available on the BRASERO website do assume that the RNA structure comparison methods are symmetric and thus do not depend on the order in which two structures are compared. It is up to the users to ensure that the methods they compare satisfy this assumption; classical approach to handle such methods will, for example, average or take the minimum of comparing the structures in both possible orders. Such approaches can easily be implemented in the

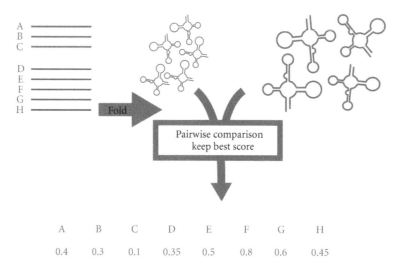

FIGURE 1: Overview of the BRASERO protocol. The benchmark (left part) is composed of positive (red) and negative (blue) sets of RNA sequences, that are folded and then compared to the reference set (right part). Each comparison tool can be parameterized to specify if it is distance based, in which case lower scores are better, or similarity based, in which case higher scores are better.

short JAVA class that has to be written to assess a comparison method (see below).

3. Illustration: Comparison Models and the SRP Family

We illustrate here a typical use of the BRASERO website, by comparing several programs based on computing an edit distance or an alignment between pairs of RNA secondary structures, applied on a benchmark for the RNA family of Signal Recognition Particle (SRP). We compare six tools: RNAdistance [19], RNAforester [10], MiGaL [8], TreeMatching [12], Gardenia [9], NestedAlign [20], and RNAStrAT [11]. These tools rely on different models of secondary structures, such as ordered trees, multilayers models, arc-annotated sequences, but are all based on the edit distance and alignment approach pioneered in [19, 21–23]. As these tools also rely on a different usage of the primary sequence conservation, we also included BLAST [24] for comparison. For each software, the default parameters were used.

RNAforester is an ordered trees local/global alignment algorithm. It uses a special tree encoding that allows to break nucleotide pairings under certain conditions. MiGaL uses a multilevel representation of the secondary structure composed by four layers coded by rooted ordered trees. The layers model different structural levels from multiloop network to the sequence of nucleotides composing the RNA. The algorithm successively applies edit distance computations to each layer. TreeMatching is based on a quotiented tree representation of the secondary structure which is an autosimilar structure composed of two rooted ordered trees on two different scales (nucleotides and structural elements). The core of the method relies on the comparison of both scales simultaneously: it computes an edit distance between quotiented trees at the macroscopic scale using edit costs defined as edit distances between subtrees at the

microscopic scale. Gardenia and NestdAlign use an arc-annotated-based representation, that allows for complex edit operations, such as arc breaking or arc altering. They allow local and global alignment features. Gardenia notably allows affine gap scores, while NestedAlign implements an original local alignment algorithm. RNAStrAT performs the comparison in two steps. First, it compares stems of the two structures using an alignment algorithm with complex edit operations. Then it finds an optimal mapping between the different stems. All tools were used with the default parameters (in particular their default scoring scheme). We applied all tools on a benchmark available on BRASERO for the SRP family benchmark, with noise obtained from viral genomes (details are available on the website). Results are illustrated in Figure 2. Note the choice of the scoring scheme for a given tool may greatly impact the final results and should be evaluated independently before using BRASERO.

We can observe on Figure 2 a clear separation between the software tools based on the principle of computing a global alignment of arc-annotated sequences, and the software tools based on multilayer or hierarchical approaches, that rely on more local alignments. The later seem to perform better, that is, to have a better classification power for the SRP family. Without providing a full analysis of the obtained results, which is beyond the scope of this note, a possible explanation could be that the SRP family exhibits much less sequence and structure conservation than other RNA families (such as tRNA) and that multilayer approaches are able to break down the task of aligning two structures into corresponding sub-structures. This observation, together with its interpretation, can then be used directly in restricting the set of software tools/models to consider when analyzing SRP secondary structures, but also in a longer term perspective by orienting further research specific to this family towards methods based on a multilayer approach.

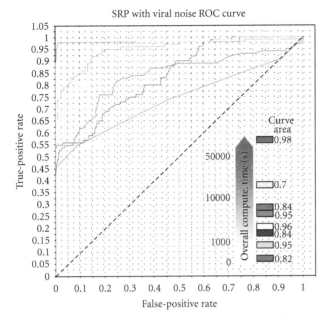

FIGURE 2: SRP benchmark with 8 pairwise edit distance/alignment methods. ROC curve and computation time. By increasing computation time: BLAST, RNAdistance, Gardenia, NestedAlign, RNAStrAT, Migal, RNAforester, and TreeMatching.

4. Conclusion

BRASERO provides useful tools and benchmarks for comparing RNA secondary structures software tools. Application can be in helping researchers decide on which tool to use either for comparing new RNA secondary structures with a specific family, or in assessing good parameters for pairwise comparison software tools in mining large sets of RNA secondary structures.

Further developments will consist in increasing the number of benchmarks and allowing users to provide their own benchmarks, and in developing additional analysis tools.

Acknowledgments

This work was funded by the ANR (Agence Nationale pour la Recherche) project BRASERO (ANR-06-BLAN-0045). Additional funding was provided by the Pacific Institute for Mathematical Sciences (PIMS, UMI CNRS 3069) and the Natural Sciences and Engineering Research Council of Canada (NSERC).

References

[1] E. Zhu, F. Zhao, G. Xu et al., "MirTools: microRNA profiling and discovery based on high-throughput sequencing," *Nucleic Acids Research*, vol. 38, no. 2, Article ID gkq393, pp. W392–W397, 2010.

[2] C. M. Sharma, S. Hoffmann, F. Darfeuille et al., "The primary transcriptome of the major human pathogen Helicobacter pylori," *Nature*, vol. 464, no. 7286, pp. 250–255, 2010.

[3] I. Irnov, C. M. Sharma, J. Vogel, and W. C. Winkler, "Identification of regulatory RNAs in Bacillus subtilis," *Nucleic Acids Research*, vol. 38, no. 19, Article ID gkq454, pp. 6637–6651, 2010.

[4] L. Childs, Z. Nikoloski, P. May, and D. Walther, "Identification and classification of ncRNA molecules using graph properties," *Nucleic Acids Research*, vol. 37, no. 9, article e66, 2009.

[5] P. Menzel, J. Gorodkin, and P. F. Stadler, "The tedious task of finding homologous noncoding RNA genes," *RNA*, vol. 15, no. 12, pp. 2075–2082, 2009.

[6] P. P. Gardner, J. Daub, J. Tate et al., "Rfam: wikipedia, clans and the "decimal" release," *Nucleic Acids Research*, vol. 39, supplement 1, pp. D141–D145, 2011.

[7] M. Andronescu, V. Bereg, H. H. Hoos, and A. Condon, "RNA STRAND: the RNA secondary structure and statistical analysis database," *BMC Bioinformatics*, vol. 9, article 340, 2008.

[8] J. Allali and M. F. Sagot, "A multiple layer model to compare RNA secondary structures," *Software—Practice and Experience*, vol. 38, no. 8, pp. 775–792, 2008.

[9] G. Blin, A. Denise, S. Dulucq, C. Herrbach, and H. Touzet, "Alignments of RNA structures," *IEEE/ACM Transactions on Computational Biology and Bioinformatics*, vol. 7, no. 2, pp. 309–322, 2010.

[10] M. Höchsmann, T. Töller, R. Giegerich, and S. Kurtz, "Local similarity in RNA secondary structures.," *Proceedings/IEEE Computer Society Bioinformatics Conference*, vol. 2, pp. 159–168, 2003.

[11] V. Guignon, C. Chauve, and S. Hamel, "RNA StrAT: RNA Structure Analysis Toolkit," in *16th Annual International Conference on Intelligent Systems for Molecular Biology (ISMB 2008)*, p. D31, 2008.

[12] A. Ouangraoua, P. Ferraro, L. Tichit, and S. Dulucq, "Local similarity between quotiented ordered trees," *Journal of Discrete Algorithms*, vol. 5, no. 1, pp. 23–35, 2007.

[13] N. R. Markham and M. Zuker, "DINAMelt web server for nucleic acid melting prediction," *Nucleic Acids Research*, vol. 33, no. 2, pp. W577–W581, 2005.

[14] S. Janssen and R. Giegerich, "Faster computation of exact RNA shape probabilities," *Bioinformatics*, vol. 26, no. 5, Article ID btq014, pp. 632–639, 2010.

[15] I. L. Hofacker, "Vienna RNA secondary structure server," *Nucleic Acids Research*, vol. 31, no. 13, pp. 3429–3431, 2003.

[16] D. L. Wheeler, T. Barrett, D. A. Benson et al., "Database resources of the National Center for Biotechnology Information," *Nucleic Acids Research*, vol. 35, no. 1, pp. D5–D12, 2007.

[17] E. A. Feingold, P. J. Good, M. S. Guyer et al., "The ENCODE (ENCyclopedia of DNA Elements) Project," *Science*, vol. 306, no. 5696, pp. 636–640, 2004.

[18] Y. Ponty, M. Termier, and A. Denise, "GenRGenS: software for generating random genomic sequences and structures," *Bioinformatics*, vol. 22, no. 12, pp. 1534–1535, 2006.

[19] B. A. Shapiro and K. Zhang, "Comparing multiple RNA secondary structures using tree comparisons," *Computer Applications in the Biosciences*, vol. 6, no. 4, pp. 309–318, 1990.

[20] C. Herrbach, "Etude algorithmique et statistique de la comparaison des structures secondaires d'ARN," Ph.D. thesis, Université Bordeaux 1, 2007.

[21] K. Zhang and D. Shasha, "Simple fast algorithms for the editing distance between trees and related problems," *SIAM Journal on Computing*, vol. 18, no. 6, pp. 1245–1262, 1989.

[22] T. Jiang, L. Wang, and K. Zhang, "Alignment of trees—an alternative to tree edit," *Theoretical Computer Science*, vol. 143, no. 1, pp. 137–148, 1995.

[23] T. Jiang, G. Lin, B. Ma, and K. Zhang, "A general edit distance between RNA structures," *Journal of Computational Biology*, vol. 9, no. 2, pp. 371–388, 2002.

[24] S. F. Altschul, W. Gish, W. Miller, E. W. Myers, and D. J. Lipman, "Basic local alignment search tool," *Journal of Molecular Biology*, vol. 215, no. 3, pp. 403–410, 1990.

6

A Multilevel Gamma-Clustering Layout Algorithm for Visualization of Biological Networks

Tomas Hruz,[1] **Markus Wyss,**[2] **Christoph Lucas,**[1] **Oliver Laule,**[2]
Peter von Rohr,[2] **Philip Zimmermann,**[2] **and Stefan Bleuler**[2]

[1] *Institute of Theoretical Computer Science, ETH Zurich, 8092 Zurich, Switzerland*
[2] *NEBION AG, Hohlstraße 515, 8048 Zurich, Switzerland*

Correspondence should be addressed to Markus Wyss; mw@nebion.com

Academic Editor: Guohui Lin

Visualization of large complex networks has become an indispensable part of systems biology, where organisms need to be considered as one complex system. The visualization of the corresponding network is challenging due to the size and density of edges. In many cases, the use of standard visualization algorithms can lead to high running times and poorly readable visualizations due to many edge crossings. We suggest an approach that analyzes the structure of the graph first and then generates a new graph which contains specific semantic symbols for regular substructures like dense clusters. We propose a multilevel gamma-clustering layout visualization algorithm (MLGA) which proceeds in three subsequent steps: (i) a multilevel γ-clustering is used to identify the structure of the underlying network, (ii) the network is transformed to a tree, and (iii) finally, the resulting tree which shows the network structure is drawn using a variation of a force-directed algorithm. The algorithm has a potential to visualize very large networks because it uses modern clustering heuristics which are optimized for large graphs. Moreover, most of the edges are removed from the visual representation which allows keeping the overview over complex graphs with dense subgraphs.

1. Introduction

The development in systems biology has brought a strong interest in considering an organism as a large and complex network of interacting parts. Many subsystems of living organisms can be modeled as complex networks. One important example is a network of biochemical reactions which constitutes a complex system responsible for homeostasis in the living cell. An abstract network model of the biochemical processes within the cell can be constructed such that reactions are represented as nodes and metabolites (and enzymes) as edges. In the past, this system was studied mainly on a subsystem level through metabolic pathways. Recently, it has become important to consider the metabolic system as one complex network to understand deeper phenomena involving interactions across multiple pathways.

The need to study the whole network consisting of thousands of reactions, metabolites, and enzymes requires a visualization system allowing biologists to study the overall structure of the system. Such a visualization should allow navigation and comprehension of the global system structures. In the present paper, we propose a visualization algorithm for very large networks arising in systems biology and we illustrate its usage on two complex biological networks. The first case study is a metabolic network of *Arabidopsis thaliana* and the second case study is a gene correlation network of *Mus musculus* based on mRNA expression measurements.

Biological networks are usually represented as graphs because such model can provide an insight into their structure. The goal of the subsequent visualization is to present the information contained in the graph in a clear and structured way. For instance, closely related nodes of a subsystem should be positioned together. This can be achieved using a cost function which formalizes the visualization criteria and which controls the drawing algorithm. Several standard algorithms exist to achieve this goal using continuous optimization of the cost function, but the optimization of a discrete cost function remains hard to solve.

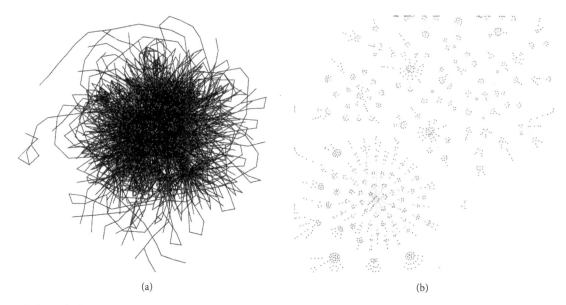

(a)

(b)

FIGURE 1: *Arabidopsis thaliana* metabolic network visualized with (a) a force-directed algorithm with all edges shown, (b) the MLGA method which combines γ-clustering with the force-directed algorithm. The underlying network has 1199 reactions (nodes) and 4386 metabolites (edges).

A widely used graph drawing method for larger graphs is the force-directed layout algorithm [1, 2]. Basically, the graph is modeled as a physical system. A force is calculated on every node: a repulsive force between every pair of nodes and an attractive force if an edge exists between two nodes. The forces direct the system into a steady state which defines a final layout. However, the method has several disadvantages for large graphs with many edges. First, a straightforward implementation needs to calculate the forces between each node-pair in each iteration. Second, for complex graphs too many iterations are needed to find an optimal layout. Third, a drawback results from the node degree distribution in biological networks which tends to be skewed (scale-free). Few nodes have a high degree while a large number of nodes have a small degree. The attractive forces will stick together the nodes with many interactions in a small area which prevents the identification of the network structure in the dense parts of the network; see Figure 1(a). The repulsive force against the other nodes leads to a scattered layout. To overcome these disadvantages, other graph visualization methods have emerged which are discussed later. On the other hand, for a very specific class of graphs like trees, a modified version of force-directed algorithm can be still a suitable method.

The visualization of very large biological networks was considered in [3]. The large graph layout algorithm (LGL) separates the graph into connected components, lays out each connected component separately, and integrates these layouts into one coordinate system. A grid variant of the spring-based algorithm [1] is used to draw the graph for each connected component. To separate dense parts of each component, the minimum spanning tree (MST) is calculated to define the order in which nodes are included in the layout computation. Beginning from a root node of the MST, new nodes with increasing edge distance from the root are

iteratively added to the layout. The new nodes are placed randomly on spheres away from the current layout. At each iteration, the spring-based layout algorithm is executed until the layout is at rest. Under certain conditions, this node placement strategy reduces cluttering and retains the structure of core components; moreover, it separates highly connected components. This layout phase is illustrated in [3, page 181, Figure 1]. However, in some situations, the LGL algorithm can even obfuscate the true structure of the graph. Consider the situation where in the graph two cliques are connected by a matching. The MST algorithm will represent this subgraph as a star having many paths of length two from the center and one path of length three leading to the center of the second clique. The rendering according to LGL would lead to a situation where the first clique is placed in the interior of the second clique. Such starting configuration can easily lead to a situation where the force-directed algorithm cannot separate the cliques; moreover, the edges of the second clique would cross the rest of the graph. The problem is that in this situation the MST algorithm reduces the second clique to one edge. In such cases a different solution would be needed as we describe later.

The problem of fast visualization for protein interaction networks was studied in [4]. The method uses an approach with a grouping phase, and a layout phase. In the grouping phase the algorithm identifies the connected components of the graph and uniformly selects pivot nodes in each component. The selection of the pivot nodes is controlled by a set of rules based on empirical parameters. In the layout phase, the pivot nodes define an initial layout of the connected components. Afterwards, the layout of each connected component is refined separately. The authors show that the method is faster than many other algorithms; however, a certain disadvantage of this algorithm is the choice of pivot nodes involving many parameters and a complex set of rules. The rules and its parameters are heuristically identified to give a uniform distribution of the nodes within the connected component. Another drawback is that the method per se cannot visualize, the structure of dense subgraphs because of too many edge crossings (see [4, page 1887, Figure 3]). To improve the visualization the authors introduce visual operations to collapse the cliques (and complete bipartite subgraphs) to reduce the number of edges and nodes. Additionally, the problem of finding maximal clique (or complete bipartite subgraph) is NP hard together with its approximation there is almost no chance to have fast identification heuristics for large graphs. Our algorithm improves the situation in this respect because relaxing requested density of the subgraph through γ-clustering (where $0 \leq \gamma \leq 1$ is the cluster density) allows much more efficient heuristics for large graphs (order 10^6 nodes and edges [5]).

A global optimization method was explored in [6] where the authors describe a layout algorithm for metabolic networks. Nodes of the graph are placed on a square grid. A discrete cost function between a pair of nodes is introduced based on their relation and position on the grid. By minimizing the total cost, a layout is generated. A simulated annealing heuristic is used to optimize the cost function by choosing better layouts among possible candidates. Due to the computationally costly calculation of the layout, the approach is applicable to networks with a few hundred nodes only. The authors showed that the algorithm works well on sparse or planar graphs and clarifies the network structure as the cost function of the method places closely related nodes together. But this layout algorithm would place dense parts of the graph in the same area leading to many edge crossings. Additionally, as no reduction in the number of edges or nodes is performed, the identification of the graph structure would be very hard for large graphs with many edges.

2. MLGA Approach

The experience with the existing visualization methods has shown that it is necessary to provide a structural view of dense networks. Representing networks with a large number of nodes and edges in a two-dimensional area results in many edge crossings. Dense subgraphs prevent the recognition of the network structure if drawn directly. Apart from other technical problems, this is the main shortcoming of most layout algorithms. We believe that the future progress in visualization of large and dense networks lies in algorithms which analyze the structure of the graph first and then generate a new graph which contains specific semantic symbols for regular substructures like dense clusters. Additionally, the algorithms may allow for drilling down and interactively show all edges for a given substructure, described below (see section visual representation and operation). Dense clusters are ideal candidates for graph preprocessing because they can be simply described, efficiently searched, and if they are replaced with a specific symbol they significantly reduce the complexity of the resulting low-dimensional (planar or three dimensional) picture because they contain most of the edges. Moreover, we focus on the graph clustering algorithms

because the underlying dimension of graphs can be very high providing difficulties for other clustering algorithms.

Graph clustering is a large field with many algorithms developed over the years [7]; however, there is no universal solution for all cases. Even a definition of a cluster comes in many flavors with different algorithmic consequences. Therefore, it is important to consider a certain class of graphs which is sufficiently general in the context of bioinformatics but allows for using an efficient clustering method. Recently new clustering methods emerged based on the idea of so-called γ-clusters [5] or (α, β)-clusters [8]. These methods use fast heuristics which allow for clustering efficiently large graphs. The existence of such methods inspired the general idea behind our research to use clustering algorithms to build a hierarchical structure of a given graph which can be much better visualized and which tells the users more about the structure of the underlying biological network. In the following, we focus on γ-clusters but other graph clustering methods could be used as well.

3. Algorithm

The MLGA method introduces multilevel γ-clustering and a specific tree transformation with a force-directed layout algorithm to visualize the structure of highly complex biological networks. First, the original graph is preprocessed using a γ-clustering algorithm described in [5] to identify the clusters. For every cluster, a new cluster node is created and these new nodes are linked with new edges if there are edges between the underlying cluster nodes as illustrated in Figure 2.

This process constructs the first hierarchical layer above the original graph. Then, the clustering algorithm is recursively applied to the cluster nodes itself to generate a cluster hierarchy. Afterwards, this hierarchy is transformed to a tree showing only the shortest paths from a root node through the intermediate cluster nodes to the nodes of the initial graph. Finally, a modified version of the force-directed algorithm visualizes the tree structure of the remaining graph. This combination of preprocessing and layout algorithm eases the identification of the cluster structure and their interactions, see Figure 1(b).

For the clustering step, we prefer γ-clustering to (α, β)-clustering or to other more complex methods because it would be much more difficult to control the clustering parameters during the transitions between the hierarchy levels. The only parameter which has to be specified for our algorithm at every hierarchical level is the parameter γ. It can be seen that the density of the graph grows when the algorithm proceeds to the higher levels. On the other hand, the number of nodes decreases very rapidly so that after few steps there is only one clique left. As a consequence, it is not meaningful to use the same clustering parameters as the algorithm recursively proceeds up the hierarchy. For more complex clustering algorithms, it would be very difficult to define a good clustering parameters if the parameter space has more dimensions. In our case, the sequence of the values for the parameter γ must be growing. As we discuss later, the actual values can be empirically determined and moreover 3-4 values are sufficient for large graphs.

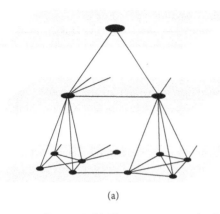 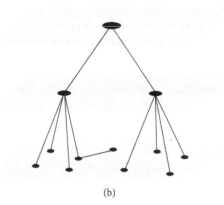

(a)   (b)

FIGURE 2: (a) The construction of a cluster hierarchy and (b) the transformation to a tree.

4. Algorithmic Phases

Let $G = (V, E)$ be an undirected graph G with the vertex set V and edge set E. A γ-cluster for $0 \leq \gamma \leq 1$, also described as γ-clique or dense subgraph, is a subset $S \subseteq V$ such that for its edge set $E(S)$ and the vertex set $V(S)$ the following is true:

$$|E(S)| \geq \gamma \binom{|V(S)|}{2}. \quad (1)$$

Finding a γ-clique of maximal cardinality in G is the maximal γ-clique problem. The 1-clique problem is NP hard and is proved to be hard to approximate [9].

To identify the clusters on one hierarchical level, we use a heuristic developed in [5] to detect γ-clusters for very large graphs. Reference [5] introduced a potential function on a vertex set relative to a given γ-cluster and derived an algorithm to discover maximal γ-clusters. The time complexity of the algorithm is $O(|S||V|^2)$ with S the set of vertexes of the maximal γ-cluster detected. Further, the authors use a greedy randomized adaptive search procedure (GRASP) version of the algorithm with edge pruning. The feasibility of the resulting method was demonstrated by applying it to telecommunication data with millions of vertexes and edges.

5. γ-Cluster Detection

To find all γ-clusters on one level in the graph a variant (Algorithm 1) of the GRASP approach of [5] is used. The cluster construction procedure *construct_dsubg* is the nonbipartite case for finding a high cardinality cluster of specified density γ in a graph with nodes V and edges E. Our algorithm repeatedly applies the detection algorithm to the highest hierarchical level of the new graph. It terminates if no more γ-clusters are found or the number of clusters with a cluster-size below a given minimum size is reached.

6. Hierarchy Creation

The cluster detection algorithm is repeatedly applied to the graph and the clusters to build a hierarchy; see Figure 2(a). Each node of the graph has an attribute level which is

```
input: V: Vertices
input: E: Edges
input: γ: density of cluster
begin
    initialize empty list of clusters C;
    count ← 0;
    cluster ← construct_dsubg(γ, V, E);
    while cluster ≠ ∅ ∧ count < max_count do
        size ← |cluster|;
        if size ≥ min_size then
            add cluster to C;
            count ← 0;
        else
            count ← count + 1;
        end
        set V to V without nodes of cluster;
        set E to E without edges within cluster;
        cluster ← construct_dsubg(γ, V, E);
    end
end
```

ALGORITHM 1: createClusters.

initially assigned to zero. First, the cluster detection algorithm retrieves the clusters of this initial graph. Afterwards, the algorithm iteratively creates the clusters of the next level i among the clusters one level below $i - 1$ (Algorithm 2). To control the density of the clusters on each level a γ_i-value is specified. At each level an edge between the cluster nodes is created if an edge exists between the nodes one level below. Additionally, a new edge is generated between the cluster and the nodes belonging to the cluster. The algorithm terminates if no more clusters are found. This phase resembles hierarchical clustering where new nodes are introduced for hierarchically different clusters but the γ-clustering is based on a completely different density measure and merges multiple nodes in one step. Consequently, this leads to a much lower tree depth (as described in the following section) compared to the hierarchical clustering which generates a binary tree.

```
begin
    level ← 0;
    nodes ← getNodes(level);
    γ ← getGammaValue(level);
    clusters ← createClusters(nodes, γ);
    while clusters ≠ ∅ do
        create one node on the next level for each cluster;
        create edges between clusters and nodes;
        level ← level + 1;
        nodes ← getNodes(level);
        γ ← getGammaValue(level);
        clusters ← createClusters(nodes, γ);
    end
end
```

ALGORITHM 2: createMultiLevelClusters.

7. Tree Transformation

To gain the structure of the cluster hierarchy, a tree transformation is performed; see Figure 2(b). In the transformation (Algorithm 3), a hidden root node is connected to all cluster nodes at the highest level as their parent. Afterwards, only the edges belonging to the shortest path from the root node to each node is shown. If the shortest path is not unique a path will be chosen at random. The distance for each node is calculated beginning from the root using a breath-first search. The parent of a node will be set to the neighbor node with the shortest distance. If the node belongs to a cluster node at one level above, the parent is set to this cluster.

8. Layout Algorithm

A modified version of a force-directed algorithm [2] is used to lay out the transformed graph. Our method introduces different edge length on each level. Longer edges are assigned to higher levels than on lower levels. This results in a natural visualization of the hierarchy. Furthermore, the initial positions of the nodes are specifically calculated. The nodes of the graph are located on concentric circles with the hidden root node at the center. Nodes immediately connected to the root are positioned at the next inner circle and so on. A segment of the circle is assigned to each node within which its location is calculated. Recursively, a fraction of this segment is assigned to the children of the node on the next circle. This initial setup reduces the rendering time and guides the layout algorithm to visualize the tree structure. A random initial positioning may result in a local minimum of the force-directed layout with many edge crossings which would disrupt the tree representation. Additionally, the repulsive forces are ignored beyond a given distance depending on the size of the drawing area. This restriction prevents disconnected components of the graph from separating too far. To suppress the well-known oscillation problem [10] of force-directed algorithms a dumping heuristics is used where we compute an average of the previous node positions during the force calculation.

```
begin
    create root;
    set parent of highest level nodes to root;
    candidates ← highest level nodes;
    foreach node ∈ candidates do
        if node belongs to a cluster one level above then
            node.parent ← cluster;
        else
            set node.parent to the neighbor with shortest
            distance to the root;
        end
        node.dist ← node.parent.dist + 1;
        foreach neighbor of node except node.parent do
            if neighbor has already been visited then
                hide edge;
            else
                candidates ← candidates ∪ neighbor;
            end
        end
    end
end
```

ALGORITHM 3: treeTransformation.

As the graph is transformed to a tree, other layout algorithms can be used in the this phase. Reference [11] uses a level-based approach which horizontally aligns nodes with the same distance from the root node. As only a few levels are created for our initial graph the resulting drawing would have a much larger width than height. A ringed circular approach like [12] where the children of the nodes are plotted on the periphery of a circle has a better space efficiency on the 2D plane than [11]. But a visual inspection of the resulting graph in [12, page 11, Figure 7 (left)] shows that the force-directed layout distributes the children of a node more evenly.

9. Visual Representation and Operation

After the creation of the cluster hierarchy and the tree transformation many initial edge connections are hidden. In the presentation of the resulting graph the nodes of the inital graph are colored depending on the number of edges in the initial graph. Additionally cluster nodes and edges are visualized with different symbols and colors (Figure 3).

Our implementation of the visualization tool offers two operations to get deeper insight into the original graph. First, all edges between a selected node and its direct neighbors can be highlighted (Figure 4(b)). If the marked node is a cluster node, all connections to the nodes of the cluster will be shown. During the tree transformation, most of these connections were eliminated and a direct connection between two nodes in different clusters was replaced by an indirect connection between the cluster nodes. The second operation will display all edges between the nodes forming a γ-cluster node (Figure 4(c)) which allows the user to temporarily alter the view between the star-shaped cluster node and the real connections of the cluster.

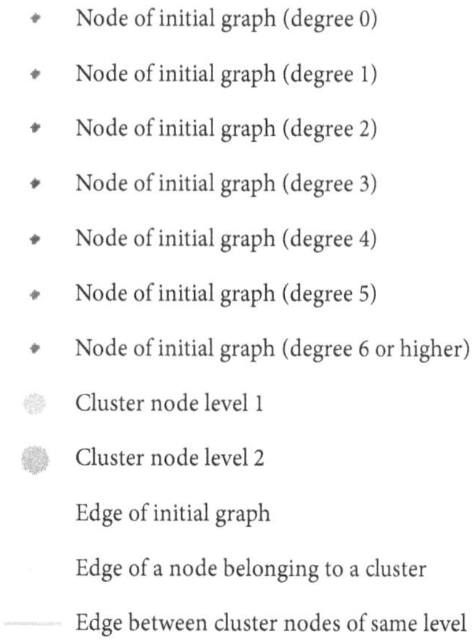

♦ Node of initial graph (degree 0)

♦ Node of initial graph (degree 1)

♦ Node of initial graph (degree 2)

♦ Node of initial graph (degree 3)

♦ Node of initial graph (degree 4)

♦ Node of initial graph (degree 5)

♦ Node of initial graph (degree 6 or higher)

● Cluster node level 1

● Cluster node level 2

Edge of initial graph

Edge of a node belonging to a cluster

——— Edge between cluster nodes of same level

FIGURE 3: Semantic symbols used in MLGA visualization. Nodes and edges are color encoded, nodes of the initial graph are colored according to their degree and cluster nodes are enlarged at each level of the hierarchy.

10. Computation Speed and Memory Requirements

Retrieving a γ-clique with the clustering algorithm of [5] has a running time of $O(|S||V|^2)$ with $|S|$ the size of the detected clique and $|V|$ the size of the initial graph. As the algorithm is recursively applied to the remaining nodes of the graph, a time complexity of at most $O(|V|^3)$ results on each level of the hierarchy. The number of levels depends on the number of clusters found on each level. It ranges from the worst case where two nodes are clustered together $\log_2 |V|$ down to 1 if all nodes are in the same cluster. Therefore, the total runtime order has an upper limit $O((\log_2 |V|)^4)$ and a lower limit $O(|V|^3)$. The tree transformation of the resulting hierarchy uses breath-first search. As new nodes and edges are introduced during the hierarchy creation its runtime ranges from $O(4|V| + |E|)$ down to $O(|V| + |E|)$ in terms of the inital number of nodes $|V|$ and initial number of edges $|E|$.

The implemented version of force-directed layout algorithm needs a runtime of $O(|V|^2)$. A specialized tree layout algorithm like [11] has a runtime of order $O(|V|)$ and [12] an order $O(|V|)$ or $O(|V| \log |V|)$ if an optimal solution for the circle size is required.

The memory required by the algorithm mainly depends on the graph representation. For biological networks a representation between the worst case $O(4|V|+|E|)$ and $O(|V|+|E|)$ space is suitable.

11. Results

11.1. Metabolic Networks. To provide experimental justification of the proposed method, we extracted the metabolic network for *Arabidopsis thaliana* from Genevestigator [13]. The network has 932 nodes and 2315 edges. The edges represent metabolites and the nodes represent biochemical reactions. We used two versions of the network as illustrated in Figure 5(a) where the second version in Figure 5(b) contains additionally the regulatory pathways with enzymes as edges leading to 1199 nodes and 4386 edges.

The application of multi-level γ-clustering to visualize the *A. thaliana* biochemical network (Figure 5(a)) revealed that both global view and lucidity were sustained, which is also true when regulatory pathways were added to the network (Figure 5(b)). We looked at plant isoprenoid biosynthesis, in particular at the synthesis of brassinosteroids (BRs), a class of plant hormones which are essential for the regulation of plant growth and development [14, 15]. All individual reaction steps, leading to BRs, were found structured according to metabolite flux through the pathway as part of a level 2 cluster, also containing upstream pathways as well as reactions leading to other isoprenoid end products (Figure 5(a)). After inclusion of regulatory elements and signal-transduction chains, multi-level γ-clustering assigned the biochemical reactions from brassinosteroid biosynthesis to clusters containing reactions known to be regulated by BRs and elements that are involved in the regulation of this biosynthetic pathway. As an example, the known fact that BRs act synergistically with auxins to promote cell elongation [16] is nicely reflected in the MLGA drawn network (Figure 5(b)).

11.2. Gene Interaction Networks. The MLGA method can also be successfully used to analyze gene interaction networks. Gene interaction networks are constructed as graphs where nodes represent genes and edges represent interactions between genes on various biological levels, as for example, interactions between the corresponding proteins or regulatory and causal interactions obtained from gene expression experiments. There is a long-term research into methods how to obtain networks which identify different kinds of gene interaction networks based on different types of input data [17–22]. However, as we illustrate later, even if a simplified network generation method was used, our visualization algorithm was able to identify correctly the biologically meaningful subsystems from a genomewide correlation network.

To generate the gene correlation networks, we used a *Mus musculus* dataset from the Genevestigator database. The data consisted of 3157 publicly available Affymetrix arrays. Each array measured the expression values of 12488 genes. The gene correlation matrix was calculated using the Pearson correlation and afterwards a network was generated, where an edge was introduced between two genes if the correlation value between the genes was above a certain threshold. Two networks were constructed using a threshold of 0.72 in Figure 6(a) and 0.80 in Figure 6(b).

We use a well-known ribosomal gene complex [23–25] to illustrate the possibilities of MLGA to discover interesting structures in the correlation network. An inspection of the cluster highlighted in Figure 6(a) shows that it contains genes which are documented to belong to the ribosomal cluster. Moreover, our method has a structural stability in a wide range of graph density. This can be seen comparing Figures 6(a) and 6(b). Figure 6(a) has lower threshold; therefore, it contains 38 889 edges and 2774 nodes compared to

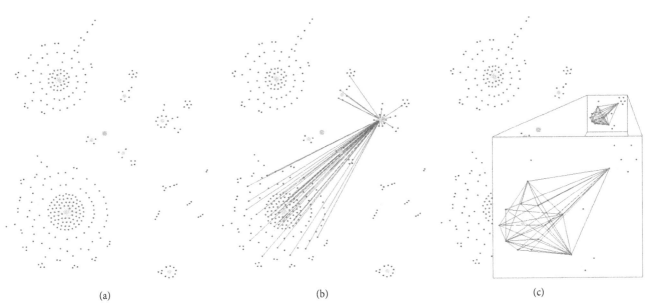

FIGURE 4: (a) A part of a gene correlation network of *Arabidopsis thaliana* drawn with MLGA, (b) showing all edges connected to the γ-cluster node at the top right and (c) displaying all edges between the nodes defining the cluster. The inset shows a magnification of the edges of the selected cluster.

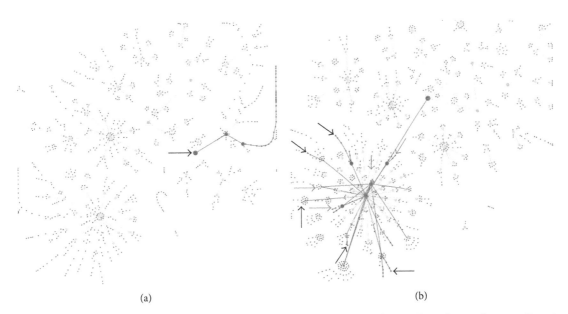

FIGURE 5: MLGA applied to (a) A. thaliana biochemical network without signaling effects and regulatory elements. Reactions directly involved in the synthesis of brassinosteroids are highlighted with the red color and direct connections are depicted by red edges. The level 2 cluster, indicated by an arrow, combines the major parts of isoprenoid biosynthesis, resulting from the nonmevalonate pathway. (b) A. thaliana biochemical network including signaling effects and regulatory elements. Reactions directly involved in brassinosteroid and auxin metabolism/signaling are highlighted with red and direct connections are depicted by red edges. Black arrows point to reactions involved in brassinosteroid metabolism/signaling. Green arrows point to reactions involved in auxin metabolism/signaling.

8659 edges and 1232 nodes in Figure 6(b). In both cases the ribosomal cluster can be clearly identified.

12. Discussion

Visualization methods often contain parameters which must be empirically identified. In [4], the selection of pivot nodes is determined by a set of empirical values to achieve a uniform distribution of these nodes in the network. Afterwards, the layout is computed with respect to the selected pivot nodes. In our method, the only important empirically set parameters are the cluster densities γ on each hierarchical level. This influences the granularity of the visualization and the subsequent tree transformation supports the recovering

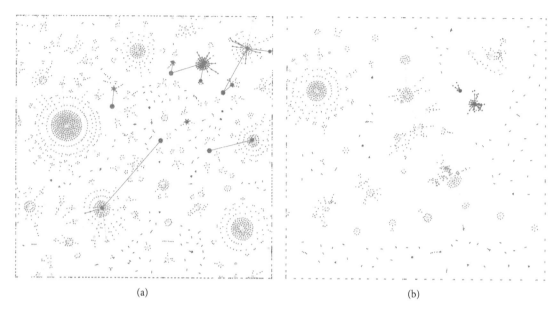

(a)   (b)

FIGURE 6: MLGA applied to (a) *Mus musculus* gene correlation network generated with a threshold of 0.72. (b) The gene correlation network generated with a threshold of 0.80. The red highlighted nodes and direct connections belong to the ribosomal cluster.

of the network structure. The computational experience has shown that it is recommended to use a slightly smaller γ value in the first than in the subsequent levels; we use 0.5 and 0.7, respectively. The density of the graph grows considerably over the hierarchical levels. In most of the experiments with a graph sizing up to 10^5 edges the third level was already a clique. Therefore, very few γ values are needed even for large graphs.

A different approach in a similar direction as our research is described in [26]. The authors consider weighted graphs where vertexes with degree 1 are repeatedly removed until no more vertex of degree 1 exists. The removed nodes can be added at the end of the drawing algorithm. After that, a hierarchy of clusters is calculated on the remaining graph using an approximation of the graph distances. A cluster is formed if the pairwise shortest path of its nodes is equal to or above a threshold which depends on the hierarchy level. This leads to different definition of clusters than in our algorithm together with a different cluster heuristics. The algorithm preserves more edges than in our case making the structure of the graph more difficult to identify. Comparing the result of MLGA Figure 1(b) with [26], the structure of graphs in [26] is only partially resolved (see, e.g., [26, page 2, Figure 1]). Similarly as in our case a version of force-directed algorithm is used in the last stage to refine the visualization. A higher weight is assigned to the edges between the nodes of a cluster than to the edges between clusters. This forces the nodes of a cluster to be drawn close to each other. In our approach, the additional cluster node and the desired edge length have a similar effect.

In addition to complexity problems for large graphs (NP-hard approximation), the algorithms based on identification of cliques have also a drawback that it is often not clear which cliques are relevant. This problem is particularly present in cases of graphs with dense subgraphs, where we obtain

a system of large cliques with similar sizes which have additionally large intersections. In particular, in the presence of noise where every measurement defines a graph which differs in a small percentage of edges, it is difficult to decide during visualization based on cliques which part of the graph can be emphasized as structurally important. An interesting development is represented by [27] where the authors concentrate on intersections of large clusters under a condition that these intersections are cliques. They identify so-called "atom subgraphs" which represent clique minimal separator decomposition (a separator is a set of vertexes whose removal will disconnect the graph into several parts). However, the relaxation from cliques to dense clusters in our method improves also on the intersection problem because our method would glue the cliques with large intersection into one cluster.

13. Conclusion

As discussed, many approaches try to improve the layout of complex networks through better placement of the nodes alone. In our work, we pursue a different line of research towards efficient visualization algorithms for large biological networks. Our approach does not aim at rendering all edges in a network, but we focus on the discovery and visualization of important structural features. This approach is combined with complementary visual operations which allow to drill-down into the details of structurally identified elements. The MLGA method is successful in identifying the biologically relevant structures and allows for processing very large graphs as we illustrated on two different case studies of biological networks. Naturally, this paradigm opens new questions on how to further improve the visualization output and speed. Different clustering algorithms can be tried to create the multi-level structure; however, in the case of multiparameter clustering the control and analysis of the parameter values between the levels would become more difficult.

On the theoretical side, the next question to consider is how to provide a provably good (optimal) sequence of γ values. Another question is whether the surprisingly good structure identification features of our algorithm could be traced back to the scale-free character of many biological networks.

Disclosure

All materials, source code, and small case studies data can be freely downloaded from http://www.pw.ethz.ch/research/projects/complexnetworks/. Very large datasets are available on request.

Acknowledgments

The authors would like to thank Professor Peter Widmayer for the ongoing support of this project. This work was also supported by Commission for Technology and Innovation of the Swiss Federation under Grant 9428.1 PFLS-LS.

References

[1] T. Kamada and S. Kawai, "An algorithm for drawing general undirected graphs," *Information Processing Letters*, vol. 31, no. 1, pp. 7–15, 1989.

[2] T. M. J. Ffuchterman and E. M. Reingold, "Graph drawing by force-directed place-ment," *Software*, vol. 21, no. 11, pp. 1129–1164, 1991.

[3] A. T. Adai, S. V. Date, S. Wieland, and E. M. Marcotte, "LGL: creating a map of protein function with an algorithm for visualizing very large biological networks," *Journal of Molecular Biology*, vol. 340, no. 1, pp. 179–190, 2004.

[4] K. Han and B.-H. Ju, "A fast layout algorithm for protein interaction networks," *Bioinformatics*, vol. 19, no. 15, pp. 1882–1888, 2003.

[5] J. Abello, M. Resende, and S. Sudarsky, "Massive quasi-clique detection," in *LATIN 2002: Theoretical Informatics*, S. Rajsbaum, Ed., vol. 2286 of *Lecture Notes in Computer Science*, pp. 598–612, Springer, Berlin, Germany, 2002.

[6] W. Li and H. Kurata, "A grid layout algorithm for automatic drawing of biochemical networks," *Bioinformatics*, vol. 21, no. 9, pp. 2036–2042, 2005.

[7] S. E. Schaeffer, "Graph clustering," *Computer Science Review*, vol. 1, pp. 27–64, 2007.

[8] N. Mishra, R. Schreiber, I. Stanton, and R. Tarjan, "Clustering social networks," in *Algorithms and Models For the Web-Graph*, A. Bonato and F. Chung, Eds., vol. 4863 of *Lecture Notes in Computer Science*, pp. 56–67, Springer, Berlin, Germany, 2007.

[9] J. Hastad, "Clique is hard to approximate within $n^{1-\varepsilon}$," *Acta Mathematica*, vol. 182, pp. 105–142, 1999.

[10] A. Frick, A. Ludwig, and H. Mehldau, "A fast adaptive layout algorithm for undirected graphs (extended abstract and system demonstration)," in *Graph Drawing*, R. Tamassia and I. Tollis, Eds., vol. 894 of *Lecture Notes in Computer Science*, pp. 388–403, Springer, Berlin, Germany, 1995.

[11] E. M. Reingold and J. S. Tilford, "Tidier drawings of trees," *IEEE Transactions on Software Engineering*, vol. SE-7, no. 2, pp. 223–228, 1981.

[12] S. Grivet, D. Auber, J. P. Domenger, and G. Melancon, "Bubble tree drawing algorithm," in *Computer Vision and Graphics*, K. Wojciechowski, B. Smolka, H. Palus, R. Kozera, W. Skarbek, and L. Noakes, Eds., vol. 32 of *Computational Imaging and Vision*, pp. 633–641, Springer, Dordrecht, The Netherlands, 2006.

[13] T. Hruz, O. Laule, G. Szabo et al., "Genevestigator v3: a reference expression database for the meta-analysis of transcriptomes," *Advances in Bioinformatics*, vol. 2008, Article ID 420747, 5 pages, 2008.

[14] T. Asami, Y. K. Min, K. Sekimata et al., "Mode of action of brassinazole: a specific inhibitor of brassinosteroid biosynthesis," *ACS Symposium Series*, vol. 774, pp. 269–280, 2001.

[15] J.-X. He, J. M. Gendron, Y. Yang, J. Li, and Z.-Y. Wang, "The GSK3-like kinase BIN2 phosphorylates and destabilizes BZR1, a positive regulator of the brassinosteroid signaling pathway in Arabidopsis," *Proceedings of the National Academy of Sciences of the United States of America*, vol. 99, no. 15, pp. 10185–10190, 2002.

[16] K. J. Halliday, "Plant hormones: the interplay of brassinosteroids and auxin," *Current Biology*, vol. 14, no. 23, pp. R1008–R1010, 2004.

[17] K. Y. Yip, R. P. Alexander, K.-K. Yan, and M. Gerstein, "Improved reconstruction of in silico gene regulatory networks by integrating knockout and perturbation data," *PLoS ONE*, vol. 5, no. 1, Article ID e8121, 2010.

[18] M. Mutwil, B. Usadel, M. Schütte, A. Loraine, O. Ebenhöh, and S. Persson, "Assembly of an interactive correlation network for the Arabidopsis genome using a novel Heuristic Clustering Algorithm," *Plant Physiology*, vol. 152, no. 1, pp. 29–43, 2010.

[19] D. Marbach, R. J. Prill, T. Schaffter, C. Mattiussi, D. Floreano, and G. Stolovitzky, "Revealing strengths and weaknesses of methods for gene network inference," *Proceedings of the National Academy of Sciences of the United States of America*, vol. 107, no. 14, pp. 6286–6291, 2010.

[20] S. De Bodt, S. Proost, K. Vandepoele, P. Rouzé, and Y. Van de Peer, "Predicting protein-protein interactions in Arabidopsis thaliana through integration of orthology, gene ontology and co-expression," *BMC genomics*, vol. 10, p. 288, 2009.

[21] D. R. Rhodes, S. A. Tomlins, S. Varambally et al., "Probabilistic model of the human protein-protein interaction network," *Nature Biotechnology*, vol. 23, no. 8, pp. 951–959, 2005.

[22] A. de la Fuente, N. Bing, I. Hoeschele, and P. Mendes, "Discovery of meaningful associations in genomic data using partial correlation coefficients," *Bioinformatics*, vol. 20, no. 18, pp. 3565–3574, 2004.

[23] J.-F. Rual, K. Venkatesan, T. Hao et al., "Towards a proteome-scale map of the human protein-protein interaction network," *Nature*, vol. 437, no. 7062, pp. 1173–1178, 2005.

[24] K. Ishii, T. Washio, T. Uechi, M. Yoshihama, N. Kenmochi, and M. Tomita, "Characteristics and clustering of human ribosomal protein genes," *BMC Genomics*, vol. 7, article 37, 2006.

[25] O. Atias, B. Chor, and D. A. Chamovitz, "Large-scale analysis of Arabidopsis transcription reveals a basal co-regulation network," *BMC Systems Biology*, vol. 3, p. 86, 2009.

[26] R. Bourqui, D. Auber, and P. Mary, "How to draw clustered weighted graphs using a multilevel force-directed graph

drawing algorithm," in *Proceedings of the 11th International Conference Information Visualization (IV '07)*, pp. 757–764, July 2007.

[27] B. Kaba, N. Pinet, G. Lelandais, A. Sigayret, and A. Berry, "Clustering gene expression data using graph separators," *In Silico Biology*, vol. 7, no. 4-5, pp. 433–452, 2007.

7

A Topology-Based Metric for Measuring Term Similarity in the Gene Ontology

Gaston K. Mazandu and Nicola J. Mulder

Computational Biology Group, Department of Clinical Laboratory Sciences, Institute of Infectious Disease and Molecular Medicine, University of Cape Town, Cape Town 7925, South Africa

Correspondence should be addressed to Nicola J. Mulder, nicola.mulder@uct.ac.za

Academic Editor: Satoru Miyano

The wide coverage and biological relevance of the Gene Ontology (GO), confirmed through its successful use in protein function prediction, have led to the growth in its popularity. In order to exploit the extent of biological knowledge that GO offers in describing genes or groups of genes, there is a need for an efficient, scalable similarity measure for GO terms and GO-annotated proteins. While several GO similarity measures exist, none adequately addresses all issues surrounding the design and usage of the ontology. We introduce a new metric for measuring the distance between two GO terms using the intrinsic topology of the GO-DAG, thus enabling the measurement of functional similarities between proteins based on their GO annotations. We assess the performance of this metric using a ROC analysis on human protein-protein interaction datasets and correlation coefficient analysis on the selected set of protein pairs from the CESSM online tool. This metric achieves good performance compared to the existing annotation-based GO measures. We used this new metric to assess functional similarity between orthologues, and show that it is effective at determining whether orthologues are annotated with similar functions and identifying cases where annotation is inconsistent between orthologues.

1. Introduction

Worldwide DNA sequencing efforts have led to a rapid increase in sequence data in the public domain. Unfortunately, this has also yielded a lack of functional annotations for many newly sequenced genes and proteins. From 20% to 50% of genes within a genome [1] are still labeled unknown, uncharacterized, or hypothetical, and this limits our ability to exploit these data. Therefore, automatic genome annotation, which consists of assigning functions to genes and their products, has to be performed to ensure that maximal benefit is derived from these sequencing efforts. This requires a systematic description of the attributes of genes and proteins using a standardized syntax and semantics in a format that is human readable and understandable, as well as being interpretable computationally. The terms used for describing functional annotations should have definitions and be placed within a structure of relationships. Therefore, an ontology is required in order to represent annotations of known genes and proteins and to use these to predict functional annotations of those which are identified but as yet uncharacterized.

By capturing knowledge about a domain in a shareable and computationally accessible form, ontologies can provide defined and computable semantics about the domain knowledge they describe [2]. In biology, ontologies are expected to produce an efficient and standardized functional scheme for describing genes and gene products. Generally, such an ontology should be designed to cover a wide range of organisms, ensuring the integration of biological phenomena occurring in a wide variety of biological systems. In addition, it must be dynamic in nature in order to enable the design to incorporate new knowledge of gene and protein roles over time. One of the biggest accomplishments in this area is the creation of the gene ontology (GO) [3], which currently serves as the dominant and most popular functional classification scheme [4, 5] for functional representation and annotation of genes and their products. The construction of the gene ontology (GO) [3] arose from the necessity for organizing and unifying biology and information about genes and proteins shared by different organisms. At its outset, GO aims at producing a dynamic, structured and controlled vocabulary describing the role of genes and their products in any organism, thus allowing humans and computers to resolve language ambiguity.

GO provides three key biological aspects of genes and their products in a living cell, namely, complete description of the tasks that are carried out by individual proteins, their broad biological goals, and the subcellular components, or locations where the activities are taking place. GO consists of three distinct ontologies, molecular function (MF), biological process (BP), and cellular component (CC), each engineered as a directed acyclic graph (DAG), allowing a term (node) to have more than one parent. Traditionally, there were two types of relationships between a parent and a child. The "is_a" relation means that a child is a subclass or an instance of the parent, and the "part_of" relation indicates the child is a component of a parent. Thus, each edge in a GO-DAG represents either an "is_a" or a "part_of" association. However, another relationship has emerged, namely, "regulates", which includes "positively_regulates" and "negatively_regulates", and provides for relationships between regulatory terms and their regulated parents [6]. As we are only interested in the GO-DAG topology in the sense that where a term occurs, its parents also occur, regardless of whether the term regulates the parent term or not, we only use the relations "is_a" and "part_of" here, and these are treated equally. The is_a relationships are more prominent, constituting approximately 88% for BP, 99% for MF, and 81% for CC, of all the relationships, so the impacts of part_of relationships are less significant.

The GO has been widely used and deployed in several protein function prediction analyses in genomics and proteomics. This growth in popularity is mainly due to the fundamental organization principles and functional aspects of its conception displayed by its wide coverage and biological relevance. Specific tools, such as the AmiGO browser [7, 8], have been developed for making GO easy to use and have significantly contributed to the large expansion of GO in the experimental and computational biology fields. Nowadays, GO is the most widely adopted ontology by the life science community [9], and this superiority has been proven by successes resulting from its use in protein function prediction. The GO annotation (GOA-UniProtKB) project arose in order to provide high-quality annotations to gene products and is applied in the UniProt knowledgebase (UniProtKB) [10–13]. It also provides a central dataset for annotation in other major multispecies databases, such as Ensembl and NCBI [14].

Considering its wide use, the issues related to its design and usage have been qualified as critical points [15] to be taken into account for effectively deploying GO in genome annotation or analysis. One of the issues is associated with the depth of GO, which often reflects the vagaries in different levels of biological knowledge, rather than anything intrinsic about the terms [2]. Consequently, two genes or proteins may be functionally similar but technically annotated with different GO Ids. Although several approaches have been designed

to assess the similarity and correlation between genes [16–21] using their sequences or gene expression patterns from high-throughput biology technologies, some methods exist for measuring functional similarities of genes based on their GO annotations but these have their drawbacks. An effective approach should be able to consider the issue related to the depth of the GO-DAG raised previously and provide a clear relation of how similar a parent and child are using only the GO-DAG topology. This should apply to gene or protein GO annotations derived from different sources and be independent of the size of the GO-DAG, as GO is still expanding.

Several GO term similarity measures have been proposed for characterizing similar terms, each having its own strengths and weaknesses. These similarity measures are partitioned into edge- and node-based approaches according to Pesquita et al. [9]. Edge-based similarity measures are based mainly on counting the number of edges in the graph to get the path between two terms [22, 23]. Among them, we have the longest shared path (LP) approach implemented in the GOstats package of Bioconductor [24] and the IntelliGO approach suggested by Benabderrahmane et al. [25]. Although these approaches use only the intrinsic structure of the hierarchy under consideration, they generally suffer from the fact that they consider only the distance between terms, ignoring their position characteristics within the hierarchy. Thus, nodes at the same level have the same semantic distance to the root of the hierarchy, producing a biased semantic similarity between terms. In order to alleviate this issue, edges can be weighted differently depending on their level in the hierarchy to influence the similarity scores [26]. Unfortunately, using these edge weighting approaches does not completely resolve the problem [9]. The node-based approaches use the concept of information content, also called semantic value, to compare the properties of the terms themselves and relations to their ancestors or descendants, and these measures are referred to as IC-based (information content-based) approaches [27].

Here we introduce a new semantic similarity measure of GO terms based only on the GO-DAG topology to determine functional closeness of genes and their products based on the semantic similarity of GO terms used to annotate them. This measure incorporates position characteristic parameters of GO terms to provide an unequivocal difference between more general terms at the higher level, or closer to the root, and more specific terms at the lower level, or further from root node. This provides a clearer topological relationship between terms in the hierarchical structure. This new measure is a hybrid node- and edge-based approach, overcoming not only the issue related to the GO-DAG depth, as stated previously, but also the issues related to the dependence on the annotation statistics of node-based approaches and those related to edge-based approaches in which nodes and edges at the same level are evenly distributed.

2. Materials and Methods

In this section we survey existing annotation- and topology-based approaches and set up a novel GO semantic similarity metric in order to measure GO term closeness in the hierarchy of the GO-directed acyclic graph (DAG). This novel GO term semantic similarity measure is derived in order to ensure effective exploitation of the large amounts of biological knowledge that GO offers. This, in turn, provides a measurement of functional similarity of proteins on the basis of their annotations from heterogeneous data using semantic similarities of their GO terms.

2.1. Existing GO-IC-Based Semantic Similarity Approaches.

We are interested in the IC-based approaches, and unlike the graph-based or hybrid approach introduced by Wang et al. [28], which is based on the intrinsic structure of the GO-DAG, that is, only uses the GO-DAG topology to compute the semantic similarity, other measures do not consider only the topology. Most of them are adapted from Resnik [29] or Lin's [30] methods, in which the information content (or semantic value) of a term conveying its biological description and specificity is based on the annotation statistics related to the term [2, 31], and thus they have a natural singularity problem caused by orphan terms. Here these approaches are referred to as Resnik-related approaches. In these approaches, the more often the term is used for annotation, the lower its semantic value, and as pointed out by Wang et al., this may lead to different semantic values of the GO terms for GO annotation data derived from different sources. However, each biological term in the ontology is expected to have a fixed semantic value when used in genome annotation. The semantic value is defined as the biological content of a given term, and this is particularly a problem in the hierarchical structure of the GO-DAG if the information will be used to predict functions of uncharacterized proteins in the genome, since one source can annotate a given protein with a term at a low level and another source with a term at a higher level in the hierarchy. Furthermore, the description and specificity of a given term in GO essentially depends on its GO annotation specification, translated by its position in the GO-DAG structure or topology.

To overcome these limitations, Wang introduced a topology-based semantic similarity measure in which the semantic value of a term z is given by

$$\mathrm{IC}_W(z) = \sum_{t \in T_z} S_z(t),\qquad(1)$$

where T_z denotes the set of ancestors of the term z including z, and $S_z(t)$ is calculated as follows:

$$S_z(t) = \begin{cases} 1, & \text{if } t = z, \\ \max\{\omega_e * S_z(t') : t' \in \mathcal{C}_h(t)\}, & \text{otherwise,} \end{cases}\qquad(2)$$

with $\mathcal{C}_h(t)$ being the set of children of the term t, and ω_e the semantic contribution factor for "is_a" and "part_a" relations set to 0.8 and 0.6, respectively. The semantic similarity of the two GO terms is given by

$$S_W(x, y) = \frac{\sum_{t \in T_x \cap T_y} \left(S_x(t) + S_y(t) \right)}{\mathrm{IC}_W(x) + \mathrm{IC}_W(y)}.\qquad(3)$$

It has been shown that the Wang et al. approach performs better than Resnik's approach in clustering gene pairs according to their semantic similarity [27, 28].

On the edge-based similarity approaches, Zhang et al. [32] introduced a GO-topology-based approach to assess protein functional similarity for retrieving functionally related proteins from a specific proteome, overcoming the common issue of other edge-based approaches mentioned previously. This was achieved by computing a measure called the D value, which depends only on the children of a given GO term and is numerically equal to the sum of D values of all its children. Thus, the D value of a GO term is calculated using a recursive formula starting from leaves in the hierarchical structure, where the D-value of all leaves are equal and set to the inverse multiplicative of the count of the root obtained by recursively summing the counts of all the direct children from the bottom up, with the count of the leaf set to 1. Note that the count of a given nonleaf term is just the number of all paths from that term node to all leaves connected to the term. In this approach, the D value for a pair of terms x and y is given by

$$D(x, y) = \min\{D(z) : z \in \mathcal{A}(x, y)\}.\qquad(4)$$

However, a general limitation common to all these semantic similarity measures is that none of them fully address the issue related to the depth of the GO-DAG as stated previously; that is, the depth sometimes reflects vagaries in different levels of knowledge. An example is where the structure is just growing deeper in one path without spreading sideways. In the context of the GO-DAG, such a term is sometimes declared obsolete and automatically replaced by its parent. Thus, to consider this issue, we are introducing a topological identity or synonym term measure based on term topological information in which a parent term having only one child and that child term having only that parent are assumed to be topologically identical and they are assigned the same semantic value. This provides an absolute difference between more general terms closer to the root and more specific terms further from the root node, depending on the topology of the GO-DAG, that is, whether a branch splits into more than one possible path of specificity. Furthermore, this is consistent with the human language in which the semantic similarity between a parent term and its child depends on the number of children that the parent term possesses and also the number of parents that the child term has. Intuitively a parent having more children loses specificity and this parent is no longer relevant to be used for its child specification, thus leading to a lower similarity score between this parent and each of its children.

To illustrate this, let us consider the hierarchical structure in Figure 1 where "a", "b", "c", "d", and "e" are terms used to annotate proteins in a given genome and these terms are linked by the relation "is_a". For the Zhang et al. approach, the semantic values of "b" and "d" are the same, which is 1.09861 ($-\ln(1/3)$), but it fails to distinguish between "d" and "e", which would be expected to have different semantic values. The Wang et al. approach will assign different semantic values to "b" and "d"; the semantic value of

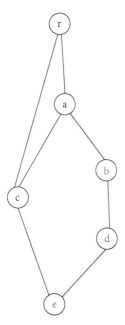

FIGURE 1: Fictitious hierarchical structure illustrating the computation of term semantic values. Terms are nodes with "r" as a root.

"b" is 2.44 and that of "d" is 2.952, although they are topologically identical in the sense that there is no other option going down the DAG except to "d". For annotation-based approaches, if we consider a genome, for example, which has been annotated by two different labs, referred to as heterogeneous sources, it is likely that the terms "b" and "d" will not occur at the same frequency, in which case "b" and "d" will have different semantic values. For this new measure, the term "b" has only one child "d", which has only one parent "b" (no sideways spread) and therefore the term "d" does not have additional value compared to "b" in the illustration in Figure 1. This means that "b" and "d" are topologically identical (synonymous) and have the same fixed semantic value, equal to 1.38629. This is different to the semantic value of the term "e", which is 3.46574 as "e" could be "derived" from two different branches.

2.2. GO Term Topological Information and New GO Term Similarity Approach. Translating the biological content of a given GO term into a numeric value, called the semantic value or topological information, on the basis of its location in the GO-DAG, requires knowledge of the topological position characteristics of its immediate parents. This leads to a recursive formula for measuring topological information of a given GO term, in which the child is expected to be more specific than its parents. The more children a term has, the more specific its children are compared to that term, and the greater the biological difference. In addition, the more parents a term has, the greater the biological difference between this term and each of its parent terms. The three separate ontologies, namely, molecular function (MF), biological process (BP), and cellular component (CC) with GO Ids GO: 0003674, GO: 0008150, and GO: 0005575 respectively, are roots for the complete ontology, located at

level 0, the reference level, and are assumed to be biologically meaningless. Unless specified explicitly, in the rest of this work the level of a term is considered to be the length of the longest path from the root down to that term in order to avoid a given term and its child having the same level. $\mathcal{N}_{GO}$ and $\mathcal{L}_{GO}$ will, respectively, express the set of GO terms and links, $(x, y) \in \mathcal{L}_{GO}$ represents the link or association between a given parent x and its child y, and the level of the link (x, y) is the level of its source node x. Finally, $[x, y] \in \mathcal{N}_{GO}$ indicates that the level of term x is lower than that of y.

Definition 1. The topological information $IC_T(z)$ of a given term $z \in \mathcal{N}_{GO}$ is computed as

$$IC_T(z) = -\ln(\mu(z)), \qquad (5)$$

where $\mu(z)$ is a topological position characteristic of z, recursively obtained using its parents gathered in the set $\mathcal{P}_z = \{x : (x, z) \in \mathcal{L}_{GO}\}$, and given by

$$\mu(z) = \begin{cases} 1, & \text{if } z \text{ is a root,} \\ \displaystyle\prod_{x \in \mathcal{P}_z} \frac{\mu(x)}{\mathcal{C}_x}, & \text{otherwise,} \end{cases} \qquad (6)$$

with $\mathcal{C}_x$ being the number of children of parent term x.

A topological position is thus a function $\mu : \mathcal{N}_{GO} \to [0, 1]$, such that for any term $t \in \mathcal{N}_{GO}$, $\mu(t)$ defines a reachability measure of an instance of term t. Obviously, μ is monotonically increasing as one moves towards the root; that is, if t_1 is_a t_2, then $\mu(t_1) \le \mu(t_2)$. For the top node or root, the reachability measure is 1. Furthermore, this reachability measure takes into account information of parents of the term under consideration through their reachability measures and that of every parent's children by incorporating the number of children that each parent term has in order to quantify how specific a given child is compared to each of its parent terms.

Note that, in general, the information we possess about something is a measure of how well we understand it and how well ordered it is. $\mu(z)$ provides a precise indicator of all we know about the term z in the DAG structure. As μ is decreasing when moving towards leaves and a strictly positive defined function, the multiplicative inverse of μ is an increasing function. This implies that $1/\mu(z)$ is a measure of how we understand the term z and how ordered it is in the DAG, which merely means that the inverse of $\mu(z)$ measures the information we possess about the term z in the context of the DAG structure. The formula in (5) is a logarithmic weighting of the inverse of $\mu(z)$, referred to as topological information and measuring what we know about the term z in the DAG structure.

To illustrate the way this approach works, consider the hierarchical structure shown in Figure 2. In this DAG from top to bottom, we have the following.

(i) The topological position characteristic of the root 0 is $\mu(0) = 1$, and so its topological information is $IC_T(1) = -\ln(1) = 0$.

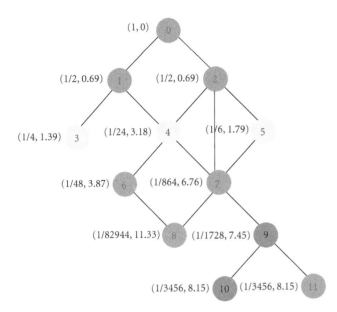

FIGURE 2: Hierarchical structure illustrating how our approach works. Nodes are represented by integers from 0 to 11 with 0 as a root. The numbers beside each node represent its topological position characteristic and information content.

(ii) As 1 and 2 have only parent 0, which has only these two children with $\mu(0) = 1$, this yields $\mu(1) = 1/2 = \mu(2)$, and so their topological information is $IC_T(1) = -\ln(1/2) = 0.69315 = IC_T(2)$.

(iii) 3 has only one direct parent 1 with $\mu(1) = 1/2$ and this parent has two children, we have $\mu(3) = 1/4$, and its topological information is then $IC_T(3) = -\ln(1/4) = 1.38639$.

(iv) 4 has two direct parents 1 and 2. 1 has two children with $\mu(1) = 1/2$ and 2 has three children with $\mu(2) = 1/2$. Thus, its topological position characteristic is the product of topological position characteristics of its parents, respectively, divided by the number of children for each parent $\mu(4) = 1/4 * 1/6 = 1/24$ and its topological information is $IC_T(4) = -\ln(1/24) = 3.17806$.

(v) 5 has only one direct parent 2, which has three children and $\mu(2) = 1/2$. Its topological position characteristic is $\mu(5) = 1/6$ and its topological information is $IC_T = -\ln(1/6) = 1.79176$.

Unlike edge-based approaches where nodes and edges are uniformly distributed, and edges at the same level of the ontology correspond to the same semantic distance between terms [9], in this new approach these parameters depend on the topological position characteristic of terms, which are not necessarily the same. In this illustration, nodes 3, 4, and 5 are at the same level but they do not have the same topological position characteristic, thus leading to different topological information or semantic values. Furthermore, the aforemetioned illustration reveals that the product in formula (6) of topological position characteristic must be carefully considered when implementing the approach, since

the exponential tail-off with increasing depth is severe depending on the density of the hierarchical structure under consideration. Here, we suggest computing $\mu(z)$ iteratively when performing this product, and every time the multiplication is done, the obtained value must immediately be converted to a pair of numbers (α, β) such that $\mu(z) = \alpha 10^\beta$ with $0.1 \leq \alpha < 1$ and $\beta < 0$. This means that every time the product is performed, the new value is converte to this format so that in the end, the topological position characteristic is just given by (α, β) such that $\mu(z) = \alpha 10^\beta$ and $IC_T = -\ln(\alpha) - \beta \ln(10)$.

Definition 2. Let $[x, y] \in \mathcal{N}_{GO}$; x and y are topologically identical or synonym terms and denoted by $x \stackrel{GO}{=} y$, if the following properties are satisfied.

(i) $IC_T(x) = IC_T(y)$ or $\mu(x) = \mu(y)$.

(ii) There exists one path p_{xy} from x to y.

Therefore, two GO terms are equal if and only if they are either the same or topologically identical terms. Suppose that there exists a path p_{xy} from term x to term y, x is a more general term compared to y, or y is more specific compared to x and denoted by $x \stackrel{GO}{<} y$ if $IC_T(x) < IC_T(y)$ or $\mu(y) < \mu(x)$.

The topological position μ provides a new way of assessing the intrinsic closeness of GO terms. Two terms in the GO-DAG may share multiple ancestors as a GO term can have several parents through multiple paths. Therefore, we define the topological position $\mu_s(x, y)$ of x and y as that of their common ancestor with the smallest topological position characteristic, that is,

$$\mu_s(x, y) = \min\{\mu(t) : t \in \mathcal{A}(x, y)\}, \qquad (7)$$

where $\mathcal{A}(x, y) = \mathcal{A} \cup \{x, y\}$ with $\mathcal{A}$ being the set of ancestral terms shared by both terms x and y. Finally, the semantic similarity score of the two GO terms is given by

$$S_{GO}(x, y) = \frac{IC_T(x, y)}{\max\{IC_T(x), IC_T(y)\}}, \qquad (8)$$

with $IC_T(x, y) = -\ln \mu_s(x, y)$ being the topological information shared by the two concepts x and y.

The semantic similarity measure S_{GO} proposed here is referred to as the GO-universal similarity measure [33], as it induces a distance or a metric, d_{GO}, given by $d_{GO}(x, y) = 1 - S_{GO}(x, y)$ (see Supplementary Material available online at doi:10.1155/2012/975783), which in Information Theory is known as a universal metric [34]. The more topological information two concepts share, the smaller their distance and the more similar they are. Moreover, the similarity formula in (8) emphasizes the importance of the shared GO terms by giving more weight to the shared ancestors corrected by the maximum topological information, and thus measuring how similar each GO term is to the other. Thus, for two GO terms sharing less informative ancestors the distance is greater and the similarity is smaller, while for two GO terms sharing more informative ancestors, they are closer and their similarity is higher.

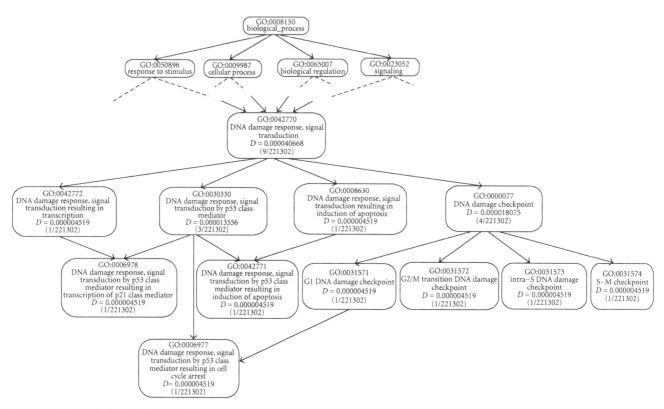

FIGURE 3: Subgraph of the GO BP. Each box represents a GO term with GO ID, D value (Zhang et al. measure). This is used to illustrate our approach and compare its effectiveness to the Zhang et al. approach.

To illustrate the GO-universal approach, we use (5) and (6) to compute the reachability measure $\mu(z)$ and topological information measure $\mathrm{IC}_T(z)$ of GO terms z in a minimum spanning graph shown in Figure 3 adapted from [32]. Results are shown in Table 1 for our approach and the Zhang et al. approach. To relate the scale of Zhang et al. to ours, the D value of a given term is considered to be the probability of usage or occurrence of the term in the structure as suggested by Zhang et al. This means that the information content (IC) of a term x is calculated as

$$\mathrm{IC}_Z(x) = -\ln(D(x)). \qquad (9)$$

Moreover, two approaches, Resnik and Lin's approaches, are used for scaling the semantic similarity measure induced by IC_Z between 0 and 1. The uniform Resnik's measure is given by

$$S_{ZuR}(x, y) = \max\{\mathrm{IC}_{Zu}(a) : a \in \mathcal{A}(x, y)\}, \qquad (10)$$

where $\mathrm{IC}_{Zu}(a)$ is the uniform $\mathrm{IC}_Z(a)$ obtained by dividing $\mathrm{IC}_Z(a)$ by the maximum scale whose value is $\ln N$ where N is the total number of terms within the ontology under consideration. $\mathrm{IC}_{Zu}(a)$ is therefore computed as follows:

$$\mathrm{IC}_{Zu}(a) = \frac{\mathrm{IC}_Z(a)}{\ln N}, \qquad (11)$$

where N is the number of terms in the ontology under consideration. Lin's semantic similarity measure is given by

$$S_{ZL}(x, y) = \max\left\{ \frac{2 \times \mathrm{IC}_Z(a)}{\mathrm{IC}_Z(x) + \mathrm{IC}_Z(y)} : a \in \mathcal{A}(x, y) \right\}. \qquad (12)$$

As we can see, the more specific the term, that is, the further it is from the root node, the higher its topological information, meaning that children are more informative or more specific than their parents, and for two GO terms in the same path, the more specific one will either be more informative or topologically identical to that closer to the root. This is not the case for the Zhang et al. approach, in which the semantic values of the terms at the same level tend to be uniform and a child term is not necessarily more specific than a given parent term, independent of the number of parents that the child term has. Our method distinguishes these different local topologies.

We calculate the semantic similarity between every two consecutive GO terms in Figure 3 and results are given in Table 2 for three different approaches. The formula in (6) shows that, for our approach, the contribution of a given parent to the term depends on the parent reachability measure. The smaller the reachability measure of that parent and the fewer children it possesses, the higher its similarity compared to another parent of the term. From the results in Table 2, we see that GO:0042771 is more similar to GO:0008630 than to GO:0030330, both of which are its

TABLE 1: Names and characteristics of GO terms in Figure 3, including topological position characteristics μ and information content IC_T from our approach and IC_Z and IC_{Zu} from the Zhang et al. approach.

GO Id	Level	μ	IC_T	IC_Z	IC_{Zu}
GO:0042770	6	0.0456910e-27	6.525565e+01	10.11006	0.71747
GO:0042772	7	0.1142274e-28	6.664195e+01	12.30729	0.87340
GO:0030330	7	0.1142274e-28	6.664195e+01	11.20867	0.79544
GO:0000077	7	0.0171747e-34	8.235221e+01	10.92099	0.77502
GO:0008630	10	0.0335723e-86	2.014164e+02	12.30729	0.87340
GO:0006978	8	0.0434930e-57	1.343825e+02	12.30729	0.87340
GO:0006977	9	0.0419985e-79	1.850743e+02	12.30729	0.87340
GO:0042771	11	0.1278292e-116	2.691569e+02	12.30729	0.87340
GO:0031571	8	0.1103023e-50	1.173338e+02	12.30729	0.87340
GO:0031572	8	0.0735349e-50	1.177393e+02	12.30729	0.87340
GO:0031573	8	0.4293676e-36	8.373851e+01	12.30729	0.87340
GO:0031574	8	0.2206046e-50	1.166406e+02	12.30729	0.87340

TABLE 2: Semantic similarity values between child-parent pairwise terms in Figure 3 from the Wang et al. and Zhang et al. approaches are compared to our approach. S_W refers to the semantic similarity between two GO terms obtained using the Wang semantic similarity approach from G-SESAME (Gene Semantic Similarity Analysis and Measurements) Tools. D values, S_Z, S_{ZuR}, and S_{ZL} refer to the Zhang et al. approach and S_{GO} refers to the semantic similarity approach developed here.

Parent GO Id	Child GO Id	S_{GO}	S_W	S_Z	S_{ZuR}	S_{ZL}
GO:0042770	GO:0042772	0.97920	0.940	10.11006	0.71747	0.90199
GO:0042770	GO:0030330	0.97920	0.940	10.11006	0.71747	0.94847
GO:0042770	GO:0008630	0.32398	0.704	10.11006	0.71747	0.90199
GO:0042770	GO:0000077	0.79240	0.802	10.11006	0.71747	0.96144
GO:0042772	GO:0006978	0.49591	0.882	12.30729	0.87340	1.00000
GO:0030330	GO:0006978	0.49591	0.889	11.20867	0.79544	0.95328
GO:0030330	GO:0006977	0.36008	0.615	11.20867	0.79544	0.95328
GO:0030330	GO:0042771	0.24760	0.696	11.20867	0.79544	0.95328
GO:0008630	GO:0042771	0.74832	0.931	12.30729	0.87340	1.00000
GO:0000077	GO:0031571	0.70186	0.830	10.92099	0.77502	0.94032
GO:0000077	GO:0031572	0.69945	0.850	10.92099	0.77502	0.94032
GO:0000077	GO:0031573	0.98344	0.948	10.92099	0.77502	0.94032
GO:0000077	GO:0031574	0.70603	0.870	10.92099	0.77502	0.94032
GO:0031571	GO:0006977	0.63398	0.774	12.30729	0.87340	1.00000

parents. This is topologically explained by the lower reachability of GO:0008630 compared to GO:0030330 and the higher number of children the term GO:0030330 possesses. This reduces its influence on each of its children, becoming less relevant for it to represent a given child due to the lower similarity between them. Furthermore, GO:0006977 is more similar to GO:0031571 than to GO:0030330. This is numerically due to the influence of GO:0030330, reflected by its reachability measure, which is lower than that of GO:0031571. It is topologically caused by the higher level of the term GO:0031571 compared to the level of GO:0030330, and therefore gives the term GO:0031571 a higher biological content property than GO:0030330 for better representing the child term GO:0006977.

Table 2 also includes the semantic similarity between every two consecutive GO terms computed using the Zhang et al. and Wang et al. methods. These results show that Wang's semantic similarity measure between a given term and its immediate child is always greater than 0.6, which is the semantic factor of "part_of" relations, and is independent of the characteristics of the position of these terms in the GO-DAG, including the number of children belonging to the parent term and their levels. This shows how our approach provides a scalable and consistent measurement method, in which the semantic similarity of two terms is completely determined by their reachability measures and that of their highest informative ancestor, that is, the ancestor with the smallest reachability measure. Using the intrinsic topology property of the GO-DAG, the semantic similarity measure of two terms is in agreement with the GO consortium vocabulary, in the sense that two terms whose most common informative ancestor is close to the root share less topological information compared to those having the highest common informative ancestor far from the root.

2.3. Functional Similarity of Proteins Based on GO Similarity. A given protein may perform several functions, thus requiring several GO terms to describe these functions. For characterized or annotated pairwise proteins with known GO terms, functional closeness or GO similarities based on their annotations and consequently the distances between these proteins can be evaluated using the Czekanowski-Dice approach [35] as follows:

$$
\begin{aligned}
&S_{\mathcal{F}}(p_1, p_2) \\
&= \frac{2 \times \left| T_{\mathrm{GO}}^X(p_1) \cap T_{\mathrm{GO}}^X(p_2) \right|}{\left| T_{\mathrm{GO}}^X(p_1) \cup T_{\mathrm{GO}}^X(p_2) \right| + \left| T_{\mathrm{GO}}^X(p_1) \cap T_{\mathrm{GO}}^X(p_2) \right|},
\end{aligned}
\tag{13}
$$

where $T_{\mathrm{GO}}^X(p)$ is the set of GO terms of a given protein p for a given ontology $X = \mathrm{MF}, \mathrm{BP}, \mathrm{CC}$, and $|T_{\mathrm{GO}}^X(p)|$ stands for its number of elements.

Czekanowski-Dice's measure is not convenient for using in the case of GO term sets, since GO terms may be similar at some level without being identical. This aspect cannot be captured in Czekanowski-Dice's measure which only requires the contribution from the GO terms exactly matched between the sets of GO terms of these proteins. One can attempt to avoid this difficulty by incorporating the true path rule in the computation of the intersection and union of GO term sets for proteins. However, in most cases where these proteins are annotated by successive GO terms in the GO-DAG, this may lead to the situation where the number of elements in the union of these sets is equal to that of their intersection plus one, in which case, the functional closeness of these proteins is forced to converge to 1, independently of the biological contents of the GO terms in the GO-DAG.

To overcome this problem, we set up a functional similarity between proteins which emphasizes semantic similarity between terms in their sets of GO terms considered to be uniformly distributed. This functional similarity is given by

$$
\begin{aligned}
S_{\mathcal{F}}(p_1, p_2) = \frac{1}{2}\Bigg[& \frac{1}{\left| T_{\mathrm{GO}}^X(p_1) \right|} \sum_{t \in T_{\mathrm{GO}}^X(p_1)} S_{\mathrm{GO}}\left(t, T_{\mathrm{GO}}^X(p_2)\right) \\
& + \frac{1}{\left| T_{\mathrm{GO}}^X(p_2) \right|} \sum_{t \in T_{\mathrm{GO}}^X(p_2)} S_{\mathrm{GO}}\left(t, T_{\mathrm{GO}}^X(p_1)\right) \Bigg],
\end{aligned}
\tag{14}
$$

where $S_{\mathrm{GO}}(t, T_{\mathrm{GO}}^X(p)) = 1 - d_{\mathrm{GO}}(t, T_{\mathrm{GO}}^X(p))$, with $d_{\mathrm{GO}}(t, T_{\mathrm{GO}}^X(p))$ being the distance between a given term t and a set of terms $T_{\mathrm{GO}}^X(p)$ for a given protein p, mathematically defined as follows:

$$
d_{\mathrm{GO}}\left(t, T_{\mathrm{GO}}^X(p)\right) = \min\left\{ d_{\mathrm{GO}}(t, s) : s \in T_{\mathrm{GO}}^X(p) \right\}.
\tag{15}
$$

Thus, owing to the fact that $d_{\mathrm{GO}}(s, t) = 1 - S_{\mathrm{GO}}(t, s)$, we obtain

$$
S_{\mathrm{GO}}\left(t, T_{\mathrm{GO}}^X(p)\right) = \max\left\{ S_{\mathrm{GO}}(t, s) : s \in T_{\mathrm{GO}}^X(p) \right\}.
\tag{16}
$$

This shows that the functional closeness formula emphasizes the importance of the shared GO terms by assigning more weight to similarities than differences. Thus, for two proteins that do not share any similar GO terms, the functional closeness value is 0, while for two proteins sharing exactly the same set of GO terms, the functional closeness value is 1. The functional similarity between proteins in (14) is a value that ranges between 0 and 1 and indicates the percentage of similarity the two proteins share, on average, based on their annotations. For example, a functional similarity between two proteins of 0.9 means that these proteins are 90% similar, on average, based on their annotations.

Note that the approach used here to combine GO term topological information for calculating protein functional similarity scores was used in the context of annotation-based approaches and is referred to as the best match average (BMA) approach. This approach has been suggested to be better than the average (Avg) [2] or maximum (Max) [19] approaches from a biological point of view [36, 37]. However, even Avg and Max approaches can also be used to combine GO term semantic similarity scores produced using this new measure to quantify protein functional similarity depending on the application. Furthermore, the GO-universal metric can be used in the context of the SimGIC approach [9, 38] derived from the Jaccard index based on the Tversky ratio model of similarity [39], which uses GO term IC directly in order to compute protein functional similarity scores, and referred to as SimUIC. These approaches are generally referred to as term-based approaches. The GO term topological information scores can also be used to construct protein functional similarity schemes relying on other Tversky ratio models, for example, using the Dice index, referred to as SimDIC, and SimUIX which uses a universal index, given by

$$
\mathrm{SimDIC}(p, q) = \frac{2 \times \sum_{x \in T_{\mathrm{GO}}^X(p) \cap T_{\mathrm{GO}}^X(q)} \mathrm{IC}_T(x)}{\sum_{x \in T_{\mathrm{GO}}^X(p)} \mathrm{IC}_T(x) + \sum_{x \in T_{\mathrm{GO}}^X(q)} \mathrm{IC}_T(x)},
$$

$$
\mathrm{SimUIX}(p, q) = \frac{\sum_{x \in T_{\mathrm{GO}}^X(p) \cap T_{\mathrm{GO}}^X(q)} \mathrm{IC}_T(x)}{\max\left\{ \sum_{x \in T_{\mathrm{GO}}^X(p)} \mathrm{IC}_T(x), \sum_{x \in T_{\mathrm{GO}}^X(q)} \mathrm{IC}_T(x) \right\}}.
\tag{17}
$$

3. Results and Discussion

We have developed a semantic value measurement approach for GO terms using the intrinsic topology of the GO-DAG and taking into account issues related to the depth of the structure. We evaluate our method against the Wang et al. and Zhang et al. topology-based methods for a specific subgraph of the GO-DAG and then use UniProt data to compare our similarity scores to those of annotation-based approaches. Note that the Zhang et al. approach has recently been shown to perform equally to the Resnik measure and to perform better than the Wang et al. measure [40] and the relevance approach which is the Lin enhancement measure suggested by Schlicker et al. [31].

3.1. Evaluation of the New Approach. We have seen Section 2 that the GO-universal similarity measure produces effective semantic similarity scores based on the intrinsic topology of the GO-DAG by making explicit use of topological relationships between different terms, thus producing a clearer representation of these relations. As discussed previously, the biggest limitation of existing approaches based on Resnik's algorithm is that they are constrained by the annotation statistics related to the terms. On the other hand, although, like ours, Wang's measure is based only on the intrinsic topology of the GO-DAG, one of the drawbacks of their approach is that it raises a scalability issue since it requires complete knowledge of the sub-GO-DAG of the two terms for which the semantic similarity is being computed and that of all their common ancestors. However, since GO is expanding and increasing in size, the term relationships are becoming more and more important. Thus, a semantic similarity measurement approach should be effective independent of the size of the GO-DAG.

Another negative aspect of Wang's approach is that it essentially relies on the semantic factors of "is_a" and "part_of" relations, and it is not clear for which values of these semantic factors the semantic similarity measure yields the optimal value of biological content of terms. Moreover, these semantic factors make the similarity value between a given child and its direct parent independent of the number of children that the parent term has (shown in (3)). Wang's semantic similarity measure between a given term and its immediate child term depends solely on the semantic relationship ("part_of" or "is_a") and is completely independent of the position characteristics in the hierarchical structure. However, considering the GO-DAG, the semantic similarity between a given term and its child should not only depend on the number of parents the child term possesses, but also on the number of children that the parent term possesses. The more children a term has, the smaller the semantic similarity to each of its children, which is logical.

The Zhang approach, which depends only on the children of a given term, often fails to effectively differentiate a child from its parents, yielding an equal D value and IC for these terms. It also tends to produce a uniform semantic similarity between a parent and its children (see Table 2 in Section 2), which is overestimated to 1 when using Lin's approach, whereas these GO terms are biologically and topologically different. This means that the approach ignores the fact that a child is more specific than the parent by assigning them the same semantic value and consequently the approach fails to distinguish proteins annotated by these terms, which leads to an overestimation of functional similarity between these proteins. This case occurs, for instance, for the child-parent GO terms: GO:0006978 and GO:0042772, GO:0042771 and GO:0008630, and GO:0006977 and GO:0031571, all of which have identical values. These observations suggest that a given similarity approach relying on the intrinsic topology of the hierarchical structure should consider both GO term parents and children in its conception.

3.2. Performance Evaluation of the GO-Universal Metric. We first evaluated the performance of the new metric by assessing its ability to capture functional coherence in a human protein-protein interaction network in terms of how interacting proteins are functionally related to each other. Expert-curated and experimentally determined human protein-protein interactions (PPIs) were retrieved from the IntAct database [41], the Database of Interacting Proteins (DIP) [42], the Biomolecular Interaction Network Database (BIND) [43], the Mammalian Protein-Protein Interaction Database (MIPS) [44], the Molecular INTeraction database (MINT) [45], and the Biological General Repository for Interaction Datasets (BioGRIDs) [46]. These networks were integrated into a single network where we only considered interactions predicted by at least two different approaches to alleviate the issue of false positives, as a specific approach may incorrectly identify an interaction [47]. This has produced a protein-protein interaction network with 4918 proteins out of 25831 found in the complete list of reviewed proteins from the UniProt database at http://www.uniprot.org/ and 9707 interactions out of 29430 combined interactions from these protein interaction databases. Protein annotations were retrieved via GOA-UniProtKB [13] using UniProt protein accessions.

For our performance evaluation, we only used proteins annotated with BP terms in the network produced. This is because two proteins that interact physically are more likely to be involved in similar biological processes [40] but there is no guarantee that they share molecular functions [48]. Among 25831 proteins found in the complete list of reviewed proteins in human, 10620 proteins are annotated with GO BP terms. After removing all uncharacterized proteins with respect to the BP ontology from the network, 6417 direct interactions remain if we exclude annotations inferred electronically (IEA) and 7712 direct interactions remain when using all GO evidence codes (http://www.geneontology.org/GO.evidence.shtml). This was used as a positive control set. Lack of complete knowledge about protein interaction sets makes the generation of a negative control set challenging, since the fact that two proteins are not known to interact may simply be because this interaction has not yet been detected [47]. One of the models suggests generating a set of negatives from randomly selecting pairs from all proteins in the dataset under consideration [49, 50]. Thus, negative datasets with equal numbers of protein pairs as in the positive interaction dataset were built by randomly choosing annotated human protein pairs in the proteome. In our context, this is relevant as the probability of randomly selecting a true protein-protein interaction is very low (less than 0.052%).

The classification power of the new metric was tested by receiver operator characteristic (ROC) curve analysis [51] which measures the true positive rate or sensitivity against the false positive rate or 1-specificity. The best match average version of the new metric is compared to the best match average under the Lin measure and that using the Resnik measure which has been shown to perform better than others [52]. Our functional similarity measure inferred using Jaccard index weighted by topological information (SimUIC)

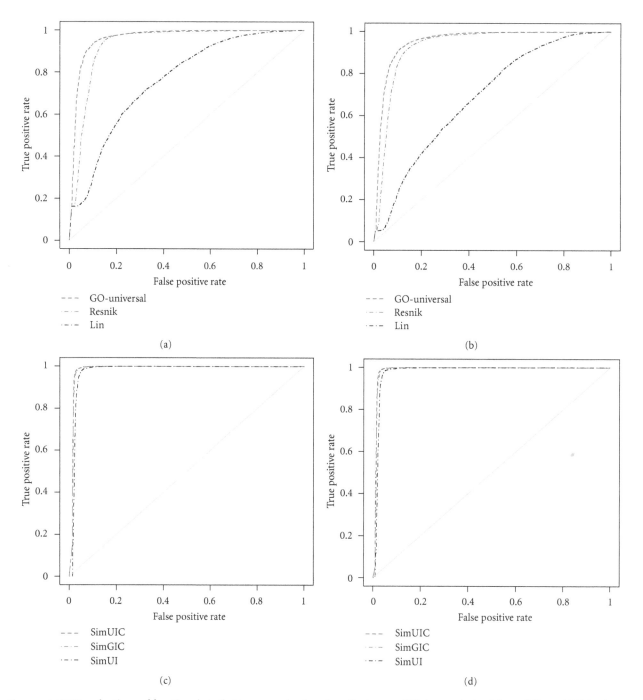

FIGURE 4: ROC evaluations of functional similarity approaches based on the human PPI dataset derived from different PPI databases.

is compared to SimGIC and SimUI. The SimUI approach refers to the union-intersection protein similarity measure, which is also implemented in the GOstats package [24]. It is a particular case of simGIC or SimUIC which assumes that all GO terms occur at equal frequency, in which case, only the topology of the GO-DAG is needed. This implies that the SimUI approach assigns equal semantic value or information content to all terms in the GO-DAG. The area under the ROC curve (AUC) is used as a measure of discriminative power, the larger the upper AUC value, the more powerful the measure is, and a realistic classifier must have an AUC

larger than 0.5. Results found using the ROCR package under the R programming language [53, 54] are shown in Figures 4(a) and 4(b) for the BMA approach and Figures 4(c) and 4(d) for measures inferred from the Jaccard index (term-based approaches), and their AUCs and precisions are shown in Table 3.

These results indicate that all the approaches perform well. In the context of term-based approaches, the new approach performs as well as the SimGIC approach, which is the best annotation-based measure in this case, in terms of AUC, but it performs slightly better than the SimGIC

TABLE 3: Area under ROC curves (AUCs) and precision for the human PPI dataset. For each group, the top score is in bold.

Approaches	Area under curve (AUC)		Precision		Accuracy	
	Excluding IEA	Including IEA	Excluding IEA	Including IEA	Excluding IEA	Including IEA
GO-universal	**0.962**	**0.954**	**0.841**	**0.772**	**0.885**	**0.816**
Resnik	0.933	0.931	0.724	0.701	0.713	0.739
Lin	0.763	0.691	0.610	0.568	0.481	0.549
SimUIC	**0.983**	**0.986**	**0.930**	0.916	**0.977**	**0.979**
SimGIC	**0.983**	**0.986**	0.922	**0.917**	0.974	0.974
SimUI	0.975	0.978	0.866	0.845	0.926	0.937

approach in terms of precision excluding IEA and accuracy. When considering protein functional similarity approaches derived from GO term semantic similarity scores (first three rows of Table 3), the new approach outperforms the best annotation-based approach, namely, BMA under Resnik, particularly in precision, and accuracy. This also shows that the new metric is less sensitive to outliers compared to annotation-based approaches, on top of the fact that it only uses the intrinsic topology (structure) of the GO-DAG without requiring annotation data. Thus, the new metric performs better overall than the existing approaches, specifically providing the best performances in the context of annotation-based approaches, namely, BMA under Resnik and SimGIC. Note that the performance of Resnik and SimGIC approaches is related to the corpus under consideration because of its dependence on the frequencies of GO term occurrences in the corpus. This shallow annotation problem constitutes a serious drawback to these approaches, specifically for organisms with sparse GO annotations [55] and may negatively affect their performances [52]. The use of the whole set of annotations may solve this problem but could, in turn, increase the complexity of these annotation-based approaches as the number of protein annotations increases daily. This would potentially hamper the performance of these approaches in their running time, since reading the annotation file takes time.

Looking at the two main groups of protein functional similarity approaches, term-based approaches perform better than those using GO term semantic similarity scores. This is in part due to the fact that models of protein functional similarity approaches using GO term semantic similarity scores are based on statistical measures of closeness (Avg, Max), which are known to be sensitive to scores that lie at abnormal distances from the majority of scores, or outliers. This means that these measures may produce biases which affect protein functional similarity scores. Furthermore, we investigate if the performance can be improved by leaving out GO annotations with IEA evidence codes. Interestingly, no significant improvement is achieved when leaving out GO annotations with IEA evidence code suggesting that these IEA annotations are in fact of high quality [33, 56]. This also justifies observations made by Guzzi et al. [52] concerning the use of all types of GO evidence codes when assessing a given GO-based semantic similarity approach. Finally, as expected among term-based approaches, SimUIC

and SimGIC approaches perform better than the SimUI approach.

3.3. Comparison of the GO-Universal Metric with State-of-the-Art Measures. We assess the effectiveness of the new metric compared to other topology-based approaches, namely, the Wang and Zhang approaches, the Resnik-related functional similarity measures, and SimGIC. We used a dataset of proteins with known relationships downloaded from the Collaborative Evaluation of Semantic Similarity Measures (CESSMs) online tool [57] at http://xldb.di.fc.ul.pt/tools/cessm/. The set of interacting proteins was extracted from UniProt [58, 59] with GO annotations being obtained from GOA-UniProtKB [13]. CESSM is an online tool for evaluating protein GO-based semantic similarity measures or functional similarity metrics, integrating several functional similarity approaches. The CESSM tool has made the comparison of new semantic measures against previously developed annotation-based metrics possible using Pearson's correlation measures with sequence, Pfam domain and Enzyme Commission (EC) similarity, as well as measuring resolution. Correlation measures how effective the new approach is in capturing sequence, Pfam, and EC similarity. Resolution, which is defined as the relative intensity with which variations in the sequence similarity scale are translated into the semantic similarity scale, provides an indication of how sensitive the approach is to differences in the annotations [36]. This implies that a metric with a higher correlation and resolution performs better, since it captures sequence, Pfam, and EC similarity well and it is likely to be an unbiased metric.

To evaluate the new metric, we ran the CESSM online tool and results are shown in Table 4 for BP and MF. These results indicate that our approach effectively captures sequence, Pfam, and EC similarity in terms of Pearson's correlation, especially for the BP ontology. According to the Pesquita et al. performance classification [36], the SimGIC measure provides the best overall performance among all annotation-based approaches, followed by the Resnik under BMA approach. For the BP ontology, overall our approach outperforms the existing annotation-based approaches, by appearing in the top two measures for all four parameters tested, unlike any of the other measures. It consistently shows one of the highest correlation with sequence, Pfam

TABLE 4: Comparison of performance of our approach with Wang et al., Zhang et al. and annotation-based ones using Pearson's correlation with enzyme Commission (eC), Pfam and sequence similarity, and resolution. Results are obtained from the CESSM online tool. For each ontology, the top two best scores among 12 approaches are in bold.

Ontology	Approaches		Similarity measure correlation			Resolution
			EC	PFAM	Seq Sim	
BP	GO-Universal		**0.44287**	**0.53919**	**0.76797**	**0.90067**
	Wang et al.	(BMA)	0.43266	**0.46692**	0.63356	**0.90966**
	Zhang et al.		0.21944	0.26495	0.20270	0.30148
	Resnik	Avg	0.30218	0.32324	0.40685	0.33673
		Max	0.30756	0.26268	0.30273	0.64522
		BMA	**0.44441**	0.45878	0.73973	0.90041
	Term-based	SimUIC	0.38458	0.43693	0.74410	0.84503
		SimGIC	0.39811	0.45470	**0.77326**	0.83730
MF	GO-Universal		**0.73886**	0.60285	0.55163	0.52905
	Wang et al.	(BMA)	**0.65910**	0.49101	0.37101	0.33109
	Zhang et al.		0.49753	0.41147	0.32235	0.39865
	Resnik	Avg	0.39635	0.44038	0.50143	0.41490
		Max	0.45393	0.18152	0.12458	0.38056
		BMA	0.60271	0.57183	**0.66832**	**0.95771**
	Term-based	SimUIC	0.65826	**0.62510**	0.60512	**0.96928**
		SimGIC	0.62196	**0.63806**	**0.71716**	0.95590

and EC similarity and also provides one of the two best resolutions, thus achieving overall best performance. For the MF ontology, our approach generally performs well producing good Pearson's correlation compared to the existing annotation-based approaches, and specifically outperforming existing annotation-based approaches in terms of EC and Pfam similarity. It is among the top measures for three out of four parameters, specifically providing high resolution under SimUIC. The new approach consistently outperforms the Wang and Zhang approaches, except for resolution, where the Wang et al. approach performs marginally better for BP. Overall, this shows the improved consistency and relevance of the new metric compared to the existing ones, and our approach has the advantage of being independent of annotation data.

3.4. Assessing Functional Similarity between Protein Orthologues Using the GO-Universal Metric. Orthologous proteins in different species are thought to maintain similar functions. Therefore, we used protein sequence data together with protein GO annotations to determine the extent to which sequence similarities between protein orthologues are translated into similarities between their GO annotations through the GO-universal metric using protein orthologues between human (*Homo sapiens*) and mouse (*Mus musculus* strain C57BL/6) as a case study. Protein orthologue pairs were retrieved from the Ensembl website [60, 61] at http://www.ensembl.org/index.html, GO-association data were downloaded from the GOA site, and the protein sequence files were retrieved from UniProtKB [58, 59, 62].

In order to produce sequence similarity data, an all-against-all BLASTP [63, 64] was performed under the BLOSUM62 amino acid substitution matrix [65]. We obtained

TABLE 5: Proportion in percentage of Human-Mouse orthologue pairs sharing high functional similarity.

Approach	Using all GO evidence codes		Leaving out IEA and ISS	
	BP	MF	BP	MF
GO-Universal	76	82	12	49
Resnik	76	80	13	38

BLAST bit scores of these pairwise orthologues in order to compute their sequence similarity scores using the approach suggested in [66]. After removing protein pairs with at least one nonannotated protein, 10691 protein pairs annotated with molecular function terms and 10675 pairs with biological process terms remained. We investigated the power of the GO-universal metric to assess functional similarity between orthologues. We found that 82% of orthologue pairs shared high functional similarity (score ≥ 0.7) in MF annotation and 76% in BP annotation. These results are shown in Table 5, together with proportions achieved by the Resnik approach when using all GO evidence codes, as well as results for both approaches when leaving out IEA and ISS (inferred from sequence or structural similarity) evidence codes. The number of ortholog pairs with GO annotations when IEA and ISS annotations are removed drops to less than 4000 pairs, and the percentage of these pairs sharing high functional similarity drops significantly, particularly for BP. The negative impact of removing IEA annotations has been reported previously [52] and may be due to the fact that IEA and ISS annotations tend to be to higher level GO terms compared to manual mappings.

The high proportion of functionally similar protein orthologues observed in the full dataset was expected, since

TABLE 6: Some human-mouse protein orthologue pairs without GO-based functional similarity.

	Protein ID	Organism	Annotation information			
			GO ID	GO name	Code	Source
BP	A1Z1Q3	Homo sapiens	GO:0042278	Purine nucleoside metabolic process	IDA	UniProtKB
	Q3UYG8	Mus musculus	GO:0007420	Brain development	IEP	UniProtKB
	Q96EQ8	Homo sapiens	GO:0032480	Negative regulation of type I interferon production	TAS	Reactome
			GO:0045087	Innate immune response	TAS	Reactome
	Q9D9R0	Mus musculus	GO:0016567	Protein ubiquitination	EXP	GOC
	O00451	Homo sapiens	GO:0007169	Transmembrane receptor protein tyrosine kinase signaling pathway	TAS	PINC
			GO:0035860	Glial cell-derived neurotrophic factor receptor signaling pathway	TAS	GOC
	O08842	Mus musculus	GO:0007399	Nervous system development	IMP	MGI
	Q9BS16		GO:0000087	M phase of mitotic cell cycle	TAS	Reactome
		Homo sapiens	GO:0000236	Mitotic prometaphase	TAS	Reactome
			GO:0000278	Mitotic cell cycle	TAS	Reactome
			GO:0006334	Nucleosome assembly	TAS	Reactome
			GO:0034080	Cenh3-containing nucleosome assembly at centromere	TAS	Reactome
	Q9ESN5	Mus musculus	GO:0045944	Positive regulation of transcription from RNA polymerase II promoter	IDA	MGI
	O15347	Homo sapiens	GO:0006310	DNA recombination	ISS	UniProtKB
			GO:0007275	Multicellular organismal development	TAS	PINC
	O54879	Mus musculus	GO:0045578	Negative regulation of B cell differentiation	IDA	MGI
			GO:0045638	Negative regulation of myeloid cell differentiation	IDA	MGI
	Q9NP31		GO:0001525	Angiogenesis	IEA	UniProtKB
		Homo sapiens	GO:0007165	Signal transduction	TAS	PINC
			GO:0007275	Multicellular organismal development	IEA	UniProtKB
			GO:0030154	Cell differentiation	IEA	UniProtKB
	Q9QXK9	Mus musculus	GO:0008283	Cell proliferation	IMP	occurs_in (CL:0000084)
	Q9C035	Homo sapiens	GO:0009615	Response to virus	IEA	UniProtKB
			GO:0044419	Interspecies interaction between organisms	IEA	UniProtKB
			GO:0070206	Protein trimerization	IDA	UniProtKB:Q9C035-1
	P15533	Mus musculus	GO:0006351	Transcription, DNA-dependent	IEA	UniProtKB
			GO:0006355	Regulation of transcription, DNA-dependent	IEA	UniProtKB
MF	Q86XR7	Homo sapiens	GO:0004871	Signal transducer activity	IMP	UniProtKB
	Q8BJQ4	Mus musculus	GO:0005515	Protein binding	IPI	BHF-UCL
	Q99218	Homo sapiens	GO:0030345	Structural constituent of tooth enamel	IDA	BHF-UCL
	P63277		GO:0005515	Protein binding	IPI	MGI, BHF-UCL
			GO:0008083	Growth factor activity	IMP	BHF-UCL
		Mus musculus	GO:0042802	Identical protein binding	IPI	BHF-UCL
			GO:0043498	Cell surface binding	IMP	BHF-UCL
			GO:0046848	Hydroxyapatite binding	IDA	BHF-UCL
	P45379		GO:0003779	Actin binding	IDA	UniProtKB
			GO:0005523	Tropomyosin binding	IDA	UniProtKB
		Homo sapiens	GO:0030172	Troponin C binding	IPI	UniProtKB
			GO:003113	Troponin I binding	IPI	UniProtKB

TABLE 6: Continued.

	Protein ID	Organism	Annotation information			
			GO ID	GO name	Code	Source
MF			GO:0016887	Atpase activity	IDA	UniProtKB:P45379-1-6-7-8
	P50752	Mus musculus	GO:0005200	Structural constituent of cytoskeleton	IDA	occurs_in (CL:0000193)
	Q9H0E3	Homo sapiens	GO:0003713	Transcription coactivator activity	IDA	UniProtKB
			GO:0004402	Histone acetyltransferase activity	IDA	UniProtKB
	Q8BIH0	Mus musculus	GO:0005515	Protein binding	IPI	UniProtKB
	Q5T9L3	Homo sapiens	GO:0004871	Signal transducer activity	ISS	UniProtKB
	Q6DID7	Mus musculus	GO:0005515	Protein binding	IPI	UniProtKB
			GO:0017147	Wnt-protein binding	IDA	UniProtKB
	A8CG34	Homo sapiens	GO:0005515	Protein binding	IPI	UniProtKB
	Q8K3Z9	Mus musculus	GO:0017056	Structural constituent of nuclear pore	IEA	ENSEMBL
	O15446	Homo sapiens	GO:0003899	DNA-directed RNA polymerase activity	IEA	UniProtKB
	Q76KJ5	Mus musculus	GO:0005515	Protein binding	IPI	MGI

many of the GO annotations probably arose from homology-based annotation transfer [67, 68]. We were also interested in finding orthologues with very low protein functional similarity scores based on their GO annotations. The new metric was able to detect such cases, which are contrary to the belief in function conservation between orthologues. Some examples are shown in Table 6 together with their GO annotations, GO evidence codes, and sources. There are several possible reasons for this, including protein misannotations, the use of more general GO terms for one and more specific terms for the other protein, or simply the lack of relevant biological knowledge about these proteins. For biological process, in particular, in the examples in Table 6, the differing terms are not conflicting processes, so it may be that the other terms are correct but have just not yet been added, or they may be organism specific. This example provides an illustration of a biological application of the metric and how it can be used to identify possible incorrect or missing annotations.

4. Conclusions

In this work, we have set up a new approach to measure the closeness of terms in the gene ontology (GO), thus translating the difference between the biological contents of terms into numeric values using topological information shared by these terms in the GO-DAG. Like other measures, this enables us to measure functional similarities of proteins on the basis of their GO annotations derived from heterogeneous data sources using semantic similarities of their GO terms. We compare our method to two similar measures and show its advantages. The similarity measure which we defined shows consistent behaviour in that going down the DAG (away from the root) increases specificity, thus providing an effective semantic value for GO terms that reflects functional relationships between GO annotated proteins.

The relevance of this measure is evident when considering the GO hierarchy, as it makes explicit use of the two main relationships between different terms in the DAG, which makes it possible to provide a more precise view of the similarities between terms. This measure yields a simple and reliable semantic similarity between GO terms and functional similarity measure for sets of GO terms or proteins. We have validated this new metric using ROC analysis on human PPI datasets and a selected protein dataset from UniProt with their GO annotations obtained from GOA-UniProt and analysis by the Collaborative Evaluation of Semantic Similarity Measures (CESSM) online tool. Results show that this new GO-semantic value measure that we have introduced constitutes an effective solution to the GO metric problem for the next generation of functional similarity metrics.

As a biological use case, we have applied the GO-universal metric to determine functional similarity between orthologues based on their GO annotations. In most cases functional conservation was shown, but we did identify some orthologues annotated with different functions. This suggests that the new metric can be used to track protein annotation errors or missing annotations. We are currently applying it to assess the closeness of InterPro entries using their mappings to GO. This measure will also be used to design a retrieval tool for genes and gene products based on their GO annotations, providing a new tool for gene clustering and knowledge discovery on the basis of GO annotations. Given a source protein or a set of GO terms, this engine will be able to retrieve functionally related proteins from a specific proteome based on their functional closeness, or identify genes and gene products matched by these functions or very similar functions.

Conflict of Interests

The authors declare that they have no conflict of interests.

Authors' Contributions

N. J. Mulder generated and supervised the project, and finalized the manuscript. G. K. Mazandu analyzed, designed and implemented the model, and wrote the paper. N. J. Mulder and G. K. Mazandu analyzed data, read, and approved the final paper and N. J. Mulder approved the production of this paper.

Acknowledgments

Any work dependent on open-source software owes debt to those who developed these tools. The authors thank everyone involved with free software, from the core developers to those who contributed to the documentation. Many thanks to the authors of the freely available libraries, in particular, the GO Consortium who made this work possible. This work has been supported by the Claude Leon Foundation Postdoctoral Fellowship, the National Research Foundation (NRF) in South Africa, and Computational Biology (CBIO) research group at the Institute of Infectious Disease and Molecular Medicine, University of Cape Town.

References

[1] F. Enault, K. Suhre, and J. M. Claverie, "Phydbac "gene function predictor": a gene annotation tool based on genomic context analysis," *BMC Bioinformatics*, vol. 6, p. 247, 2005.

[2] P. W. Lord, R. D. Stevens, A. Brass, and C. A. Goble, "Investigating semantic similarity measures across the gene ontology: the relationship between sequence and annotation," *Bioinformatics*, vol. 19, no. 10, pp. 1275–1283, 2003.

[3] M. Ashburner, C. A. Ball, J. A. Blake et al., "Gene ontology: tool for the unification of biology," *Nature Genetics*, vol. 25, no. 1, pp. 25–29, 2000.

[4] X. Mao, T. Cai, J. G. Olyarchuk, and L. Wei, "Automated genome annotation and pathway identification using the KEGG Orthology (KO) as a controlled vocabulary," *Bioinformatics*, vol. 21, no. 19, pp. 3787–3793, 2005.

[5] Q. Zheng and X. J. Wang, "GOEAST: a web-based software toolkit for gene ontology enrichment analysis," *Nucleic acids research*, vol. 36, pp. W358–363, 2008.

[6] GO-Consortium, "The gene ontology in 2010: extensions and refinements," *Nucleic Acids Research*, vol. 38, no. 1, Article ID gkp1018, pp. D331–D335, 2009.

[7] GO-Consortium, "The gene ontology (GO) project in 2006," *Nucleic Acids Research*, vol. 34, pp. D322–D326, 2006.

[8] S. Carbon, A. Ireland, C. J. Mungall et al., "AmiGO: online access to ontology and annotation data," *Bioinformatics*, vol. 25, no. 2, pp. 288–289, 2009.

[9] C. Pesquita, D. Faria, A. O. Falcão, P. Lord, and F. M. Couto, "Semantic similarity in biomedical ontologies," *PLoS Computational Biology*, vol. 5, no. 7, Article ID e1000443, 2009.

[10] E. Camon, M. Magrane, D. Barrell et al., "The gene ontology annotation (GOA) project: implementation of GO in SWISS-PROT, TrEMBL, and interpro," *Genome Research*, vol. 13, no. 4, pp. 662–672, 2003.

[11] E. Camon, D. Barrell, V. Lee, E. Dimmer, and R. Apweiler, "The gene ontology annotation (GOA) database—an integrated resource of GO annotations to the UniProt knowledgebase," *In Silico Biology*, vol. 4, no. 1, pp. 5–6, 2004.

[12] E. Camon, M. Magrane, D. Barrell et al., "The gene ontology annotation (GOA) Database: sharing knowledge in Uniprot with gene oncology," *Nucleic Acids Research*, vol. 32, pp. D262–D266, 2004.

[13] D. Barrell, E. Dimmer, R. P. Huntley, D. Binns, C. O'Donovan, and R. Apweiler, "The GOA database in 2009—an integrated gene ontology annotation resource," *Nucleic Acids Research*, vol. 37, no. 1, pp. D396–D403, 2009.

[14] E. C. Dimmer, R. P. Huntley, D. G. Barrell et al., "The gene ontology—providing a functional role in proteomic studies," *Proteomics*, vol. 8, supplement 23-24, pp. 2–11, 2008.

[15] L. N. Soldatova and R. D. King, "Are the current ontologies in biology good ontologies?" *Nature Biotechnology*, vol. 23, no. 9, pp. 1095–1098, 2005.

[16] J. Shon, J. Y. Park, and L. Wei, "Beyond similarity-based methods to associate genes for the inference of function," *Drug Discovery Today*, vol. 1, no. 3, pp. 89–96, 2003.

[17] F. Shi, Q. Chen, and X. Niu, "Functional similarity analyzing of protein sequences with empirical mode decomposition," in *Proceedings of the 4th International Conference on Fuzzy Systems and Knowledge Discovery (FSKD '07)*, vol. 2, pp. 766–770, 2007.

[18] T. Kambe, T. Suzuki, M. Nagao, and Y. Yamaguchi-Iwai, "Sequence similarity and functional relationship among eukaryotic ZIP and CDF transporters," *Genomics, Proteomics and Bioinformatics*, vol. 4, no. 1, pp. 1–9, 2006.

[19] J. L. Sevilla, V. Segura, A. Podhorski et al., "Correlation between gene expression and GO semantic similarity," *IEEE/ACM Transactions on Computational Biology and Bioinformatics*, vol. 2, no. 4, pp. 330–338, 2005.

[20] T. J. Hestilow and Y. Huang, "Clustering of gene expression data based on shape similarity," *Eurasip Journal on Bioinformatics and Systems Biology*, vol. 2009, Article ID 195712, 2009.

[21] W. Wang, J. M. Cherry, Y. Nochomovitz, E. Jolly, D. Botstein, and H. Li, "Inference of combinatorial regulation in yeast transcriptional networks: a case study of sporulation," *Proceedings of the National Academy of Sciences of the United States of America*, vol. 102, no. 6, pp. 1998–2003, 2005.

[22] Z. Wu and M. S. Palmer, "Verb semantics and lexical selection," in *Proceedings of the 32nd Annual Meeting of the Association for Computational Linguistics (ACL '94)*, pp. 133–138, 1994.

[23] V. Pekar and S. Staab, "Taxonomy learning: factoring the structure of a taxonomy into a semantic classification decision," in *Proceedings of the 19th International Conference on Computational Linguistics*, pp. 1–7, Association for Computational Linguistics, Morristown, NJ, USA, 2002.

[24] R. Gentleman, Visualizing and Distances Using GO, http://bioconductor.org/packages/2.6/bioc/vignettes/GOstats/inst/, doc/GOvis.pdf, 2005.

[25] S. Benabderrahmane, M. Smail-Tabbone, O. Poch, A. Napoli, and M. D. Devignes, "IntelliGO: a new vector-based semantic similarity measure including annotation origin," *BMC Bioinformatics*, vol. 11, p. 588, 2010.

[26] M. H. Seddiqui and M. Aono, "Metric of intrinsic information content for measuring semantic similarity in an ontology," in *Proceedings of the 7th Asia-Pacific Conference on Conceptual Modelling (APCCM '10)*, vol. 110, pp. 89–96, Brisbane, Australia, 2010.

[27] G. Yu, F. Li, Y. Qin, X. Bo, Y. Wu, and S. Wang, "GOSemSim: an R package for measuring semantic similarity among GO terms and gene products," *Bioinformatics*, vol. 26, no. 7, Article ID btq064, pp. 976–978, 2010.

[28] J. Z. Wang, Z. Du, R. Payattakool, P. S. Yu, and C. F. Chen, "A new method to measure the semantic similarity of GO terms," *Bioinformatics*, vol. 23, no. 10, pp. 1274–1281, 2007.

[29] P. Resnik, "Semantic similarity in a taxonomy: an information-based measure and its application to problems of ambiguity in natural language," *Journal of Artificial Intelligence Research*, vol. 11, pp. 95–130, 1999.

[30] D. Lin, "An information-theoretic definition of similarity," in *Proceedings of the 15th International Conference on Machine Learning*, pp. 296–304, 1998.

[31] A. Schlicker, F. S. Domingues, J. Rahnenfuhrer, and T. Lengauer, "A new measure for functional similarity of gene products based on gene ontology," *BMC Bioinformatics*, vol. 7, p. 302, 2006.

[32] P. Zhang, J. Zhang, H. Sheng, J. J. Russo, B. Osborne, and K. Buetow, "Gene functional similarity search tool (GFSST)," *BMC Bioinformatics*, vol. 7, p. 135, 2006.

[33] G. K. Mazandu and N. J. Mulder, "Using the underlying biological organization of the MTB functional network for protein function prediction," *Infection, Genetics and Evolution*, vol. 12, no. 5, pp. 922–932, 2011.

[34] M. Li, X. Chen, X. Li, B. Ma, and P. M. B. Vitányi, "The similarity metric," *IEEE Transactions on Information Theory*, vol. 50, no. 12, pp. 3250–3264, 2004.

[35] D. Martin, C. Brun, E. Remy, P. Mouren, D. Thieffry, and B. Jacq, "GOToolBox: functional analysis of gene datasets based on gene ontology," *Genome Biology*, vol. 5, no. 12, p. R101, 2004.

[36] C. Pesquita, D. Faria, H. Bastos, A. E. N. Ferreira, A. O. Falcão, and F. M. Couto, "Metrics for GO based protein semantic similarity: a systematic evaluation," *BMC Bioinformatics*, vol. 9, supplement 5, p. S4, 2008.

[37] M. Alvarez, X. Qi, and C. Yan, "A shortest-path graph kernel for estimating gene product semantic similarity," *Journal of Biomedical Semantics*, vol. 2, no. 3, pp. 1–9, 2011.

[38] C. Pesquita, D. Faria, H. Bastos, A. O. Falcão, and F. M. Couto, Evaluating GO-based Semantic Similarity Measures, http://xldb.fc.ul.pt/xldb/publications/Pesquita.etal:EvaluatingGO-basedSemantic:2007_document.pdf, 2007.

[39] A. Tversky, "Features of similarity," *Psychological Review*, vol. 84, no. 4, pp. 327–352, 1977.

[40] S. Jain and G. D. Bader, "An improved method for scoring protein-protein interactions using semantic similarity within the gene ontology," *BMC Bioinformatics*, vol. 11, p. 562, 2010.

[41] B. Aranda, P. Achuthan, Y. Alam-Faruque et al., "The IntAct molecular interaction database in 2010," *Nucleic Acids Research*, vol. 38, no. 1, Article ID gkp878, pp. D525–D531, 2009.

[42] I. Xenarios, L. Salwinski, X. J. Duan et al., "DIP, the database of interacting proteins: a research tool for studying cellular networks of protein interactions," *Nucleic Acids Research*, vol. 30, no. 1, pp. 303–305, 2002.

[43] G. D. Bader, I. Donaldson, C. Wolting, B. F. F. Ouellette, T. Pawson, and C. W. V. Hogue, "BIND—the biomolecular interaction network database," *Nucleic Acids Research*, vol. 29, no. 1, pp. 242–245, 2001.

[44] P. Pagel, S. Kovac, M. Oesterheld et al., "The MIPS mammalian protein-protein interaction database," *Bioinformatics*, vol. 21, no. 6, pp. 832–834, 2005.

[45] A. Ceol, C. A. Aryamontri, L. Licata et al., "Mint, the molecular interaction database: 2009 update," *Nucleic Acids Research*, vol. 38, supplement 1, pp. D532–D539, 2010.

[46] C. Stark, B. J. Breitkreutz, A. Chatr-Aryamontri et al., "The BioGRID interaction database: 2011 update," *Nucleic Acids Research*, vol. 39, no. 1, pp. D698–D704, 2011.

[47] G. K. Mazandu and N. J. Mulder, "Generation and analysis of large-scale data-driven mycobacterium tuberculosis functional networks for drug target identification," *Advances in Bioinformatics*, vol. 2011, Article ID 801478, 14 pages, 2011.

[48] P. Hu, G. Bader, D. A. Wigle, and A. Emili, "Computational prediction of cancer-gene function," *Nature Reviews Cancer*, vol. 7, no. 1, pp. 23–34, 2007.

[49] L. V. Zhang, S. L. Wong, O. D. King, and F. P. Roth, "Predicting co-complexed protein pairs using genomic and proteomic data integration," *BMC Bioinformatics*, vol. 5, p. 38, 2004.

[50] A. Ben-Hur and W. S. Noble, "Choosing negative examples for the prediction of protein-protein interactions," *BMC Bioinformatics*, vol. 7, supplement 1, p. S2, 2006.

[51] T. Sing, O. Sander, N. Beerenwinkel, and T. Lengauer, "ROCR: visualizing classifier performance in R," *Bioinformatics*, vol. 21, no. 20, pp. 3940–3941, 2005.

[52] P. H. Guzzi, M. Mina, C. Guerra, and M. Cannataro, "Semantic similarity analysis of protein data: assessment with biological features and issues," *Briefings in Bioinformatics*, Advance Access, 17 pages, 2012.

[53] R Development Core Team, *R: A Language and Environment for Statistical Computing*, R Foundation for Statistical Computing, Vienna, Austria, 2010.

[54] R Development Core Team, *R: A Language and Environment for Statistical Computing*, R Foundation for Statistical Computing, Vienna, Austria, 2011.

[55] M. Mistry and P. Pavlidis, "Gene ontology term overlap as a measure of gene functional similarity," *BMC Bioinformatics*, vol. 9, p. 327, 2008.

[56] E. B. Camon, D. G. Barrell, E. C. Dimmer et al., "An evaluation of GO annotation retrieval for BioCreAtIvE and GOA," *BMC Bioinformatics*, vol. 6, supplement 1, p. S17, 2005.

[57] C. Pesquita, D. Pessoa, D. Faria, and F. Couto, CESSM: Collaborative Evaluation of Semantic Similarity Measures. JB2009: Challenges in Bioinformatics: 1–5, 2009.

[58] E. Jain, A. Bairoch, S. Duvaud et al., "Infrastructure for the life sciences: design and implementation of the UniProt website," *BMC Bioinformatics*, vol. 10, p. 136, 2009.

[59] UniProt-Consortium, "The universal protein resource (UniProt) in 2010," *Nucleic Acids Research*, vol. 38, no. 1, Article ID gkp846, pp. D142–D148, 2009.

[60] P. Flicek, M. R. Amode, D. Barrell et al., "Ensembl 2011," *Nucleic Acids Research*, vol. 39, no. 1, pp. D800–D806, 2011.

[61] R. J. Kinsella, A. Kähäri, S. Haider et al., "Ensembl biomarts: a hub for data retrieval across taxonomic space," *Database (Oxford)*, bar030, 2011.

[62] R. Apweiler, A. Bairoch, C. H. Wu et al., "UniProt: the universal protein knowledgebase," *Nucleic Acids Research*, vol. 32, pp. D115–D119, 2004.

[63] S. F. Altschul, W. Gish, W. Miller, E. W. Myers, and D. J. Lipman, "Basic local alignment search tool," *Journal of Molecular Biology*, vol. 215, no. 3, pp. 403–410, 1990.

[64] S. F. Altschul, T. L. Madden, A. A. Schäffer et al., "Gapped BLAST and PSI-BLAST: a new generation of protein database search programs," *Nucleic Acids Research*, vol. 25, no. 17, pp. 3389–3402, 1997.

[65] S. F. Altschul, "Amino acid substitution matrices from an information theoretic perspective," *Journal of Molecular Biology*, vol. 219, no. 3, pp. 555–565, 1991.

[66] G. K. Mazandu and N. J. Mulder, "Scoring protein relationships in functional interaction networks predicted from sequence data," *PLoS ONE*, vol. 6, no. 4, Article ID e18607, 2011.

[67] S. P. Calderon-Copete, G. Wigger, C. Wunderlin et al., "The Mycoplasma conjunctivae genome sequencing, annotation and analysis," *BMC Bioinformatics*, vol. 10, supplement 6, p. S7, 2009.

[68] W. C. Wong, S. Maurer-Stroh, and F. Eisenhaber, "More than 1,001 problems with protein domain databases: transmembrane regions, signal peptides and the issue of sequence homology," *PLoS Computational Biology*, vol. 6, no. 7, p. e1000867, 2010.

8

An Overview of the Statistical Methods Used for Inferring Gene Regulatory Networks and Protein-Protein Interaction Networks

Amina Noor,[1] **Erchin Serpedin,**[1] **Mohamed Nounou,**[2] **Hazem Nounou,**[3]
Nady Mohamed,[4] **and Lotfi Chouchane**[4]

[1] *Electrical and Computer Engineering Department, Texas A&M University, College Station, TX 77843-3128, USA*
[2] *Chemical Engineering Department, Texas A&M University at Qatar, 253 Texas A&M Engineering Building, Education City, P.O. Box 23874, Doha, Qatar*
[3] *Electrical Engineering Department, Texas A&M University at Qatar, 253 Texas A&M Engineering Building, Education City, P.O. Box 23874, Doha, Qatar*
[4] *Department of Genetic Medicine, Weill Cornell Medical College in Qatar, P.O. Box 24144, Doha, Qatar*

Correspondence should be addressed to Amina Noor; amina@neo.tamu.edu

Academic Editor: Yufei Huang

The large influx of data from high-throughput genomic and proteomic technologies has encouraged the researchers to seek approaches for understanding the structure of gene regulatory networks and proteomic networks. This work reviews some of the most important statistical methods used for modeling of gene regulatory networks (GRNs) and protein-protein interaction (PPI) networks. The paper focuses on the recent advances in the statistical graphical modeling techniques, state-space representation models, and information theoretic methods that were proposed for inferring the topology of GRNs. It appears that the problem of inferring the structure of PPI networks is quite different from that of GRNs. Clustering and probabilistic graphical modeling techniques are of prime importance in the statistical inference of PPI networks, and some of the recent approaches using these techniques are also reviewed in this paper. Performance evaluation criteria for the approaches used for modeling GRNs and PPI networks are also discussed.

1. Introduction

Postgenomic era is marked by the availability of a deluge of genomic data and has, thus, enabled the researchers to look towards new dimensions for understanding the complex biological processes governing the life of a living organism [1–5]. The various life sustaining functions are performed via a collaborative effort involving DNA, RNA, and proteins. Genes and proteins interact with themselves and each other and orchestrate the successful completion of a multitude of important tasks. Understanding how they work together to form a cellular network in a living organism is extremely important in the field of molecular biology. Two important problems in this considerably nascent field of computational biology are the inference of gene regulatory networks and the inference of protein-protein interaction networks. This paper first looks at how the genes and proteins interact with

themselves and then discusses the inference of an integrative cellular network of genes and proteins combined.

Gene regulation is one of the many fascinating processes taking place in a living organism whereby the expression and repression of genes are controlled in a systematic manner. With the help of the enzyme RNA polymerase, DNA transcribes into mRNA which may or may not translate into proteins. It is found that in certain special cases mRNA is reverse-transcribed to DNA. The processes of transcription and translation are schematically represented in Figure 1, where the interactions in black show the most general framework and the interactions depicted in red occur less frequently. Transcription factors (TFs), which are a class of proteins, play the significant role of binding onto the DNA and thereby regulate their transcription. Since the genes may be coding for TFs and/or other proteins, a complex network of genes and proteins is formed. The level of activity of a gene

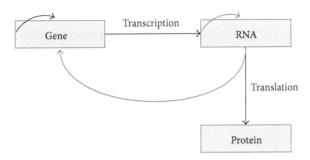

FIGURE 1: Central dogma of molecular biology.

is measured in terms of the amount of resulting functional product, and is referred to as gene expression. The recent high-throughput genomic technologies are able to measure the gene expression values and have provided large-scale data sets, which can be used to obtain insights into how the gene networks are organized and operated. One of the most encountered representations of gene regulatory networks is in terms of a graph, where the genes are depicted by its nodes and the edges represent the interactions between them.

The gene regulatory network (GRN) inference problem consists in understanding the underlying system model [6–10]. Simply stated, given the gene expression data, the activation or repression actions by a set of genes on the other genes need to be identified. There are several issues associated with this problem, including the choice of models that capture the gene interactions sufficiently well, followed by robust and reliable inference algorithms that can be used to derive decisive conclusions about the network. The inferred networks vary in their sophistication depending on the extent and accuracy of the prior knowledge available and the type of models used in the process. It is also important that the gene networks thus inferred should possess the highly desirable quality of reproducibility in order to have a high degree of confidence in them. A sufficiently accurate picture of gene interactions could pave the way for significant breakthroughs in finding cures for various genetic diseases including cancer.

Protein-protein interactions (PPIs) are of enormous significance for the workings of a cell. Insights into the molecular mechanism can be obtained by finding the protein interactions with a high degree of accuracy [11, 12]. The protein interaction networks not only consist of the binary interactions, rather, in order to carry out various tasks, proteins work together with cohorts to form protein complexes. It should be emphasized that a particular protein may be a part of different protein complexes, and hence the inference problem is much more complicated. The existing high-throughput proteomic data sets enable the inference of protein-protein interactions. However, it is found that the protein-protein interactions obtained by using different methods may not be equivalent, indicating that a large number of false positives and negatives are present in the data. Similar to the representation of gene regulatory networks, protein-protein interaction networks will also be modeled in terms of graphs, where the proteins denote the nodes and the edges signify whether an interaction is present between the adjacent nodes.

Many statistical methods have been applied extensively to solve various bioinformatics problems in the last decade. There are several papers that provide excellent review of various statistical and computational techniques for inferring genomic and proteomic networks [2, 12]. However, it is important to understand the fundamental similarities and differences that characterize the two inference problems. This paper provides an overview of the most recent statistical methods proposed for the inference of GRNs and PPI networks. For gene network inference, three large classes of modeling and inferencing techniques will be presented, namely, probabilistic graphical modeling approaches, information theoretic methods, and state-space representation models. Clustering and probabilistic graphical modeling methods which comprise the largest class of statistical methods using PPI data are reviewed for the protein-protein interaction networks. Through a concise review of these contemporary algorithms, our goal is to provide the reader with a sufficiently rich understanding of the current state-of-the-art techniques used in the field of genomic and proteomic network inference.

The rest of this paper is organized as follows. Section 2 describes some of the data sets available for the inference of genomic and proteomic networks. Section 3 reviews the recent statistical methods employed to infer gene regulatory networks. Protein-protein network inferencing techniques are reviewed in Section 4. The methods for obtaining an integrated network with gene network and protein-protein as subnetworks are given in Section 5. The inferred network evaluation is discussed in Section 6. Finally, conclusions are drawn in Section 7.

2. Available Biological Data

The postgenomic era is distinguished by the availability of huge amount of biological data sets which are quite heterogenous in nature and difficult to analyze [3]. It is expected that these data sets can aid in obtaining useful knowledge about the underlying interactions in gene-gene and protein-protein networks. This section reviews some of the main types of data used for the inference of genomic and proteomic networks, including, gene expression data, protein-protein interaction data, and ChIP-chip data.

2.1. Gene Expression Data. Of all the available datasets, gene expression data is the most widely used for gene regulatory network inference. Gene expression is the process that results in functional transcripts, for example, RNA or proteins, while utilizing the information coded on the genes. The level of gene expression is an important indicator of how active a gene is and is measured in the form of gene expression data. Similarity in the gene expression profiles of two genes advocates some level of correlation between them. In this paper, the gene expression data is denoted by means of a random variable $\mathbf{x}(t)$, where t stands for the time index.

2.1.1. cDNA-Microarray Data. One way of generating cDNA-microarray data is via the DNA microarray technology, which

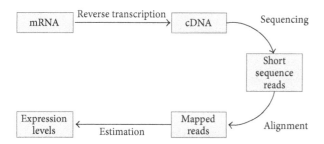

FIGURE 2: Expression estimation in RNA-Seq.

is by far the most popular method employed for this purpose. The number of data samples is in general much smaller than the number of genes. A main drawback associated with cDNA-microarray data is the noise in the observed gene expressions. Although the gene expression values should be continuous, the inability to measure them accurately suggests the use of discretized values.

2.1.2. RNA-Seq Data. The recent advancement of sequencing technologies has provided the ability to acquire more accurate gene expression levels [13]. RNA-Seq is a novel technology for mapping and quantifying transcriptomes, and it is expected to replace all the contemporary methods because of its superiority in terms of time, complexity, and accuracy. The gene expression estimation in RNA-Seq begins with the reverse transcription of RNA sample into cDNA samples, which undergo high-throughput sequencing, resulting in short sequence reads. These reads are then mapped to the reference genome using a variety of available alignment tools. The gene expression levels are estimated using the mapped reads, and several algorithms have been proposed in the recent literature to find efficient and more accurate estimates of the gene expression levels. This process is summarized in Figure 2. The gene expression data obtained in this manner has been found to be much more reproducible and less noisy as compared to the cDNA microarrays. The next subsection describes the data used for PPI network inference.

2.2. Protein-Protein Interaction Data. Large-scale PPI data have been produced in recent years by high-throughput technologies like yeast two-hybrid and tandem affinity purification, which provide stable and transient interactions, and mass spectrometry, which indicates the protein complexes [11, 12]. These data sets, in addition to being incomplete also consist of false positives, and, therefore, the interactions found in various data sets may not agree with each other. Owing to this disagreement, it is imperative to make use of statistical methods to infer the PPI networks by finding reliable and reproducible interactions and predict the interactions not found yet in the currently available data.

2.3. ChIP-Chip Data. ChIP-chip data, which is an abbreviation of chromatin immunoprecipitation and microarray (chip), investigates the interactions between DNA and proteins. This data provides information about the DNA-binding

proteins. Since some of the genes encode for transcription factors (TFs) which in turn regulate some other genes and/or proteins, this information comes in hand for the inference of gene networks [10] and the integrated network. However, generating the ChIP-chip data for large genome would be technically and financially difficult.

2.4. Other Data Sets. Apart from the data sets described above, gene deletion and perturbation data are worth mentioning here. Perturbation data set is generated by performing an initial perturbation and then letting the system to react to it [14]. The gene expression values at the following time instants and at steady-state are measured, thereby obtaining the response of the genes to the specific perturbation which could be the increase or decrease of the expression level of all or certain genes. Gene deletion dataset, as the name indicates, involves deleting a gene and measuring the resulting expression level of other genes. This data may effectively uncover simple direct relationships [14].

3. Modeling and Inferring Gene Regulatory Networks

Gene regulatory networks capture the interactions present among the genes. Accurate and reliable estimation of gene networks is significantly crucial and can reap far-reaching benefits in the field of medicinal biology, for example, in terms of developing personalized medicines. The following subsections review the main statistical methods used for inference of gene regulatory networks. First, the important class of probabilistic graphical models is presented.

3.1. Probabilistic Graphical Modeling Techniques. Probabilistic graphical models have emerged as a useful tool for reverse engineering gene regulatory networks. A gene network is represented by a graph $\mathbf{G} = (V, E)$, where V represents the set of vertices (genes), and E denotes the set of edges connecting the vertices. The vertices of the graph are modeled as random variables and the edges signify the interaction between them. The expression value of gene i is denoted by X_i, and the total number of genes in the network is denoted by N. The following subsections briefly describe some of the robust and popular graphical modeling techniques for gene network inference.

3.1.1. Bayesian Networks. Bayesian networks model the gene regulatory networks as directed acyclic graphs (DAGs). To simplify the inference process, the probability distribution of DAG-networks is generally factored in terms of the conditional distributions of each random variable given its parents:

$$P(\mathbf{X}) = \prod_{i=1}^{N} P(X_i \mid Pa(X_i)), \qquad (1)$$

where $Pa(X_i)$ denotes the parent of node X_i. The gene regulatory network is inferred by using the Bayesian network learning techniques. This is done by maximizing the probability $P(\mathbf{G} \mid \mathbf{D})$, where $\mathbf{D}$ denotes the available gene expression data. Several scoring metrics have been proposed to obtain the best graph structure [15]. The network, thus, obtained is unique to the extent of equivalence class; that is, the independence relationships are uniquely identified.

The gene expression data available to date consist of very few data points, while the number of genes is substantially larger, rendering the system to be underdetermined. As an alternative to finding the complete networks, scientists have proposed looking at certain important features, for example, Markov relations and order relations. If a gene X is present in the minimal network blanketing the gene Y, then a Markov relation is said to be established. A relationship between two genes is referred to as an ordered relation if a particular gene X appears to be a parent of another gene Y in all the equivalent networks. By aggregating this information, it is possible to infer the underlying regulatory structure robustly and reliably. The network structure inferred in this manner looks at the static interactions only. In order to cater for the dynamic interactions inherent in gene networks, dynamic Bayesian networks (DBNs) have been used [16, 17].

3.1.2. Qualitative Probabilistic Networks. A novel method of modeling gene networks is via the usage of qualitative probabilistic networks (QPNs), which represent the qualitative analog of the DBNs [18]. The structural and independence properties of QPNs are the same as those of Bayesian networks. However, instead of being concerned about the local conditional probabilities of the random variables, the former class of models looks at how the changes in probabilities of the random variables affect the probabilities of their immediate parents. This change is measured in qualitative terms instead of quantitative values, that is, whether the probabilities increase, decrease, or stay the same as shown in Figure 3.

Two important properties of QPNs are the qualitative influences and the qualitative synergies. A positive influence denoted by $I^{+}(X, Y)$ indicates the greater possibility of Y having a higher value when that of X is high and vice versa, irrespective of all other variables; that is,

$$I^{+}(X, Y) \quad \text{iff } P(y \mid x, W) > P(y \mid -x). \quad (2)$$

In the case of three variables, QPNs look at the synergies. A positive additive synergy, denoted by $S^{+}(\{X, Y\}, Z)$, exists when the combined effect of the parent nodes is greater on the child node than their individual effects given by

$$S^{+}(\{X, Y\}, Z) \quad \text{iff } P(z \mid x, y, W) + P(z \mid -x, -y, W)$$
$$> P(z \mid x, -y, W) + P(z \mid -x, y, W). \quad (3)$$

QPNs, thus, provide more insight into the gene networks by indicating whether a particular gene is a promoter or an inhibitor.

3.1.3. Graphical Gaussian Models. Graphical Gaussian models, also known as covariance selection or concentration

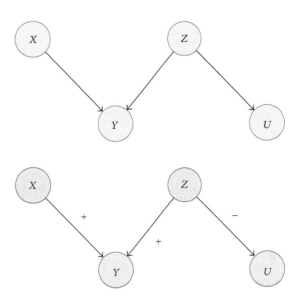

FIGURE 3: Qualitative probabilistic network (red) for a Bayesian network (blue).

graph models, provide a simple and effective way of characterizing the gene interactions [19, 20]. This method relies on assessing the conditional dependencies among genes in terms of partial correlation coefficients among the gene expressions and results in an undirected network. A covariance matrix is estimated using the available gene expression data sets. Suppose that $\mathbf{X} \in \mathbb{R}^{n \times n}$ denotes the gene expression data matrix, where the rows correspond to observations and the columns correspond to genes, then an estimate of the covariance matrix is obtained by

$$\widehat{\mathbf{W}} = \frac{1}{N-1} \mathbf{X}^{T} \mathbf{X}. \quad (4)$$

Assuming invertibility of $\widehat{\mathbf{W}}$, the partial correlations can be determined as

$$\widehat{\rho}_{ij} = -\frac{\widehat{w}_{ij}}{\sqrt{\widehat{w}_{ii} \widehat{w}_{jj}}}, \quad (5)$$

where $\widehat{\rho}_{ij}$ denotes the partial correlation between genes i and j.

3.1.4. Graphical LASSO Algorithm. A major drawback of the covariance-matrix-estimation-based methods is their unreliability due to the small number of data samples. Making use of the fact that gene networks are inherently sparse, it is possible to obtain the dependencies between genes by means of a penalized linear regression approach [20]. The graphical Least Absolute Shrinkage and Selection Operator (LASSO) algorithm solves the network inference problem efficiently by maximizing the following penalized likelihood function:

$$\frac{2}{n} l(\mathbf{W}) = \log(\det(\mathbf{W})) - \text{trace}(\widehat{\mathbf{W}}\mathbf{W}) - \rho \|\mathbf{W}\|_{1}, \quad (6)$$

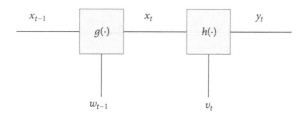

FIGURE 4: State-Space model.

where ρ controls the sparsity of the network, notation $\| \cdot \|_1$ represents the l_1-norm, and $\mathbf{W}$ denotes the covariance matrix. This minimization can be carried out by using block gradient descent methods, the details of which can be found in [20] and the references therein.

3.2. State-Space Representation Models. One of the earliest and widely used methods of modeling gene networks is by employing the state-space representation models [21]. As opposed to other classes, all the methods belonging to this class model the dynamic evolution of the gene network. These models generally consist of two sets of equations, the first set of equations representing the evolution of the hidden state variables denoted by $\mathbf{z}(t)$, and the second set of equations relating the hidden state variables with the observed gene expression data, denoted by $\mathbf{x}(t)$ as depicted in Figure 4. The functions $g(\cdot)$ and $h(\cdot)$ describe the evolution of hidden and observed variables, respectively. Next, in this section we will describe various models for gene network inference using the state-space representation model.

3.2.1. Linear State-Space Model. The simplest model for state-space equations is the linear Gaussian model given by [21, 22]:

$$\begin{aligned} \mathbf{z}(t) &= \mathbf{A}\mathbf{z}(t-1) + v(t), \\ \mathbf{x}(t) &= \mathbf{C}\mathbf{z}(t) + \mathbf{w}(t), \end{aligned} \tag{7}$$

where $\mathbf{A}$ is a matrix representing the regulatory relations between the genes, and t stands for the discrete time points. Difference equations are used in place of differential equations because discrete observations are available in the gene expression data. The noise components $v(t)$ and $\mathbf{w}(t)$ represent the system and the measurement noise, respectively, and are assumed to be Gaussian. The noise models the uncertainty present in the estimated gene expression data. The matrix $\mathbf{C}$ is generally considered to be an identity matrix. Inference in gene networks modeled by the state-space representation (7) can be performed using standard Kalman filter updates. The simplicity of the state-space model avoids overfitting of the network, and therefore, it provides reliable results.

3.2.2. Nonlinear Models. While it is useful to represent gene networks by simple models to ease the computational complexity, it is also imperative to incorporate nonlinear effects into the system equations, since the genes are known to interact nonlinearly [23]. A particular function that is frequently used to capture the nonlinear effects is the sigmoid

squash function defined below in (9) [24]. The nonlinear state-space representation model capturing the gene interactions is described by the following system of equations:

$$\mathbf{z}(t) = \mathbf{A}\mathbf{z}(t-1) + \mathbf{B}f\left(\mathbf{z}(t-1), \boldsymbol{\mu}\right) + \mathbf{I}_0 + v(t), \tag{8}$$

where the jth entry of vector function $f(\cdot)$ is given by the sigmoid squash function:

$$f_j\left(z_j, \mu_j\right) = \frac{1}{1 + e^{-\mu_j z_j}}, \tag{9}$$

where μ is a parameter to be identified. Matrix $\mathbf{A}$ represents the linear relationships between the genes, while matrix $\mathbf{B}$ characterizes the nonlinear interactions. The problem, thus, boils down to the estimation of the following unknowns in the system:

$$\theta = \left[\mathbf{A}, \mathbf{B}, \boldsymbol{\mu}, \mathbf{I}_0\right], \tag{10}$$

where $\mathbf{I}_0$ models the constant bias. One way of solving these equations is by using the extended Kalman filter (EKF) [24], which is a popular algorithm for solving nonlinear state-space equations. EKF algorithm provides the solution by approximating the nonlinear system by its first-order linear approximation. Other variants of Kalman filter algorithm like the cubature Kalman filter (CKF), unscented Kalman filter (UKF), and particle filter algorithm are also used to solve such inference problems [25].

However, for many studies, the considered nonlinear model is comprised of a large number of unknowns and in order to estimate these unknown variables with considerable accuracy, data sets consisting of a large number of samples are required. The availability of smaller data sets represents an insurmountable obstacle in the reliable estimation of a large number of unknowns. This problem can be partially avoided by simplifying the model to include only nonlinear terms, and thus reducing the number of unknown parameters to the bare minimum [25] and by approximating μ to be one. The system of equations corresponding to such a parsimonious scenario is then given by

$$\mathbf{z}(t) = \mathbf{B}f\left(\mathbf{z}(t-1)\right) + v(t), \tag{11}$$

where f is the function defined previously.

3.2.3. Models with Sparsity Constraints. A crucial feature for many gene networks is their inherent sparsity; that is, all genes in the network are connected to a few other genes only. Therefore, matrices $\mathbf{A}$ and $\mathbf{B}$ depicting the regulatory relations between the genes are expected to contain only very few nonzero values as compared to the size of these matrices. Therefore, one may apply shrinkage-based methods like LASSO [25, 26] for parameter estimation and parsimonious model selection. One of the ways for inferring models with sparsity constraints is to perform dual estimation, which involves estimating the states and the parameters one by one. The hidden states can be estimated using the particle filter algorithm, and once all the estimates for the hidden states are obtained, they can be stacked together to form a matrix and thus the following system of equations is obtained to perform the parameter estimation:

$$\begin{bmatrix} z_{n1} \\ z_{n2} \\ \vdots \\ z_{nI} \end{bmatrix} = \begin{bmatrix} f(z_{0,1}) & \cdots & f(z_{0,N}) \\ f(z_{1,1}) & \cdots & \vdots \\ \vdots & \ddots & \\ f(z_{I-1,1}) & & f(z_{I-1,N}) \end{bmatrix} \begin{bmatrix} b_{n1} \\ b_{n2} \\ \vdots \\ b_{nN} \end{bmatrix} + \begin{bmatrix} v_{n1} \\ v_{n2} \\ \vdots \\ v_{nI} \end{bmatrix}, \tag{12}$$

which can be expressed compactly in vector/matrix-form representation as

$$\mathbf{z}_n = \mathbf{\Phi}\mathbf{b}_n + v_n. \tag{13}$$

LASSO operates on this system of equations and produces a parameter vector $\mathbf{b}_n$ by minimizing the criterion [27]:

$$\min_{\mathbf{b}_n} \frac{1}{2}\|\mathbf{z}_n - \mathbf{\Phi}\mathbf{b}_n\|_2^2 + \rho\|\mathbf{b}_n\|_1. \tag{14}$$

The parameter estimates obtained using LASSO-based algorithms appear to be more reliable than the estimates provided by other approaches [25].

3.2.4. State-Space Models for Time-Delayed Dependencies.
The state-space models discussed so far do not consider time delays whereas it has been found that time-delayed interactions are present in gene networks [28] due to the time required for the processes of transcription and translation to take place. One of the ways to model this phenomenon is by adopting the following state-space model:

$$\mathbf{z}(t) = \mathbf{A}\mathbf{z}(t-1) + \mathbf{B}\mathbf{u}(t-\tau) + v(t),$$
$$\mathbf{x}(t) = \mathbf{C}\mathbf{z}(t) + \mathbf{w}(t). \tag{15}$$

In this state-space model, the input is considered to be the expression profile of a regulator such as a transcription factor. Here, $\mathbf{A}$ stands for the $N \times N$ state transition matrix, while $N \times p$ matrix $\mathbf{B}$ captures the effect of p regulators on the system. The value of the time delay τ is obtained by finding the best fit over a range of possible values using Akaike's information criterion (AIC) in order to avoid overfitting the network.

3.3. Information Theoretic Methods.
Information theoretic methods have provided some of the most robust and reliable algorithms for gene network inference and form the basis of a standard in this field [29–31]. A particular advantage associated with these methods is their ability to work with minimal assumptions about the underlying network. This is in contrast with the probabilistic graphical modeling techniques as well as the state-space models, both of which have their own set of assumptions. As highlighted previously, a Markov network provides an undirected network, while Bayesian networks are not able to incorporate cycles or feedback loops. State-space models apart from the linear Gaussian model make critical assumptions on the model structure. These drawbacks are not present in the case of information theoretic methods. The following discussion presents the main information theoretic approaches for inferring gene regulatory networks.

3.3.1. Finding the Correlation between Genes.
Two of the most fundamental concepts in information theory are mutual information and entropy. Mutual information between two random variables X and Y is defined as [32]

$$I(X;Y) = \sum_{x,y}\left[p(x,y)\log\frac{p(x,y)}{p(x)p(y)}\right] \\ = H(X) + H(Y) - H(X,Y), \tag{16}$$

where H denotes the entropy or the uncertainty present in a random variable, and it is given by

$$H(X) = -\sum_x p(x)\log p(x). \tag{17}$$

Mutual information measures the correlation between two random variables. In the context of gene network inference, a higher mutual information between two genes indicates a higher dependency, and therefore, a possible interaction between them. Some of the most important and robust algorithms for gene network inference make use of the mutual information for finding the interacting genes [29, 30].

3.3.2. Identifying Indirect Interactions between Genes.
If the mutual information between two genes is greater than a certain threshold, it indicates some correlation between them. However, this information alone is not sufficient to decide whether the genes are connected directly or indirectly via an intermediate gene. The data processing inequality (DPI) provides some insight to assess whether such a scenario holds. In case of three genes forming a Markov chain as shown in Figure 5, DPI can be expressed as

$$I(X;Y) \le \min[I(X;Z), I(Y;Z)]. \tag{18}$$

Using this inequality, it is found that the interaction with the least mutual information is an indirect one. This method is employed in ARACNE [29], which has become a standard algorithm for gene network inference. However, DPI fails to hold in situations where one of the three genes is a parent gene to the other two genes. Conditional mutual information has been proposed to be used in such cases [30]. Conditional mutual information is defined as

$$I(X;Y \mid Z) = \sum_{X,Y,Z}\left[p(x,y,z)\log\frac{p(x,y \mid z)}{p(x \mid z)\cdot p(y \mid z)}\right] \\ = H(X,Z) + H(Y,Z) - H(Z) - H(X,Y,Z). \tag{19}$$

If $I(X;Y \mid Z)$ is much less than $I(X;Y)$, it implies that Z is a parent of the genes X and Y as shown in Figure 5. In case the two quantities are almost equal, it means that the gene Z does not have any influence on the other two genes. Therefore, by employing the idea of conditional mutual information, indirect interactions in the case of common cause can be sifted.

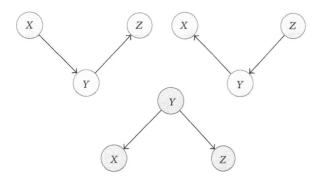

FIGURE 5: Markov chain (blue) and common cause (red).

3.3.3. Finding the Directed Networks.

Calculating the mutual information using static data does not provide any information about the directed relationships. On the other hand, using time series data may indicate the directionality of interactions as well [33]. Mutual information for time series data can be expressed as

$$I\left(X_{t+1}; Y_t\right) = \sum_{x_{t+1}, y_t} \left[p\left(x_{t+1}, y_t\right) \log \frac{p\left(x_{t+1}, y_t\right)}{p\left(x_{t+1}\right) p\left(y_t\right)} \right]. \tag{20}$$

If a high value is obtained for $I(X_{t+1}; Y_t)$, it signifies a directed relationship from gene Y to X. While using these methods, the determination of the significance threshold is of considerable importance and can be estimated based on the prior knowledge about the network.

The information theoretic quantities discussed so far are symmetric (or bidirectional) and do not provide any information about the directionality by themselves. Some new metrics have been proposed recently to infer asymmetric or one-directional relationships such as the ϕ-mixing coefficient defined as [34]:

$$\phi\left(Y \mid X\right) = \max_{S \subseteq A, T \subseteq B} \left| \Pr\left\{Y \in T \mid X \in S\right\} - \Pr\left\{Y \in T\right\} \right|. \tag{21}$$

In other words, this coefficient provides a measure of independence or difference between two genes X and Y. DPI also holds true for the ϕ-mixing metric, and therefore, it can be used to identify the indirect interactions as in the case of mutual information.

3.3.4. Time-Delayed Dependencies.

Another way of finding directed relationships is by detecting the time-delayed dependencies by using time series data. The time instants at which the mutual information goes above or drops below the thresholds τ_{up} and τ_{down}, respectively, are noted [35]. These instants are called the initial change of expression (IcE) times and are defined as

$$\text{IcE}\left(x_a\right) = \arg\min_j \left\{ \frac{x_a^j}{x_a^0} \geq \tau_{\text{up}} \text{ or } \frac{x_a^j}{x_a^0} \leq \tau_{\text{down}} \right\}. \tag{22}$$

It can be seen that a gene x_a can be a regulator for gene x_b if and only if (iff) $\text{IcE}(x_a) < \text{IcE}(x_b)$. The mutual information in this case is given by

$$I^k\left(x_a; x_b\right) = \sum_{i=1} \left[p\left(x_a^i, x_b^{i+k}\right) \log \frac{p\left(x_a^i, x_b^{i+k}\right)}{p\left(x_a^i\right) p\left(x_b^{i+k}\right)} \right], \tag{23}$$

where the delay is denoted by k. The next step consists in finding the maximum of the mutual information values calculated for all the time delays; that is,

$$I\left(x_a, x_b\right) = \max_k \left\{ I^k\left(x_a, x_b^{(k)}\right) \right\} \tag{24}$$

for $k = 1, 2, \ldots$, while $\text{IcE}\left(x_a\right) \leq \text{IcE}\left(x_b\right)$.

If the value of the maximum mutual information is greater than a prespecified threshold, it is concluded that a directed relationship exists from x_a to x_b. The calculation of threshold is very important in all the information theoretic methods which is selected on the basis of the predetermined P-value [29]. This helps to obtain networks with the required significance value.

3.3.5. Model Selection.

An important and necessary step in the implementation of the above-mentioned algorithms is the model selection. A network formed by using mutual information alone will result in an overfitted structure, and therefore, model selection becomes imperative. Minimum description length (MDL) principle was proposed as a general approach for model selection. MDL states that the network with the shortest coding length should be selected. For a network with a large number of nodes, the coding length will be large and vice versa. MDL principle provides a trade-off and aids in selecting only the significant interactions between the genes. MDL was applied in various ways in finding the coding length of the network and the probability densities associated with it [33]. Another way of using this principle is in conjunction with the maximum likelihood (ML) principle which results in a more general algorithm [36]. Further details on this algorithm can be found in [36]. Thus, it appears that the tools of information theory are quite powerful in modeling and inferring gene regulatory networks.

4. Inferring the Protein-Protein Interaction Networks

Having examined the gene network inference problem, this section describes the statistical methods that are used to find reliable and complete protein-protein interaction networks. As opposed to gene networks which are mostly inferred using the expression data or the likes of it, inference of PPI networks can be carried out in various ways such as phylogenetic profiling and identification of structural patterns. This paper focuses only on the methods that employ PPI data to make inference. The given data in this scenario are the protein-protein interactions. However, such data sets consist of a large number of false positives and negatives and are far from being complete and homogeneous. Therefore, only a small overlap is found between the PPI data sets obtained from various sources. However, it is observed that the interactions predicted by more than one method are more reliable [37]. One of the challenges is the large number of interactions indicated by the PPI data as opposed to the considerably fewer interactions assumed to be present in reality. Therefore, the problem in this scenario is to find more reliable interactions and predict the yet unknown interactions. In addition, the protein interactions can be of different types ranging from stable ones to transient ones [37].

It is to be noted that as opposed to the gene networks, a lot of work can still be done for protein-protein network inference using the probabilistic methods. In a living organism, several proteins work together to carry out various tasks forming a protein complex. Most of the PPI data consists of binary interactions only and it is very rare to find interactions between more than two proteins simultaneously. Hence, identification of protein complexes is of prime importance to gain a better understanding of the cellular network.

Detecting protein complexes is a fundamental area of study of protein networks [38], for which various clustering methods were applied. One of the various ways of identifying the protein complexes include graph segmentation, where the graph is clustered into subgraphs using cost-based search algorithms. Another approach is broadly categorized as conservation across species [38], where alignment tools are used to find the complexes that are common in multiple data sets coming from different species. In what follows, some of the recently proposed probabilistic graphical-modeling- and clustering-based methods are described.

4.1. Markov Networks.

The available PPI data look mostly at the binary interactions, and interactions of three or more genes are hard to find. However, it is important to look at the interacting proteins holistically. Markov networks are probabilistic graphical modeling techniques which result in undirected graphs. Suppose $\mathbf{X} = \{X_1, \ldots, X_N\}$ is a vector of random variables modeling the proteins. Their joint distribution is captured in terms of the potentials $\psi_c \in \Psi$. The random variables $\mathbf{X}_c$ that are connected to each other are called the scope for the particular potential ψ_c. The joint probability distribution is then given by

$$P(\mathbf{X} = \mathbf{x}) = \frac{1}{Z} \prod_{c \in C} e^{\psi_c(\mathbf{x}_c)},$$ (25)

where Z is the normalizing constant also called the partition function. In this way, a compact representation of the probability distribution is obtained. The network structure is learned by using the independence properties of Markov networks using the available PPI data. The details of this method can be found in [37].

4.2. Bayesian Networks.

Another way of modeling PPI networks is by means of Bayesian networks (BNs) [39], which represent a probabilistic graphical modeling technique. The inference algorithm is based on finding the conditional probability densities $P(X_i \mid C)$, where C denotes the class variable, and X_i denotes the ith node in the network. A

particular strength of BNs is their ability to estimate model parameters even in the presence of incomplete data, which is often the case with the PPI networks. This fact makes BN a perfectly suited method for modeling protein networks. One way of estimating the model parameters is via the Expectation Maximization (EM) algorithm [39]. The joint probability distribution is expressed as

$$P(C, X_1, \ldots, X_N) = P(C) \prod_i P(X_i \mid C).$$ (26)

Assuming all the random variables to be independent of each other, the posterior density is given by

$$P(C \mid X_1, \ldots, X_N) = P(C) \prod_i \frac{P(X_i \mid C)}{P(X_i)}.$$ (27)

Once the model parameters are known, prediction can be made about random variables for which the data may not be available. Therefore, this algorithm provides a suitable method for finding protein complexes.

4.3. Graphical Clustering Methods.

One of the ways of graph clustering is based on supervised learning [12, 38]. The subgraphs are modeled using Bayesian networks, and the features consist of topological patterns of graphs and biological properties. Rather than assuming the widely used cliqueness property, which considers all the nodes to be connected with each other, the algorithm looks for the properties that are inferred from already known complexes. Two important features are the label C indicating whether a subgraph is a complex and the number of nodes N. The other feature descriptors including degree statistics, graph density, and degree correlation statistics are indicated by $X_1, \ldots, X_m$ and are considered independent given C and N. The number of nodes in and off itself is an important feature. Its importance can be seen from the fact that a larger number of nodes in a subgraph indicate a lesser probability of it being a clique. All the subgraphs are assigned scores by making use of these properties. One way of finding how probable it is for a subgraph to be a protein complex is to perform simple hypothesis testing by calculating the following conditional probability [12, 38]:

$$\begin{aligned} L &= \log \frac{p(c_1 \mid x_1, \ldots, x_m)}{p(c_0 \mid x_1, \ldots, x_m)} \\ &= \log \frac{p(n \mid c_1) \prod_{k=1}^m p(x_k \mid n, c_1)}{p(n \mid c_0) \prod_{k=1}^m p(x_k \mid n, c_0)}, \end{aligned}$$ (28)

where the posterior probabilities are calculated via Bayes rule as

$$\begin{aligned} & p(c_i \mid n, x_1, \ldots, x_m) \\ &= \frac{p(n, x_1, \ldots, x_m \mid c_i = 1) \, p(c_i = 1)}{p(n, x_1, \ldots, x_m)} \\ &= \frac{p(x_1, \ldots, x_m \mid n, c_i = 1) \, p(n \mid c_i = 1) \, p(c_i = 1)}{p(n, x_1, \ldots, x_m)}. \end{aligned}$$ (29)

These probability densities can be calculated using maximum likelihood methods. By comparing the obtained score to a predetermined threshold, some of the subgraphs can be labeled to be complexes. This algorithm takes the weighted matrix of PPI data as input, where the weights are assigned using the likelihood of any particular interaction. Several other graphical-clustering-based methods are surveyed in [12].

4.4. Matrix Factorization Methods for Clustering.

Nonnegative matrix factorization (NMF) is a method widely used in problems of clustering. Application of this technique has been proposed recently in [40], where an ensemble of nonnegative factored matrices obtained using protein-protein interaction data are combined together to perform soft clustering. The importance of this step lies in the fact that a particular object may belong to multiple classes. Hence, the various algorithms reported in the literature performing hard clustering may not be of much benefit in such scenarios. This ensemble NMF method is observed to classify the proteins in accordance with the functions they perform and also identify the multiple groups they belong to.

The algorithm produces τ base clusterings by factorizing the symmetric data matrix S of protein interactions in the following manner [40]:

$$\min_{V>0}\left\|S - VV^T\right\|_F^2, \tag{30}$$

where $\|\cdot\|_F$ denotes the Frobenius norm. The factors V produced in this manner are not unique. Let k_i be the number of clusters in the ith base cluster, each with a different value in order to promote diversity. Once the ensemble of factored matrices is available, the next step is to construct the graph by combining the information present in them. Parameter $l = k_1 + \cdots + k_\tau$ gives the total number of basis vectors which are denoted by $V = \{v_1, \ldots, v_l\}$. Each vector denotes a node on the graph, and the edge weight is calculated using the Pearson correlation for a pair of vector (v_i, v_j) given by

$$\text{cor}\left(v_i, v_j\right) = \frac{1}{2}\left(\frac{\left(v_i - \bar{v}_i\right)^T \left(v_j - \bar{v}_j\right)}{\left\|v_i - \bar{v}_i\right\|_2 \cdot \left\|v_j - \bar{v}_j\right\|_2} + 1\right). \tag{31}$$

Having looked at the GRNs and PPI network inference problems individually, we now proceed to review the recent advancements in the joint modeling of the two networks.

5. An Integrated Cellular Network

The advances in reverse engineering of GRNs and PPI networks have paved the way for joint estimation of GRNs and PPI networks [41]. This is a step towards the inference of an integrated network consisting of genes, proteins, and transcription factors, indicating interactions among themselves and each other. Figure 6 shows the schematic of an integrated cellular network. In this section, we review two important ways of estimating a joint network.

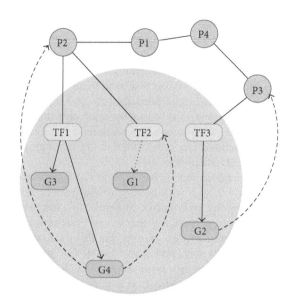

FIGURE 6: An integrated cellular network.

5.1. Probabilistic Graphical Models for Joint Inference.

Reference [41] proposed an interesting method for estimating GRNs and PPI networks simultaneously. Suppose that the gene expression is denoted by x and PPI data is represented by y. The algorithm provides an undirected protein network G_p and a directed gene network G_r, modeled using Markov and Bayesian networks, respectively, by maximizing their joint distribution; that is,

$$P\left(G_r, G_p \mid X, Y\right) \propto P\left(G_r, G_p, X, Y\right)$$
$$= P\left(X \mid G_r\right) P\left(Y \mid G_p\right) P\left(G_r, G_p\right), \tag{32}$$

where $P(X \mid G_r, G_p) = P(X \mid G_r)$ and $P(Y \mid Gr, G_p) = P(Y \mid G_p)$. The inference on Markov and Bayesian networks is performed in the same manner as explained in the previous sections. The two subnetworks are estimated iteratively till the algorithm converges. Further details on this algorithm can be found in [41].

5.2. Joint Estimation Using State-Space Model.

State-space model can also be used to obtain an integrated network of gene and protein-protein interactions [42, 43]. A novel approach employing nonlinear model is proposed in [43], where the system parameters are estimated using constrained leastsquares. The gene expression is assumed to follow a dynamic model given by

$$x_i(t+1) = x_i(t) + \sum_{j=1}^N a_{ij}s_i(t) - \lambda_i z_i(t) + k_i + w_i(t), \tag{33}$$

where

$$s_j(t) = f_i\left(y_j(t)\right) = \frac{1}{1 + \exp\left\{-\left(y_j(t) - \mu_j\right)/\sigma_j\right\}}, \tag{34}$$

and y_j denotes the protein activity profile of jth transcription factor, and its mean and standard deviations are represented by μ_j and σ_j, respectively. The magnitude of a_{ij} indicates the strength of relationship between the jth TF and ith gene, and the sign suggests whether it is an excitatory or inhibitory relationship. The model in (33) suggests that the gene expression level at tth time instant depends upon the gene expression level at the previous time instant as well as the protein activity level. The degradation effect of gene expression is modeled by λ_i, k_i is a constant representing the basal level, and $w_i(t)$ is the Gaussian noise modeling the uncertainties in the model and the errors in the data.

The protein activity level follows the following dynamic model:

$$
y_n(t+1) = y_n(t) + \sum_{m=1}^{M} b_{nm} y_n(t) y_m(t)
$$
$$
+ \alpha_n x_n(t) - \beta_n y_n(t) + h_n + \nu_n(t),
$$
(35)

where b_{ij} gives the relationship between the proteins, α_n indicates the translation effect of mRNA to protein, and $\nu_n(t)$ is the Gaussian noise. The unknown parameters for both the models are given by

$$
\theta_i = \begin{bmatrix} a_{i1} & \cdots & a_{iN} & \lambda_i & k_i \end{bmatrix}^T,
$$
$$
\phi_n = \begin{bmatrix} b_{n1} & \cdots & b_{nM} & \alpha_n & \beta_n & h_n \end{bmatrix}^T
$$
(36)

and are estimated by solving a constrained least squares problem [43]. Once the individual subnetworks are obtained, they are merged together to form one cellular network with the TFs connecting them together.

The problem of inferring an integrated network is in relatively initial stages, and several avenues of research are still open. Moreover, comparison studies are needed so as to determine the merits and demerits of the different methods in use.

6. Performance Evaluation

The inference accuracy can be assessed using the knowledge of a gold-standard network or the true network. In order to benchmark the algorithms, the correctly identified edges or true positives (TPs) need to be calculated. In addition, the number of false positives (FPs), or the edges incorrectly indicated to be present, and false negatives (FNs) which is the missed detection should also be counted [10]. With these values in hand, true positive rate or recall; that is, TPR = TP/(TP+FN), false positive rate; that is, FPR = FP/(FP+TN), and positive predictive value; that is, PPV = TP/(TP + FP), also called the precision, can be calculated. These quantities enable us to view the performance graphically by the area under the ROC curve which plots FPR versus the TPR. These criteria are most widely used as the fidelity criterion for gene network inference algorithms.

While it is possible to identify the gene regulatory relationships experimentally, it would not only be technically prohibitive but also proved to be very costly. For this

reason, several *in silico* and *in vivo* networks have been generated to assist in benchmarking the network inference algorithms. Foremost among these are the DREAM (dialogue on reverse engineering assessment and methods) [44] and IRMA (*in vivo* reverse engineering and modeling assessment) [45] datasets. Reference [10] provides a unified survey of some of the important algorithms in gene network inference algorithms using these datasets.

7. Discussions and Conclusions

This paper reviews the main statistical methods used for inference of gene and protein-protein networks. PPI network inference can be carried out in a wide variety of ways by exploiting phylogenetics information and sequencing data. This paper focused only on those inference methods that employ PPI data.

For the inference of gene regulatory networks, the problem can be simply stated as follows: given the gene expression data, find the interactions between the genes. Three major classes of statistical methods were reviewed in this paper: probabilistic graphical models, state-space models, and information theoretic methods. For all these methods, modeling as well as inferencing techniques was discussed. It is observed that much progress has been made in the field of GRN inference. However, almost all of the proposed network inference methods in the literature work with only the popular gene expression data sets. An interesting part of future work could be integrating different data sets and biological knowledge available to come up with better and more robust algorithms.

Comparing the three broad classes of statistical methods reviewed in the paper, it is found that the information theoretic methods have advantages over the other methods in terms of minimal modeling assumptions and, therefore, are capable of modeling more general networks. Graphical modeling techniques assume the network to be acyclic in case of Bayesian network modeling and provide an undirected graph when using Markov networks. The state-space nonlinear models work with nonlinear functions which may not be the true representative of the underlying network, thereby resulting in less robust algorithms.

In case of PPI network prediction, the most popular statistical method is clustering. In addition, probabilistic graphical modeling techniques are also used. However, several important avenues of research are still open. Since the Markov networks and Bayesian networks are able to model PPI networks efficiently, other probabilistic graphical techniques such as factor graphs could potentially be used for solving this inference problem. Clustering methods are more suited to the PPI network inference problem as the main emphasis is on the identification of protein complexes. It is found that certain important and popular modeling techniques may fail to model PPI networks [46]. Also, clustering methods based on mutual information could be used [47].

Several statistical methods have been proposed to infer an integrated network of transcription regulation and protein-protein interaction. A state-space model for integrated network inference involves parameter estimation which indicates the strength of the inhibitory and excitatory regulations. As the cellular networks are known to be sparse, employing sparsity-constrained least squares for parameter estimation as proposed in [25] is expected to result in more robust inference algorithms.

Recent years have shown tremendous and rapid progress in the field of cellular network modeling. With the amount and types of data sets increasing, algorithms combining multiple datasets are necessary for future.

Acknowledgments

This paper was made possible by QNRF-NPRP Grant no. 09-874-3-235 and support from NSF Grant no. 0915444. The statements made herein are solely the responsibility of the authors.

References

[1] X. Zhou and S. T. C. Wong, *Computational Systems Bioinformatics*, World Scientific, 2008.

[2] Y. Huang, I. M. Tienda-Luna, and Y. Wang, "Reverse engineering gene regulatory networks: a survey of statistical models," *IEEE Signal Processing Magazine*, vol. 26, no. 1, pp. 76–97, 2009.

[3] X. Zhou, X. Wang, and E. R. Dougherty, *Genomic Networks: Statistical Inference from Microarray Data*, John Wiley & Sons, 2006.

[4] H. Kitano, "Computational systems biology," *Nature*, vol. 420, no. 6912, pp. 206–210, 2002.

[5] B. Mallick, D. Gold, and V. Baladandayuthapani, *Bayesian Analysis of Gene Expression Data*, Wiley, 2009.

[6] H. D. Jong, "Modeling and simulation of genetic regulatoy systems: a literature review," *Journal of Computational Biology*, vol. 9, no. 1, pp. 67–103, 2002.

[7] X. Cai and X. Wang, "Stochastic modeling and simulation of gene networks," *IEEE Signal Processing Magazine*, vol. 24, no. 1, pp. 27–36, 2007.

[8] H. Hache, H. Lehrach, and R. Herwig, "Reverse engineering of gene regulatory networks: a comparative study," *Eurasip Journal on Bioinformatics and Systems Biology*, vol. 2009, Article ID 617281, 2009.

[9] F. Markowetz and R. Spang, "Inferring cellular networks—a review," *BMC Bioinformatics*, vol. 8, article S5, 2007.

[10] C. A. Penfold and D. L. Wild, "How to infer gene networks from expression profiles, revisited," *Interface Focus*, vol. 3, pp. 857–870, 2011.

[11] J. Wang, M. Li, Y. Deng, and Y. Pan, "Recent advances in clustering methods for protein interaction networks," *BMC Genomics*, vol. 11, no. supplement 3, article S10, 2010.

[12] X. Li, M. Wu, C. K. Kwoh, and S. K. Ng, "Computational approaches for detecting protein complexes from protein interaction networks: a survey," *BMC Genomics*, vol. 11, no. 1, article S3, 2010.

[13] A. Mortazavi, B. A. Williams, K. McCue, L. Schaeffer, and B. Wold, "Mapping and quantifying mammalian transcriptomes by RNA-Seq," *Nature Methods*, vol. 5, no. 7, pp. 621–628, 2008.

[14] K. Y. Yip, R. P. Alexander, K. K. Yan, and M. Gerstein, "Improved reconstruction of in silico gene regulatory networks by integrating knockout and perturbation data," *PLoS ONE*, vol. 5, no. 1, Article ID e8121, 2010.

[15] D. Koller and N. Friedman, *Probabilistic Graphical Models: Principles and Techniques*, MIT Press, 2009.

[16] K. Murphy and S. Mian, "Modeling gene expression data using dynamic Bayesian networks," Tech. Rep., University of California, Berkeley, Calif, USA, 2001.

[17] Y. Zhang, Z. Deng, H. Jiang, and P. Jia, "Inferring gene regulatory networks from multiple data sources via a dynamic Bayesian network with structural EM," in *DILS*, S. C. Boulakia and V. Tannen, Eds., vol. 4544 of *Lecture Notes in Computer Science*, pp. 204–214, Springer, 2007.

[18] Z. M. Ibrahim, A. Ngom, and A. Y. Tawfik, "Using qualitative probability in reverse-engineering gene regulatory networks," *IEEE Transactions on Computational Biology and Bioinformatics*, vol. 8, no. 2, pp. 326–334, 2011.

[19] N. Kramer, J. Schafer, and A. Boulesteix, "Regularized estimation of large-scale gene association networks using graphical gaussian models," *BMC Bioinformatics*, vol. 10, no. 1, p. 384, 2009.

[20] P. Menéndez, Y. A. I. Kourmpetis, C. J. F. ter Braak, and F. A. van Eeuwijk, "Gene regulatory networks from multifactorial perturbations using graphical lasso: application to the DREAM4 challenge," *PLoS ONE*, vol. 5, no. 12, Article ID e14147, 2010.

[21] F.-X. Wu, W.-J. Zhang, and A. J. Kusalik, "Modeling gene expression from microarray expression data with state-space equations," in *Pacific Symposium on Biocomputing*, R. B. Altman, A. K. Dunker, L. Hunter, T. A. Jung, and T. E. Klein, Eds., pp. 581–592, World Scientific, 2004.

[22] Z. Wang, F. Yang, D. W. C. Ho, S. Swift, A. Tucker, and X. Liu, "Stochastic dynamic modeling of short gene expression time-series data," *IEEE Transactions on Nanobioscience*, vol. 7, no. 1, pp. 44–55, 2008.

[23] M. Quach, N. Brunel, and F. D'alché-Buc, "Estimating parameters and hidden variables in non-linear state-space models based on ODEs for biological networks inference," *Bioinformatics*, vol. 23, no. 23, pp. 3209–3216, 2007.

[24] Z. Wang, X. Liu, Y. Liu, J. Liang, and V. Vinciotti, "An extended kalman filtering approach to modeling nonlinear dynamic gene regulatory networks via short gene expression time series," *IEEE/ACM Transactions on Computational Biology and Bioinformatics*, vol. 6, no. 3, pp. 410–419, 2009.

[25] A. Noor, E. Serpedin, M. N. Nounou, and H. N. Nounou, "Inferring gene regulatory networks via nonlinear state-space models and exploiting sparsity," *IEEE/ACM Transactions on Computational Biology and Bioinformatics*, vol. 9, no. 4, pp. 1203–1211, 2012.

[26] A. Noor, E. Serpedin, M. Nounou, and H. Nounou, "Inferring gene regulatory networks with nonlinear models via exploiting sparsity," in *IEEE International Conference on Acoustics, Speech and Signal Processing (ICASSP '12)*, pp. 725–728, March 2012.

[27] R. Tibshirani, "Regression shrinkage and selection via the lasso," *Journal of the Royal Statistical Society B*, vol. 58, pp. 267–288, 1996.

[28] C. Koh, F. X. Wu, G. Selvaraj, and A. J. Kusalik, "Using a state-space model and location analysis to infer time-delayed Regulatory Networks," *Eurasip Journal on Bioinformatics and Systems Biology*, vol. 2009, Article ID 484601, 3 pages, 2009.

[29] A. A. Margolin, I. Nemenman, K. Basso et al., "ARACNE: an algorithm for the reconstruction of gene regulatory networks in a mammalian cellular context," *BMC Bioinformatics*, vol. 7, no. supplement 1, article S7, 2006.

[30] W. Zhao, E. Serpedin, and E. R. Dougherty, "Inferring connectivity of genetic regulatory networks using information-theoretic criteria," *IEEE/ACM Transactions on Computational Biology and Bioinformatics*, vol. 5, no. 2, pp. 262–274, 2008.

[31] A. Noor, E. Serpedin, M. N. Nounou, H. N. Nounou, N. Mohamed, and L. Chouchane, "Information theoretic methods for modeling of gene regulatory networks," in *IEEE Symposium on Computational Intelligence in Bioinformatics and Computational Biology (CIBCB '12)*, pp. 418–423, 2012.

[32] T. Cover and J. Thomas, *Elements of Information Theory*, Wiley Interscience, 2006.

[33] W. Zhao, E. Serpedin, and E. R. Dougherty, "Inferring gene regulatory networks from time series data using the minimum description length principle," *Bioinformatics*, vol. 22, no. 17, pp. 2129–2135, 2006.

[34] M. Vidyasagar, "Probabilistic methods in cancer biology," *Childhood*, vol. 20, pp. 82–89, 2011.

[35] P. Zoppoli, S. Morganella, and M. Ceccarelli, "TimeDelay-ARACNE: reverse engineering of gene networks from time-course data by an information theoretic approach," *BMC Bioinformatics*, vol. 11, no. 1, article 154, 2010.

[36] J. Dougherty, I. Tabus, and J. Astola, "Inference of gene regulatory networks based on a universal minimum description length," *Eurasip Journal on Bioinformatics and Systems Biology*, vol. 2008, Article ID 482090, 2008.

[37] A. Jaimovich, G. Elidan, H. Margalit, and N. Friedman, "Towards an integrated protein-protein interaction network: a relational Markov network approach," *Journal of Computational Biology*, vol. 13, no. 2, pp. 145–164, 2006.

[38] Y. Qi, F. Balem, C. Faloutsos, J. Klein-Seetharaman, and Z. Bar-Joseph, "Protein complex identification by supervised graph local clustering," *Bioinformatics*, vol. 24, no. 13, pp. i250–i268, 2008.

[39] J. R. Bradford, C. J. Needham, A. J. Bulpitt, and D. R. Westhead, "Insights into protein-protein interfaces using a Bayesian network prediction method," *Journal of Molecular Biology*, vol. 362, no. 2, pp. 365–386, 2006.

[40] D. Greene, G. Cagney, N. Krogan, and P. Cunningham, "Ensemble non-negative matrix factorization methods for clustering protein-protein interactions," *Bioinformatics*, vol. 24, no. 15, pp. 1722–1728, 2008.

[41] N. Nariai, Y. Tamada, S. Imoto, and S. Miyano, "Estimating gene regulatory networks and protein-protein interactions of Saccharomyces cerevisiae from multiple genome-wide data," *Bioinformatics*, vol. 21, no. supplement 2, pp. ii206–ii212, 2005.

[42] C. W. Li and B. S. Chen, "Identifying functional mechanisms of gene and protein regulatory networks in response to a broader range of environmental stresses," *Comparative and Functional Genomics*, vol. 2010, Article ID 408705, 2010.

[43] Y. C. Wang and B. S. Chen, "Integrated cellular network of transcription regulations and protein-protein interactions," *BMC Systems Biology*, vol. 4, no. 1, article 20, 2010.

[44] http://wiki.c2b2.columbia.edu/dream.

[45] I. Cantone, L. Marucci, F. Iorio et al., "A yeast synthetic network for in vivo assessment of reverse-engineering and modeling approaches," *Cell*, vol. 137, no. 1, pp. 172–181, 2009.

[46] R. Schweiger, M. Linial, and N. Linial, "Generative probabilistic models for protein-protein interaction networks-the biclique perspective," *Bioinformatics*, vol. 27, no. 13, pp. i142–i148, 2011.

[47] X. Zhou, X. Wang, and E. R. Dougherty, "Construction of genomic networks using mutual-information clustering and

reversible-jump Markov-chain-Monte-Carlo predictor design," *Signal Processing*, vol. 83, no. 4, pp. 745–761, 2003.

9

Statistical Analysis of Terminal Extensions of Protein β-Strand Pairs

Ning Zhang,[1] Shan Gao,[2] Lei Zhang,[3] Jishou Ruan,[2] and Tao Zhang[3]

[1] *Department of Biomedical Engineering, Tianjin University, Tianjin Key Lab of BME Measurement, Tianjin 300072, China*
[2] *College of Mathematical Sciences and LPKM, Nankai University, Tianjin 300071, China*
[3] *College of Life Sciences, Nankai University, Tianjin 300071, China*

Correspondence should be addressed to Jishou Ruan; jsruan@nankai.edu.cn and Tao Zhang; zhangtao@nankai.edu.cn

Academic Editor: Bhaskar Dasgupta

The long-range interactions, required to the accurate predictions of tertiary structures of β-sheet-containing proteins, are still difficult to simulate. To remedy this problem and to facilitate β-sheet structure predictions, many efforts have been made by computational methods. However, known efforts on β-sheets mainly focus on interresidue contacts or amino acid partners. In this study, to go one step further, we studied β-sheets on the strand level, in which a statistical analysis was made on the terminal extensions of paired β-strands. In most cases, the two paired β-strands have different lengths, and terminal extensions exist. The terminal extensions are the extended part of the paired strands besides the common paired part. However, we found that the best pairing required a terminal alignment, and β-strands tend to pair to make bigger common parts. As a result, 96.97% of β-strand pairs have a ratio of 25% of the paired common part to the whole length. Also 94.26% and 95.98% of β-strand pairs have a ratio of 40% of the paired common part to the length of the two β-strands, respectively. Interstrand register predictions by searching interacting β-strands from several alternative offsets should comply with this rule to reduce the computational searching space to improve the performances of algorithms.

1. Introduction

The issue of protein structure prediction is still extremely challenging in bioinformatics [1, 2]. Usually, structural information for protein sequences with no detectable homology to a protein of known structure could be obtained by predicting the arrangement of their secondary structural elements [3]. As we know, the two predominant protein secondary structures are α-helices and β-sheets. However, a combination of the early suitable α-helical model systems and sustained researches have resulted in a detailed understanding of α-helix, while comparatively little is known about β-sheet [4]. Tertiary structures of β-sheet-containing proteins are especially difficult to simulate [3, 5]. Unlike α-helices, β-sheets are more complex resulting from a combination of two or more disjoint peptide segments, called β-strands. Therefore, the β-sheet topology is very useful for elucidating protein folding

pathways [6, 7] for predicting tertiary structures [3, 8–11], and even for designing new proteins [12–14].

As fundamental components, β-sheets are plentifully contained in protein domains. In a β-sheet, multiple β-strands held together linked by hydrogen bonds and can be classified into parallel and antiparallel direction styles. Adjacent β-strands bring distant residues on sequences into close special contact with one another and constitute a specific mode of amino acid pairing [1, 15–17], interactions (like DNA base pairing). There is a growing recognition of the importance of the strand-to-strand interactions among β-sheets [18]. Several studies, including statistical studies examining frequencies of nearest-neighbor amino acids in β-sheets, found a significantly different preference for certain interstrand amino acid pairs at nonhydrogen-bonded and hydrogen-bonded sites [1, 17, 19, 20], Dou et al. [21] created a comprehensive database of interchain β-sheet (ICBS) interactions. We also developed the SheetsPair database [22] to compile both the interchain and the intrachain amino acid pairs.

Generally speaking, previous work on β-sheets mainly focused on the interresidue contacts or amino acid partners [23–28]. Prediction of inter-residue contacts in β-sheets is interesting, while the prediction by ab initio structure is also useful to understand protein folding [29, 30]. Our previous studies showed that the interstrand amino acid pairs played a significant role to determine the parallel or antiparallel orientation of β-strands [15], and the statistical results could possibly be used to predict the β-strand orientation [16]. Cheng and Baldi [11] introduced BETAPRO method to predict and assemble β-strands into a β-sheet, in which a single misprediction of one amino acid pairing from the first stage could be amplified by the next stages and results in serious wrong set of partner assignments between β-strands. However, those studies can be viewed as initial steps of β-sheet studies relative to predict strand level pairing [25]. In this paper, to go one step further, we investigate the β-strand pairing on the strand level for exploring the rules of how β-strands form a β-sheet.

Many results have shown the importance of statistical analysis in protein structure studies [15, 16]. In particular, statistical information could provide a starting point for de novo computational design methods that are now becoming successful for short, single-chain proteins [14], as well as methods of protein structure predictions and understanding of protein folding mechanisms [31, 32]. Fooks et al. [1] also indicated that such statistical analysis results would be useful for protein structure prediction. Therefore, we advocate using the tools of statistics and informatics to study β-sheet and generate new rules for algorithm development. In this study, we focused on the terminal extensions of paired β-strands.

2. Results

2.1. Dataset. All protein structure data used in this study were taken from a PISCES [33, 34] dataset generated on May 16, 2009. In the dataset, the percentage identity cutoff is 25%, the resolution cutoff is 2.0 angstroms, and the R-factor cutoff is 0.25. Secondary structures were assigned from the experimentally determined tertiary structures by using the DSSP program. Besides proteins containing disordered regions [35–37], all data were further preprocessed according to the following criteria: (i) no β-sheet-containing protein chains were removed; (ii) protein chains with nonstandard three-letter residue names (such as DPN, EFC, ABA, C5C, PLP, etc.) were removed, since these indicate that the protein chains have covalently bounded ligands or modified residues; (iii) protein chains with uncertain structures or incorrect data were removed. Since β-bulges tend to be isolated and rare [11], we did not consider β-bulges in this study either, as several previous studies did [1, 3]. Finally, 2,315 protein chains were extracted, containing 19,214 β-strand pairs. Note that in the special case of β-bulges, no amino acid pair is assigned.

2.2. The β-Sheet Structure. The β-sheets, where two or more β-strands are arranged in a specific conformation, are illustrated in Figure 1(a), by a protein example (PDB code 1HZT). Adjacent strands, or the so-called strand pairs, can either run in the same (parallel) or in the opposite (antiparallel) direction styles. In protein 1HZT, there are 3 β-sheets called A, B, and C, formed by 10 different β-strands numbered from 1 to 10, making 7 different β-strand pairs, respectively. The 10 β-strands can be named by the β-sheet each belongs to and the index numbers in the order of partnership. For example, the 3 β-strands forming β-sheet A can be called "A1," "A2," and "A3," while other 4 β-strands forming β-sheet B can be called "B1," "B2," "B3," and "B4," respectively. "A1-A2," "A2-A3," "B1-B2," "B2-B3," and "B3-B4" are all β-strand pairs. Sequences of the 10 β-strands with their initial and ending residue numbers are also given in Figure 1(b).

2.3. Different Lengths of Paired β-Strands. For a β-strand pair, the terminal of one β-strand does not always align with the terminal of the other (Figure 2), making "terminal extensions" besides the common paired parts. Note that only amino acids in the common part construct amino acid pairs.

Why "terminal extensions" exist widely in β-strand pairs? We firstly investigated the lengths of two paired β-strands and then calculated the percent of each case whether the "terminal extensions" exist or not. Results are shown in Table 1.

As shown in Table 1, the two paired β-strands having the same length only account for 29.53% of all samples. In other 70.47% percent of samples, lengths of the two paired β-strands are different.

2.4. Statistical Results of Variables. We define the following variables.

(1) Let SL_1 and SL_2 represent the lengths of two paired β-strands, respectively. Length of the β-strand with smaller strand number (strand numbers can be obtained from PDB database) is defined as SL_1, while length of the other β-strand is defined as SL_2.

(2) Let PL stand for the length of the common part, which is often smaller than SL_1 and SL_2.

(3) Terminal extensions can be found in either of the two β-strands. We define the lengths of the two terminal extensions Et_1 and Et_2, respectively. Length of the terminal extension of the β-strand with length SL_1 is defined as Et_1 while the other as Et_2.

(4) Let EL represent the whole length; $EL = PL + Et_1 + Et_2$.

Then, the paring ratio R could be calculated by

$$R = \frac{PL}{EL} \times 100\% = \frac{PL}{PL + Et_1 + Et_2} \times 100\%. \quad (1)$$

The ratio of the common paired part to the length of each β-strand ($i = 1, 2$) could be calculated by

$$Rt_i = \frac{PL}{SL_i} \times 100\%, \quad i = 1, 2. \quad (2)$$

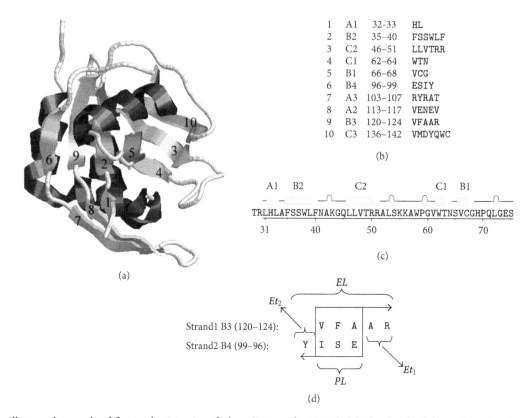

1	A1	32–33	HL
2	B2	35–40	FSSWLF
3	C2	46–51	LLVTRR
4	C1	62–64	WTN
5	B1	66–68	VCG
6	B4	96–99	ESIY
7	A3	103–107	RYRAT
8	A2	113–117	VENEV
9	B3	120–124	VFAAR
10	C3	136–142	VMDYQWC

(b)

A1 B2   C2   C1 B1

TRLHLAFSSWLFNAKGQLLVTRRALSKKAWPGVWTNSVCGHPQLGES

31   40   50   60   70

(c)

EL

Et_2

Strand1 B3 (120–124):   V F A A R
Strand2 B4 (99–96):   Y I S E

Et_1

PL

(d)

FIGURE 1: An illustrated example of β-strand pairing in a β-sheet (PDB code: 1HZT). (a) The sketch of the tertiary structure of the protein produced by using RASMOL. Protein 1HZT is an α/β protein with 10 β-strands numbered from 1 to 10, forming seven different strand pairs. (b) The sequences of the 10 β-strands with their initial and ending residue numbers. (c) The 10 β-strands in the linear primary sequence. (d) An example of a β-strand partnership graph. The pairing is between strands "B3" and "B4," with the light gray box representing the common pairing part.

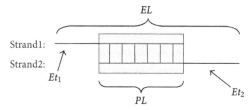

FIGURE 2: A schematic diagram of terminal extensions of β-strand pairs. The two blank lines represent the two β-strands, respectively. The light gray box represents the common pairing part of the two β-strands with amino acid pairing.

A small percent of β-strand pairs have no "terminal extensions," the R, Rt_1, and Rt_2 values for which will be 100%.

We calculated PL, Et_1, Et_2, EL for all β-strand pairs in the present dataset. Table 2 gives the range of these variables as well as the averages and standard deviations.

We also calculated R, Rt_1, and Rt_2 for all β-strand pairs in the present dataset. The distribution of these variables is shown in Figure 3.

3. Discussion

3.1. Strands Tend to Align Their Terminals. For the 70.47% of samples with different strand lengths, although they have different lengths, the differences are not big for most of them. Only a small percent of samples (below 2.09%) have the difference above 5. In these cases, it is obvious that they cannot align the terminals (with both $Et_1 = 0$ and $Et_2 = 0$). They have two ways to choose from: either align to only one terminal making another "terminal extension", or align to none of the two terminals making both "terminal extensions." However, it can be seen from Table 1 that most β-strands tend to be in the former case. For example, in case of the length difference 1, the former case accounts for 85.18% while the latter only 14.82%. It is consistent with the case of same-length strand pairs, in which β-strands tend to align their terminals with each other. Interestingly, it is suggested that β-strands tend to align their terminals. In different-length strand pairs, they still retain one terminal alignment, although they can not align both ends.

3.2. Small "Terminal Extensions". From Table 2, it can be seen that lengths of β-strands are not very long, ranging from 1 to 25 with an average length about 4-5 amino acids. The averages and the standard deviations are similar between lengths of the two paired β-strands (SL_1 and SL_2).

The length of the common part PL has a range similar to that of lengths of β-strands. This indicates that although "terminal extensions" exist, common pairing parts occupy most of β-strands, while "terminal extensions" occupy least.

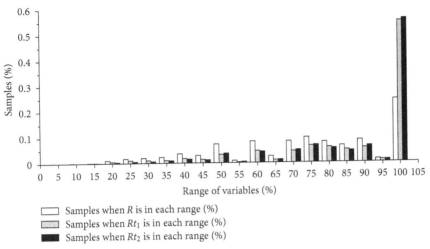

FIGURE 3: Distribution of R, Rt_1, and Rt_2 variables in the current dataset.

TABLE 1: Statistical results of lengths of two paired β-strands and percent of samples in each case whether the two "terminal extensions" exist or not.

Abs $(SL_1 - SL_2)^*$	Number of pairs	Percent	Percent of $Et_1 = 0$ and $Et_2 = 0$	Percent of $Et_1 = 0$ and $Et_2 > 0$	Percent of $Et_1 > 0$ and $Et_2 = 0$	Percent of $Et_1 > 0$ and $Et_2 > 0$
0	5673	29.53%	82.95%	0.00%	0.00%	17.05%
1	5633	29.32%	0.00%	40.48%	44.70%	14.82%
2	3170	16.50%	0.00%	30.57%	41.10%	28.33%
3	1798	9.36%	0.00%	28.59%	31.15%	40.27%
4	1016	5.29%	0.00%	26.77%	29.82%	43.41%
5	618	3.22%	0.00%	29.13%	27.51%	43.37%
6	401	2.09%	0.00%	30.42%	25.69%	43.89%
7	323	1.68%	0.00%	25.39%	32.51%	42.11%
8	247	1.29%	0.00%	16.19%	30.36%	53.44%
9	101	0.53%	0.00%	26.73%	24.75%	48.51%
10	69	0.36%	0.00%	20.29%	39.13%	40.58%
>10	165	0.86%	0.00%	15.15%	27.27%	57.58%

* Absolute value of the difference of $SL_1 - SL_2$.

TABLE 2: Statistical results of variables of β-strand pairs in the current dataset.

	Minimum value	Maximum value	Average	Standard deviation
SL_1	1	25	4.99	2.82
SL_2	1	25	4.90	2.80
PL	1	23	4.86	2.26
Et_1	0	18	1.15	1.79
Et_2	0	22	1.03	1.64
EL	2	29	7.03	3.09

The fact that the maximum value of EL is 29, only a little bigger than that of lengths of β-strands, and the fact that in average both the "terminal extensions" only have about 1 amino acid ($Et_1 = 1.05$ and $Et_2 = 1.03$) also support this assumption.

Figure 3 gives percent of samples for R, Rt_1, and Rt_2 in each range of their possible values (from 0% to 100%), respectively. It can be seen that the distributions of Rt_1 and Rt_2 are similar. More than half of the β-strand pairs have these two variables above 95% (or in the range (95–100)). Big Rt_1 or Rt_2 means big common part of β-strands, or small "terminal extensions." Rare β-strand pairs have smaller values of R, Rt_1, and Rt_2, which indicates that most β-strands do not pair by means of small "common part" or big "terminal extensions." It could be concluded from the results that β-strands tend to pair with bigger pairing common parts, leaving smaller "terminal extensions."

3.3. Possible Reasons for β-Strand Extensions. Why "terminal extensions" exist so widely in β-strand pairs? The fact that lengths of two paired β-strands are not the same in most cases as shown in Table 1 may be one of the possible reasons. If paired β-strands have the same lengths, most of them

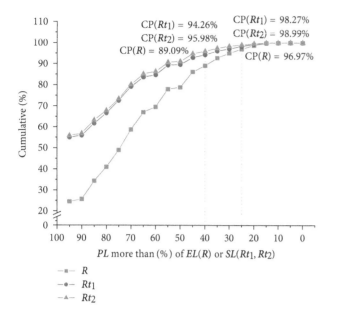

FIGURE 4: Cumulative percentages (CPs) of R, Rt_1, and Rt_2 calculated from the present dataset. The horizontal axis denotes the percentage of common paired region PL to EL (for curve R) or to SL (for curves Rt_1 and Rt_2). Points on the R curve denote the cumulative percentages of samples whose $R = PL/EL$ equals or is bigger than the corresponding abscissa value. Points on the Rt_1 and Rt_2 curves denote the cumulative percentages of samples whose $Rt_1 = PL/Rt_1$ or $Rt_2 = PL/Rt_2$ equals or is bigger than the corresponding abscissa value, respectively.

(82.95%) tend to align their terminals with each other, leaving no "terminal extensions."

A β-strand is led to pair with another by several kinds of potential forces. Steward and Thornton [3] indicated that a single β-strand was still able to recognize a noninteracting β-strand with greater accuracy than that in the case of between two random sequences. The potential forces include hydrogen bonds, van der Waals forces, electrostatic interaction, ionic bonds, hydrophobic effects, and so forth. Parisien and Major [38] revealed that among all the forces, the most important one was the construction of a hydrophobic face. It is conceivable that one residue of a β-strand prefers to pair with the residue of another resulting in a stable state of hydrophobic effects. Optimizing such interactions may result in extensions, which could be the second reason, since more often than not the "terminal alignment" is not the case of optimized pairing style.

A third possible reason could be due to the nucleation events that initiate the β-sheet folding. Amino acids in the central part could pair firstly and then fold to extend to terminals.

Another reason is the roles of the nonpaired terminal amino acids in stabilizing the β-sheet structure. Several other studies have identified their key roles in modulating protein folding rates, stability, and folding mechanism [39–43]. Therefore, the β-strand terminals could also be important factors for a β-sheet formation.

3.4. Ratio Rule of Pairing Strand Alignment.
To quantify the pairing common part of paired β-strands, we calculated the cumulative percent of variables R, Rt_1, and Rt_2 and depicted them in Figure 4.

From Figure 4, it can be seen that when $Rt_1 \geq 40\%$ and $Rt_2 \geq 40\%$, the cumulative percentages reach 94.26% and 95.98%, respectively, while when $R \geq 40\%$ only 89.89%. When $R \geq 25\%$, the cumulative percentages reach up to 96.97%. Therefore, a rule can be made of the alignment of β-strand pair as follows:

$$R \geq 25\%, \qquad Rt_i \geq 40\%, \quad i = 1, 2. \tag{3}$$

Almost all samples (above 94%) obey this rule.

In a β-strand alignment prediction algorithm, all possible pairings should be examined and scored; it is a time-consuming task. Kato et al. [44] stated that prediction of planar β-sheet structures was NP-hard in the present state of our knowledge (http://en.wikipedia.org/wiki/NP-hard). However, this previous rule should be used as a constraint of the relative positions in β-strand alignment to reduce the computational searching space, which could be used to develop high-speed β-strand topology prediction algorithms.

4. Conclusion

At the most straightforward level, full "identification" of a β-strand pair could consist of (i) finding the interacting partner β-strand(s), (ii) predicting the relative orientation (i.e. parallel or antiparallel), and (iii) shifting the relative positions of the two interacting β-strands [15, 16]. In this study, we focused on the third aspect. The formation of protein structure and protein folding mechanism are very complex, and the mechanisms of β-sheet formation are unclear [45]. However, simple rules could contribute to developing new algorithms in the step of full prediction of β-sheet and understanding of protein folding pathways in ongoing research.

In this study, to go one step further, we studied β-sheets on the strand level instead of amino acid level. Statistical analyses of the terminal extensions of paired β-strands were performed and a simple rule "$R \geq 25\%$ and $Rt_i \geq 40\%$, $i = 1, 2$" was made. Steward and Thornton [3] developed an information theory approach to predict the relative offset positions by shifting one β-strand up to 10 residues either side of that observed. Such a rule could be used in similar studies. We certainly believe that the conclusions presented in this study could contribute to predict protein structures and to develop β-sheet prediction methods.

Conflict of Interests

The authors have declared that no conflict of interests exists.

Acknowledgment

This work was supported by Grants from the National Natural Science Foundation of China (nos. 31171053, 11232005, 81171342, 68075049, and 10671100).

References

[1] H. M. Fooks, A. C. R. Martin, D. N. Woolfson, R. B. Sessions, and E. G. Hutchinson, "Amino acid pairing preferences in parallel β-sheets in proteins," *Journal of Molecular Biology*, vol. 356, no. 1, pp. 32–44, 2006.

[2] M. Dorn and O. N. de Souza, "A3N: an artificial neural network n-gram-based method to approximate 3-D polypeptides structure prediction," *Expert Systems with Applications*, vol. 37, no. 12, pp. 7497–7508, 2010.

[3] R. E. Steward and J. M. Thornton, "Prediction of strand pairing in antiparallel and parallel β-sheets using information theory," *Proteins*, vol. 48, no. 2, pp. 178–191, 2002.

[4] M. Jäger, M. Dendle, A. A. Fuller, and J. W. Kelly, "A cross-strand Trp-Trp pair stabilizes the hPin1 WW domain at the expense of function," *Protein Science*, vol. 16, no. 10, pp. 2306–2313, 2007.

[5] M. Kuhn, J. Meiler, and D. Baker, "Strand-loop-strand motifs: prediction of hairpins and diverging turns in proteins," *Proteins*, vol. 54, no. 2, pp. 282–288, 2004.

[6] J. S. Merkel and L. Regan, "Modulating protein folding rates in vivo and in vitro by side-chain interactions between the parallel β strands of green fluorescent protein," *Journal of Biological Chemistry*, vol. 275, no. 38, pp. 29200–29206, 2000.

[7] Y. Mandel-Gutfreund, S. M. Zaremba, and L. M. Gregoret, "Contributions of residue pairing to β-sheet formation: conservation and covariation of amino acid residue pairs on antiparallel β-strands," *Journal of Molecular Biology*, vol. 305, no. 5, pp. 1145–1159, 2001.

[8] S. M. Zaremba and L. M. Gregoret, "Context-dependence of amino acid residue pairing in antiparallel β-sheets," *Journal of Molecular Biology*, vol. 291, no. 2, pp. 463–479, 1999.

[9] I. Ruczinski, C. Kooperberg, R. Bonneau, and D. Baker, "Distributions of beta sheets in proteins with application to structure prediction," *Proteins*, vol. 48, no. 1, pp. 85–97, 2002.

[10] B. Rost, J. Liu, D. Przybylski et al., "Prediction of protein structure through evolution," in *Handbook of Chemoinformatics: From Data to Knowledge*, J. Gasteiger and T. Engel, Eds., pp. 1789–1811, John Wiley & Sons, New York, NY, USA, 2003.

[11] J. Cheng and P. Baldi, "Three-stage prediction of protein β-sheets by neural networks, alignments and graph algorithms," *Bioinformatics*, vol. 21, supplement 1, pp. i75–i84, 2005.

[12] C. K. Smith and L. Regan, "Construction and design of betasheets," *Accounts of Chemical Research*, vol. 30, no. 4, pp. 153–161, 1997.

[13] T. Kortemme, M. Ramirez-Alvarado, and L. Serrano, "Design of a 20-amino acid, three-stranded β-sheet protein," *Science*, vol. 281, no. 5374, pp. 253–256, 1998.

[14] B. Kuhlman, G. Dantas, G. C. Ireton, G. Varani, B. L. Stoddard, and D. Baker, "Design of a novel globular protein fold with atomic-level accuracy," *Science*, vol. 302, no. 5649, pp. 1364–1368, 2003.

[15] N. Zhang, J. Ruan, G. Duan, S. Gao, and T. Zhang, "The interstrand amino acid pairs play a significant role in determining the parallel or antiparallel orientation of β-strands," *Biochemical and Biophysical Research Communications*, vol. 386, no. 3, pp. 537–543, 2009.

[16] N. Zhang, G. Duan, S. Gao, J. Ruan, and T. Zhang, "Prediction of the parallel/antiparallel orientation of beta-strands using amino acid pairing preferences and support vector machines," *Journal of Theoretical Biology*, vol. 263, no. 3, pp. 360–368, 2010.

[17] E. G. Hutchinson, R. B. Sessions, J. M. Thornton, and D. N. Woolfson, "Determinants of strand register in antiparallel β-sheets of proteins," *Protein Science*, vol. 7, no. 11, pp. 2287–2300, 1998.

[18] J. S. Nowick, "Exploring β-sheet structure and interactions with chemical model systems," *Accounts of Chemical Research*, vol. 41, no. 10, pp. 1319–1330, 2008.

[19] A. G. Cochran, R. T. Tong, M. A. Starovasnik et al., "A minimal peptide scaffold for β-turn display: optimizing a strand position in disulfide-cyclized β-hairpins," *Journal of the American Chemical Society*, vol. 123, no. 4, pp. 625–632, 2001.

[20] S. J. Russell and A. G. Cochran, "Designing stable β-hairpins: energetic contributions from cross-strand residues," *Journal of the American Chemical Society*, vol. 122, no. 50, pp. 12600–12601, 2000.

[21] Y. Dou, P. F. Baisnée, G. Pollastri, Y. Pécout, J. Nowick, and P. Baldi, "ICBS: a database of interactions between protein chains mediated by β-sheet formation," *Bioinformatics*, vol. 20, no. 16, pp. 2767–2777, 2004.

[22] N. Zhang, J. Ruan, J. Wu, and T. Zhang, "Sheetspair: a database of amino acid pairs in protein sheet structures," *Data Science Journal*, vol. 6, no. 15, pp. S589–S595, 2007.

[23] Q. Zhang, S. Yoon, and W. J. Welsh, "Improved method for predicting β-turn using support vector machine," *Bioinformatics*, vol. 21, no. 10, pp. 2370–2374, 2005.

[24] J. Cheng and P. Baldi, "Improved residue contact prediction using support vector machines and a large feature set," *BMC Bioinformatics*, vol. 8, article 113, 2007.

[25] P. Baldi, G. Pollastri, C. A. Andersen, and S. Brunak, "Matching protein beta-sheet partners by feedforward and recurrent neural networks.," in *Proceedings of International Conference on Intelligent Systems for Molecular Biology (ISMB '00)*, vol. 8, pp. 25–36, 2000.

[26] O. Grana, D. Baker, R. M. MacCallum et al., "CASP6 assessment of contact prediction," *Proteins*, vol. 61, no. 7, pp. 214–224, 2005.

[27] I. Halperin, H. Wolfson, and R. Nussinov, "Correlated mutations: advances and limitations. A study on fusion proteins and on the Cohesin-Dockerin families," *Proteins*, vol. 63, no. 4, pp. 832–845, 2006.

[28] P. J. Kundrotas and E. G. Alexov, "Predicting residue contacts using pragmatic correlated mutations method: reducing the false positives," *BMC Bioinformatics*, vol. 7, article 503, 2006.

[29] G. Z. Zhang, D. S. Huang, and Z. H. Quan, "Combining a binary input encoding scheme with RBFNN for globulin protein inter-residue contact map prediction," *Pattern Recognition Letters*, vol. 26, no. 10, pp. 1543–1553, 2005.

[30] J. Cheng and P. Baldi, "Improved residue contact prediction using support vector machines and a large feature set," *BMC Bioinformatics*, vol. 8, article 113, 2007.

[31] C. A. Rohl, C. E. M. Strauss, K. M. S. Misura, and D. Baker, "Protein structure prediction using rosetta," *Methods in Enzymology*, vol. 383, pp. 66–93, 2004.

[32] J. Lee, S. Y. Kim, and J. Lee, "Protein structure prediction based on fragment assembly and parameter optimization," *Biophysical Chemistry*, vol. 115, no. 2-3, pp. 209–214, 2005.

[33] G. Wang and R. L. Dunbrack, "PISCES: a protein sequence culling server," *Bioinformatics*, vol. 19, no. 12, pp. 1589–1591, 2003.

[34] G. Wang and R. L. Dunbrack, "PISCES: recent improvements to a PDB sequence culling server," *Nucleic Acids Research*, vol. 33, no. 2, pp. W94–W98, 2005.

[35] F. Ferron, S. Longhi, B. Canard, and D. Karlin, "A practical overview of protein disorder prediction methods," *Proteins*, vol. 65, no. 1, pp. 1–14, 2006.

[36] R. Linding, L. J. Jensen, F. Diella, P. Bork, T. J. Gibson, and R. B. Russell, "Protein disorder prediction: implications for structural proteomics," *Structure*, vol. 11, no. 11, pp. 1453–1459, 2003.

[37] B. Liu, L. Lin, X. Wang, X. Wang, and Y. Shen, "Protein long disordered region prediction based on profile-level disorder propensities and position-specific scoring matrixes," in *Proceedings of IEEE International Conference on Bioinformatics and Biomedicine (BIBM '09)*, pp. 66–69, November 2009.

[38] M. Parisien and F. Major, "Ranking the factors that contribute to protein β-sheet folding," *Proteins*, vol. 68, no. 4, pp. 824–829, 2007.

[39] M. S. Searle and B. Ciani, "Design of β-sheet systems for understanding the thermodynamics and kinetics of protein folding," *Current Opinion in Structural Biology*, vol. 14, no. 4, pp. 458–464, 2004.

[40] K. S. Rotondi and L. M. Gierasch, "Local sequence information in cellular retinoic acid-binding protein I: specific residue roles in β-turns," *Biopolymers*, vol. 71, no. 6, pp. 638–651, 2003.

[41] J. Kim, S. R. Brych, J. Lee, T. M. Logan, and M. Blaber, "Identification of a key structural element for protein folding within β-hairpin turns," *Journal of Molecular Biology*, vol. 328, no. 4, pp. 951–961, 2003.

[42] J. Karanicolas and C. L. Brooks, "The structural basis for biphasic kinetics in the folding of the WW domain from a formin-binding protein: lessons for protein design?" *Proceedings of the National Academy of Sciences of the United States of America*, vol. 100, no. 7, pp. 3954–3959, 2003.

[43] K. S. Rotondi, L. F. Rotondi, and L. M. Gierasch, "Native structural propensity in cellular retinoic acid-binding protein I 64–88: the role of locally encoded structure in the folding of a β-barrel protein," *Biophysical Chemistry*, vol. 100, no. 1-3, pp. 421–436, 2003.

[44] Y. Kato, T. Akutsu, and H. Seki, "Dynamic programming algorithms and grammatical modeling for protein beta-sheet prediction," *Journal of Computational Biology*, vol. 16, no. 7, pp. 945–957, 2009.

[45] B. Wathen and Z. Jia, "Protein β-sheet nucleation is driven by local modular formation," *Journal of Biological Chemistry*, vol. 285, no. 24, pp. 18376–18384, 2010.

10

Gap Detection for Genome-Scale Constraint-Based Models

J. Paul Brooks,[1,2] **William P. Burns,**[1] **Stephen S. Fong,**[1,3]
Chris M. Gowen,[1,3] **and Seth B. Roberts**[1,3]

[1] Center for the Study of Biological Complexity, Virginia Commonwealth University, P.O. Box 843083, Richmond, VA 23284, USA

[2] Department of Statistical Sciences and Operations Research, Virginia Commonwealth University, P.O. Box 843083, Richmond, VA 23284, USA

[3] Department of Chemical and Life Science Engineering, Virginia Commonwealth University, P.O. Box 843083, Richmond, VA 23284, USA

Correspondence should be addressed to J. Paul Brooks, jpbrooks@vcu.edu

Academic Editor: T. Akutsu

Constraint-based metabolic models are currently the most comprehensive system-wide models of cellular metabolism. Several challenges arise when building an *in silico* constraint-based model of an organism that need to be addressed before flux balance analysis (FBA) can be applied for simulations. An algorithm called FBA-Gap is presented here that aids the construction of a working model based on plausible modifications to a given list of reactions that are known to occur in the organism. When applied to a working model, the algorithm gives a hypothesis concerning a minimal medium for sustaining the cell in culture. The utility of the algorithm is demonstrated in creating a new model organism and is applied to four existing working models for generating hypotheses about culture media. In modifying a partial metabolic reconstruction so that biomass may be produced using FBA, the proposed method is more efficient than a previously proposed method in that fewer new reactions are added to complete the model. The proposed method is also more accurate than other approaches in that only biologically plausible reactions and exchange reactions are used.

1. Introduction

Flux balance analysis (FBA) is the use of a linear program (LP) to model the flow of metabolites through the network of reactions in a cell [1]. FBA simulations give insight into the relative rates at which reactions occur when the cell is optimized for a specific objective. A fundamental assumption of FBA is that organisms can function optimally (often as a result of adaptive evolution) in that they make optimal use of scarce resources to serve the needs of the organism. This characterization of cell behavior naturally leads to a math programming modeling paradigm. FBA has been used to predict growth rates, gene essentiality, and other features of multiple organisms [2–5].

Several related challenges are encountered in the building of metabolic reconstructions. To apply FBA to a constraint-based model, both a reaction network (representing organism-specific biochemical capabilities) and an objective (representing a desired or measurable physiological goal) need to be specified. Currently, complete reaction networks for organisms are not known. There may be reactions in a cell that must be active for the production of biomass that have not been cataloged in biological databases or documented in the literature. Another challenge is modeler error; the modeler can mistakenly omit a reaction or transport process that is necessary for the production of biomass. Aside from establishing a model that can produce biomass, a common difficulty in using FBA models is that of finding a culture medium that can allow the *in silico* cell to send flux through the biomass reaction.

Several methods for restoring functionality in broken FBA models, those incapable of a desired level of flux through the biomass reaction, have been previously proposed. GapFind [6] is a procedure that determines which metabolites in a network cannot be produced, and GapFill [6] determines a minimal set of reactions to add from a universal database so that a specified set of metabolites may be produced. These optimization-based procedures have already been integrated into the Model SEED metabolic reconstruction pipeline with some success [7]. Reed et al. [8] utilize a method that adds a minimum-sized set of reactions from a universal database that allows for a specified level of biomass production in the resulting model. MetaFlux [9] is an automated approach to find missing reactions, exchange reactions, and biomass metabolites. OptStrain [10] determines the maximum possible yield of a desired product based on the inclusion of all reactions in a universal database and then finds the minimum number of reactions from the database needed to achieve the optimal yield. Segrè et al. [11] use the Forward Propagation and Backward Propagation/Backtracking algorithms [12] to first determine the metabolites that can be produced in a model, and then find the precursors of essential nonproducible metabolites that cannot be produced.

Several investigators have proposed methods for filling gaps in metabolic networks outside of the FBA paradigm, including searching through a network of metabolites and reactions for logically possible paths [13, 14] and using logic programming to construct pathways [15]. These methods do not ensure that the mass balancing constraints of FBA models are satisfied, nor do they consider the effects of generated pathways on the production of biomass. Thus, the application of these methods does not guarantee the generation of a constraint-based model that produces biomass when FBA is applied.

A fundamental assumption of FBA modeling is that metabolites remain at constant concentration within the cell. Throughout this paper, we use the term *metabolite* to refer to any molecule whose concentration is of interest, including byproducts of metabolism, coenzymes, and protons. Let v_j be the flux through reaction j, for each $j \in R$, which is the number of times that a reaction occurs per unit time. Let S_{ij} be the stoichiometric coefficient for metabolite i in reaction j, for each $i \in M$ and $j \in R$, with the convention that S_{ij} is negative for molecules i that are reactants for reaction j, positive for metabolites i that are products for reaction j, and 0 otherwise. Metabolites may participate in a unidirectional or reversible *exchange reaction*. For our purposes, it will be helpful to distinguish *source reactions* from *escape reactions* and assign variables b_i^{src} and b_i^{esc} for the fluxes through these reactions. We wish to restrict transport fluxes to zero for any metabolite unless its concentration changes in the cell due to transport processes. The conservation of mass for metabolite i may be stated as follows:

$$\sum_{j \in R} S_{ij} v_j + b_i^{\text{src}} - b_i^{\text{esc}} = 0. \tag{1}$$

The set of reactions R may include a (potentially artificial) *biomass* reaction which reflects the objective of the cell in terms of which metabolites are emphasized for production or consumption by other processes. The objective

$$\max v_{\text{biomass}} \tag{2}$$

can be added to the model, reflecting the desire to maximize flux through the biomass reaction. Maximizing flux through

the biomass reaction is one of several possible objectives that one could assign to a cell. FBA models with this particular objective have been shown to reflect the behavior of single-celled organisms during cell growth. Assessing whether positive biomass production is possible is an effective method for testing the completeness of a metabolic reconstruction. If an FBA model is incapable of producing biomass, then there is likely a gap in the reaction network.

Upper and lower bounds on each reaction flux are specified. If possible, these bounds are based on experimentally observed fluxes and free energy considerations, as for the *S. cerevisiae* and *E. coli* models [16–18]. If not, then a common lower and upper bound for all reactions can be assigned, and the fluxes returned by FBA give the investigator an idea of the relative activity of the reactions in the network for a given biomass reaction; the actual flux values in this latter case are less important than the ratios. For example if $v_j/v_k \geq 4$, the model indicates that a mechanism for maximizing biomass production exists wherein reaction j is at least 4 times as active as reaction k. If we generate (1) for metabolites and reactions within a cell and add the flux bounds, we obtain the linear programming-based FBA model. The general model can be expressed compactly as follows:

$$\max v_{\text{biomass}}$$
$$Sv + b^{\text{src}} - b^{\text{esc}} = 0,$$
$$L \leq v \leq U, \tag{3}$$
$$L^{\text{src}} \leq b^{\text{src}} \leq U^{\text{src}},$$
$$L^{\text{esc}} \leq b^{\text{esc}} \leq U^{\text{esc}}.$$

In this paper, we propose a new approach to address the challenges of building FBA models called FBA-Gap. The procedure identifies gaps in the metabolic network that are preventing flux through a specified objective, which in our case is the biomass reaction that represents cellular growth. Given a metabolic reconstruction and a biomass reaction, the goal is to find the most plausible modification of the metabolic reconstruction so that the model is capable of sending flux through the biomass reaction. FBA-Gap uses mathematical optimization to determine a minimum cost set of additional exchange reactions needed such that the flux through the biomass reaction can exceed a given threshold. Costs are assigned to source and escape reactions *a priori* based on their plausibility and distance to the biomass reaction. In general, exchange reactions for metabolites that exist in the extracellular compartment are given a low cost, while exchange reactions for metabolites that exist only in cytosolic and intracellular compartments are given a high cost. The output is a minimum cost set of exchange reactions and a flux distribution for the expanded reaction network. If the model is robust and has no detrimental gaps, the selected exchange reactions will correspond to missing transport reactions for uptake of metabolites from *in silico* culture medium or for discharge of byproducts into the extracellular space. However, if the model has internal gaps in the reaction network, exchange reactions will be added for internal metabolites that are furthest from the biomass reaction.

Our method is a departure from previous gap-filling methods in that we place an increased emphasis on the accuracy of the final model. The approach is to preserve the set of reactions in the initial model and to direct the model builder to a set of reactions that lead to a biomass-producing model and can be added with high confidence. In the GapFind/GapFill framework, reactions are added until *every* metabolite in the model is produced, and many additional reactions may be added to a model that are not required for the production of biomass. We will demonstrate that the proposed method is less computationally intensive than GapFind/GapFill. In the method described in [8], hereafter referred to as GapReed, reactions may be added to the model which are downstream/upstream of the actual gap. In other words, there is no attempt to ensure that modifications address gaps in the "backbone" of the network; the gaps may be masked by implausible exchange reactions or secondary pathways. The emphasis in our method is directing the modeler to the gaps in the backbone of the network that can be addressed by adding high-confidence reactions to the model.

The cost structure in FBA-Gap for the artificial exchange reactions is crucial to the proper identification of gaps in the metabolic network. Our approach is to identify the gaps that are furthest distance from the biomass reaction, utilizing as much of the existing network as possible. A trivial "fix" to any constraint-based model would be to add exchange reactions for every component of the biomass reaction, which would always result in a solution that has no biological relevance. Measuring distance in a metabolic network is a well-studied problem. Distances between metabolites in a metabolic network have been used to establish and refute scale-freeness [19, 20]. Investigators have noted difficulties associated with the inclusion of coenzymes in distance calculations, not the least of which is specifying which metabolites are coenzymes [13]. Some of these coenzymes are ubiquitous so that every metabolite appears near every other metabolite. Solutions to these difficulties include the introduction of compartments [13], excluding the most common metabolites from distance calculations [21], and using the Euclidean distance of attribute vectors for metabolites [14]. In FBA-Gap, the length of a path in the metabolic network is based on the number of reactions in which each metabolite occurs, penalizing paths that pass through often-occurring metabolites. Gaps where coenzymes play a prominent role can be discovered, but preference is given to other gaps.

In the remainder of the paper, we describe the FBA-Gap method for building metabolic reaction networks and demonstrate its effectiveness in computational experiments. The method is used to help create a new metabolic reconstruction for a cellular organism based on a partial reconstruction. We compare the accuracy and computation time of FBA-Gap to existing gap-filling methods for this model. We then remove the exchange reactions from several existing models of organisms and apply FBA-Gap, yielding a hypothesis for minimal media for each organism. Finally, we delete a portion of the internal reactions of a working model, and apply FBA-Gap to detect the resulting gaps in the network.

2. Materials and Methods

FBA-Gap takes as input an FBA model and a lower bound for the flux through the artificial biomass reaction (to ensure growth). Whereas FBA can be considered a generalized maximum flow on a hypergraph, consider an analogy with maximum flows on graphs (Figure 1(a)). Intuitively, a gap corresponds to a missing arc. The main idea behind FBA-Gap is to find a minimum-cost set of artificial exchange reactions so that biomass may be produced. Note that for the graph in Figure 1(b), artificially adding flow to any of nodes C, D, or E will ensure positive flow along the artificial arc. Given that we would like to fill the gap, we would benefit the most by knowing the needed exchange reaction that is furthest from the biomass reaction. This desire leads us to define a notion of *distance from the biomass reaction* and a corresponding cost structure that will lead us to the gaps.

Integer Programming Model. Let

$$x_i = \begin{cases} 1 & \text{if a source reaction is added for metabolite } i \\ 0 & \text{o.w.} \end{cases}$$

$$y_i = \begin{cases} 1 & \text{if an escape reaction is added for metabolite } i \\ 0 & \text{o.w.} \end{cases} \tag{4}$$

for $i \in R$. Then a minimum-cost set of exchange reactions for which a minimum threshold of flux through the biomass is attained can be determined by solving the following mixed-integer program:

$$
\begin{aligned}
\min \quad & (c^{\text{src}})^T x + (c^{\text{esc}})^T y, \\
\text{s.t.} \quad & Sv + b^{\text{src}} - b^{\text{esc}} = 0, \\
& L \le v \le U, \\
& (L^{\text{src}})^T x \le b^{\text{src}} \le (U^{\text{src}})^T x, \\
& (L^{\text{esc}})^T y \le b^{\text{esc}} \le (U^{\text{esc}})^T y.
\end{aligned} \tag{5}
$$

Note that a positive lower bound for the biomass reaction, L_{biomass}, is specified in the set of flux lower bounds. The first constraint ensures that a valid flux distribution is derived, that is, the mass balance constraints are satisfied. The last two constraints ensure that if the flux along a exchange reaction is positive, then an appropriate cost is enforced. The remaining constraint contains bounds for the reactions fluxes. Solving (5) is shown to be *NP-Complete* (see in the Supplementary Material available online at doi:10.1155/2012/323472). The selection of exchange metabolites that are most biologically plausible and/or furthest from the biomass reaction is ensured by a cost structure that is described in the next section.

Cost Structure for Exchange Reactions. First, we assign costs to extracellular metabolites. Extracellular metabolites are

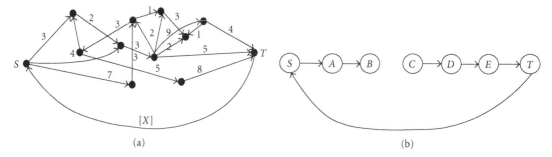

(a)   (b)

FIGURE 1: (a) An illustration of a maximum flow problem on a graph. The numbers above the arcs are capacities, and we wish to maximize flow from the source S to the sink T; equivalently, we wish to maximize flow along the artificial arc (T, S) such that the flow at each node is balanced. (b) An example of a small maximum flow problem with a gap such that no flow along arc (T, S) is possible.

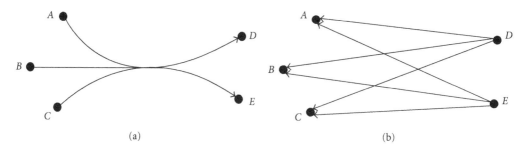

(a)   (b)

FIGURE 2: (a) An example of a hyperarc in the hypergraph H corresponding to a reaction $A + B + C \rightarrow D + E$, and (b) the corresponding arcs in G, the graph used for calculating distances.

substances that are either postulated to exist in the culture medium or are secreted by the cell. Adding a source reaction for such a metabolite is plausible if experimental culture media that support growth are likely to contain the substance, and adding an escape reaction is plausible if the cell likely secretes the metabolite. A low cost of 1 is assigned for biologically plausible exchange reactions for extracellular metabolites, and a cost of 20 is assigned for implausible exchange reactions for extracellular metabolites (Table S1). Therefore, up to 20 plausible exchange reactions will be selected before 1 implausible exchange reaction. The costs for artificial exchange reactions for internal metabolites are assigned based on the distance of a metabolite to the biomass reaction. Distance to the biomass reaction is defined as follows. Assume for the moment that all stoichiometric coefficients are 1. Let $H = (M, R)$ where $R \subseteq 2^{|M|} \times 2^{|M|}$ is the directed hypergraph associated with the reaction network for an organism, where each reaction corresponds to a hyperarc (Figure 2(a)). Define a directed graph $G = (M, \mathcal{R})$ as follows. For every hyperarc $r \in R$ with tail nodes T_r and head nodes H_r, and for every $i \in T_r$ and $j \in H_r$, there is an arc $(j, i) \in \mathcal{R}$ (Figure 2(b)). An intuitive definition for the distance of a metabolite to the biomass reactants (products) is the minimum length of a directed path in G from the metabolite to a biomass reactant (product). This distance measure does not work well because, for example, a large proportion of reactions in a cell involve cofactors such as ATP. Every metabolite is either involved in a reaction where ATP is produced or consumed or will be near such a reaction

by this distance measure. Therefore, every metabolite will appear to be near the biomass reaction.

To remedy this effect, we penalize paths that pass through these often-occurring cofactor metabolites. Instead of measuring graph distance by the number of arcs, we define the distance along an arc (i, j) in $\mathcal{R}$ by $d(i, j) = \deg(i)$, where $\deg(i)$ is the degree of i. Note that the degree of node i in G is precisely the number of reactions in which metabolite i participates. The distance of a metabolite to the biomass reactants d_i^{src} is the length of the shortest directed path in G to a biomass reactant, which can be determined by applying Dijkstra's algorithm [22]. The analogous distance to the biomass products is denoted d_i^{esc}. Let $d_{\max}^{\text{src}}$ ($d_{\max}^{\text{esc}}$) be the maximum distance among all metabolites with a directed path to the biomass reactants (products) in G. To penalize the source transport reactions that are near the biomass reactants, we define the cost for internal metabolite i to be $d_{\max}^{\text{src}} - d_i^{\text{src}} + 20$. The penalty of 20 in the cost formula ensures that the cost of an artificial exchange reaction for an internal metabolite is at least as high as the cost for an exchange reaction for an extracellular metabolite. Escape reactions are penalized in an analogous fashion. Dijkstra's shortest path algorithm is polynomial time and is computationally easy for the networks considered here. The computational complexity of the proposed method is dominated by solving instances of (5). We note here that our cost structure is less likely to find gaps involving ubiquitous but important backbone metabolites. However, the ubiquity of these metabolites in reactions that are already in the draft model indicates that they are unlikely to be responsible for a lack of biomass production in the *in silico* organism. We choose to penalize the inclusion of cofactors rather than simply removing them from the directed graph because determining which metabolites are cofactors can present a challenge [13]. The focus of the proposed method is on creating a high-confidence model that produces biomass, even if "secondary" pathways are involved; subsequent analyses with a working FBA model can help to identify remaining gaps in primary pathways.

Applying FBA-Gap to Broken Models. The trivial solution of zero flux on all reactions, including the biomass reaction, is always feasible for (3). A broken model is one for which the optimal objective value for (3) is lower than desired. The process of applying FBA-Gap to a broken model involves three stages: calculating distances to the biomass reaction, reviewing the output of FBA-Gap, and systematically adding reactions from a universal database. In the first stage, Dijkstra's algorithm is applied as described in the previous section to determine the distances of metabolites to biomass products and reactants. The distances are initialized to be infinite. If after application of the shortest path algorithm, the distance of a metabolite to biomass reactants, is still infinite, then there is no path in G to the biomass reactants for that metabolite, and the metabolite will never be selected by solving (5) as having a source reaction. By construction of G, there is no sequence of reactions in H beginning with a reaction that produces i and ending with a reaction that produces a biomass reactant. Therefore, adding a source reaction for i will only increase the objective value of (5) without helping to increase biomass production. Similarly, a metabolite i with $d_i^{esc} = \infty$ after application of the shortest path algorithm will never be selected by solving (5) as having an escape reaction. The corresponding binary variables in (5) for these metabolites can be fixed to zero to reduce computation time. Further, the knowledgeable modeler can review this list to find metabolites that are known to be involved in the production of biomass and fill in gaps along known pathways.

The next stage includes the solution of the integer program (5). The problem is NP-hard and is related to the closed hemisphere problem (see Supplementary Material), suggesting that heuristics for the latter may be adapted to solve challenging instances. Action can be taken to reduce the computational time of solving the integer program directly. The modeler can fix the binary variables to 0 or 1 corresponding to exchange reactions that should not be eligible for selection and exchange reactions that should be selected, respectively. This feature can be used to allow the modeler to specify a particular carbon source for the cell or facilitate discovery of solutions corresponding to secretion of a particular substance. Specifying certain exchange reactions is analogous to determining the list of exchanges to be "tried" as in the MetaFlux procedure [9]. In FBA-Gap, if too many binary variables are fixed to zero, there is a risk that the integer program becomes infeasible. If a feasible solution exists, the output includes a set of exchange reactions, fluxes

on those exchange reactions, and fluxes for all other reactions in the network that will provide the desired flux through the biomass reaction. If no feasible solution exists, then the minimum biomass flux must be reduced and/or the bounds on reaction fluxes in the network need to be expanded.

If a feasible solution contains only biologically plausible exchange reactions for extracellular metabolites, then the source reactions can indicate components of a culture medium for the organism. Biologically plausible exchange reactions are those that are for metabolites likely to exist in the culture medium and transportable across the cell membrane. If a feasible solution includes exchange reactions for internal metabolites (e.g., metabolites in the cytoplasm), then the selected exchange reactions give an indication of the location of gaps in the reaction network. The modeler can then consult the appropriate diagram in a publicly available biochemical pathway database, for example, KEGG [23], BioCyc [24], or Reactome [25]. The search for missing reactions is facilitated by the authors' software MetModel GUI (Figure 3). The software includes a searchable and sortable database of metabolic reactions that can be added to a model, as well as capabilities for searching the reactions in a user's model. After adding new reactions to the model, the integer program (5) is resolved and the process of adding reactions is repeated until the model uses only low-cost exchange reactions. A flowchart of the steps in FBA-GAP is depicted in Figure 4.

Small Example. Consider the reaction network depicted in Figure 5. Table 1 contains the distance-to-biomass calculation. Metabolites $B, F, G, H,$ and I will not be selected as having source reactions, and metabolites $A, B, C, D, E,$ and H will not be selected as having escape reactions because they are infinite distance from the biomass reactants and products, respectively. The instance of (5) would be

$$\min \quad x_A + 20x_C + 21x_D + 21x_E + 21y_F + 20y_G + y_I,$$

$$\text{s.t.} \quad -v_{A \to E} + b_A^{src} = 0,$$

$$-v_{C \to D} + b_C^{src} = 0,$$

$$-v_{DE \to F} + v_{C \to D} + b_D^{src} = 0,$$

$$-v_{DE \to F} + v_{A \to E} + b_E^{src} = 0,$$

$$-v_{F \to GI} + v_{DE \to F} - b_F^{esc} = 0, \qquad (6)$$

$$v_{F \to GI} - b_G^{esc} = 0,$$

$$v_{F \to GI} - b_I^{esc} = 0,$$

$$0 \le b_i^{src} \le U_i^{src} x_i, \quad i \in \{A, C, D, E\},$$

$$0 \le b_i^{esc} \le U_i^{esc} y_i, \quad i \in \{F, G, I\},$$

$$L \le v \le U,$$

with the additional restriction that the variables x_i and y_i are binary. Included in the last set of constraints is a nonzero

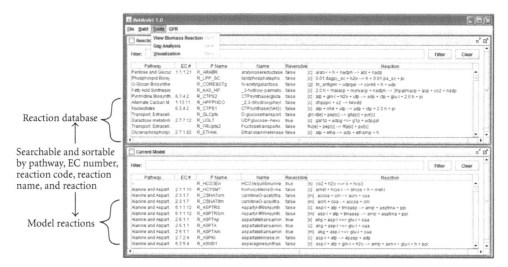

Reaction database

Searchable and sortable
by pathway, EC number,
reaction code, reaction
name, and reaction

Model reactions

FIGURE 3: Screenshot of MetModel GUI, software for building FBA models. The top frame contains the universal reaction database, and the bottom frame contains the set of reactions in the current working model.

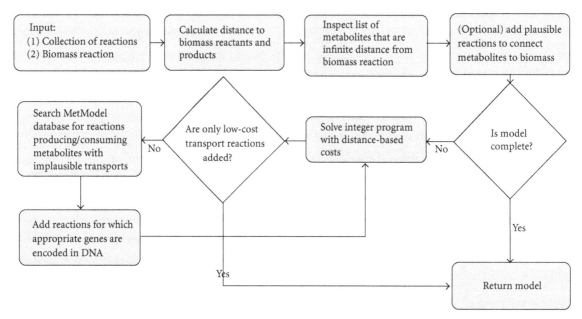

FIGURE 4: Flowchart of steps in building metabolic reconstructions using FBA-Gap. Determining if a model is complete involves checking if biomass is produced using only biologically plausible exchange reactions.

lower bound on $v_{DE \to F}$ which requires biomass production. The algorithm selects an artificial source reaction for metabolite C and an artificial escape for metabolite G. A source reaction for C is selected rather than a reaction for D, because C is further from the biomass reaction and therefore the cost is less. The selected source reactions will indicate to the modeler that reactions $B \leftrightarrow C$ and $G \leftrightarrow H$ are missing from the model. The reactions can be found hypothetically by searching through the database in MetModel GUI (Figure 3) or by searching the relevant pathway in another database. Adding these reactions and

solving the new instance of (5) produces a solution that indicates that biologically plausible exchange reactions can be added for A, B, I, and H in order to produce biomass.

3. Results

Application to a Partial Metabolic Reconstruction. To illustrate the ability of FBA-Gap to aid in the construction of new FBA models, we apply the methodology to a new multicompartment model for *Cryptococcus neoformans*. *C. neoformans* is a fungus that can cause meningitis in humans.

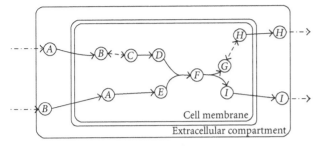

FIGURE 5: An example of a "broken" FBA model. The biomass reaction is indicated by a bold line, reactions included in the model are indicated by solid lines, reactions omitted from the model (gaps) are indicated by dashed lines, and plausible exchange reactions omitted from the model are indicated by dotted/dashed lines.

TABLE 1: Distances of metabolites to biomass reactants and biomass products for the network depicted in Figure 5.

Distance to biomass reactants	Distance to biomass products
$d_A^{\mathrm{src}} = 1$	$d_A^{\mathrm{esc}} = \infty$
$d_B^{\mathrm{src}} = \infty$	$d_B^{\mathrm{esc}} = \infty$
$d_C^{\mathrm{src}} = 1$	$d_C^{\mathrm{esc}} = \infty$
$d_D^{\mathrm{src}} = 0$	$d_D^{\mathrm{esc}} = \infty$
$d_E^{\mathrm{src}} = 0$	$d_E^{\mathrm{esc}} = \infty$
$d_F^{\mathrm{src}} = \infty$	$d_F^{\mathrm{esc}} = 0$
$d_G^{\mathrm{src}} = \infty$	$d_G^{\mathrm{esc}} = 1$
$d_H^{\mathrm{src}} = \infty$	$d_H^{\mathrm{esc}} = \infty$
$d_I^{\mathrm{src}} = \infty$	$d_I^{\mathrm{esc}} = 1$

Because no metabolic reconstruction of *C. neoformans* has been previously carried out, we assign a generic biomass reaction previously used for *B. subtilis* [26] using only central metabolites that occur in the cytosol:

$$1.241\,3\,\mathrm{pg} + 2.097\,\mathrm{AcCoa} + 1.236\,\mathrm{Akg} + 35.115\,\mathrm{ATP}$$

$$+\, 0.397\,\mathrm{e4p} + 0.428\,\mathrm{g3p} + 0.712\,\mathrm{g6p} + 0.542\,\mathrm{Gly}$$

$$+\, 14.405\,\mathrm{NADPH} + 8.066\,\mathrm{NH_4} + 1.785\,\mathrm{oaa} + 0.642\,\mathrm{pep}$$

$$+\, 1.640\,\mathrm{Pi} + 2.994\,\mathrm{Pyr} + 0.445\,\mathrm{r5p}$$

$$+\, 0.262\,\mathrm{Ser\text{-}l} + 0.195\,\mathrm{SO_4}$$

$$\longrightarrow 2.852\,\mathrm{CO_2} + 3.015\,\mathrm{NADH}. \tag{7}$$

We begin with a partial reconstruction based on evidence from genome annotations and scientific literature. The ability of the model to produce biomass is not considered during this step. The initial model consists of 576 reactions and 712 metabolites with compartments corresponding to the cytosol, mitochondria, and peroxisome. This initial curation was carried out over several weeks. We then solve (5) to find gaps in the model with a time limit of 120 seconds. The MetModel GUI database and KEGG are explored to find reactions that fill the gaps by producing and consuming metabolites with artificial exchange reactions. An internal

reaction is added to the model only if it is present in the MetModel GUI database and if KEGG specifies that a gene encodes an enzyme that catalyzes the reaction in the organism. After adding reactions, (5) is solved again, and additional reactions are added. The process is repeated as long as plausible reactions can be added.

Four rounds of solving (5) and manually adding reactions from the MetModel GUI database/KEGG are conducted (Tables S4–S7). Figure 6 illustrates how the searchable and sortable reaction database in MetModel GUI facilitates adding high-confidence reactions. After the first round of solving (5), cytoplasmic cyclic AMP is selected for an artificial source reaction. Browsing the MetModel GUI database reveals that the only reaction producing cyclic AMP, R_ADNCYC, is already included in the model. Upon inspection of the pathway containing R_ADNCYC, we discover an adjacent reaction, R_ADNK1, that is missing from the model and may be added because the corresponding enzyme is encoded in the *C. neoformans* genome. Cytoplasmic coenzyme A is also selected for an artificial source reaction. Inspection of the initial partial reconstruction reveals that much of fatty acid metabolism is omitted. Rather than adding the new pathways, we leave the artificial transport reaction as a placeholder. The artificial and plausible exchange reactions in Table S7 are sufficient to create a working model. In the final round of gap analysis, nine plausible source reactions, seven plausible escape reactions, and an artificial transport reaction for cytoplasmic coenzyme A are added to the model. The first round of solving (5) is terminated at the time limit of 120 seconds with a feasible solution. The remaining three rounds take less than one second to find a provably optimal solution. For a given metabolite, MetModel GUI instantly returns a list of potential reactions. For metabolites involved in reactions that form the backbone of the metabolic network, the list is typically short. Combined with searching the KEGG database, a round of FBA-Gap takes around ten minutes, and the completion of the partial reconstruction for *C. neoformans* takes around one hour.

Comparison to Other Gap-Filling Algorithms. In this section, FBA-Gap is compared to GapReed [8] and GapFind/GapFill [6] to demonstrate differences in results and computation time using the *C. neoformans* partial reconstruction. GapReed and GapFind/GapFill are implemented with a universal database curated from existing metabolic reconstructions.

When using GapFind/GapFill in these experiments, GapFind is applied to find all nonproducible metabolites in a model, and GapFill is applied to each nonproducible metabolite to find reactions to add so that the metabolite is produced. If GapFill is infeasible, an exchange reaction is added for that metabolite. Integer programming instances for all methods are solved using Gurobi (http://www.gurobi.com/) with a time limit of 600 seconds.

GapFind determines that only nine metabolites are producible and therefore there are 703 downstream unproducible metabolites. Solving the integer program for

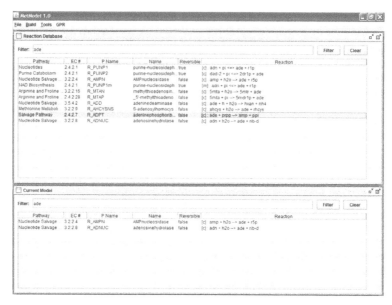

FIGURE 6: Searching for a gap-filling reaction is facilitated by a searchable and sortable database in MetModel GUI software. The initial model is unable to process ade^c. The reaction database in MetModel GUI has 10 reactions that involve ade^e. The KEGG database indicates that an enzyme for R_ADPT is encoded in the genome for *C. neoformans* and can be added to the model with confidence.

GapFind and the 703 integer programs for GapFill takes 50,169 seconds (about 14 hours). GapFill adds 550 reactions from the reaction database and 182 exchange reactions for metabolites.

The integer program for GapReed terminates at the time limit of 600 seconds. Source exchange reactions are added for nine cytosolic metabolites, one escape exchange reaction is added, and one reaction from the reaction database is added. The source exchange reactions are for cytoplasmic Gln-L, SO$_4$, FDP, O$_2$, NADPH, Gly, PRPP, ATP, and Acetyl-CoA. The escape reaction is for cytoplasmic CO$_2$, and the added reaction is the peroxidative reaction catalyzed by catalase ($2H_2O_2 \rightarrow 2H_2O + O_2$).

GapFind/GapFill and GapReed are more conducive to an automated implementation than FBA-Gap, but in this example, one can see some of the pitfalls of an automated approach. GapFind/GapFill adds many internal reactions and exchange reactions for cytosolic metabolites so that there is a high probability that implausible reactions are present in the final model. Further, GapFind/GapFill requires significantly more computation time. GapReed adds exchange reactions for more implausible cytosolic metabolites than FBA-Gap. A hybrid computational/manual curation approach such as FBA-Gap is able to derive a biomass-producing model with higher-confidence reactions for our partial reconstruction for *C. neoformans* than these two established methods.

Application to Existing Models. FBA-Gap is applied to four existing models with exchange reactions removed. The metabolic reconstructions used in this experiment are for *Trypanosoma cruzi* [27], *Bacillus subtilis* [26], *Heliocbacter pylori* (iIT341 GSM/GPR) [2], and *Escherichia coli* (iJR904 GSM/GPR) [28]. The results of applying the procedure

provide a hypothesis for a defined culture medium for each organism.

The hypothesized culture media are summarized in Table S2. *T. cruzi* is a protozoan parasite of humans that causes Chagas disease. The reconstruction is a multi-compartment model of central metabolism for *T. cruzi*. FBA-Gap selects biologically realistic source and escape reactions. The source reactions correspond to the transport of extracellular metabolites that are plausible constituents of a culture medium for sustaining *T. cruzi* and the escape reactions correspond to metabolites that are likely secreted by *T. cruzi*. *B. subtilis* is a Gram-positive bacterium found in soil. As with the *T. cruzi* model, FBA-Gap selects biologically realistic exchange reactions for production of biomass. For the *E. coli* reconstruction, one undesirable escape reaction is selected (clpn_ec^c) that is unique to the *E. coli* model. This metabolite occurs in only one reaction in the model and is a reactant in the biomass reaction. Therefore, a simple remedy is to increase the stoichiometric coefficient in the biomass reaction. For the *h. pylori* reconstruction, a single implausible escape reaction is selected for rhcys^c. Upon investigation of the network around this metabolite, we discover that there are reactions converting rhcys^c to dhptd^c and dhptd^c to hmfurn^c, but there are no reactions consuming hmfurn^c. There are no reactions consuming hmfurn^c in our universal database, so we can either add it as a reactant in the biomass reaction or add an escape reaction to remove it from the cell.

Recovering Deleted Reactions from an Existing Model. FBA-Gap is applied to an existing model with internal reactions deleted to evaluate the ability to find the resulting gaps in the network. In this experiment, we deleted a random sample of 222 internal reactions (15% of all reactions) from the *B. subtilis* model (Table S9). Solving (5) for the resulting model takes two seconds. FBA-Gap suggests 15 exchange reactions, all of which are source reactions (Table S10). Because we know which reactions are deleted from the model, we cannot properly evaluate how many of the deleted reactions a modeler would have added based on the suggested exchange reactions. Of the 15 metabolites in the selected artificial exchange reactions, 14 occur in at least one of the deleted reactions (93%), indicating that FBA-Gap does find the backbone metabolites that are next to the gaps. Of the 222 deleted reactions, 17 of them contain metabolites that are selected for artificial exchange reactions. Not all of the 222 deleted reactions are required to produce biomass, so it is likely that adding a subset of the deleted reactions would be sufficient for the resulting FBA model to produce biomass.

4. Discussion

This paper presents an optimization-based method for "debugging" metabolic reconstructions called FBA-Gap. We demonstrate the effectiveness of the procedure in helping to find gaps in a model for *C. neoformans*. FBA-Gap produces a more accurate reconstruction than an application of existing methods for filling gaps and requires less computation time. However, in contrast to other methods, FBA-Gap also involves manually selecting and approving which reactions to add to a model so that the overall time may be longer. As noted by Latendresse et al. [9], a fully automated gap-filling procedure likely leads to significant errors. The motivation behind FBA-Gap is to reduce the manual effort required by allowing the modeler to select from among a few suggested modifications to a model. The distance measure used in pricing artificial exchange reactions helps to indicate the location of gaps; these weights could also be incorporated into a procedure like MetaFlux [9], a more automated procedure that also has the capability of suggesting modifications to the biomass reaction. The FBA-Gap procedure provides hypotheses for defined culture media for organisms based on previously published models. One weakness of FBA-Gap is the computational complexity of solving (5). Finding optimal solutions to these integer programs is NP-Complete, but specialized solution methods may facilitate the computation of good solutions.

List of Abbreviations

FBA: flux balance analysis
LP: linear program.

Acknowledgments

This research is partially supported by NASA Award NNX09AR44A. The authors would like to thank the VCU Center for High Performance Computing for computational infrastructure and support.

References

[1] N. D. Price, J. L. Reed, and B. Ø. Palsson, "Genome-scale models of microbial cells: evaluating the consequences of constraints," *Nature Reviews Microbiology*, vol. 2, no. 11, pp. 886–897, 2004.

[2] I. Thiele, T. D. Vo, N. D. Price, and B. Ø. Palsson, "Expanded metabolic reconstruction of *Helicobacter pylori* (iIT341 GSM/GPR): an in silico genome-scale characterization of single- and double-deletion mutants," *Journal of Bacteriology*, vol. 187, no. 16, pp. 5818–5830, 2005.

[3] J. S. Edwards, R. U. Ibarra, and B. O. Palsson, "In silico predictions of *Escherichia coli* metabolic capabilities are consistent with experimental data," *Nature Biotechnology*, vol. 19, no. 2, pp. 125–130, 2001.

[4] A. R. Joyce, J. L. Reed, A. White et al., "Experimental and computational assessment of conditionally essential genes in *Escherichia coli*," *Journal of Bacteriology*, vol. 188, no. 23, pp. 8259–8271, 2006.

[5] J. Förster, I. Famili, B. Ø. Palsson, and J. Nielsen, "Large-scale evaluation of in silico gene deletions in *Saccharomyces cerevisiae*," *OMICS A Journal of Integrative Biology*, vol. 7, no. 2, pp. 193–202, 2003.

[6] V. S. Kumar, M. S. Dasika, and C. D. Maranas, "Optimization based automated curation of metabolic reconstructions," *BMC Bioinformatics*, vol. 8, article 212, 2007.

[7] C. S. Henry, M. Dejongh, A. A. Best, P. M. Frybarger, B. Linsay, and R. L. Stevens, "High-throughput generation, optimization and analysis of genome-scale metabolic models," *Nature Biotechnology*, vol. 28, no. 9, pp. 977–982, 2010.

[8] J. L. Reed, T. R. Patel, K. H. Chen et al., "Systems approach to refining genome annotation," *Proceedings of the National Academy of Sciences of the United States of America*, vol. 103, no. 46, pp. 17480–17484, 2006.

[9] M. Latendresse, M. Krummenacker, M. Trupp, and P. D. Karp, "Construction and completion of flux balance models from pathway databases," *Bioinformatics*, vol. 28, pp. 388–396, 2012.

[10] P. Pharkya, A. P. Burgard, and C. D. Maranas, "OptStrain: a computational framework for redesign of microbial production systems," *Genome Research*, vol. 14, no. 11, pp. 2367–2376, 2004.

[11] D. Segrè, J. Zucker, J. Katz et al., "From annotated genomes to metabolic flux models and kinetic parameter fitting," *OMICS A Journal of Integrative Biology*, vol. 7, no. 3, pp. 301–316, 2003.

[12] P. R. Romero and P. Karp, "Nutrient-related analysis of pathway/genome databases," *Pacific Symposium on Biocomputing*, pp. 471–482, 2001.

[13] M. Arita, "Metabolic reconstruction using shortest paths," *Simulation Practice and Theory*, vol. 8, no. 1-2, pp. 109–125, 2000.

[14] D. C. McShan, S. Rao, and I. Shah, "PathMiner: predicting metabolic pathways by heuristic search," *Bioinformatics*, vol. 19, no. 13, pp. 1692–1698, 2003.

[15] T. Gaasterland and E. Selkov, "Reconstruction of metabolic networks using incomplete information," in *Proceedings of the 3rd International Conference on Intelligent Systems in Molecular Biology*, pp. 127–135, 1995.

[16] A. M. Feist and B. Ø. Palsson, "The growing scope of applications of genome-scale metabolic reconstructions using *Escherichia coli*," *Nature Biotechnology*, vol. 26, no. 6, pp. 659–667, 2008.

[17] E. P. Gianchandani, M. A. Oberhardt, A. P. Burgard, C. D. Maranas, and J. A. Papin, "Predicting biological system objectives de novo from internal state measurements," *BMC Bioinformatics*, vol. 9, article 43, 2008.

[18] M. J. Herrgård, S. S. Fong, and B. Ø. Palsson, "Identification of genome-scale metabolic network models using experimentally

measured flux profiles," *PLoS Computational Biology*, vol. 2, no. 7, article e72, 2006.

[19] H. Jeong, B. Tombor, R. Albert, Z. N. Oltval, and A. L. Barabásl, "The large-scale organization of metabolic networks," *Nature*, vol. 407, no. 6804, pp. 651–654, 2000.

[20] M. Arita, "The metabolic world of *Escherichia coli* is not small," *Proceedings of the National Academy of Sciences of the United States of America*, vol. 101, no. 6, pp. 1543–1547, 2004.

[21] P. Kharchenko, L. Chen, Y. Freund, D. Vitkup, and G. M. Church, "Identifying metabolic enzymes with multiple types of association evidence," *BMC Bioinformatics*, vol. 7, article 177, 2006.

[22] E. W. Dijkstra, "A note on two problems in connexion with graphs," *Numerische Mathematik*, vol. 1, no. 1, pp. 269–271, 1959.

[23] M. Kanehisa and S. Goto, "KEGG: kyoto encyclopedia of genes and genomes," *Nucleic Acids Research*, vol. 28, no. 1, pp. 27–30, 2000.

[24] R. Caspi and P. D. Karp, "Using the MetaCyc pathway database and the BioCyc database collection," *Current Protocols in Bioinformatics*, chapter 1, unit 1.17, 2007.

[25] I. Vastrik, P. D'Eustachio, E. Schmidt et al., "Reactome: a knowledge base of biologic pathways and processes," *Genome Biology*, vol. 8, no. 3, article R39, 2007.

[26] M. Dauner and U. Sauer, "Stoichiometric growth model for riboflavin-producing bacillus subtilis," *Biotechnology and Bioengineering*, vol. 76, no. 2, pp. 132–143, 2001.

[27] S. B. Roberts, J. L. Robichaux, A. K. Chavali et al., "Proteomic and network analysis characterize stage-specific metabolism in *Trypanosoma cruzi*," *BMC Systems Biology*, vol. 3, article 52, 2009.

[28] J. L. Reed, T. D. Vo, C. H. Schilling, and B. O. Palsson, "An expanded genome-scale model of *Escherichia coli* K-12 (iJR904 GSM/GPR)," *Genome Biology*, vol. 4, no. 9, p. R54, 2003.

11

Reverse Engineering Sparse Gene Regulatory Networks Using Cubature Kalman Filter and Compressed Sensing

Amina Noor,[1] Erchin Serpedin,[1] Mohamed Nounou,[2] and Hazem Nounou[3]

[1] *Department of Electrical and Computer Engineering, Texas A&M University, College Station, TX 77843-3128, USA*
[2] *Chemical Engineering Department, Texas A&M University at Qatar, 253 Texas A&M Engineering Building, Education City, P.O. Box 23874, Doha, Qatar*
[3] *Electrical Engineering Department, Texas A&M University at Qatar, 253 Texas A&M Engineering Building, Education City, P.O. Box 23874, Doha, Qatar*

Correspondence should be addressed to Amina Noor; amina@neo.tamu.edu

Academic Editor: Yufei Huang

This paper proposes a novel algorithm for inferring gene regulatory networks which makes use of cubature Kalman filter (CKF) and Kalman filter (KF) techniques in conjunction with compressed sensing methods. The gene network is described using a state-space model. A nonlinear model for the evolution of gene expression is considered, while the gene expression data is assumed to follow a linear Gaussian model. The hidden states are estimated using CKF. The system parameters are modeled as a Gauss-Markov process and are estimated using compressed sensing-based KF. These parameters provide insight into the regulatory relations among the genes. The Cramér-Rao lower bound of the parameter estimates is calculated for the system model and used as a benchmark to assess the estimation accuracy. The proposed algorithm is evaluated rigorously using synthetic data in different scenarios which include different number of genes and varying number of sample points. In addition, the algorithm is tested on the DREAM4 *in silico* data sets as well as the *in vivo* data sets from IRMA network. The proposed algorithm shows superior performance in terms of accuracy, robustness, and scalability.

1. Introduction

Gene regulation is one of the most intriguing processes taking place in living cells. With hundreds of thousands of genes at their disposal, cells must decide which genes are to express at a particular time. As the cell development evolves, different needs and functions entail an efficient mechanism to turn the required genes on while leaving the others off. Cells can also activate new genes to respond effectively to environmental changes and perform specific roles. The knowledge of which gene triggers a particular genetic condition can help us ward off the potential harmful effects by switching that gene off. For instance, cancer can be controlled by deactivating the genes that cause it.

Gene expression is the process of generating functional gene products, for example, mRNA and protein. The level of gene functionality can be measured using microarrays or gene chips to produce the gene expression data [1]. More accurate estimation of gene expression is now possible using the RNA-Seq method. Intelligent use of such data can help improve our understanding of how the genes are interacting in a living organism [2–4]. Gene regulation is known to exhibit several modes; a couple of important ones include transcription regulation and posttranscription regulation [5]. While the theoretical applications of gene regulation are extremely promising, it requires a thorough understanding of this complex process. Different genes may cooperate to produce a particular reaction, while a gene may repress another gene as well. The potential benefits of gene regulation can only be reaped if a complete and accurate picture of genetic interactions is available. A network specifying different interconnections of genes can go a long way in understanding the gene regulation mechanism. The control and interaction of genes can be described through a *gene regulatory network*. Such a network depicts various interdependencies among genes where nodes of the network represent the genes, and the edges between them correspond to an interaction among them. The strength of these interactions represents the extent to which a gene is affected by other genes in the network. A key ingredient of this approach is an accurate and representative modeling of gene networks. Precise modeling of a regulatory network coupled with efficient inference and intervention algorithms can help in devising personalized medicines and cures for genetic diseases [6].

Various methods for gene network modeling have been proposed recently in the literature with varying degrees of sophistication [7–10]. These techniques can be broadly classified as static and dynamic modeling schemes. Static modeling includes the use of correlation, statistical independence for clustering [11–13], and information theoretic criteria [14–16]. On the other hand, dynamic models provide an insight into the temporal evolution of gene expressions and hence yield a more quantitative prediction on gene network behavior [17–20]. In order to incorporate the stochasticity of gene expressions, statistical techniques have been applied [13]. A rich literature is also available on the Bayesian modeling of gene networks [21–26]. Promoted in part by the Bayesian methods, the state-space approach is a popular technique to model the gene networks [27–33], whereby the hidden states can be estimated using the Kalman filter. In the case of nonlinear functions, the extended Kalman filter (EKF) and particle filter represent feasible approaches [33, 34]. However, the EKF relies on the first-order linear approximations of nonlinearities, while the particle filter may be computationally too complex. A comprehensive review of these methods can be found in [35].

In this paper, the gene network is modeled using a state-space approach, and the cubature Kalman filter (CKF) is used to estimate the hidden states of the nonlinear model [36, 37]. The gene expressions are assumed to evolve following a sigmoid squash function, whereas a linear function is considered for the expression data. The noise is assumed to be Gaussian for both the state evolution and gene expression measurements. As the gene network is assumed sparse, any simple mean square error minimization technique will not suffice for the estimation of static parameters. Therefore, a compressed sensing-based Kalman filter (CSKF) [38] is used in conjunction with CKF for reliable estimation of parameters. In case of statistical inference, it is essential to obtain some guarantees on the performance of estimators. In this regard, the Cramér-Rao lower bound (CRB) of the parameter estimates is used as a benchmarking index to assess the mean square error (MSE) performance of the proposed estimator which is evaluated here for a parameter vector. The performance of the proposed algorithm is tested on synthetically generated random Boolean networks in various scenarios. The algorithm is also tested using DREAM4 data sets and IRMA networks [39, 40].

The main contributions of this paper can be summarized as follows.

(1) CKF is proposed for the estimation of states, and a compressed sensing-based Kalman filter is used for the estimation of system parameters. The genes are

known to interact with few other genes only necessitating the use of sparsity constraint for more accurate estimation. The proposed algorithm carries out online estimation of parameters and is therefore computationally efficient and is particularly suitable for large gene networks.

(2) The Cramér-Rao lower bound is calculated for the estimation of unknown parameters of the system. The performance of the proposed algorithm is compared to CRB. This comparison is significant as it shows room for improvement in the estimation of parameters.

(3) The proposed algorithm is compared with the EKF algorithm. Using the false alarm errors, true connections, and Hamming distance as fidelity criteria, rigorous simulations are carried out to assess the performance of the algorithm with the increase in the number of samples. In addition, receiver operating characteristic (ROC) curves are plotted to evaluate the algorithms for different network sizes. It is observed that the proposed algorithm outperforms EKF in terms of accuracy and precision. The proposed algorithm is then applied to the DREAM4 10-gene and 100-gene data sets to assess the algorithm accuracy. The underlying gene network for the IRMA data sets is also inferred.

The rest of this paper is organized as follows. Section 2 describes the underlying system model for the gene expressions. The proposed CKF algorithm in combination with CSKF for gene network inference is formulated in Section 3. The derivation of CRB is shown in Section 4, and the simulation results and their interpretation are presented in Section 5. Finally, conclusions are drawn in Section 6.

2. System Model

Gene regulatory networks can be modeled as static or dynamical systems. In this work, state-space modeling is considered which is an instance of a dynamic modeling approach and can effectively cope with time variations. The states represent gene expressions, and their evolution in time, in general, can be expressed as

$$\mathbf{x}_k = g\left(\mathbf{x}_{k-1}\right) + \mathbf{w}_k \quad k = 1, \ldots, K, \tag{1}$$

where K is the total number of data points available, $\mathbf{w}_k$ is assumed to be a zero-mean Gaussian random variable with covariance $\mathbf{Q}_k = \sigma_w^2 \mathbf{I}$, and the function $g(\cdot)$ represents the regulatory relationship between the genes and is generally nonlinear. The microarray data is a set of noisy observations and is commonly expressed as a linear Gaussian model [41]

$$\mathbf{y}_k = h\left(\mathbf{x}_k\right) + \mathbf{v}_k, \tag{2}$$

where $\mathbf{v}_k$ is Gaussian-distributed random variable with zero mean and covariance $\mathbf{S}_k = \sigma_v^2 \mathbf{I}$ and incorporates the uncertainty in the microarray experiments. In order to capture the gene interactions effectively, the following nonlinear state evolution model is assumed [33, 34]:

$$x_{k,n} = \sum_{m=1}^{N} b_{nm} f\left(x_{k-1,m}\right) + w_{k,n}, \tag{3}$$

$$k = 1,\ldots,K, \ n = 1,\ldots,N,$$

where N is the total number of genes in the network and $f(\cdot)$ is the sigmoid squash function

$$f\left(x_{k-1,m}\right) = \frac{1}{1 + e^{-x_{k-1,m}}}. \tag{4}$$

This particular choice for the nonlinear function ensures that the conditional distribution of the states remains Gaussian [41]. The multiplicative constants b_{nm} quantify the positive or negative relations between various genes in the network. A positive value of b_{nm} implies that the mth gene is activating the nth gene, whereas a negative value implies repression [34, 42]. The absolute value of these parameters indicates the strength of interaction.

The model given in (3) and (4) in the absence of any constraints may be unidentifiable and may result into overfitted solutions [43]. Assumptions on network structures are, therefore, necessary to obtain a connectivity matrix that agrees with the biological knowledge. In a gene regulatory network (GRN), the genes are known to interact with few other genes only. To this end, the coefficients b_{nm}s are estimated using sparsity constraints, as explained in the next section.

A discrete linear Gaussian model for the microarray data is considered which can be expressed at the kth time instant as [41]

$$\mathbf{y}_k = \mathbf{x}_k + \mathbf{v}_k. \tag{5}$$

Stacking the unknown parameters together, the parameter vector to be estimated is

$$\mathbf{b} \triangleq [\phi_1, \phi_2,\ldots,\phi_N], \tag{6}$$

where $\phi_n = [b_{n1},\ldots,b_{nN}]$. Plugging the values of states from (3) into (5), it follows that

$$\mathbf{y}_k = \mathbf{R}_k \mathbf{b} + \mathbf{e}_k, \tag{7}$$

where

$$\mathbf{R}_k \triangleq \begin{bmatrix} \tilde{\mathbf{f}}_k & \mathbf{0} & \mathbf{0} & \mathbf{0} \\ \mathbf{0} & \tilde{\mathbf{f}}_k & \mathbf{0} & \mathbf{0} \\ \mathbf{0} & \mathbf{0} & \ddots & \mathbf{0} \\ \mathbf{0} & \mathbf{0} & \mathbf{0} & \tilde{\mathbf{f}}_k \end{bmatrix}, \tag{8}$$

$$\tilde{\mathbf{f}}_k \triangleq \left[f\left(x_{k,1}\right) \cdots f\left(x_{k,N}\right)\right]. \tag{9}$$

Thus, the gene network inference problem boils down to the estimation of system parameters $\mathbf{b}$ using the observations $\mathbf{y}_k$, where the effective noise $\mathbf{e}_k$ is the sum of system and observation noises. The next section describes the proposed inference algorithm for sparse networks.

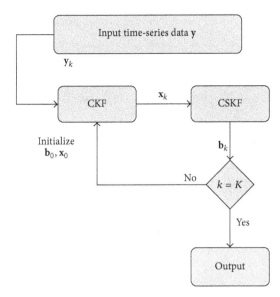

FIGURE 1: Block diagram of network inference methodology CKFS.

3. Method

In this section, the methodology proposed to infer the system parameters in (3) is described. The proposed cubature Kalman filter with sparsity constraints (CKFS) approach is succinctly illustrated in Figure 1. The specific details of this algorithm are as next presented.

3.1. Cubature Kalman Filter.
Kalman filter is a Bayesian filter which provides the optimal solution to a general linear state space inference problem depicted by (1) and (2) and assumes a recursive *predictive-update* process. The underlying assumption of Gaussianity for the predictive and the likelihood densities simplifies the Kalman filter algorithm to a two-step process, consisting of prediction and update of the mean and covariance of the hidden states. However, the presence of nonlinear functions in the state and measurement equations requires calculation of multidimensional integrals of the form *nonlinear function × Gaussian density* [36], which in general is computationally prohibitive. Several solutions to this problem have been proposed including the EKF, which linearizes the nonlinear function by taking its first-order Taylor approximation, and the unscented Kalman filter (UKF), which approximates the probability density function (PDF) using a nonlinear transformation of the random variable. Recently, a new approach, CKF, has been proposed which evaluates the integrals numerically using spherical-radial cubature rules [36].

The next two subsections briefly explain the working of Bayesian filtering and the CKF solution for the nonlinear multidimensional integrals.

3.1.1. Time Update.
Let the observations up to the time instant k be denoted by $\mathbf{d}_k$; that is, $\mathbf{d}_k \triangleq [\mathbf{y}_1^T,\ldots,\mathbf{y}_k^T]^T$. In the prediction phase, also called the time update of the Bayesian filter,

the mean and covariance of the Gaussian posterior density are computed as follows:

$$\widehat{\mathbf{x}}_{k|k-1} = E\left[\mathbf{f}\left(\mathbf{x}_{k-1}\right) \mid \mathbf{d}_{k-1}\right],$$
$$\mathbf{P}_{xx,k|k-1} = E\left[\mathbf{f}\left(\mathbf{x}_k\right)\mathbf{f}^T\left(x_k\right)\right] - \widehat{\mathbf{x}}_{k|k-1}\widehat{\mathbf{x}}_{k|k-1}^T + \mathbf{Q}_{k-1}, \tag{10}$$

where E denotes the expectation operator and $\mathbf{x}_{k-1}$ is normally distributed with parameters $(\widehat{\mathbf{x}}_{k-1|k-1}, \mathbf{P}_{xx,k-1|k-1})$. The third equality is a consequence of the zero-mean nature of Gaussian noise $\mathbf{w}$ and its independence from $\mathbf{d}_k$. The estimates $\widehat{\mathbf{x}}_{k-1|k-1}$ and $\mathbf{P}_{xx,k-1|k-1}$ are assumed to be available from the previous iteration. Here, $\mathbf{P}_{xx,k|k-1}$ is an estimate of the error covariance matrix.

3.1.2. Measurement Update. Since the measurement noise is also Gaussian, the likelihood density is given by $\mathbf{y}_{k-1} \mid \mathbf{d}_{k-1} : \mathcal{N}(\mathbf{z}_{k-1}; \widehat{\mathbf{y}}_{k|k-1}, \mathbf{P}_{xx,k|k-1})$. As the measurements become available at the kth time instant, the mean and covariance of the likelihood density are calculated as follows:

$$\widehat{\mathbf{y}}_{k|k-1} = E\left[\mathbf{y}_k \mid \mathbf{d}_{k-1}\right],$$
$$\mathbf{P}_{yy,k|k-1} = E\left[\mathbf{x}_k\mathbf{x}_k^T\right] - \widehat{\mathbf{y}}_{k|k-1}\widehat{\mathbf{y}}_{k|k-1}^T + \mathbf{S}_{k-1}. \tag{11}$$

The updated posterior density, obtained from the conditional joint density of states, and the measurements can be expressed as

$$\left(\left[\mathbf{x}_k^T\mathbf{y}_k^T\right]^T\mathbf{d}_{k-1}\right)$$
$$\sim \mathcal{N}\left(\begin{pmatrix}\widehat{\mathbf{x}}_{k|k-1}\\\widehat{\mathbf{y}}_{k|k-1}\end{pmatrix},\begin{pmatrix}\mathbf{P}_{xx,k|k-1} & \mathbf{P}_{xy,k|k-1}\\\mathbf{P}_{xy,k|k-1}^T & \mathbf{P}_{yy,k|k-1}\end{pmatrix}\right), \tag{12}$$

where

$$P_{xy,k|k-1} = E\left[\mathbf{x}_k\mathbf{x}_k^T\right] - \widehat{\mathbf{x}}_{k|k-1}\widehat{\mathbf{y}}_{k-1}^T \tag{13}$$

is the cross-covariance matrix between the states and the measurements. Hence, the states and the corresponding error covariance matrix are updated by calculating the innovation $\mathbf{z}_k - \widehat{\mathbf{z}}_{k|k-1}$ and the Kalman gain $\mathbf{K}_{G,i}$

$$\widehat{\mathbf{x}}_{k|k} = \widehat{\mathbf{x}}_{k|k-1} + \mathbf{K}_{G,k}\left(\mathbf{y}_k - \widehat{\mathbf{y}}_{k|k-1}\right),$$
$$P_{xx,k|k} = P_{xx,k|k-1} - \mathbf{K}_{G,k}P_{yy,k|k-1}\mathbf{K}_{G,k}^T, \tag{14}$$
$$\mathbf{K}_{G,k} = P_{xy,k|k-1}P_{yy,k|k-1}^{-1}.$$

The next subsection briefly describes the computation of high-dimensional integrals present in the equations above.

3.1.3. Computation of Integrals Using Spherical-Radial Cubature Points. In order to determine the expectations in (10), using a numerical integration method, a spherical-radial cubature rule is applied. This method calculates the cubature points $\mathbf{X}_{j,k-1|k-1}$ as follows [36]:

$$\mathbf{X}_{j,k-1|k-1} = \mathbf{U}_{k-1|k-1}\zeta_j + \widehat{\mathbf{x}}_{k-1|k-1}, \tag{15}$$

where $\zeta_j = \sqrt{\ell/2}[1]_j$, $j = 1, \ldots, \ell$, $\ell = 2N$ denotes the total number of cubature points and $\mathbf{U}_{k-1|k-1}$ stands for the square root of the error covariance matrix; that is,

$$\mathbf{P}_{xx,k-1|k-1} = \mathbf{U}_{k-1|k-1}\mathbf{U}_{k-1|k-1}^T. \tag{16}$$

The cubature points are updated via the state equation

$$\mathbf{X}_{j,k|k-1}^* = g\left(\mathbf{X}_{j,k-1|k-1}\right). \tag{17}$$

The propagated cubature points yield the state and error covariance estimates

$$\widehat{\mathbf{x}}_{k|k-1} = \frac{1}{\ell}\sum_{j=1}^{\ell}\mathbf{X}_{j,k|k-1}^*,$$
$$\mathbf{P}_{xx,k|k-1} = \frac{1}{\ell}\sum_{j=1}^{\ell}\mathbf{X}_{j,k|k-1}^*\mathbf{X}_{j,k|k-1}^{*T}$$
$$- \widehat{\mathbf{x}}_{k|k-1}\widehat{\mathbf{x}}_{k|k-1}^T + \mathbf{Q}_{k-1}. \tag{18}$$

The integrals in (11) and (14) can be evaluated in a similar manner. The next subsection explains the estimation of parameters in the system.

3.2. Estimation of Sparse Parameters Using Kalman Filter. The state estimates are obtained using the CKF as described in the previous subsection. In order to estimate the unknown parameters in the system model, one of the most commonly used methods involves stacking the parameters with the states and estimating them together. The estimation process performed in this manner is called *joint estimation*. Another method for the estimation of parameters consists of a two-step recursive process which is termed *dual estimation*. This process estimates the states in the first step, and with the assumption that states are known, parameters are estimated in the second step. These steps are repeated until the algorithm converges to the true values or until the amount of available observations is exhausted. This paper makes use of the latter technique.

The vector $\mathbf{b}$ as defined in (6) is assumed to be evolving as a Gauss-Markov model. As discussed previously, the states are assumed to be known at this step. The system evolution equations can therefore be expressed as

$$\mathbf{b}_k = \mathbf{b}_{k-1} + \boldsymbol{\eta}_{k-1},$$
$$\mathbf{y}_k = \mathbf{R}_k\mathbf{b}_k + \mathbf{e}_k, \tag{19}$$

where $\boldsymbol{\eta}_k$ stands for the i.i.d Gaussian noise and $\mathbf{R}_k$ is as defined in (8). It is observed that (19) is a system of linear equations with additive Gaussian noise, and therefore, the Kalman filter is the optimal choice for the estimation of parameter vector. The standard *predict* and *update* steps involved in Kalman filter are summarized as follows:

$$\hat{\mathbf{b}}_{k|k-1} = \hat{\mathbf{b}}_{k-1|k-1} + \boldsymbol{\eta}_k,$$

$$\mathbf{P}_{bb,k|k-1} = \mathbf{P}_{bb,k-1|k-1} + \boldsymbol{\Sigma}_{\eta_k},$$

$$\mathbf{u}_k = \mathbf{y}_k - \mathbf{R}_{f_k}\hat{\mathbf{b}}_k,$$

$$\mathbf{K}_G = \mathbf{P}_{bb,k|k-1}\mathbf{R}_{f_k}^T \left(\mathbf{R}_{f_k}\mathbf{P}_{bb,k|k-1}\mathbf{R}_{f_k}^T + \sigma_e^2\mathbf{I}^{-1} \right), \quad (20)$$

$$\hat{\mathbf{b}}_{k|k} = \hat{\mathbf{b}}_{k|k-1} + \mathbf{K}_G\mathbf{u}_k,$$

$$\mathbf{P}_{bb,k|k} = \left(\mathbf{I} - \mathbf{K}_G\mathbf{R}_{f_k} \right)\mathbf{P}_{bb,k|k-1},$$

where $\mathbf{K}_G$ denotes the Kalman gain and $\mathbf{P}$ represents the error covariance matrix.

The Kalman filter algorithm is based on an l_2-norm minimization criterion. As the gene networks are known to be highly sparse, the parameter vector is expected to have only a few nonzero values. A more accurate approach for estimating such a vector would be to introduce an additional constraint on its l_1-norm which is the core idea in compressed sensing [38, 44]. Such an l_1-norm constraint provides a unique solution to the underdetermined set of equations [45]. Therefore, instead of a simple l_2 norm minimization, the following constrained optimization problem is considered:

$$\min_{\hat{\mathbf{b}}_k} \left\| \hat{\mathbf{b}}_k - \mathbf{b}_k \right\|_2^2 \quad \text{s.t.} \quad \left\| \hat{\mathbf{b}}_k \right\| \le \epsilon. \quad (21)$$

The importance of this constraint can be judged by the fact that without it, the system would be rendered unidentifiable [43].

The problem (21) can be solved using a pseudomeasurement (PM) method which incorporates the inequality constraint (21) in the filtering process by assuming an artificial measurement $\|\mathbf{b}_k\|_1 - \epsilon = 0$. This is concisely expressed as

$$0 = \overline{\mathbf{R}}\hat{\mathbf{b}}_k - \epsilon, \quad \overline{\mathbf{R}}_\tau = \left[\text{sign}\left(\hat{\mathbf{b}}_\tau(1)\right), \dots, \text{sign}\left(\hat{\mathbf{b}}_\tau(N)\right) \right]. \quad (22)$$

The value of the covariance matrix $\boldsymbol{\Sigma}_\epsilon = \sigma_\epsilon^2\mathbf{I}$ of the pseudonoise ϵ is selected in a similar manner as the process noise covariance in the EKF algorithm. However, it is found that large values of variances, that is, $\sigma_\epsilon^2 \ge 100$, prove sufficient in most cases [38]. Further details on selecting these parameters can be found in [38, 46]. The PM method solves (21) in a recursive manner for K_τ iterations using the following steps:

$$\mathbf{K}_G^\tau = \mathbf{P}_\tau\overline{\mathbf{R}}_\tau^T\left(\overline{\mathbf{R}}_\tau\mathbf{P}_\tau\overline{\mathbf{R}}_\tau^T + \boldsymbol{\Sigma}_\epsilon\right)^{-1},$$

$$\hat{\mathbf{b}}_{\tau+1} = \left(\mathbf{I} - \mathbf{K}_G^\tau\overline{\mathbf{R}}_\tau\right)\hat{\mathbf{b}}_\tau, \quad (23)$$

$$\mathbf{P}_{\tau+1} = \left(\mathbf{I} - \mathbf{K}_G^\tau\overline{\mathbf{R}}_\tau\right)\mathbf{P}_\tau.$$

At each kth time instant, $\mathbf{P}_{bb,k|k}$ and $\hat{\mathbf{b}}_{k|k}$ obtained from (20) are considered as initial values; that is, $\hat{\mathbf{b}}^1 = \hat{\mathbf{b}}_{k|k}$ and $\mathbf{P}_1 = \mathbf{P}_{bb,k|k}$ which is the error covariance matrix. The value of

---

(1) Input time series data set **y**.
(2) Initialize $I, K, \phi_0, \mathbf{x}_0$.
(3) **for** $k = 1, \dots, K$ **do**
(4)   Find the state estimates using CKF following the time and measurement update steps in Section 3.
(5)   Estimate parameters $\hat{\mathbf{b}}_k$ from $\mathbf{x}_k$ and $\mathbf{y}_k$ using (20).
(6)   **for** $\tau = 1, \dots, K_\tau$ **do**
(7)   Update the parameters $\hat{\mathbf{b}}_k$ using (23).
(8)   **end for**
(9) **end for**
(10) **return**

ALGORITHM 1: Network inference: CKFS.

K_τ is equal to the number of constraints, that is, the expected number of nonzero $\mathbf{b}_{mn}$s in the system. Possible ways for calculating K_τ include minimum description length (MDL) principle and Bayesian information criterion (BIC).

3.3. Inference Algorithm. The network inference algorithm is summarized in Algorithm 1. The algorithm consists of a recursive process which repeats itself for the number of observations present in the time-series data. For each time sample, the state estimate is obtained using the CKF, and the parameter estimate is obtained using the KF. Since the parameters are expected to be sparse, the estimates are then refined further using the CSKF algorithm. This iterative process results in a simple and accurate algorithm for gene network inference while considering a complex nonlinear model.

4. Cramér-Rao Bound

The performance of an estimator can be judged by comparing it with theoretical lower bounds proposed in parameter estimation theory. The CRB establishes a lower bound on the MSE of an unbiased estimator [47]. In particular, the CRB states that the covariance matrix of the estimator $\hat{\mathbf{b}}$ is lower bounded by

$$\mathbb{E}\left[\left(\hat{\mathbf{b}} - \mathbf{b}\right)\left(\hat{\mathbf{b}} - \mathbf{b}\right)^T\right] \succeq \left[\mathbf{I}\left(\mathbf{b}\right)\right]^{-1}, \quad (24)$$

where the matrix inequality $\succeq$ is to be interpreted in the semidefinite sense and $\mathbf{I}(\mathbf{b})$ is the Fisher information matrix (FIM)

$$\mathbf{I}\left(\mathbf{b}\right) = \mathbb{E}\left[\left(\frac{\partial \ln f\left(\mathbf{y} \mid \mathbf{b}\right)}{\partial \mathbf{b}}\right)\left(\frac{\partial \ln f\left(\mathbf{y} \mid \mathbf{b}\right)}{\partial \mathbf{b}}\right)^T\right]. \quad (25)$$

The CRB for gene network inference can be calculated as follows. By stacking all the observations for $k = 1, \dots, K$, (7) can be written compactly in the matrix form

$$\mathbf{y} = \mathbf{Rb} + \mathbf{e}, \quad (26)$$

where $\mathbf{y} = [\mathbf{y}_1^T, \ldots, \mathbf{y}_K^T]^T$, $\mathbf{R} = [\mathbf{R}_1^T, \ldots, \mathbf{R}_K^T]^T$, and $\mathbf{e} = [\mathbf{e}_1^T, \ldots, \mathbf{e}_K^T]^T$. The PDF $p(\mathbf{y} \mid \mathbf{b})$ is expressed as

$$p(\mathbf{y} \mid \mathbf{b}) = C \exp\left(-\frac{(\mathbf{y} - \mathbf{Rb})^T (\mathbf{y} - \mathbf{Rb})}{2\sigma_e^2}\right), \quad (27)$$

where C is a constant. The derivative of $\ln p(\mathbf{y} \mid \mathbf{b})$ can be expressed as

$$\frac{\partial \ln p(\mathbf{y} \mid \mathbf{b})}{\partial \mathbf{b}} = -\frac{\partial}{\partial \mathbf{b}}\left[\frac{(\mathbf{y} - \mathbf{Rb})^T (\mathbf{y} - \mathbf{Rb})}{\sigma_e^2}\right]$$
$$= \frac{\mathbf{R}^T \mathbf{y} - \mathbf{R}^T \mathbf{Rb}}{\sigma_e^2}. \quad (28)$$

It now follows that

$$\left(\frac{\partial \ln p(\mathbf{y} \mid \mathbf{b})}{\partial \mathbf{b}}\right)\left(\frac{\partial \ln p(\mathbf{y} \mid \mathbf{b})}{\partial \mathbf{b}}\right)^T$$
$$= \frac{\mathbf{R}^T (\mathbf{y} - \mathbf{Rb})(\mathbf{y} - \mathbf{Rb})^T \mathbf{R}}{\sigma_e^4}. \quad (29)$$

By taking the expectation of (29), the FIM in (25) is given by

$$\mathbf{I}(\mathbf{b}) = \frac{\mathbf{R}^T \mathbf{R}}{\sigma_e^2}. \quad (30)$$

The inverse of the FIM in (30) can be used to place a lower bound on the estimation error of the parameter vector $\mathbf{b}$. Figure 2 shows the comparison of MSE of CKFS algorithm with CRB as a function of number of samples K for one representative gene from the eight-gene network considered in Section 5.1. It is observed that the MSE of the estimated parameters decreases with increasing number of samples.

5. Results and Discussion

The simulation results of the CKFS algorithm are discussed in this section. The performance is first tested on synthetic data obtained from randomly generated Boolean networks under various scenarios and performance metrics. The algorithm is then assessed on the DREAM4 networks and the IRMA network.

5.1. Synthetic Data. Time-series data is produced from randomly generated Boolean networks using the system model (3) and (5). Two scenarios are considered for this purpose.

First, the comparison is performed by varying the number of sample size while keeping the network size fixed. The gene network consists of 8 genes and 20 vertices. In terms of network estimation, if the algorithm predicts an edge between two nodes which may not be present in reality, an error, referred to as *false alarm error* (F), is said to have occurred. Another situation is the indication of the absence of a vertex in the graph which in fact is present in the real network. This kind of error is termed *missed detection* (M). The summation of these two errors normalized over the total

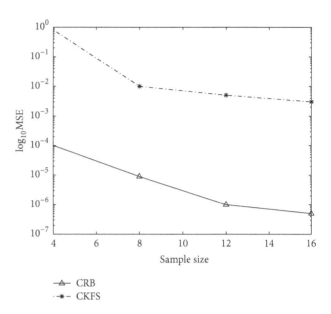

FIGURE 2: Cramér-Rao bound on the estimation of parameters. The MSE for one of the representative θ is shown here for a network consisting of 8 vertices.

number of vertices in the network yields the *Hamming distance*. It is also important to consider the probability of predicting the true connections correctly which will be assessed by the *true connections* (T) metric. An algorithm with low Hamming distance and small false alarm error is particularly desirable as predicting an edge erroneously can be troublesome for biologists. True connections indicate the reliability of the predictions. Figure 3 illustrates the performance of the CKFS algorithm and that of the EKF algorithm proposed in [34] in terms of the metrics described above. It is important to mention here that the same system model is assumed by both CKFS and EKF algorithms for the purpose of this simulation. These metrics are the same as those used in [15]. The variances of both the system and measurement noises, σ_w^2 and σ_v^2, respectively, are taken to be 10^{-5} in all the simulations and are assumed to be known. It is noticed that EKF has a slightly lower false alarm rate when the number of samples is small; however, as the number of samples increases, CKFS yields a lower false alarm error. The Hamming distance for CKFS is also smaller than EKF indicating lesser cumulative error. True connections show a consistent behavior for the two algorithms when the number of samples is increased where CKFS is able to predict connections more accurately. These experiments show the superiority of CKFS in terms of lower error rate.

To obtain a more rigorous evaluation, the performance of algorithms is then compared in a scenario which considers the sample size to be fixed and assumes networks of different sizes. The receiver operating characteristic (ROC) curves are plotted as performance measures. A higher area under the ROC curve (AUROC) shows more true positives for a given false positive, and therefore, indicates better classification. The performance of CKFS(N, E, K) and EKF(N, E, K) is shown in Figure 4, where N stands for the number of nodes,

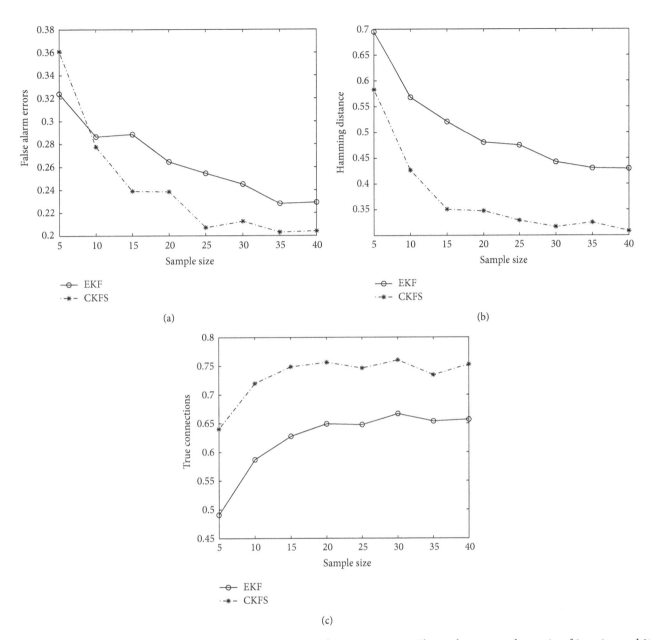

FIGURE 3: (a), (b), and (c) False alarm errors, Hamming distance, and true connections. The synthetic networks consist of 8 vertices and 20 edges. The metric is normalized over the number of edges. CKFS gives lower error and predicts more true connections with the increase in the sample size of data.

E represents the number of edges, and K denotes the time points. It is observed that the CKFS exhibits superior performance than the EKF for networks of different sizes.

The complexity of the two algorithms is compared for synthetically generated networks with number of genes equal to 10, 20, 30, and 40. The sample size is kept to 50 time points for each of these networks, and the run time for EKF and CKFS algorithms is calculated as shown in Table 1. It is noted that EKF is faster for smaller network sizes, but as the network size increases, the run time gets much larger than that for CKFS. The main reason for this is that EKF [34] estimates the states and parameters by stacking them together which requires large-sized matrix multiplications at each iteration.

The benefit associated with performing dual estimation, as in CKFS, is that the parameters are estimated separately from the states. Since the system is linear and one-to-one for parameters, inversion of much smaller matrices can be performed reducing the computational complexity of CKFS algorithm. CKFS is therefore particularly attractive for large-sized networks.

5.2. DREAM4 Gene Networks. Several *in silico* networks have been produced in order to benchmark the performance of gene network inference algorithms. dialogue on reverse engineering assessment and methods (DREAM) *in silico* networks serve as one of the popular methods used for this

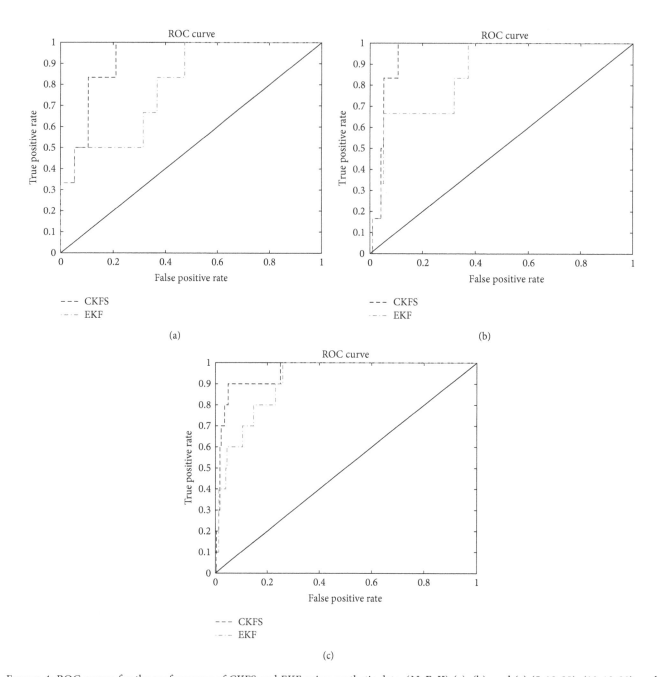

FIGURE 4: ROC curves for the performance of CKFS and EKF using synthetic data. (N, E, K) (a), (b), and (c) $(5, 10, 20)$, $(10, 12, 20)$, and $(15, 19, 20)$. The area under the ROC curve for CKFS is more than that for EKF for various sized networks.

TABLE 1: Run time in seconds for EKF and CKFS algorithms for varying network sizes for synthetically generated data. The number of sample points is fixed to 50.

Number of genes	10	20	30	40
EKF	0.16	1.9	16.5	84
CKFS	1.2	4.3	11.5	24.1

purpose [39, 48]. In this section, the performance of the CKFS algorithm is evaluated using the 10-gene and 100-gene networks released online by the DREAM4 challenge.

Five networks are produced using the known GRNs of *Escherichia coli* and *Saccharomyces cerevisiae*. The data sets for each of 10-gene network consists of 21 data points for five different perturbations. The inference is performed by using all the perturbations. The 100-gene network consists of data sets for ten perturbations. AUROC and area under the precision-recall curve (AUPR) are calculated for the five networks of both the data sets and shown in Tables 2 and 3, respectively. The quantities, *precision* and *recall*, are defined as $P = T/(T + F)$ and $R = T/(T + M)$, respectively. For comparison purposes, the values of the two quantities for time-series network identification (TSNI) algorithm that

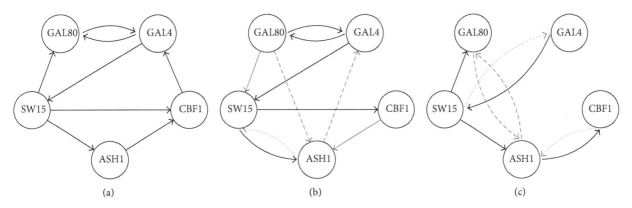

FIGURE 5: The inferred IRMA networks. (a), (b), and (c) Gold standard, inferred network using CKFS, and inferred network using ODE [39, 40]. Black arrows indicate true connections, blue arrows indicate the edges that are correct, but their directions are reversed, and red arrows indicate false positives.

TABLE 2: Area under the ROC curve (AUROC) and area under the PR curve (AUPR) for DREAM4 10-gene networks for the five different networks.

Algorithm	Network 1	Network 2	Network 3	Network 4	Network 5
ODE [39]	0.62 (0.27)	0.63 (0.32)	0.58 (0.21)	0.63 (0.23)	0.68 (0.25)
CKFS	0.63 (0.40)	0.67 (0.50)	0.72 (0.50)	0.75 (0.49)	0.81 (0.42)
Random [39]	0.55 (0.18)	0.55 (0.19)	0.55 (0.17)	0.57 (0.17)	0.56 (0.16)

TABLE 3: Area under the ROC curve (AUROC) and area under the PR curve (AUPR) for DREAM4 100-gene networks for the five different networks.

Algorithm	Network 1	Network 2	Network 3	Network 4	Network 5
ODE [39]	0.55 (0.02)	0.55 (0.03)	0.60 (0.03)	0.54 (0.02)	0.59 (0.03)
CKFS	0.67 (0.13)	0.57 (0.08)	0.60 (0.10)	0.62 (0.10)	0.60 (0.07)
Random [39]	0.50 (0.002)	0.50 (0.002)	0.50 (0.002)	0.50 (0.002)	0.50 (0.002)

exploits ordinary differential equations are also given [39]. The CKFS algorithm is found to perform significantly better than the TSNI algorithm.

5.3. IRMA Gene Network. In addition to synthetic data, it is imperative to test the algorithms using real biological data. In this subsection, the performance of the CKFS algorithm is assessed using the *in vivo* reverse-engineering and modeling assessment (IRMA) network [40]. This network consists of five genes. Galactose activates the gene expression in the network, whereas glucose deactivates it. The cells are grown in the presence of galactose and then switched to glucose to obtain the switch-off data which represents the expressive samples at 21 time points. The switch-on data consists of 16 sample points and is obtained by growing the cells in a glucose medium and then changing to galactose. The system and measurement noise variances for the CKFS are assumed to be identical as in the previous simulations. Figure 5 shows the inferred network, the gold standard, and the network inferred using TSNI. It is observed that the CKFS algorithm succeeds

to predict most of the interactions while giving lower false positives.

6. Conclusions

This paper presents a novel algorithm for inferring gene regulatory networks from time-series data. Gene regulation is assumed to follow a nonlinear state evolution model. The parameters of the system, which indicate the inhibitory or excitatory relationships between the genes, are estimated using compressed sensing-based Kalman filtering. The sparsity constraint on the parameters is crucial because the genes are known to interact with few other genes only. The use of CKF and the dual estimation of states and parameters renders the algorithm computationally efficient. The performance of CKFS is evaluated for synthetic data for different network sizes as well as varying sample points. ROC curves, Hamming distance, and true positives are used for comparing the accuracy of inferred network with EKF. It is observed that CKFS outperforms the EKF algorithm. In addition, CKFS gives advantages over EKF in terms of smaller run time for large networks. The Cramér-Rao lower bound is also determined for the parameters of the model and compared with the MSE performance of the proposed algorithm. Assessment using DREAM4 10-gene and 100-gene networks and IRMA network data corroborates the superior performance of CKFS. Future research directions include incorporating the estimation of model order in the network inference algorithm.

Acknowledgments

This work was supported by US National Science Foundation (NSF) Grant 0915444 and QNRF-NPRP Grant 09-874-3-235. The material in this paper was presented in part at the IEEE International Workshop on Genomic Signal Processing and Statistics (GENSIPS), San Antonio, TX, USA, December 2011.

References

[1] X. Zhou, X. Wang, and E. R. Dougherty, *Genomic Networks: Statistical Inference from Microarray Data*, John Wiley & Sons, New York, NY, USA, 2006.

[2] H. Kitano, "Computational systems biology," *Nature*, vol. 420, pp. 206–210, 2002.

[3] X. Zhou and S. T. C. Wong, *Computational Systems Bioinformatics*, World Scientific, River Edge, NJ, USA, 2008.

[4] X. Cai and X. Wang, "Stochastic modeling and simulation of gene networks," *IEEE Signal Processing Magazine*, vol. 24, no. 1, pp. 27–36, 2007.

[5] D. Yue, J. Meng, M. Lu, C. L. P. Chen, M. Guo, and Y. Huang, "Understanding micro-RNA regulation: a computational perspective," *IEEE Signal Processing Magazine*, vol. 29, no. 1, pp. 77–88, 2012.

[6] R. Pal, S. Bhattacharya, and M. U. Caglar, "Robust approaches for genetic regulatory network modeling and intervention: a review of recent advances," *IEEE Signal Processing Magazine*, vol. 29, no. 1, pp. 66–76, 2012.

[7] H. Hache, H. Lehrach, and R. Herwig, "Reverse engineering of gene regulatory networks: a comparative study," *Eurasip Journal on Bioinformatics and Systems Biology*, vol. 2009, Article ID 617281, 2009.

[8] T. Schlitt and A. Brazma, "Current approaches to gene regulatory network modelling," *BMC Bioinformatics*, vol. 8, no. 6, p. 9, 2007.

[9] H. D. Jong, "Modeling and simulation of genetic regulatoy systems: a literature review," *Journal of Computational Biology*, vol. 9, no. 1, pp. 67–103, 2002.

[10] I. Nachman, A. Regev, and N. Friedman, "Inferring quantitative models of regulatory networks from expression data," *Bioinformatics*, vol. 20, no. 1, pp. i248–i256, 2004.

[11] C. D. Giurcaneanu, I. Tabus, and J. Astola, "Clustering time series gene expression data based on sum-of-exponentials fitting," *EURASIP Journal on Advances in Signal Processing*, vol. 2005, no. 8, Article ID 358568, pp. 1159–1173, 2005.

[12] C. D. Giurcaneanu, I. Tabus, J. Astola, J. Ollila, and M. Vihinen, "Fast iterative gene clustering based on information theoretic criteria for selecting the cluster structure," *Journal of Computational Biology*, vol. 11, no. 4, pp. 660–682, 2004.

[13] X. Cai and G. B. Giannakis, "Identifying differentially expressed genes in microarray experiments with model-based variance estimation," *IEEE Transactions on Signal Processing*, vol. 54, no. 6, pp. 2418–2426, 2006.

[14] X. Zhou, X. Wang, and E. R. Dougherty, "Gene clustering based on cluster-wide mutual information," *Journal of Computational Biology*, vol. 11, no. 1, pp. 151–165, 2004.

[15] W. Zhao, E. Serpedin, and E. R. Dougherty, "Inferring connectivity of genetic regulatory networks using informationtheoretic criteria," *IEEE/ACM Transactions on Computational Biology and Bioinformatics*, vol. 5, no. 2, pp. 262–274, 2008.

[16] J. Dougherty, I. Tabus, and J. Astola, "Inference of gene regulatory networks based on a universal minimum description length," *Eurasip Journal on Bioinformatics and Systems Biology*, vol. 2008, Article ID 482090, 2008.

[17] L. Qian, H. Wang, and E. R. Dougherty, "Inference of noisy nonlinear differential equation models for gene regulatory networks using genetic programming and Kalman filtering," *IEEE Transactions on Signal Processing*, vol. 56, no. 7, pp. 3327–3339, 2008.

[18] W. Zhao, E. Serpedin, and E. R. Dougherty, "Inferring gene regulatory networks from time series data using the minimum description length principle," *Bioinformatics*, vol. 22, no. 17, pp. 2129–2135, 2006.

[19] X. Zhou, X. Wang, R. Pal, I. Ivanov, M. Bittner, and E. R. Dougherty, "A Bayesian connectivity-based approach to constructing probabilistic gene regulatory networks," *Bioinformatics*, vol. 20, no. 17, pp. 2918–2927, 2004.

[20] J. Meng, M. Lu, Y. Chen, S.-J. Gao, and Y. Huang, "Robust inference of the context specific structure and temporal dynamics of gene regulatory network," *BMC Genomics*, vol. 11, no. 3, p. S11, 2010.

[21] Y. Zhang, Z. Deng, H. Jiang, and P. Jia, "Inferring gene regulatory networks from multiple data sources via a dynamic Bayesian network with structural em.," in *DILS*, S. C. Boulakia and V. Tannen, Eds., vol. 4544 of *Lecture Notes in Computer Science*, pp. 204–214, Springer, New York, NY, USA, 2007.

[22] K. Murphy and S. Mian, Modeling gene expression data using dynamic Bayesian networks, University of California, Berkeley, Calif, USA, 2001.

[23] H. Liu, D. Yue, L. Zhang, Y. Chen, S. J. Gao, and Y. Huang, "A Bayesian approach for identifying miRNA targets by combining sequence prediction and gene expression profiling," *BMC Genomics*, vol. 11, no. 3, p. S12, 2010.

[24] Y. Huang, J. Wang, J. Zhang, M. Sanchez, and Y. Wang, "Bayesian inference of genetic regulatory networks from time series microarray data using dynamic Bayesian networks," *Journal of Multimedia*, vol. 2, no. 3, pp. 46–56, 2007.

[25] B.-E. Perrin, L. Ralaivola, A. Mazurie, S. Bottani, J. Mallet, and F. D'Alché-Buc, "Gene networks inference using dynamic Bayesian networks," *Bioinformatics*, vol. 19, no. 2, pp. ii138–ii148, 2003.

[26] C. Rangel, D. L. Wild, F. Falciani, Z. Ghahramani, and A. Gaiba, "A. modelling biological responses using gene expression profiling and linear dynamical systems," *Bioinformatics*, pp. 349–356, 2005.

[27] M. Quach, N. Brunel, and F. d'Alch Buc, "Estimating parameters and hidden variables in non-linear state-space models based on ODEs for biological networks inference," *Bioinformatics*, vol. 23, no. 23, pp. 3209–3216, 2007.

[28] F.-X. Wu, W.-J. Zhang, and A. J. Kusalik, "Modeling gene expression from microarray expression data with state-space

equations," in *Pacific Symposium on Biocomputing*, R. B. Altman, A. K. Dunker, L. Hunter, T. A. Jung, and T. E. Klein, Eds., pp. 581–592, World Scientific, River Edge, NJ, USA, 2004.

[29] R. Yamaguchi, S. Yoshida, S. Imoto, T. Higuchi, and S. Miyano, "Finding module-based gene networks with state-space modelsmining high-dimensional and short time-course gene expression data," *IEEE Signal Processing Magazine*, vol. 24, no. 1, pp. 37–46, 2007.

[30] O. Hirose, R. Yoshida, S. Imoto et al., "Statistical inference of transcriptional module-based gene networks from time course gene expression profiles by using state space models," *Bioinformatics*, vol. 24, no. 7, pp. 932–942, 2008.

[31] J. Angus, M. Beal, J. Li, C. Rangel, and D. Wild, "Inferring transcriptional networks using prior biological knowledge and constrained state-space models," in *Learning and Inference in Computational Systems Biology*, N. Lawrence, M. Girolami, M. Rattray, and G. Sanguinetti, Eds., pp. 117–152, MIT Press, Cambridge, UK, 2010.

[32] C. Rangel, J. Angus, Z. Ghahramani et al., "Modeling T-cell activation using gene expression profiling and state-space models," *Bioinformatics*, vol. 20, no. 9, pp. 1361–1372, 2004.

[33] A. Noor, E. Serpedin, M. N. Nounou, and H. N. Nounou, "Inferring gene regulatory networks via nonlinear state-space models and exploiting sparsity," *IEEE/ACM Transactions on Computational Biology and Bioinformatics*, vol. 9, no. 4, pp. 1203–1211, 2012.

[34] Z. Wang, X. Liu, Y. Liu, J. Liang, and V. Vinciotti, "An extended kalman filtering approach to modeling nonlinear dynamic gene regulatory networks via short gene expression time series," *IEEE/ACM Transactions on Computational Biology and Bioinformatics*, vol. 6, no. 3, pp. 410–419, 2009.

[35] A. Noor, E. Serpedin, M. Nounou, H. Nounou, N. Mohamed, and L. Chouchane, "An overview of the statistical methods used for inferring gene regulatory networks and proteinprotein interaction networks," *Advances in Bioinformatics*, vol. 2013, Article ID 953814, 12 pages, 2013.

[36] I. Arasaratnam and S. Haykin, "Cubature kalman filters," *IEEE Transactions on Automatic Control*, vol. 54, no. 6, pp. 1254–1269, 2009.

[37] A. Noor, E. Serpedin, M. N. Nounou, and H. N. Nounou, "A cubature Kalman filter approach for inferring gene regulatory networks using time series data," in *Proceedings of the IEEE International Workshop on Genomic Signal Processing and Statistics (GENSIPS '11)*, pp. 25–28, 2011.

[38] A. Carmi, P. Gurfil, and D. Kanevsky, "Methods for sparse signal recovery using kalman filtering with embedded rseudomeasurement norms and quasi-norms," *IEEE Transactions on Signal Processing*, vol. 58, no. 4, pp. 2405–2409, 2010.

[39] C. A. Penfold and D. L. Wild, "How to infer gene networks from expression profiles, revisited," *Interface Focus*, pp. 857–870, 2011.

[40] I. Cantone, L. Marucci, F. Iorio et al., "A yeast synthetic network for *in vivo* assessment of reverse-engineering and modeling approaches," *Cell*, vol. 137, no. 1, pp. 172–181, 2009.

[41] Y. Huang, I. M. Tienda-Luna, and Y. Wang, "Reverse engineering gene regulatory networks: a survey of statistical models," *IEEE Signal Processing Magazine*, vol. 26, no. 1, pp. 76–97, 2009.

[42] Z. Wang, F. Yang, D. W. C. Ho, S. Swift, A. Tucker, and X. Liu, "Stochastic dynamic modeling of short gene expression time-series data," *IEEE Transactions on Nanobioscience*, vol. 7, no. 1, pp. 44–55, 2008.

[43] H. Xiong and Y. Choe, "Structural systems identification of genetic regulatory networks," *Bioinformatics*, vol. 24, no. 4, pp. 553–560, 2008.

[44] R. Tibshirani, "Regression shrinkage and selection via the lasso," *Journal of the Royal Statistical Society B*, vol. 58, no. 1, pp. 267–288, 1996.

[45] E. J. Cands and T. Tao, "Decoding by linear programming," *IEEE Transactions on Information Theory*, vol. 51, no. 12, pp. 4203–4215, 2005.

[46] J. D. Geeter, H. V. Brussel, and J. D. Schutter, "A smoothly constrained Kalman filter," *IEEE Transactions on Pattern Analysis and Machine Intelligence*, vol. 19, no. 10, pp. 1171–1177, 1997.

[47] S. M. Kay, *Fundamentals of Statistical Signal Processing. Estimation Theory*, Prentice-Hall, New York, NY, USA, 1993.

[48] http://wiki.c2b2.columbia.edu/dream/.

12

Spectral Analysis on Time-Course Expression Data: Detecting Periodic Genes Using a Real-Valued Iterative Adaptive Approach

Kwadwo S. Agyepong,[1] Fang-Han Hsu,[1] Edward R. Dougherty,[1,2] and Erchin Serpedin[1]

[1] *Department of Electrical and Computer Engineering, Texas A&M University, College Station, TX 77843-3128, USA*
[2] *Computational Biology Division, Translational Genomics Research Institute, Phoenix, AZ 85004-2101, USA*

Correspondence should be addressed to Erchin Serpedin; serpedin@ece.tamu.edu

Academic Editor: Mohamed Nounou

Time-course expression profiles and methods for spectrum analysis have been applied for detecting transcriptional periodicities, which are valuable patterns to unravel genes associated with cell cycle and circadian rhythm regulation. However, most of the proposed methods suffer from restrictions and large false positives to a certain extent. Additionally, in some experiments, arbitrarily irregular sampling times as well as the presence of high noise and small sample sizes make accurate detection a challenging task. A novel scheme for detecting periodicities in time-course expression data is proposed, in which a real-valued iterative adaptive approach (RIAA), originally proposed for signal processing, is applied for periodogram estimation. The inferred spectrum is then analyzed using Fisher's hypothesis test. With a proper p-value threshold, periodic genes can be detected. A periodic signal, two nonperiodic signals, and four sampling strategies were considered in the simulations, including both bursts and drops. In addition, two yeast real datasets were applied for validation. The simulations and real data analysis reveal that RIAA can perform competitively with the existing algorithms. The advantage of RIAA is manifested when the expression data are highly irregularly sampled, and when the number of cycles covered by the sampling time points is very reduced.

1. Introduction

Patterns of periodic gene expression have been found to be associated with essential biological processes such as cell cycle and circadian rhythm [1], and the detection of periodic genes is crucial to advance our understanding of gene function, disease pathways, and, ultimately, therapeutic solutions. Using high-throughput technologies such as microarrays, gene expression profiles at discrete time points can be derived and hundreds of cell cycle regulated genes have been reported in a variety of species. For example, Spellman et al. applied cell synchronization methods and conducted time-course gene expression experiments on *Saccharomyces cerevisiae* [2]. The authors identified 800 cell cycle regulated genes using DNA microarrays. Also, Rustici et al. and Menges et al. identified 407 and about 500 cell cycle regulated genes in *Schizosaccharomyces pombe* and *Arabidopsis*, respectively [3, 4].

Signal processing in the frequency domain simplifies the analysis and an emerging number of studies have demonstrated the power of spectrum analysis in the detection of periodic genes. Considering the common issues of missing values and noise in microarray experiments, Ahdesmäki et al. proposed a robust detection method incorporating the fast Fourier transform (FFT) with a series of data preprocessing and hypothesis testing steps [5]. Two years later, the authors further proposed a modified version for expression data with unevenly spaced time intervals [6]. A Lomb-Scargle (LS) approach, originally used for finding periodicities in astrophysics, was developed for expression data with uneven sampling [7]. Yang et al. further improved the performance using a detrended fluctuation analysis [8]. It used harmonic regression in the time domain for significance evaluation. The method was termed "Lomb-Scargle periodogram and harmonic regression (LSPR)." Basically, these methods consists of two steps: transferring the signals into the frequency (spectral) domain and then applying a significance evaluation test for the resulting peak in the spectral density.

While numerous methods have been developed for detecting periodicities in gene expression, most of these methods suffer from false positive errors and working restrictions to a certain extent, particularly when the time-course data contain limited time points. In addition, no algorithm seems available to resolve all of these challenges. Microarray as well as other high-throughput experiments, due to high manufacturing and preparation costs, have common characteristics of small sample size [9], noisy measurements [10], and arbitrary sampling strategies [11], thereby making the detection of periodicities highly challenging. Since the number and functions of cell cycle regulated genes, or periodic genes, remain greatly uncertain, advances in detection algorithms are urgently needed.

Recently, Stoica et al. developed a novel nonparametric method, termed the "real-valued iterative adaptive approach (RIAA)," specifically for spectral analysis with nonuniformly sampled data [12]. As stated by the authors, RIAA, an iteratively weighted least-squares periodogram, can provide robust spectral estimates and is most suitable for sinusoidal signals. These characteristics of RIAA inspired us to apply it to time-course gene expression data and conduct an examination on its performance. Herein, we incorporate RIAA with a Fisher's statistic to detect transcriptional periodicities. A rigorous comparison of RIAA with several aforementioned algorithms in terms of sensitivities and specificities is conducted through simulations and simulation results dealing with real data analysis are also provided.

In this study, we found that the RIAA algorithm can provide robust spectral estimates for the detection of periodic genes regardless of the sampling strategies adopted in the experiments or the nonperiodic nature of noise present in the measurement process. We show through simulations that the RIAA can outperform the existing algorithms particularly when the data are highly irregularly sampled, and when the number of cycles covered by the sampling time points is very few. These characteristics of RIAA fit perfectly the needs of time-course gene expression data analysis. This paper is organized as follows. In Section 2, we begin with an overview of RIAA. In Section 3, a scheme for detecting periodicities is proposed, and simulation models for performance evaluation and a real data analysis for validation purposes are presented. A complete investigation of the performance of RIAA and a rigorous comparison with other algorithms are provided in Section 4.

2. RIAA Algorithm

RIAA is an iterative algorithm developed for finding the least-squares periodogram with the utilization of a weighted function. The essential mathematics involved in RIAA is introduced in this section with the algorithm input being time-course expression data; for more details regarding RIAA, the readers are encouraged to check the original paper by Stoica et al. [12].

2.1. Basics.
Suppose that the signals associated with the periodic gene expressions are composed of noise and sinusoidal components. Let $y_h(t_i)$, $i = 1, \ldots, n$, denote the time-course expression ratios of gene h at instances $t_1, \ldots, t_n$, respectively; $y_h(t_i)$ are real numbers; $\sum_{i=1}^{n} y_h(t_i) = 0$. The least-squares periodogram Φ_{lsp} is given by

$$\Phi_{lsp} = |\widehat{\alpha}(\omega)|^2, \tag{1}$$

where $\widehat{\alpha}(\omega)$ is the solution to the following fitting problem:

$$\widehat{\alpha}(\omega) = \arg\min_{\alpha(\omega)} \sum_{i=1}^{n} \left[y_h(t_i) - \alpha(\omega) e^{j\omega t_i} \right]^2. \tag{2}$$

Let $\alpha(\omega) = |\alpha(\omega)| e^{j\phi(\omega)} = \beta e^{j\theta}$, where $\beta = |\alpha(\omega)| \geq 0$ and $\theta = \phi(\omega) \in [0, 2\pi]$ refer to the amplitude and phase of $\alpha(\omega)$, respectively. The criterion in (2) can then be rewritten as

$$\sum_{i=1}^{n} \left[y_h(t_i) - \beta \cos(\omega t_i + \theta) \right]^2 + \beta^2 \sum_{i=1}^{n} \sin^2(\omega t_i + \theta). \tag{3}$$

The second term in the above equation is data independent and can be omitted from the minimization operation. Hence, the criterion (2) is simplified to

$$\left(\widehat{\beta}, \widehat{\theta} \right) = \arg\min_{\beta, \theta} \sum_{i=1}^{n} \left[y_h(t_i) - \beta \cos(\omega t_i + \theta) \right]^2. \tag{4}$$

We further apply $a = \beta \cos(\theta)$ and $b = -\beta \sin(\theta)$ and derive an equivalent of (4) as follows:

$$\left(\widehat{a}, \widehat{b} \right) = \arg\min_{a,b} \sum_{i=1}^{n} \left[y_h(t_i) - a \cos(\omega t_i) - b \sin(\omega t_i) \right]^2. \tag{5}$$

The target of interest to the fitting problem now becomes $\widehat{a}$ and $\widehat{b}$ (instead of $\alpha(\omega)$), and the solution is well known to be

$$\begin{bmatrix} \widehat{a} \\ \widehat{b} \end{bmatrix} = \mathbf{R}^{-1} \mathbf{r}, \tag{6}$$

where

$$\mathbf{R} = \sum_{i=1}^{n} \begin{bmatrix} \cos(\omega t_i)^2 & \cos(\omega t_i) \sin(\omega t_i) \\ \sin(\omega t_i) \cos(\omega t_i) & \sin(\omega t_i)^2 \end{bmatrix},$$

$$\mathbf{r} = \sum_{i=1}^{n} \begin{bmatrix} \cos(\omega t_i) \\ \sin(\omega t_i) \end{bmatrix} y_h(t_i). \tag{7}$$

After $\widehat{a}$ and $\widehat{b}$ are estimated, the least-squares periodogram can be derived.

2.2. Observation Interval and Resolution.
Prior to implementation of RIAA for periodogram estimation, the observation interval $[0, \omega_{max}]$ and the resolution in terms of grid size have to be selected. To this end, the maximum frequency ω_{max} in the observation interval without aliasing errors for sampling instances $t_1, \ldots, t_n$, can be evaluated by

$$\omega_{max} = \frac{\omega_0}{2}, \tag{8}$$

where ω_0 is given by

$$\omega_0 = \frac{2(n-1)\pi}{\sum_{i=1}^{n-1}(t_{i+1} - t_i)}. \tag{9}$$

The observation interval $[0, \omega_{max}]$ is hence chosen after ω_{max} is obtained.

To ensure that the smallest frequency separation in time-course expression data with regular or irregular sampling can be adequately detected, the grid size $\Delta\omega$ is chosen to be

$$\Delta\omega = \frac{2\pi}{t_n - t_1}, \tag{10}$$

which, in fact, is the resolution limit of the least-squares periodogram. As a result, the frequency grids ω_g considered in periodogram are

$$\omega_g = g\Delta\omega, \quad g = 1, \ldots, G, \tag{11}$$

where the number of grids G is given by

$$G = \left\lfloor \frac{\omega_{max}}{\Delta\omega} \right\rfloor. \tag{12}$$

2.3. Implementation. The following notations are introduced for the implementation of RIAA at a specific frequency ω_g:

$$\mathbf{Y} = [y_h(t_1) \quad \cdots \quad y_h(t_n)]^T,$$

$$\rho_g = [a(\omega_g) \quad b(\omega_g)]^T, \tag{13}$$

$$\mathbf{A}_g = [\mathbf{c}_g \quad \mathbf{s}_g],$$

where

$$\mathbf{c}_g = [\cos(\omega_g t_1) \quad \cdots \quad \cos(\omega_g t_n)]^T,$$

$$\mathbf{s}_g = [\sin(\omega_g t_1) \quad \cdots \quad \sin(\omega_g t_n)]^T, \tag{14}$$

and $a(\omega_g)$ and $b(\omega_g)$ denote variables a and b at frequency ω_g, respectively.

RIAA's salient feature is the addition of a weighted matrix $\mathbf{Q}_g$ to the least-squares fitting criterion. The weighted matrix $\mathbf{Q}_g$ can be viewed as a covariance matrix encapsulating the contributions of noise and other sinusoidal components in $\mathbf{Y}$ other than ω_g to the spectrum; it is defined as

$$\mathbf{Q}_g = \mathbf{\Sigma} + \sum_{m=1, m \neq g}^{G} \mathbf{A}_m \mathbf{D}_m \mathbf{A}_m^T, \tag{15}$$

where

$$\mathbf{D}_m = \frac{a^2(\omega_g) + b^2(\omega_g)}{2} \begin{bmatrix} 1 & 0 \\ 0 & 1 \end{bmatrix}, \tag{16}$$

and $\mathbf{\Sigma}$ denotes the covariance matrix of noise in expression data $\mathbf{Y}$, given by

$$\mathbf{\Sigma} = \begin{bmatrix} \sigma^2 & \cdots & 0 \\ \vdots & \ddots & \vdots \\ 0 & \cdots & \sigma^2 \end{bmatrix}. \tag{17}$$

Assuming that $\mathbf{Q}_g$ is invertible, in RIAA, a weighted least-squares fitting problem is formulated and considered for finding $\hat{a}$ and $\hat{b}$ (instead of using (5)), and it is written in the form of matrices using (13) as follows:

$$\hat{\rho}_g = \arg\min_{\rho_g} [\mathbf{Y} - \mathbf{A}_g\rho_g]^T \mathbf{Q}_g^{-1} [\mathbf{Y} - \mathbf{A}_g\rho_g]. \tag{18}$$

In Stoica et al. [12], the solution to (18) has been shown to be

$$\hat{\rho}_g = \frac{\mathbf{A}_g^T \mathbf{Q}_g^{-1} \mathbf{Y}}{\mathbf{A}_g^T \mathbf{Q}_g^{-1} \mathbf{A}_g}, \tag{19}$$

and the RIAA periodogram at $\omega = \omega_g$ can be derived by

$$\Phi_{riaa}(\omega_g) = \frac{1}{n}\hat{\rho}_g^T (\mathbf{A}_g^T \mathbf{A}_g) \hat{\rho}_g. \tag{20}$$

From (15) and (19), it is obvious that $\mathbf{Q}_g$ and $\hat{\rho}_g$ are dependent on each other. An iterative approach (i.e., RIAA) is hence a feasible solution to get the estimate $\hat{\rho}_g$ and the weighted matrix $\mathbf{Q}_g$.

The iteration for estimating spectrum starts with initial estimates $\hat{\rho}_g^0$, in which the elements $\hat{a}$ and $\hat{b}$ are given by (6) with $\omega = \omega_g$, $g = 1, \ldots, G$. After initialization, the first iteration begins. First, the elements $\hat{a}$ and $\hat{b}$ of $\hat{\rho}_g^0$ are applied to obtain $\widehat{\mathbf{D}}_m^1$ using (16). Secondly, to get a good estimate of $\hat{\sigma}^1$, the frequency ω_p at which the largest value-p is located in the temporary periodogram $\Phi^0(\omega_g)$, $g = 1, \ldots, G$, derived using (20) with $\hat{\rho}_g = \hat{\rho}_g^0$, is applied for obtaining a reversed engineered signal $\widehat{\mathbf{Y}}^0$. The elements $\hat{y}_h(t_i)$, $i = 1, \ldots, n$, in $\widehat{\mathbf{Y}}^0$ are given by

$$\hat{y}_h(t_i) = \sqrt{2P}\cos(\omega_p t_i + s), \quad i = 1, \ldots, n. \tag{21}$$

The phase of the cosine function s is unknown; however, $\hat{\sigma}^1$ is estimable using

$$\hat{\sigma}^1 = \min_{s \in [0, 2\pi]} \frac{\|\mathbf{Y} - \widehat{\mathbf{Y}}^0\|^2}{n}, \tag{22}$$

where $\| \cdot \|$ is the Euclidean norm. With estimates $\widehat{\mathbf{D}}_m^1$ and $\hat{\sigma}^1$, the estimates $\widehat{\mathbf{Q}}_g^1$, $g = 1, \ldots, G$, in the first iteration are hence given by (15). After this, $\widehat{\mathbf{Q}}_g^1$ are inserted into the right-hand side of (19) and updated estimates $\hat{\rho}_g^1$, $g = 1, \ldots, G$, are derived. The algorithm consists of repeating these steps and updating $\widehat{\mathbf{Q}}_g^k$ and $\hat{\rho}_g^k$ iteratively, where k denotes the number of iterations, until a termination criterion is reached. If the process stops at the Kth iteration, then the final RIAA periodogram is given by (20) using $\hat{\rho}_g^K$. The pseudocode in Algorithm 1 represents a concise description of the iterative RIAA process.

3. Methods

Figure 1 demonstrates our scheme for periodicity detection and algorithm comparison. The first step involves a periodogram estimation, which converts the time-course gene

Spectral Analysis on Time-Course Expression Data: Detecting Periodic Genes Using a Real-Valued Iterative Adaptive Approach

111

Algorithm RIAA

Initialization
Use (6) to obtain the initial estimates $\hat{a}$ and $\hat{b}$ in $\hat{\rho}_g^0$.

The First Iteration
Obtain $\widehat{\mathbf{D}}_m^1$ using (16) with parameters $\hat{a}$ and $\hat{b}$ given by $\hat{\rho}_g^0$. Obtain $\hat{\sigma}^1$ using (22). Using $\widehat{\mathbf{D}}_m^1$ and $\hat{\sigma}^1$ to drive the first weighted matrix $\widehat{\mathbf{Q}}_g^1$ by (15). Update estimate $\hat{\rho}_g^1$ by (19) with $\mathbf{Q}_g = \widehat{\mathbf{Q}}_g^1$.

Updating Iteration
At the kth iteration, $k = 1, 2, \ldots$, estimates $\widehat{\mathbf{Q}}_g^k$ and $\hat{\rho}_g^k$ are iteratively updated in the same way as the first iteration.

Termination
Terminate simply after 15 iterations ($K = 15$), or when the total changes in $d_g^k = \|\hat{\rho}_g^k\|$ for $g = 1, \ldots, G$, is extremely small, say, $\sqrt{\sum_{g=1}^G (d_g^k - d_g^{k-1})^2} < 0.005 \sqrt{\sum_{g=1}^G (d_g^k)^2}$, then $K = k$.

ALGORITHM 1: The pseudocode of the iterative process in RIAA.

expression ratios into the frequency domain. Three methods are considered for comparison: RIAA, LS, and a detrend LS (termed DLS), which uses an additional detrend function (developed in LSPR) before regular LS periodogram estimation is applied. The derived spectra are then analyzed using hypothesis testing. This study is conducted using a Fisher's test, with the null hypothesis that there are no periodic signals in the time domain and hence no significantly large peak in the derived spectra. The algorithm performance is evaluated and compared via simulations and receiver operating characteristic (ROC) curves. In real microarray data analysis, three published benchmark sets are utilized as standards of cell cycle genes for performance comparison.

3.1. Fisher's Test. After the spectrum of time-course expression data is obtained via periodogram estimation, a Fisher's statistic f for gene h with the null hypothesis H_0 that the peak of the spectral density is insignificant against the alternative hypothesis H_1 that the peak of the spectral density is significant is applied as

$$f_h = \frac{\max_{1 \leq g \leq G} \left(\Phi \left(\omega_g \right) \right)}{G^{-1} \sum_{g=1}^G \Phi \left(\omega_g \right)}, \qquad (23)$$

where Φ refers to the periodogram derived using RIAA, LS, or DLS. The null hypothesis H_0 is rejected, and the gene h is claimed as a periodic gene if its p-value, denoted as p_h, is less than or equal to a specific significance threshold. For simplicity, p_h is approximated from the asymptotic null distribution of f assuming Gaussian noise [13] as follows:

$$p_h = 1 - e^{-n e^{-f_h}}. \qquad (24)$$

In real data analysis, deviation might be invoked for the estimation of p_h when the time-course data is short. This issue was carefully addressed by Liew et al. [14], and, as suggested, alternative methods such as random permutation may provide less deviation and better performance. However, permutation also has limitations such as tending to be conservative [15]. While finding the most robust method for the

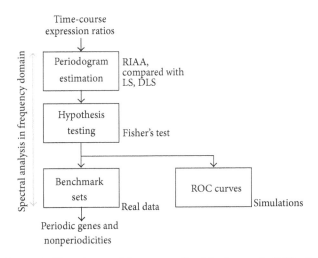

FIGURE 1: The scheme of the process for detecting periodicities in time-course expression data.

p-value evaluation remains an open question, it gets beyond the scope of this study since the algorithm comparison via ROC curves is threshold independent [16], and the results are unaffected by the deviation.

3.2. Simulations. Simulations are applied to evaluate the performance of RIAA. The simulation models and sampling strategies used for simulations are described in the following paragraphs.

3.2.1. Periodic and Nonperiodic Signals. Three models, one for periodic signals and two for nonperiodic signals, are considered as transcriptional signals. Since periodic genes are transcribed in an oscillatory manner, the expression levels y_s embedded with periodicities are assumed to be

$$y_s \left(t_i \right) = M \cos \left(\omega_s t_i \right) + \epsilon_{t_i}, \quad i = 1, \ldots, n, \qquad (25)$$

where M denotes the sinusoidal amplitude; ω_s refers to the signal frequency; ϵ_{t_i} are Gaussian noise independent and

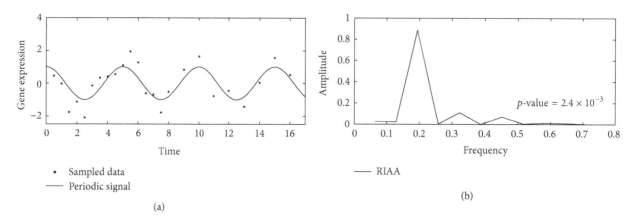

FIGURE 2: (a) A time-course periodic signal with frequency = 0.2 sampled by the bio-like sampling strategy; 16 time points are assigned to the interval (0,8], and 8 time points are assigned to the interval (8,16]. (b) The periodogram derived using RIAA. The maximum value (peak) in the periodogram locates at frequency = 0.195.

identically distributed (i.i.d.) with parameters μ and σ. For nonperiodic signals, the first model y_n is simply composed of Gaussian noise, given by

$$y_n(t_i) = \epsilon_{t_i}, \quad i = 1, \ldots, n. \tag{26}$$

Additionally, as visualized by Chubb et al., gene transcription can be nonperiodically activated with irregular intervals in a living eukaryotic cell, like pulses turning on and off rapidly and discontinuously [17]. Based on this, the second nonperiodic model y'_n incorporates one additional transcriptional burst and one additional sudden drop into the Gaussian noise, which can be written as

$$y'_n(t_i) = I_b(t_i) - I_d(t_i) + \epsilon_{t_i}, \quad i = 1, \ldots, n, \tag{27}$$

where I_b and I_d are indicator functions, equal to 1 at the location of the burst and the drop, respectively, and 0 otherwise. The transcriptional burst assumes a positive pulse while the transcriptional drop assumes a negative pulse. Both of them may be located randomly among all time points and are assumed to last for two time points. In other words, the indicator functions are equal to 1 at two consecutive time points, say, $I_b = 1$ at t_i and t_{i+1}. The burst and the drop have no overlap.

3.2.2. Sampling Strategies. As for the choices of sampling time points t_i, $i = 1, \ldots, n$, four different sampling strategies, one with regular sampling and three with irregular sampling, are considered. First, regular sampling is applied in which all time intervals are set to be $1/c$, where c is a constant. Secondly, a bio-like sampling strategy is invoked. This strategy tends to have more time points at the beginning of time-course experiments and less time points after we set the first 2/3 time intervals as $1/c$ and set the next 1/3 time intervals as $2/c$. Third, time intervals are randomly chosen between $1/c$ and $2/c$. The last sampling strategy, in which all time intervals are exponentially distributed with parameter c, is less realistic than the others but it is helpful for us to evaluate the performance of RIAA under pathological conditions.

ROC curves are applied for performance comparison. To this end, 10,000 periodic signals were generated using (25) and 10,000 nonperiodic signals were generated using either (26) or (27). Sensitivity measures the proportion of successful detection among the 10,000 periodic signals and specificity measures the proportion of correct claims on the 10,000 nonperiodic simulation datasets. Sampling time points are decided by one of the four sampling strategies and the number of time points n is chosen arbitrarily. For all ROC curves in Section 4, $c = 2$ and $n = 24$.

3.3. Real Data Analysis. Two yeast cell cycle experiments synchronized using an alpha-factor, one conducted by Spellman et al. [2] and one conducted by Pramila et al. [18], are considered for a real data analysis. The first time-course microarray data, termed dataset alpha and downloaded from the Yeast Cell Cycle Analysis Project website (http://genome-www.stanford.edu/cellcycle/), harbors 6,178 gene expression levels and 18 sampling time points with a 7-minute interval. The second time-course data, termed dataset alpha 38, is downloaded from the online portal for Fred Hutchinson Cancer Research Center's scientific laboratories (http://labs.fhcrc.org/breeden/cellcycle/). This dataset contains 4,774 gene expression levels and 25 sampling time points with a 5-minute interval. Three benchmark sets of genes that have been utilized in Lichtenberg et al. [19] and Liew et al. [20] as standards of cell cycle genes are also applied herein for performance comparison. These benchmark sets, involving 113, 352, and 518 genes, respectively, include candidates of cycle cell regulated genes in yeast proposed by Spellman et al. [2], Johansson et al. [21], Simon et al. [22], Lee et al. [23], and Mewes et al. [24] and are accessible in a laboratory website (http://www.cbs.dtu.dk/cellcycle/).

4. Results

RIAA performed well in the conducted simulations. As shown in Figure 2(a), a periodic signal (solid line) with amplitude $M = 1$ and frequency $\omega_s = 0.4\pi$ is sampled

Spectral Analysis on Time-Course Expression Data: Detecting Periodic Genes Using a Real-
Valued Iterative Adaptive Approach

113

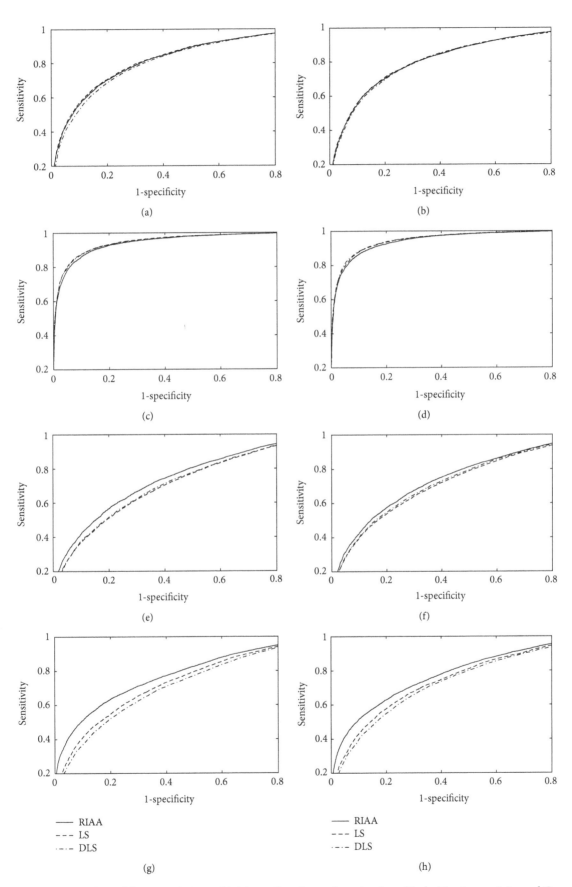

FIGURE 3: The ROC curves derived from simulations with 24 sampling time points, signal amplitude $M = 1$, $\omega_s = 0.4\pi$, and Gaussian noise $\mu = 0$ and $\sigma = 0.5$. Description of subplots is provided in Section 4.

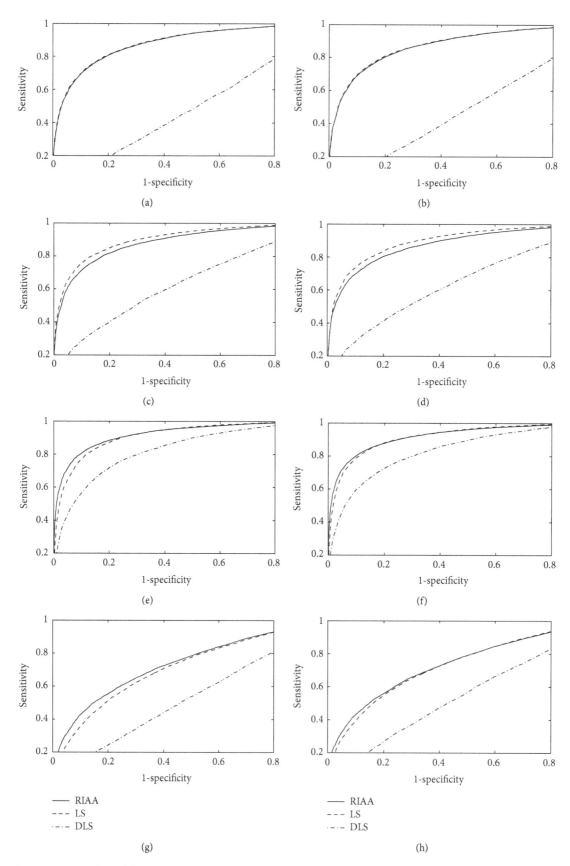

FIGURE 4: The ROC Curves derived from simulations with 24 sampling time points, signal amplitude $M = 1$, $\omega_s = 0.1\pi$, and Gaussian noise $\mu = 0$ and $\sigma = 0.5$. Description of subplots is provided in Section 4.

Spectral Analysis on Time-Course Expression Data: Detecting Periodic Genes Using a Real-Valued Iterative Adaptive Approach

115

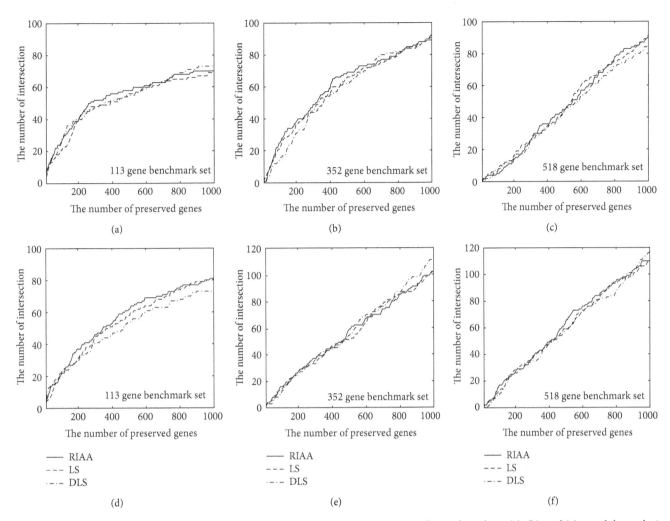

FIGURE 5: The intersection of preserved genes and the benchmark sets using RIAA, LS, and DLS algorithms. (a), (b), and (c) reveal the analysis results when dataset alpha was applied. (d), (e), and (f) reveal the analysis results when dataset alpha 38 was applied.

using the bio-like sampling strategy, which applies 16 time points in (0,8] and 8 more time points in (8,16]. Gaussian noise with parameters $\mu = 0$ and $\sigma = 0.5$ is assumed during microarray experiments. The resulting time-course expression levels (dots), at a total of 24 time points and the sampling time information were treated as inputs to the RIAA algorithm. Figure 2(b) demonstrates the result of periodogram estimation. In this example, the grid size $\Delta\omega$ was chosen to be 0.065 and a total of 11 amplitudes corresponding to different frequencies were obtained and shown in the spectrum. Using Fisher's test, the peak at the third grid (frequency = 0.195) was found to be significantly large (p-value = 2.4×10^{-3}), and hence a periodic gene was claimed.

ROC curves strongly illustrate the performance of RIAA. In Figures 3 and 4, subplots (a)-(b), (c)-(d), (e)-(f), and (g)-(h) refer to the simulations with regular, bio-like, binomially random, and exponentially random sampling strategies, respectively. Additionally, in the left-hand side subplots (a), (c), (e), and (g), nonperiodic signals were simply Gaussian noise with parameters $\mu = 0$ and $\sigma = 0.5$, while in the

right-hand side subplots (b), (d), (f), and (h), nonperiodic signals involve not only the Gaussian noise but also a transcriptional burst and a sudden drop (27). Periodic signals were generated using (25) with amplitude $M = 1$, $c = 2$, and $n = 24$. The only difference in simulation settings between Figures 3 and 4 is the frequency of periodic signals; they are $\omega_s = 0.4\pi$ and 0.1π, respectively. As shown in these figures, LS and DLS can perform well as RIAA when the time-course data are regularly sampled, or mildly irregularly sampled; however, when data are highly irregularly sampled, RIAA outperforms the others. The superiority of RIAA over DLS is particularly clear when the signal frequency is small.

Figure 5 illustrates the results of the real data analysis when these three algorithms, namely, the RIAA, LS, and DLS, were applied. On the x-axis, the numbers indicate the thresholds η that we preserved and classified as periodicities among all yeast genes; on the y-axis, the numbers refer to the intersection of η preserved genes and the proposed periodic candidates listed in the benchmark sets. Figures 5(a)–5(c) demonstrate the results derived from dataset alpha when the 113-gene benchmark set, 352-gene benchmark set, and 518-gene benchmark set were applied, respectively. Similarly, Figures 5(d)–5(f) demonstrate the results derived from dataset alpha 38. The RIAA does not result in significant differences in the numbers of intersections when compared to those corresponding to LS and DLS in most of these cases. However, RIAA shows slightly better coverage when the dataset alpha 38 and the 113-gene benchmark set was utilized (Figure 5(d)).

5. Conclusions

In this study, the rigorous simulations specifically designed to comfort with real experiments reveal that the RIAA can outperform the classical LS and modified DLS algorithms when the sampling time points are highly irregular, and when the number of cycles covered by sampling times is very limited. These characteristics, as also claimed in the original study by Stoica et al. [12], suggest that the RIAA can be generally applied to detect periodicities in time-course gene expression data with good potential to yield better results. A supplementary simulation further shows the superiority of RIAA over LS and DLS when multiple periodic signals are considered (see Supplementary Figure s1 available online at http://dx.doi.org/10.1155/2013/171530). From the simulations, we also learned that the addition of a transcriptional burst and a sudden drop to nonperiodic signals (the negatives) does not affect the power of RIAA in terms of periodicity detection. Moreover, the detrend function in DLS, designed to improve LS by removing the linearity in time-course data, may fail to provide improved accuracy and makes the algorithm unable to detect periodicities when transcription oscillates with a very low frequency.

The intersection of detected candidates and proposed periodic genes in the real data analysis (Figure 5) does not reveal much differences among RIAA, LS, and DLS. One possible reason is that the sampling time points conducted in the yeast experiment are not highly irregular (not many missing values are included), since, as demonstrated in Figures 3(a)–3(d), the RIAA just performs equally well as the LS and DLS algorithms when the time-course data are regularly or mildly irregularly sampled. Also, the very limited time points contained in the dataset may deviate the estimation of p-values [14] and thus hinder the RIAA from exhibiting its excellence. Besides, the number of true cell cycle genes included in the benchmark sets remains uncertain. We expect that the superiority of RIAA in real data analysis would be clearer in the future when more studies and more datasets become available.

Besides the comparison of these algorithms, it is interesting to note that the bio-like sampling strategy could lead to better detection of periodicities than the regular sampling strategy (as shown in Figures 3(c) and 3(d)). It might be beneficial to apply loose sampling time intervals at posterior periods to prolong the experimental time coverage when the number of time points is limited.

Acknowledgments

The authors would like to thank the members in the Genomic Signal Processing Laboratory, Texas A&M University, for the helpful discussions and valuable feedback. This work was supported by the National Science Foundation under Grant no. 0915444. The RIAA MATLAB code is available at http://gsp.tamu.edu/Publications/supplementary/agyepong 12a/.

References

[1] W. Zhao, K. Agyepong, E. Serpedin, and E. R. Dougherty, "Detecting periodic genes from irregularly sampled gene expressions: a comparison study," *EURASIP Journal on Bioinformatics and Systems Biology*, vol. 2008, Article ID 769293, 2008.

[2] P. T. Spellman, G. Sherlock, M. Q. Zhang et al., "Comprehensive identification of cell cycle-regulated genes of the yeast Saccharomyces cerevisiae by microarray hybridization," *Molecular Biology of the Cell*, vol. 9, no. 12, pp. 3273–3297, 1998.

[3] G. Rustici, J. Mata, K. Kivinen et al., "Periodic gene expression program of the fission yeast cell cycle," *Nature Genetics*, vol. 36, no. 8, pp. 809–817, 2004.

[4] M. Menges, L. Hennig, W. Gruissem, and J. A. H. Murray, "Cell cycle-regulated gene expression in Arabidopsis," *Journal of Biological Chemistry*, vol. 277, no. 44, pp. 41987–42002, 2002.

[5] M. Ahdesmäki, H. Lähdesmäki, R. Pearson, H. Huttunen, and O. Yli-Harja, "Robust detection of periodic time series measured from biological systems," *BMC Bioinformatics*, vol. 6, article 117, 2005.

[6] M. Ahdesmäki, H. Lähdesmäki, A. Gracey et al., "Robust regression for periodicity detection in non-uniformly sampled time-course gene expression data," *BMC Bioinformatics*, vol. 8, article 233, 2007.

[7] E. F. Glynn, J. Chen, and A. R. Mushegian, "Detecting periodic patterns in unevenly spaced gene expression time series using Lomb-Scargle periodograms," *Bioinformatics*, vol. 22, no. 3, pp. 310–316, 2006.

[8] R. Yang, C. Zhang, and Z. Su, "LSPR: an integrated periodicity detection algorithm for unevenly sampled temporal microarray data," *Bioinformatics*, vol. 27, no. 7, pp. 1023–1025, 2011.

[9] E. R. Dougherty, "Small sample issues for microarray-based classification," *Comparative and Functional Genomics*, vol. 2, no. 1, pp. 28–34, 2001.

[10] Y. Tu, G. Stolovitzky, and U. Klein, "Quantitative noise analysis for gene expression microarray experiments," *Proceedings of the National Academy of Sciences of the United States of America*, vol. 99, no. 22, pp. 14031–14036, 2002.

[11] Z. Bar-Joseph, "Analyzing time series gene expression data," *Bioinformatics*, vol. 20, no. 16, pp. 2493–2503, 2004.

[12] P. Stoica, J. Li, and H. He, "Spectral analysis of nonuniformly sampled data: a new approach versus the periodogram," *IEEE Transactions on Signal Processing*, vol. 57, no. 3, pp. 843–858, 2009.

[13] J. Fan and Q. Yao, *Nonlinear Time Series: Nonparametric and Parametric Methods*, Springer, New York, NY, USA, 2003.

[14] A. W. C. Liew, N. F. Law, X. Q. Cao, and H. Yan, "Statistical power of Fisher test for the detection of short periodic gene expression profiles," *Pattern Recognition*, vol. 42, no. 4, pp. 549–556, 2009.

[15] V. Berger, "Pros and cons of permutation tests in clinical trials," *Statistics in Medicine*, vol. 19, no. 10, pp. 1319–1328, 2000.

[16] A. P. Bradley, "The use of the area under the ROC curve in the evaluation of machine learning algorithms," *Pattern Recognition*, vol. 30, no. 7, pp. 1145–1159, 1997.

Spectral Analysis on Time-Course Expression Data: Detecting Periodic Genes Using a Real-Valued Iterative Adaptive Approach

117

[17] J. R. Chubb, T. Trcek, S. M. Shenoy, and R. H. Singer, "Transcriptional pulsing of a developmental gene," *Current Biology*, vol. 16, no. 10, pp. 1018–1025, 2006.

[18] T. Pramila, W. Wu, W. Noble, and L. Breeden, "Periodic genes of the yeast Saccharomyces cerevisiae: a combined analysis of five cell cycle data sets," 2007.

[19] U. Lichtenberg, L. J. Jensen, A. Fausbøll, T. S. Jensen, P. Bork, and S. Brunak, "Comparison of computational methods for the identification of cell cycle-regulated genes," *Bioinformatics*, vol. 21, no. 7, pp. 1164–1171, 2005.

[20] A. W. C. Liew, J. Xian, S. Wu, D. Smith, and H. Yan, "Spectral estimation in unevenly sampled space of periodically expressed microarray time series data," *BMC Bioinformatics*, vol. 8, article 137, 2007.

[21] D. Johansson, P. Lindgren, and A. Berglund, "A multivariate approach applied to microarray data for identification of genes with cell cycle-coupled transcription," *Bioinformatics*, vol. 19, no. 4, pp. 467–473, 2003.

[22] I. Simon, J. Barnett, N. Hannett et al., "Serial regulation of transcriptional regulators in the yeast cell cycle," *Cell*, vol. 106, no. 6, pp. 697–708, 2001.

[23] T. I. Lee, N. J. Rinaldi, F. Robert et al., "Transcriptional regulatory networks in *Saccharomyces cerevisiae*," *Science*, vol. 298, no. 5594, pp. 799–804, 2002.

[24] H. W. Mewes, D. Frishman, U. Güldener et al., "MIPS: a database for genomes and protein sequences," *Nucleic Acids Research*, vol. 30, no. 1, pp. 31–34, 2002.

13

Flux Analysis of the *Trypanosoma brucei* Glycolysis Based on a Multiobjective-Criteria Bioinformatic Approach

Amine Ghozlane,[1,2] Frédéric Bringaud,[3] Hayssam Soueidan,[4] Isabelle Dutour,[1] Fabien Jourdan,[5] and Patricia Thébault[1,2]

[1] Laboratoire Bordelais de Recherche en Informatique, UMR CNRS 5800, Université Bordeaux,
 351 Cours de la Libération, 33405 Talence Cedex, France
[2] Centre de Bioinformatique de Bordeaux, Université Bordeaux Segalen, 142 Rue Léo Saignat, 33076 Bordeaux Cedex, France
[3] Centre de Résonance Magnétique des Systèmes Biologiques, UMR 5536, Université Bordeaux Segalen, CNRS,
 146 rue Léo Saignat, 33076 Bordeaux, France
[4] The Netherlands Cancer Institute, Plesmanlaan 121, 1066 CX Amsterdam, The Netherlands
[5] Institut National de Recherche en Agronomie, UMR 1331 TOXALIM, 180 Chemin de Tournefeuille, 31027 Toulouse, France

Correspondence should be addressed to Amine Ghozlane, amine.ghozlane@labri.fr
and Patricia Thébault, patricia.thebault@labri.fr

Academic Editor: Aristotelis Chatziioannou

Trypanosoma brucei is a protozoan parasite of major of interest in discovering new genes for drug targets. This parasite alternates its life cycle between the mammal host(s) (bloodstream form) and the insect vector (procyclic form), with two divergent glucose metabolism amenable to *in vitro* culture. While the metabolic network of the bloodstream forms has been well characterized, the flux distribution between the different branches of the glucose metabolic network in the procyclic form has not been addressed so far. We present a computational analysis (called Metaboflux) that exploits the metabolic topology of the procyclic form, and allows the incorporation of multipurpose experimental data to increase the biological relevance of the model. The alternatives resulting from the structural complexity of networks are formulated as an optimization problem solved by a metaheuristic where experimental data are modeled in a multiobjective function. Our results show that the current metabolic model is in agreement with experimental data and confirms the observed high metabolic flexibility of glucose metabolism. In addition, Metaboflux offers a rational explanation for the high flexibility in the ratio between final products from glucose metabolism, thsat is, flux redistribution through the malic enzyme steps.

1. Introduction

Trypanosomes are unicellular protozoa that are ubiquitous parasites of higher eukaryotes, including insects, plants, and mammals. Among the numerous species belonging to the trypanosomatid family, *Trypanosoma brucei*, *Trypanosoma cruzi*, and *Leishmania* spp. are responsible for Human diseases. Most of these parasites live in more than one host over their life cycle and encounter very different environments, such as insect vectors' gut and vertebrate bloodstream. Consequently, the different parasitic forms have developed distinct morphologies and metabolisms.

We will consider here *T. brucei*, which belongs to the group of parasites responsible for sleeping sickness in Africa. *T. brucei* belongs to the only group of organisms that performs glycolysis in a peroxisome-like organelle, called glycosome [1]. It is widely considered that this compartmentalized glycolysis requires impermeability of glycosomal membrane to cofactors, such as $NAD(P)^+$ and $NAD(P)H$, and nucleotides (ATP, ADP, etc.) [2]. As a consequence, the intraglycosomal NAD^+/NADH and ATP/ADP balances need to be maintained, which implies that each NAD^+ or ATP molecules consumed during the first glycolytic steps have to be regenerated inside the organelle (see Figure 1).

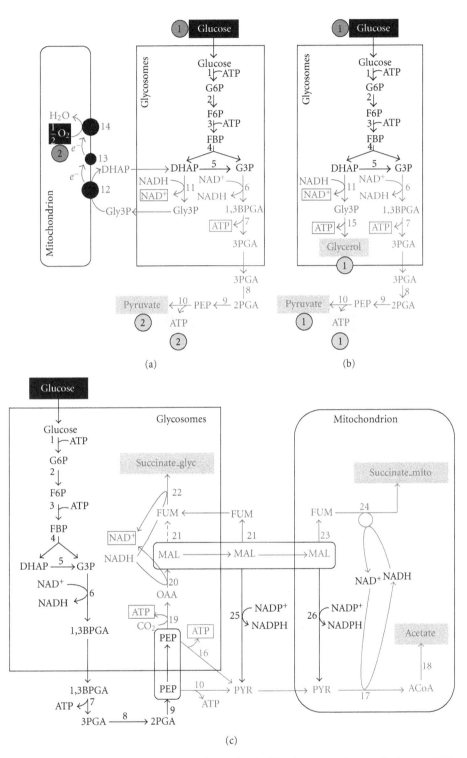

FIGURE 1: Metabolic network of glucose degradation for the bloodstream and procyclic forms of *T. brucei*.

Panels (a) and 1(b) correspond to the metabolic model of the bloodstream forms of *T. brucei* (BSF) in the aerobic and anaerobic conditions, respectively. Panel (c) represents the metabolic model for the procyclic form grown in glucose-rich medium. For both forms, the major part of the glycolytic pathway is compartmentalized in glycosomes (peroxisome-like organelles). Excreted end-products from glucose metabolism are in red, green, or purple characters on a grey rectangle as background. In Panels (a) and (b), metabolic branches consuming and regenerating NAD$^+$ are in blue and red, respectively, while the color code in Panel (c) is blue, red, and purple for the acetate, glycosomal succinate, and mitochondrial succinate branches, respectively. NAD$^+$ and ATP molecules are underlined, when consumed in the glycosomes, and boxed, when produced in the glycosomes. In aerobic conditions, BSF converts one molecule of glucose into two molecules of pyruvate with consumption of one molecule of dioxygen (Panel (a)) and net production of two molecules of ATP, while in anaerobic conditions one molecule of pyruvate, glycerol, and ATP is produced per molecule of glucose consumed (Panel (b)). Abbreviations: 1,3BPGA, 1,3-bisphosphoglycerate; DHAP, dihydroxyacetone phosphate; FBP, fructose 1,6-bisphosphate; FUM, fumarate; Gly3P, glycerol 3-phosphate; G3P, glyceraldehyde 3-phosphate; MAL, malate; OAA, oxaloacetate; PEP, phospho*enol*pyruvate; PYR, pyruvate; SUC, succinate. Individual enzymes included in the model are 1, hexokinase: 2, glucose-6-phosphate isomerase; 3, phosphofructokinase; 4, aldolase; 5, triose-phosphate isomerase; 6, glyceraldehyde-3-phosphate dehydrogenase; 7, phosphoglycerate kinase; 8, phosphoglycerate mutase; 9, enolase; 10, pyruvate kinase; 11, glycosomal glyceraldehyde-3-phosphate dehydrogenase; 12, FAD-dependent glycerol-3-phosphate dehydrogenase; 13, ubiquinone; 14, SHAM-sensitive alternative oxidase; 15, glycerol kinase; 16, pyruvate phosphate dikinase; 17, pyruvate dehydrogenase complex; 18, acetate:succinate CoA-transferase and acetyl-CoA thioesterase; 19, phospho*enol*pyruvate carboxykinase; 20, glycosomal malate dehydrogenase; 21, cytosolic (and glycosomal) fumarase; 22, glycosomal NADH-dependent fumarate reductase; 23, mitochondrial fumarase; 24, mitochondrial NADH-dependent fumarate reductase; 25, cytosolic malic enzyme; 26, mitochondrial malic enzyme.

In the mammalian host, the bloodstream forms of *T. brucei* (BSF) develop a very simple and well-known glucose-based energy metabolism, with glucose being converted into the pyruvate, which is the only end product excreted in the presence of oxygen (Figure 1(a)). In aerobiosis, equimolar amounts of pyruvate and glycerol are excreted from glucose metabolism (Figure 1(b)). In both conditions, all ATP required for the parasite development is produced in by the cytosolic pyruvate kinase (step 10 in Figure 1).

In contrast, the procyclic form of *T. brucei* (PF), which evolves in the midgut of the insect vector (tsetse fly), develops a more complex branched energy metabolism. When grown in standard rich medium, PF primarily uses glucose to provide the cell with carbon and ATP. In the course of glycolysis, phospho*enol*pyruvate (PEP) is produced in the cytosol, where it is located at a branching point (Figure 1(c)). It can be converted into pyruvate, which enters the mitochondrion to produce acetate [3, 4]. PEP can also reenter the glycosomes to be converted to succinate in either the glycosomes or the mitochondrion [5, 6]. Although the topology of the glucose metabolism network is known for the procyclic form, the flux distribution between the different branches of the network has not been addressed so far.

The main objective of this paper is to propose a bioinformatics analysis, integrating multipurposed experimental data, to investigate the flux distribution in the main branches of glucose metabolism of the PF trypanosomes. To address this question, we developed a model based on (i) the published topology of the metabolic network [7, 8], (ii) the maintenance of the glycosomal redox (NAD$^+$/NADH) and

(ATP/ADP) balances, with no exchange of these cofactors with other subcellular compartments [7], and (iii) experimental data.

2. Related Work

In the last decade, high-throughput technologies had been developed to monitor organism responses to various environmental perturbations. At the same, time many advances in bioinformatics have been made to mine these data. In particular, methods have been designed to investigate the plasticity of biological processes. To conduct such analyses, the level of abstraction of models can range from global to local and from static to dynamic, according to the biological data available (for a review, see [9]). A biological system can be modeled by a set of interconnected reactions allowing fluxes of chemical compounds (metabolites). When the organism is exposed to environmental changes, these fluxes are adjusted to preserve the homeostasis of the metabolism and to optimize biological functions such as growth rate. Several bioinformatics approaches address the problem of estimating the flux distributions accompanying these metabolic perturbations. The quality of these computed flux distributions is critical since it strongly affects the ability of subsequent *in silico* simulations to fit and predict physiological observations. Moreover, the integration of experimental data in such models helps in producing more realistic *in silico* description of biological systems.

One of the most popular formalism for modeling metabolism relies on constraint-based methods such as Flux Balance Analysis (FBA) [10, 11] that are designed to find an optimal flux distribution given a specific objective function (e.g., growth or ATP production). This mathematical framework is based on the stoichiometry of reactions, which is analyzed using linear programming to optimize fluxes toward an objective function. The resulting solution space defines all of the possible metabolic behavior of the cell under a given set of conditions, and the addition of constraints help to predict achievable cellular functions that reflect thermodynamic, kinetic, or biochemical knowledge (for a review see [12]).

To better mimic the *in vivo* system, considerable attention has been directed in recent years towards the development of variants of FBA to (1) explore differently the space solutions or/and (2) integrate experimental data.

The Optimal Metabolic Network Identification [13] and Regulatory On/Off minimization [14] methods suggest adapting the network flux structure to observed data, while the Minimization Of Metabolic Adjustment [15] approach searches for suboptimal, but more realistic solutions. To add flexibility to FBA prediction, Flux Variability Analysis (FVA) [16] proposes a feasible range of fluxes that satisfies the objective function corresponding to different genetic states. To limit the allowable functional behavior of networks, Energy Balance Analysis integrates additional thermodynamic constraints that describe energy balance and eliminate thermodynamically infeasible optima [17]. Other efforts have focused on the exploitation of integrative methods for improving the prediction of metabolic flux distributions.

Notably, integrative Omics-Metabolic Analysis [18] and integrated Flux Balance Analysis [19] quantitatively integrate proteomic and metabolomic data with genome-scale models to predict metabolic flux distributions. These methods allow for the integration of kinetics models, when available, and formulate a set of differential equations to describe the dynamics of metabolite concentrations.

However, none of the previous methods account for a multiobjective function, which is crucial since eukaryotic cells perform multiple metabolic functions. Therefore, before simulating such metabolic models, integrating biological relevant knowledge as different and multiple objectives need to be implemented. In practice, the definition of an appropriate framework is a difficult task in increasing the complexity of the flux prediction problem.

Moreover, the identification of a physiologically realistic objective function remains challenging [20] since it strongly constrains the predictive quality of the flux distribution. While it is commonly accepted to use the maximization of the biomass yield for bacteria, other objective functions may be more appropriate to predict metabolic fluxes in eukaryote cells. For instance, systems are ruled by other type of constraints, such as side compound balancing or sustaining certain metabolite concentrations within the system. Most of these constraints can be experimentally monitored and defined as an objective state.

Combining them with the flux objective function could imply several and sometimes conflicting objectives. For these reasons, recent studies investigated the flux balance problem in a multiobjective perspective [21, 22]. These theoretical articles propose algorithms to infer a flux distribution constrained by one or more target optimal output fluxes. These approaches handle several objectives with different impacts. The first step in these approaches consists of setting the bounds of the solutions space. Next, the function to optimize can be defined as a multiparametric distance that can handle data of different kinds (metabolite biomass, fluxes, etc.). The distance is then optimized by nonlinear or linear methods, adapted for multidimensional data. Finally, the aim is to find a configuration of the system, which is as close as possible to the optimal state, and where no improvement of one objective is possible without negatively impacting another objective (namely, an optimal Pareto solution). Several analyses have been carried out to infer the optimal solution when using 2, 3, or 4-objective combinations to illustrate the benefit of the addition of experimental data to mimic the reality of the cell [22]. Besides the great interest of these articles, they are not related to publicly available bioinformatic softwares.

None of the existing methods offers a qualitative or semiquantitative approach that can account for multiple constraints deduced from experimental data. Prediction of flux distribution should account for properties such as cellular homeostasis where there is no net consumption or production of key intracellular metabolites/cofactors (NAD(P)$^+$, NAD(P)H, ATP, ADP, etc.), or metabolic data, such as the ratio of excreted end-products. Therefore, we are particularly interested in a modeling system that does not require kinetic data to predict flux distribution, and that

can integrate multipurposed constraints based on the known properties of the metabolic network.

To achieve this goal, we propose and implement a heuristic algorithm that can compute the optimal flux distribution that fits results deduced from various high throughput approaches (e.g., metabolomics and fluxomics). In particular, the real values of the fluxes of most reactions are unknown and span large intervals. Therefore, the key question that our method addresses is to use experimental observations to identify the set of parameter values for which the network model would exhibit a realistic behavior.

The methodology used in this approach (called *Metaboflux*) combines a metabolic network simulator with a probabilistic metaheuristic [23] to optimize multiple flux objectives under multiple biological constraints. *Metaboflux* is freely available at http://services.cbib.u-bordeaux2.fr/metaboflux/.

3. Material and Methods

3.1. Biological Model and Data. Glucose metabolism of the BSF and PF trypanosomes differs considerably. The first model, described in the next section, corresponds to the simple and well-known glucose metabolism of BSF, with the flux distribution in the two main branches experimentally validated (Figures 1(a)-1(b)). The second model, describes the more elaborated glucose metabolism in the PF trypanosome, with three interconnected branches (Figure 1(c)). However, flux distribution between these metabolic branches has not been addressed so far.

Our bioinformatic approach will be validated through the first well-known BSF model, before being used to investigate the flux distribution in the main branches of the PF glucose metabolism.

(A) Trypanosoma brucei Bloodstream Forms (BSF). When grown in the presence of oxygen, the BSF convert glucose into pyruvate, the excreted end product, in three subcellular compartments, the glycosomes, the cytosol, and the mitochondrion [7]. For reasons of simplification, the cytosolic and mitochondrial compartments shown in the Figure 1(a) are merged in the model. The first seven glycolytic steps take place in the glycosomes (steps 1–7), while the three other steps leading to pyruvate are cytosolic (steps 8–10). It is to note that one molecule of glucose (hexose) is converted into two molecules of triose phosphate, dihydroxyacetone phosphate (DHAP), and glyceraldehyde 3-phosphate. In the glycosomes, ATP molecules consumed in steps 1 and 3 are regenerated by step 7 and NAD$^+$ consumed in step 6 is regenerated inside the organelle by conversion of DHAP into glycerol 3-phosphate (G3P) (step 11). The latter is converted back into DHAP in the mitochondrion (step 12), to form a DHAP/G3P cycle, which transfers electrons to dioxygen to produce H$_2$O (steps 12–14). Consequently, two molecules of pyruvate are produced from one molecule of glucose consumed, with a net production of two molecules of ATP in the cytosol by the pyruvate kinase (step 10). In anaerobiosis, electrons cannot be transferred to dioxygen, thus G3P is

converted into the excreted end product glycerol, with as a consequence a net production of one molecule of pyruvate and glycerol excreted by molecule of glucose consumed, with a net production of one molecule of ATP (Figure 1(b)).

(B) Trypanosoma brucei Procyclic Form (PF). Energy metabolism has been extensively studied in the PF of *T. brucei* (for a review, see [7, 8]); however, only glucose metabolism is taken into consideration in the model. Conversion of glucose into the excreted end products, succinate and acetate, implies glycosomal, cytosolic, and mitochondrial enzymatic steps [7]. As mentioned for the BSF model, the cytosolic and mitochondrial compartments shown in the Figure 1(c) are also merged in the PF model. The first six glycolytic steps take place in the glycosomes and consume 2 molecules of ATP and 2 molecules of NAD^+ per molecule of glucose consumed (steps 1–6 in Figure 1), while the three other steps leading to phospho*enol*pyruvate (PEP) are cytosolic (steps 7–9). PEP is located at a key branching point, that is, (i) one branch leads to acetate production in the mitochondrion (steps 10, 17-18) [3, 4] and (ii) the other branch is also branched with succinate being produced in both the glycosomes (steps 19–22) and the mitochondrion (steps 23-24) [24, 25]. The glycosomal succinate branch is critical for glycolysis by regenerating one molecule of ATP (step 19) and up to two molecules of NAD^+ (steps 20, 22) per molecule of succinate produced. The model also includes the essential cytosolic and mitochondrial malic enzymes (ME, steps 25 and 26, resp.) [26], which constitute a bridge between the succinate and acetate branches. It is also important to mention that (i) the tricarboxylic acid cycle is not functioning as a cycle in the PF trypanosomes and, most of acetyl-CoA produced from glucose is converted into acetate [27], (ii) most ATP is produced by substrate level phosphorylation from glucose, with a nonessential contribution of the mitochondrial F_0/F_1-ATP synthase for ATP production [4, 24, 26, 28], (iii) NADH molecules produced in the mitochondrion by the pyruvate dehydrogenase complex (step 17) are regenerated by the mitochondrial fumarate reductase (step 24), implying that the respiratory chain activity is not required to maintain the mitochondrial redox balance of glucose metabolism [6]. As a consequence, the mitochondrial tricarboxylic acid cycle, respiratory chain, and F_0/F_1-ATP synthase are not included in our model.

3.2. Metaboflux. We analyzed the behavior of both the bloodstream and procyclic form of *T. brucei* by semiquantitative modeling and simulation with stochastic Petri Nets (PN). We describe in this section the details of the design of Metaboflux (see Figure 3). Metaboflux is a new framework for the simulation and for the estimation of the parameters of PN with stochastic immediate transitions that we called Fluxes Petri Net (FPN). We first describe the formal definition of the PN variant we use. We then provide a simulation algorithm to generate sequences of markings from a model. We then outline an optimization procedure to estimate the parameters of a model so as to satisfy constraints derived from experimental data. We finally present an alternative

and faster and approximate simulation algorithm that we used to approximate the behavior of a model during the optimization steps.

3.2.1. PN Formalism. The PN formalism gives an interesting framework for simulating biological systems [29] and has been largely employed in the last decade to describe biological networks (for a review see [30]).

A PN (also called Place Transition net) is a graph-based model that can describe the dynamics of a system as a set of sequences of discrete configurations. A PN is a bipartite, directed and labeled graph. Nodes in a PN can either be a place $p \in P$ or a transition $\in T$. In the case of metabolic networks, places of a PN represent the metabolites and transitions represent enzymatic reactions, labeled by the enzyme catalyzing the reaction. Each place contains a countable (i.e., positive integer) set of tokens, representing the quantity of the corresponding metabolite. The number of tokens $i : P \rightarrow \mathbb{N}$ in every place is called a marking of the net and represents its current state. Traditionally, the number of tokens in a place p is indicated by $\#(p, i)$ or $\#(p)$ when the marking is understood. Edges in a PN are only allowed between a place and a transition or vice versa, but never between two places or two transitions. When an edge connects a place and a transition, the edge is called an input arc for the transition. When an edge connects a transition and a place, the edge is called an output arc for the transition.

A transition is enabled and can fire when all its conditions are fulfilled, namely, if all its input places contain enough tokens. When a transition is enabled, selected, and fired, tokens from its input places are consumed, and tokens are added to its output places. Every edge in a PN is labeled with a multiplicity corresponding to the stoichiometry of the reaction. More formally, the multiplicity $(p, t) \in \mathbb{R}$ of an input arc (p, t) is a positive integer value indicating the number of tokens that must be present in the place p for the transition t to be enabled. The multiplicity $m(t, p) \in \mathbb{R}$ of an output arc (p, t) is a positive integer value indicating the number of tokens that will be added to the place p if the transition t fires.

Combining ideas from Generalized Stochastic PN [31] and FBA [10, 11], we extend the PN formalism with fluxes weight. A Flux Petri Net (FPN) is a PN with an additional flux weight labeling of transitions. Formally, a flux weight is a function $w : T \rightarrow \mathbb{R}^+$ that assigns a strictly positive flux value to every transition of an FPN. During simulation, flux weights are used to compute a probability distribution over possible transitions whenever more than one transition is enabled in a given marking. The higher the flux value, the more often this reaction will fire and thus the higher the proportion of metabolites that will go through this reaction. The dynamics of an FPN is illustrated in Figure 2.

As an example of FPN, Figure 4(a) depicts the PN model of the bloodstream form of the glucose metabolic network of *T. brucei*. In this figure, places of the net are, as usual, depicted as circles. Transitions are drawn as squares and are labeled with the number of the reaction. Arcs represent input and output arcs with nonzero multiplicities. Flux weights are

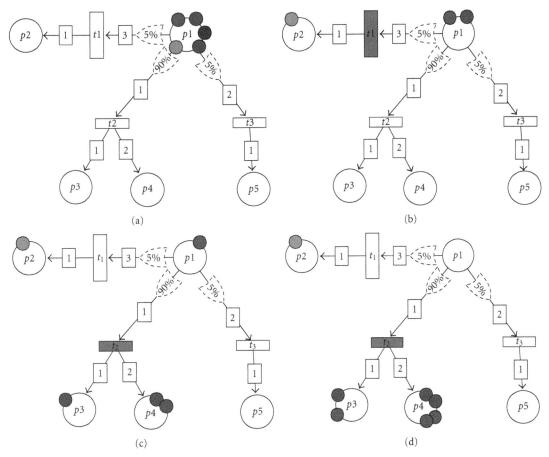

FIGURE 2: Illustration of the dynamics of a Flux Petri Net (FPN). (a) depicts the initial state of the FPN, while (b)–(d) depict its states after three transitions have been fired. This FPN comprises five places ($p1$–$p5$) and three transitions ($t1$–$t3$). The transition $t1$ consumes three tokens of $p1$, produces one token of $p2$, and has an associated flux distribution of 5%. Similarly, transition $t2$ consumes one token of $p1$, produces one token of $p3$, two tokens of $p4$, and has an associated flux of 90%. In the initial state (a), the place $p1$ contains five tokens, colored differently to be distinguishable. Since $t1$ requires three tokens of $p1$, $t2$ requires one token of $p1$, $t3$ two tokens of $p1$; that $p1$ contains five tokens; the three transitions $t1$, $t2$, and $t3$ are enabled in this configuration. The corresponding probabilities for each transition are $P(t1) = 5/(5 + 90 + 5) = 0.05$, $P(t2) = 90/(5 + 90 + 5) = 0.90$ and $P(t3) = 5/(5 + 90 + 5) = 0.05$. Suppose we select $t1$ with probability 0.05, then three tokens of $p1$ are consumed and one token of $p2$ is produced through $t1$. In the second state (b), only $t2$ and $t3$ are enabled, since the required number of tokens for $t1$ in $p1$ is not satisfied. This time, the respective probabilities associated with $t2$ and $t3$ are given by $P(t2) = 90/(90 + 5) = 0.948$, and $P(t3) = 5/(90 + 5) = 0.052$. Suppose $t2$ is selected, it consumes one token of $p1$ and produces one token of $p3$ and two of $p4$. In the third state (c), only transition $t1$ is enabled, and the FPN reaches a state (d) after firing $t1$ where no transition is enabled.

depicted in the squares bounding transitions. The default multiplicities and flux weights are 1.

To analyze the behavior of a net, we sample one possible sequence of markings with the following stochastic simulator. The simulation starts with a provided initial marking, considered as the current marking for the first iteration of the simulation.

At each iteration of the simulation loop, we update the current marking by selecting and applying an enabled transition. More formally, given a current marking : $P \to \mathbb{N}$, let $E(i) = \{t \in T \mid$ for all $p \in P$ and $m(p, t) \le \#(p)\}$ be the set of enabled transitions in the marking i. The probability $w_t(i)$ that the transition t will fire in the current marking i is given by the normalized weight $w_t(i) = w(t) / \sum_{t' \in E(i)} w(t')$. Once a transition t is selected by random choice, the next marking t' is defined by subtracting the consumed tokens

and adding the produced tokens, that is, $\#(p, i') = \#(p, i) - m(p, t) + m(t, p)$.

This simulation loop is repeated until we reach a user-provided maximal number of iterations or if there are no transition enabled in the current marking. In the case of the FPN models of the BSF and PF of the glucose metabolism of *T. brucei*, we can see that any sequence of markings will eventually reach a final marking where no transitions are enabled. Indeed, these FPNs are both bounded and contain sink places that are not inputs of any transitions. It is straightforward to see that regardless of the initial marking or of the flux weights assigned to transitions (as long as they are non zero), all the tokens in these FPNs will eventually end in one of these sink places. Therefore, after a finite number of iterations, there are no transitions that are enabled and these FPNs reach a final marking. In our simulations and

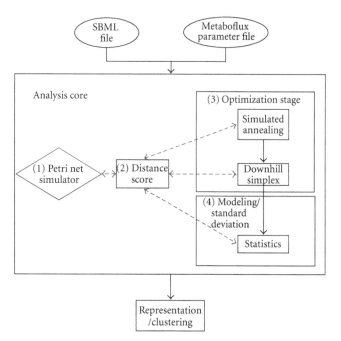

FIGURE 3: Schematic representation of Metaboflux. analysis procedure Metaboflux takes two files as input, one SBML file that describes the metabolic network topology and an XML file in Metaboflux format indicating simulation parameters. The first step launches N-analysis core by MPI (Message Passing Interface). Each analysis core solves a constrained optimization problem with a simulated annealing and downhill-simplex. These methods suggest candidate optimal fluxes valuation and submit them to the simulator. The simulator estimates the distribution of the final markings according to theses fluxes valuations and returns the corresponding distance score as a result. These steps are repeated until the optimization procedures converge to one solution.

analysis, we are thus guaranteed that these FPN will always reach a final marking.

3.2.2. Parameter Calibration of an FPN under Experimentally Observed Constraints.

We now consider the problem of fitting the predictions of an FPN to experimentally observed behavior. We first formalize the fitting problem and then indicate the computational approach we used to solve it as well as an approximate simulation algorithm. Finally, we summarize the experimental data available for the metabolic networks of the BSF and PF.

For the metabolic networks of T. brucei, available experimental data provide proportions of the final metabolites and indicate a restored balance between cofactors in the glycosome. These experimental data exclusively concern the state of the end products of the glucose metabolism of the parasite. Consequently, we are interested in the final markings of an FPN and we want them to satisfy the observed balances and proportions of end-products and cofactors. For an FPN, these final markings are completely dependent on a fluxes valuation $\vec{f}$, that is, the fluxes weights of all its transitions. Therefore, the problem of fitting the predictions of an FPN

to the expected behavior is reduced to finding $\vec{f}$ such that the final markings are in agreement with experimental evidence.

The experimental evidence we account for is of different nature and is formulated using different constraints. Experimental data indicating the expected amount of end-products (e.g., the final quantity of ATP is equal to the initial quantity, or the amount of Acetate excreted in the cytosol) are formulated using the Euclidean distance between final markings and expected quantities. These distances must be minimized. Experimental data indicating that the possible amount of end-products lies within an interval (e.g., the quantity of excreted cytosolic succinate for the PF network) are formulated using logical constraints on the final markings. These constraints must be satisfied. Experimental data indicating expected fluxes values (resp. that flux values lies within an interval) are formulated using Euclidean distances that must be minimized (resp. a constraint on the fluxes valuation that must be satisfied). These distances are summed in a distance function $D(\vec{f})$ that we want to minimize when subject to the conjunction of constraints over markings and fluxes. This function D measures the prediction error, that is, the distance between the prediction and the expected quantities.

For the T. brucei BSF model (Figures 1(a) and 1(b)), the modeled constraints are

(1) the balance of glycosomic co-factors $NAD^+/NADH$ and ATP/ADP in the final marking,

(2) an expected maximal cytosolic ATP quantity.

For the T. brucei PF model (Figure 1(c)), depending on the analysis, the modeled constraints are composed of

(1) the balance of glycosomic cofactors $NAD^+/NADH$ and ATP/ADP in the final markings,

(2) the expected proportion of excreted acetate over final acetate and succinates, that is, 50% of end products should consist of acetate,

(3) a range of acceptable glycosomal and mitochondrial succinate amount,

(4) a minimal flux value for the reaction PEP → OAA (step 19),

(5) a minimal flux value for the reaction MAL → PYR (steps 25, 26).

More details on these constraints are provided in the result section.

To find the flux valuation minimizing the prediction error, we repeatedly evaluate the distance function, and thus perform several simulations of the corresponding FPN until it reaches a final marking. Since our models and simulation algorithm are probabilistic by nature, a single flux valuation can generate multiple final markings (i.e., a distribution over final markings). We thus consider the prediction error associated with a flux valuation to be the prediction error of the average of the final marking of 100 simulation replicates.

Numerically, we solved this minimization problem by combining two nonlinear, nonderivative based optimization

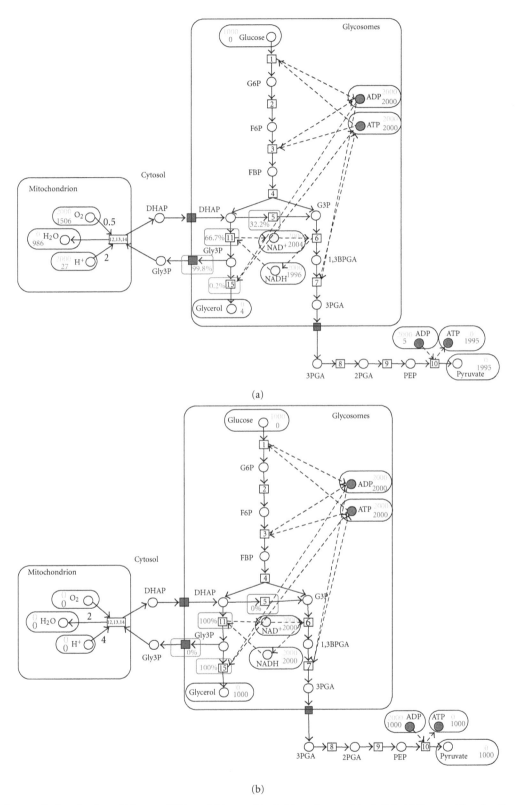

FIGURE 4: The flux prediction for the well-known BSF model in aerobiosis (a) and anaerobiosis (b). All the considered pathways are located in 3 compartments: mitochondrion, glycosomes, and cytosol. Circles represent metabolites, squares depict reactions, and blue squares are transporters. The stoichiometry is 1 by default, except for H+ and H2O (the stoichiometries of H+, H2O and O2 were multiplied by 2, resp. 4, 2 and 1). The quantity of input metabolites for the initiation stage of Metaboflux is colored in orange, and the final amount are then colored in purple. The flux percentage at branching points of the metabolic network is given in red for the DHAP node (step 5 versus step 11) and in blue for the Gly3P node (transport_1 versus step 15). The percentage values at branching points have to be considered as a subpart of the 100% of flux given for the branching point where two enzymes use the same metabolite; for instance, glycerol 3-phosphate dehydrogenase (step 11) and triose phosphate isomerase (step 5) use DHAP as substrate.

techniques. Optimization problems can be investigated in many scientific areas using metaheuristics such as Genetic algorithms or Simulated Annealing (SA) [23] processes (for a review and comparative performances see [32]). Publications have shown a better efficiency with methods based on SA processes (for instance, [32]) and influenced our choices towards an implementation of SA algorithm. However, thanks to the modular implementation of Metaboflux, a further work might investigate the impact of different solvers according to specific applications in metabolic networks.

In Metaboflux, the first technique we investigated is a global stochastic search based on SA. This method repeatedly evaluates the distance function on fluxes valuation that are chosen randomly. The probability that a candidate flux valuation is accepted as the argument of the minimum of the distance function depends on the corresponding distance value, the difference between the candidate solution and the previous candidate and a gradually decreasing value called temperature. In the first iterations, a high temperature value corresponds to a low probability of acceptance, while in later iterations, a low temperature corresponds to a high probability of acceptance. This saves the method from selecting in the first iterations a local optimum. In this study, we used the GSL [33] implementation of the SA, that we ran with an initial temperature of 10 000. We observed that even with this (relatively) very high temperature, the SA often converged to a local optimum. To avoid this issue, we used a High Performance Computing platform to run 300 individual instances with random starting fluxes valuations. For each of these instances, we use the returned candidate optimum as the starting point of an additional local optimum search based on a Nelder-Mead/downhill-simplex method.

The large amounts of metabolites present in the BSF and PF models imply that each evaluation of the function D requires thousands of iteration of the simulation loop described in the previous section. A single iteration of the simulation loop will select a transition that, once fired, will move a limited number of tokens between places. In the BSF and PF models, the stoichiometries are of 1 except for H^+ and O_2 (resp. 2 and 0.5), and thus almost all transitions will move a single token. For a model having n tokens of glucose as input, and assuming that the places are bounded by $O(n)$ tokens, the number of iterations of the simulation loop required to reach a final marking is in the order of $n * |T|$ where $|T|$ is the number of transitions in the model. Furthermore, during the minimization procedure, each flux valuation requires 100 simulation replicates. Finally, the prediction error of several thousand different fluxes valuations are evaluated before finding an optimum solution. Due to this huge number of simulation runs to be performed, using the simulation algorithm during the parameter calibration step proved to be computationally infeasible. Instead of simulating the exact semantics of FPNs, we implemented a greedy simulator that approximates their dynamics.

The greedy simulator we used during the parameter calibration step is based on the idea that the intermediate markings are not required for the minimization procedure. At each step of the simulation, the greedy simulator fires *maximally*, that is, moves as much tokens as possible by firing in one step multiple transitions. We identified three situations where multiple transitions can be lumped and fired simultaneously without modifying the final marking. The first situation is when only one transition is enabled. Consider, for example, the situation where tokens are only present in one place that is the input place of a single transition. This is the case for the initial marking where only glucose and cofactors are present. With the greedy simulation, when this single enabled transition is fired, the totality of tokens in the input place is moved to the output place(s). The second situation arises in markings where multiple transitions are enabled but are *compatible*. Two transitions are said to be compatible if they do not share any input place. In this case, the greedy simulator fires maximally all these enabled transition. The third situation arises in markings that enable incompatible transitions. In these situations, we compute for each enabled transitions the maximal number of time it can fire, by accounting for stoichiometries and the number of tokens in its input places. Let n be the minimum of these maximal numbers of times each transition can fire. The greedy simulator determines the number of times each transition fires in a single step by sampling a multinomial distribution with n trials and whose event probabilities are the (normalized) weights of the enabled transitions. These three heuristics enable a 1000-fold reduction in the number of iterations required to reach a final marking. We verified experimentally that these heuristics yields probabilities of attaining a final marking that are comparable to the exact simulation (according to a T-test, differences of the mean final marking between the exact and approximate simulators were statistically not significant at the 0.05 level).

In the analysis of the BSF model, we considered that a difference of ±9% between the predicted and expected distributions is acceptable. This variability of 9% corresponds to nonsignificant experimental differences. We determined numerically the range of values returned by the distance function when we allow for this variability between the predicted and expected markings. The corresponding distance values range from 0 to 0.2. In the subsequent analysis, we thus used a threshold of 0.2 to identify fluxes valuation yielding simulation results that are "close enough" to the experimental results.

4. Results and Discussions

The aim of this analysis is to predict the flux distribution within glucose metabolic network of *T. brucei* PF. However, before applying our approach to the PF model (4.2), we have evaluated the performance of Metaboflux to estimate the metabolic flux distribution for the well-known metabolic BSF model (4.1).

4.1. Trypanosoma brucei Bloodstream Forms (BSF). Many experimental data ranging from kinetics to metabolomics have been obtained for the glucose metabolism of BSF trypanosomes, with the objective to identify the best glycolytic drug targets [34]. Consequently, the glucose metabolic model, essential for the production of ATP and therefore fitness of the parasite, has been well characterized [34, 35]. To validate our computational analysis, we have used Metaboflux to model the complete glucose metabolic network of the parasite grown in aerobic and anaerobic conditions. To initiate the simulator, quantity of tokens has been set to 1000 for the glucose input, to 2000 for an excess of dioxygen (aerobic condition), and for both stocks of correlated molecules for ADP/ATP and NAD$^+$/NADH, within the glycosomes. As constraints implemented within the objective function of Metaboflux, the balances for ADP/ATP and NAD$^+$/NADH have been constrained within the glycosomes. As described earlier, both conditions are vital for the parasite as none transporter has been identified so far for these metabolites, which implies their sequestration within the glycosomes. Moreover, an additional objective was then specified to maximize the amounts of ATP synthesized by the cytosolic pyruvate kinase (step 10), which is the only known source of ATP in BSF [34, 35].

The simulation and optimization stage of Metaboflux has been carried out and several solutions of flux predictions have been proposed while the maximization of the ATP production was well satisfied. Considering the best solutions, which are identical for this model (even if Metaboflux allows the prediction of alternatives), three main observations can be pointed out. First, only pyruvate is produced in aerobiosis, with two molecules produced per molecules of glucose consumed (the quantity of tokens given by Metaboflux is the double of the glucose input stock), while nearly no glycerol is produced in the glycosomes (Figure 4(a)). However, in anaerobic condition, Metaboflux predicts equimolar production of pyruvate and glycerol (data not shown). Second, Metaboflux predicts that nearly two (1995 in Figure 4(a)) and one (1000 in Figure 4(b)) molecules of ATP are produced per molecule of glucose consumed in aerobic and anaerobic conditions, respectively, which fit perfectly with the BSF model. Third, flux distribution at the two branching points, DHAP and glycerol 3-phosphate (Gly3P), is also consistent with the model. In anaerobic conditions, identical metabolic fluxes are required in the glycerol and pyruvate branches (red and blue in Figure 1(b), resp.) to maintain both ATP/ADP and NAD$^+$/NADH glycosomal balances. As a consequence, all of the DHAP molecules needs to be converted to Gly3P and step 5 (conversion of DHAP into G3P) is negligible, as predicted by Metaboflux (Figure 4(b)). Similarly, the Gly3P transporter is not contributing, since Gly3P need to be converted into glycerol to maintain the glycosomal ATP balance (Figure 4(b)). In contrast, the flux distribution at these branching points is different in aerobic conditions. The DHAP/Gly3P cycle implies no glycerol in production with a full contribution of the Gly3P transporter, as predicted by Metaboflux (99.8% of the flux in Figure 4(a)). At the DHAP node, an important part of DHAP is converted into G3P, since DHAP produced from Gly3P (steps 11, 12 in Figure 1(a)) reenters into glycosomes. Altogether, these data are in accordance with the BSF experimental data provided in both incubation conditions and validate Metaboflux as an appropriate tool to study flux distribution in the different branches of glucose metabolism in the PF trypanosomes.

4.2. Trypanosoma brucei Procyclic Form (PF). The purpose of the Metaboflux method developed here is to analyze the extent of the *T. brucei* metabolic flexibility when constraining the system by five different constraints known from experimental data or assumed from the literature, that is, (i) the topology of the metabolic network shown in Figure 1(c), (ii) the ATP molecules consumed in the glycosomal steps 1 and 3 have to be generated by the glycosomal steps 16 and 19, (iii) similarly, the NAD$^+$ molecules reduced in the glycosomal step 6 have to be reoxidized in steps 20 and 22, (iv) between 56 and 86% of the total excreted succinate have to be produced in the glycosomes, and (v) conversely, 14 to 44% have to be produced in the mitochondrion. These latter two constraints were deduced from the maximum capacity estimated for both succinate production branches using reverse genetic approaches [6]. After modeling these five constraints in Metaboflux, the optimization was run with fixed proportion of acetate excretion ranging from 0 to 100%, with a 5% increment. We observed that all the constraints were accommodated for acetate proportion (given by the number of acetate tokens under the total number of excreted tokens, that is, succinate plus acetate) ranging between 26 and 95% (distance scores below 0.2) (Figure 5). Figure 5 also shows that all the constraints are accommodated with their score variations.

The model confirms that the trypanosome glucose metabolism is highly flexible in terms of utilization of the acetate versus succinate branches. Interestingly, the model is also consistent with the experimental data, since the percentage of acetate excreted from glucose metabolism varies between 26 and 80 depending on the analyses [27, 36]. This suggests that a high flexibility of flux distribution between the different branches of the network exists, although tightly constrained by the glycosomal succinate branch to maintain the organelle NAD$^+$/NADH and ATP/ADP balances.

To determine possible reasons for this flexibility, we included two additional constraints in the model to adjust the flux through PK and ME (from 1 to 80%, with a 5% increment), thus constituting a bridge between the succinate and acetate branches (steps 25 and 26). Figure 6 shows only the distance curve for each ME flux according to the proportion of acetate production. It clearly appears that restraining the flux through ME reduces the flexibility of the system. For instance, a 25% flux through ME is compatible with an acetate production (considering the total number of excreted tokens given for acetate and total succinate) ranging between 42 and 69% (Figure 6). This also shows a direct correlation between the flux through ME (between 1 and 70%) and the proportion of acetate production. However, increasing the ME flux by over 70% does not increase the flexibility of the system. The correlation between acetate production and flux distribution through the ME steps, implies that the involvement of the first step of the succinate fermentation branches (step 19) increases proportionally, as observed in Figure 7. Altogether, this analysis suggests that the flexibility of the flux distribution between the succinate and acetate branches is considerably increased by the ME activity, which are essential steps for the viability of the PF trypanosomes [26].

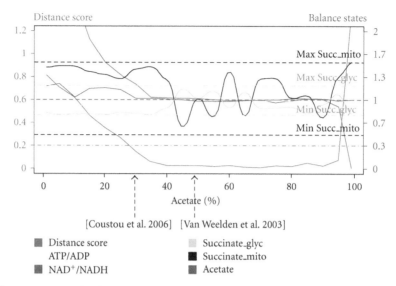

FIGURE 5: Results for the distance score and balance constraint while varying the Acetate/Succinate proportions. These curves summarize several metabolite proportions as a function of the acetate/succinate proportion. For this experiment, the model was run with 3 constraints (1) The constraints over acetate/succinate proportions ranging from 1 to 99%, with 5% increment, (2) the proportion between the two succinate pools constrained to the ratio 56–86% for succinate_glyc against 14–44% for succinate_mito, and (3) ATP/ADP and NAD+/NADH balance being required to be equilibrated. The distance score (blue curve) is a function of the satisfaction of these constraints. When the distance score is less than 0.2, we consider that all the constraints are satisfied. We see that the constraints are satisfied for a proportion of acetate/succinate ranging between 26 and 95%. This corresponds to a predicted flux flexibility of 69%. In this area of flexibility are found the experimental results given by two publications. These experimental observations are indicated by two black dashed arrows.

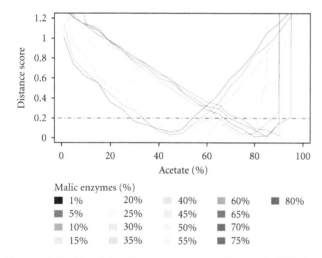

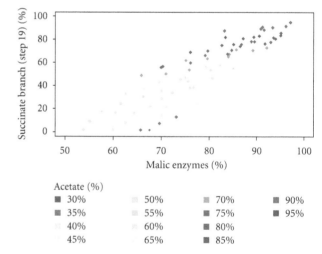

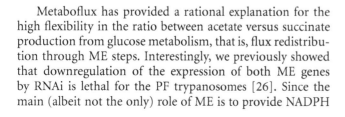

FIGURE 6: Profile of the distance scores according to the ME flux. This graphic represents the minimal distance score when the acetate proportion, the flux through PK and the flux through ME are constrained. The constraint of acetate/succinate proportion ranges from 1 to 99%, with a 5% increment. In addition to the constraints used in Figure 5, two constraints specify the flux through ME (steps 25-26) and the flux through PK (step 19).

FIGURE 7: Succinate branch/Malic enzyme. The biological constraints used for the previous analysis (Figure 5) have been also applied here. We represent the flux (%) between the succinate branch (step 19) and the ME. Only the distance points under the 0.2 limit are considered. The flux through the succinate branch increases linearly with the flux through the ME.

Metaboflux has provided a rational explanation for the high flexibility in the ratio between acetate versus succinate production from glucose metabolism, that is, flux redistribution through ME steps. Interestingly, we previously showed that downregulation of the expression of both ME genes by RNAi is lethal for the PF trypanosomes [26]. Since the main (albeit not the only) role of ME is to provide NADPH required for biosynthetic pathways and to respond to oxidative stresses, one may consider that flux through ME depends on NADPH demand. For instance, under oxidative stress conditions, redistribution of metabolic fluxes through the ME steps, to increase NADPH production in the cytosol and the mitochondrion, would lead to an increase in the acetate/succinate ratio.

5. Conclusions

This study presents a bioinformatics analysis of the flux distribution of the BSF and PF *Trypanosoma brucei* glucose metabolism under multiple and varying constraints deduced from experiments. The results suggest that the current definition of the biological model is compatible with all the constraints known from experimental data. Furthermore, our PF model predicts that there is high flexibility in the ratio of acetate to succinate production, which is consistent with data sets of various sources. Notably, our analysis suggests that the malic enzymes are the main support of this flexibility. This predicted property can be confirmed experimentally by metabolic flux analysis. These results have been obtained with the optimization of a multiobjective function that integrates heterogeneous experimental data. In addition, we demonstrate here the great potential of flux analysis to improve the quality of metabolic models. We also demonstrate that combining flux prediction with qualitative constraints derived from experimental data increases the predictive power of *in silico* flux analysis. Our models, simulation and analysis framework, shows great potential and allows for a more realistic investigation of the *T. brucei* metabolism.

Appendix

Comparison of FBA and Metaboflux

FBA and Metaboflux both aim at finding a flux distribution that fits *in vivo* observations as closely as possible. However, Metaboflux goes further by allowing the integration of biological constraints not only on fluxes but also, for instance, on metabolite biomass. In order to measure the benefit of this approach, we carried out a comparative analysis between FBA implemented in FBA-SimVis [37] and Metaboflux. To perform this evaluation, we took time-consumption and the sensitivity of predictions into consideration. Our comparative analysis is based on the metabolic network model deduced from experimental data [7, 8].

Using FBA, we integrated the proportions of acetate and succinate (excreted metabolite) by adding a supplementary reaction to the model (with a specific stoichiometry of 36, 14 and 50) thus linking together the three ways of synthesizing these metabolites. The unique objective function was specified as a biomass production reaction from these three metabolites. With Metaboflux, we run two simulations: (i) as used in FBA, an objective function was used to optimize the biomass production and (ii) a multiobjective function was used to minimize the differences given by the proportion of excreted metabolites known from experimental data. In addition, the balance scales of ADP/ATP and NAD$^+$/NADH were constrained within the glycosomes as this condition is required for maintaining the glycolytic flux in trypanosomes. The results of the three flux predictions are given in Figure 8. The flux prediction, using FBA or Metaboflux with a unique objective function, satisfies the constraints on the proportion of final metabolites (specified through the biomass production reaction); however, the balance scales of ATP/ADP and NAD$^+$/NADH were not maintained. Using Metaboflux that exploits experimental data in the multiobjective function, the constraints on balance scales and known metabolite proportions were satisfied. Contrary to FBA and Metaboflux with an objective function for the biomass production, fluxes predicted by Metaboflux integrating experimental data are relevant as they obtain the balance scales and the right excreted metabolite proportions. Detailed analysis of the flux predictions on the flux maps (Figures 8(a)–8(c)) shows that the main differences between these methods occur at branching points 1 and 2. Indeed, FBA did not use the path through the ME and distributed the flux equally between pyruvate kinase (step 10) and pyruvate phosphate dikinase (step 16). Metaboflux, on the other hand, considered pyruvate phosphate dikinase, which participates in the maintenance of the ATP/ADP balance. Consequently, 22% of the flux from glycosomal malate dehydrogenase (step 19) goes through the ME to reach the expected acetate/succinate proportion.

This analysis shows the positive contribution of multipurpose experimental data in a metabolic model using Metaboflux. The resulting conflicting constraints are integrated in Metaboflux that can deal with them as our approach is based on a nonlinear optimization. The satisfaction of such constraints is very helpful proposing the development of more realistic models for analysis. FBA is not designed to take this complexity into account and consequently seems to favour the simplest path for its flux prediction.

Metaboflux takes more time compared to FBA-SimVis (319 versus 6 seconds). The difference is mainly due to the time taken by the optimization stage of our method and is correlated to the number of branching points in the network. As the framework of FBA works with a stoichiometric matrix, the complexity of the network slightly affects its running time and such an approach has great application possibilities for exploiting genome-scale metabolic models. Metaboflux is more dependent on the complexity of networks and to deal with this issue, our method has been parallelized. This design is particularly suitable for the new development in computer hardware architectures since *n*-core processors are now available. The parallelization on the different cores will thus make the computation on individual computers faster.

Authors' Contribution

A. Ghozlane and F. Bringaud contributed equally to this work.

Acknowledgments

This work is supported by the Agence Nationale de la Recherche (ANR) program METABOTRYP of the ANR-MIME-2007 call and SYSTRYP of the ANR-BBSRC-2007 call and the CBiB. H. Souedan is supported by a grant from BBSRC through the ERA-SysBio-Plus Program. Experiments presented in this paper were carried out using the PLAFRIM experimental testbed, being developed under the INRIA PlaFRIM development action with support from

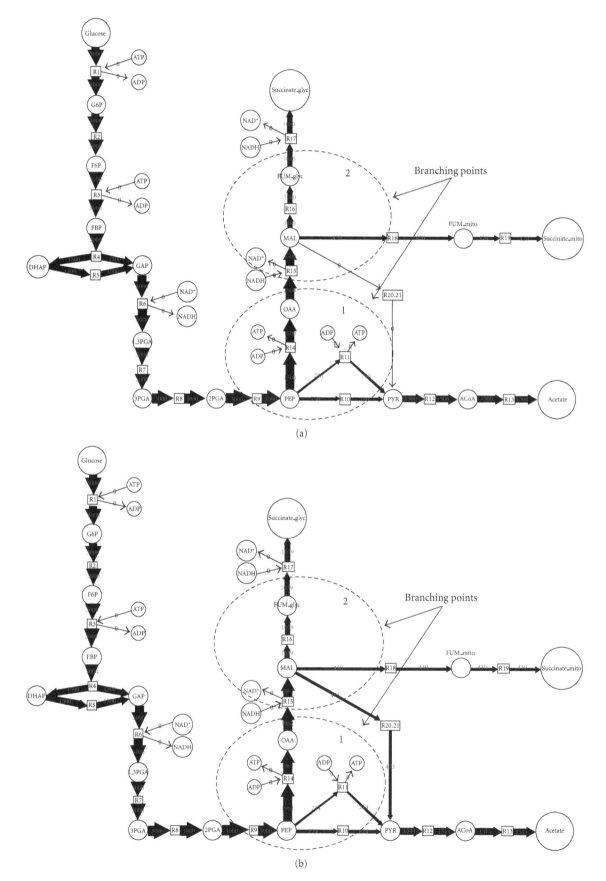

FIGURE 8: Continued.

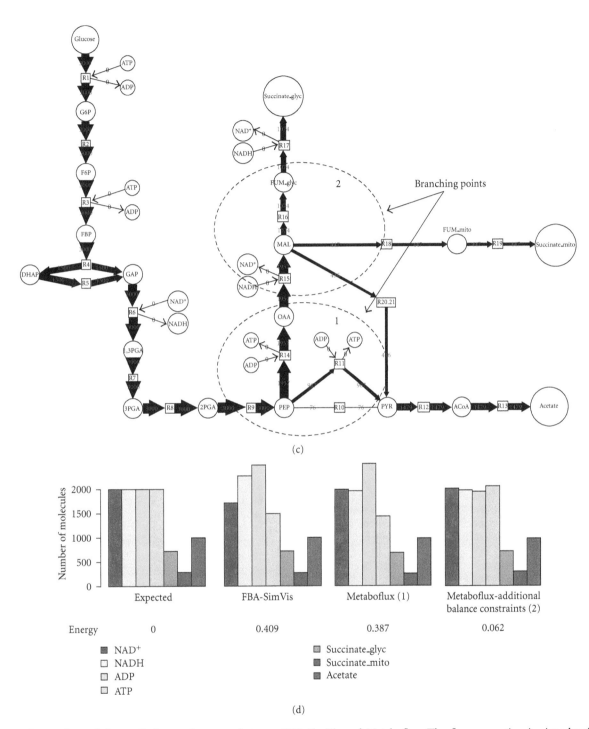

FIGURE 8: Comparison of the prediction performance between FBA-SimVis and Metaboflux. The flux proportion is given by the edge size, circles stands for metabolites, and square for enzymes. (a) Flux map obtained by FBA-SimVis. (b) Flux map obtained by Metaboflux using a single objective function. (c) Flux map obtained by Metaboflux with additional constraints on balance states and experimental knowledge. (d) Histogram that gives the expected proportion (considering experimental data), and proportions obtained with Metaboflux using the FBA-SimVis flux results as constraints and Metaboflux. The metabolite biomasses were deduced from the number tokens given by Metaboflux. Deduced from empirical measurements, the glucose biomass was set to 1000 tokens and ATP, ADP, NADH, and NAD$^+$ were set to 2000. Experimental data given as ratios of excreted metabolites were used to specify expected number of tokens. The balance ratio of ATP, ADP, NADH, and NAD$^+$ was specified by an equality equation.

LABRI and IMB and other entities: Conseil Régional d'Aquitaine, FeDER, Université de Bordeaux and CNRS (see https://plafrim.bordeaux.inria.fr/doku.php). The authors thank Macha Nikolski for helpful discussion, as well as Jean Pierre Mazat for critical reading of the paper.

References

[1] F. R. Opperdoes and P. Borst, "Localization of non glycolytic enzymes in a microbody like organelle in *Trypanosoma brucei*: the glycosome," *FEBS Letters*, vol. 80, no. 2, pp. 360–364, 1977.

[2] B. M. Bakker, F. I. C. Mensonides, B. Teusink, P. Van Hoek, P. A. M. Michels, and H. V. Westerhoff, "Compartmentation protects trypanosomes from the dangerous design of glycolysis," *Proceedings of the National Academy of Sciences of the United States of America*, vol. 97, no. 5, pp. 2087–2092, 2000.

[3] L. Rivière, S. W. H. Van Weelden, P. Glass et al., "Acetyl: succinate CoA-transferase in procyclic *Trypanosoma brucei*. Gene identification and role in carbohydrate metabolism," *Journal of Biological Chemistry*, vol. 279, no. 44, pp. 45337–45346, 2004.

[4] Y. Millerioux, P. Mor, M. Biran et al., "ATP synthesis-coupled, -uncoupled acetate production from acetyl-CoA by the mitochondrial acetate:succinate CoA-transferase, acetyl-CoA thioesterase in *Trypanosoma*," *Journal of Biological Chemistry*, vol. 287, no. 21, pp. 17186–17197, 2012.

[5] S. Besteiro, M. P. Barrett, L. Rivière, and F. Bringaud, "Energy generation in insect stages of *Trypanosoma brucei*: metabolism in flux," *Trends in Parasitology*, vol. 21, no. 4, pp. 185–191, 2005.

[6] V. Coustou, S. Besteiro, L. Rivière et al., "A mitochondrial NADH-dependent fumarate reductase involved in the production of succinate excreted by procyclic *Trypanosoma brucei*," *Journal of Biological Chemistry*, vol. 280, no. 17, pp. 16559–16570, 2005.

[7] F. Bringaud, L. Rivière, and V. Coustou, "Energy metabolism of trypanosomatids: adaptation to available carbon sources," *Molecular and Biochemical Parasitology*, vol. 149, no. 1, pp. 1–9, 2006.

[8] F. Bringaud, C. Ebikeme, and M. Boshart, "Acetate and succinate production in amoebae, helminths, diplomonads, trichomonads and trypanosomatids: common and diverse metabolic strategies used by parasitic lower eukaryotes," *Parasitology*, vol. 137, no. 9, pp. 1315–1331, 2010.

[9] V. Lacroix, L. Cottret, P. Thébault, and M. F. Sagot, "An introduction to metabolic networks and their structural analysis," *IEEE/ACM Transactions on Computational Biology and Bioinformatics*, vol. 5, no. 4, pp. 594–617, 2008.

[10] D. A. Fell and J. R. Small, "Fat synthesis in adipose tissue. An examination of stoichiometric constraints," *Biochemical Journal*, vol. 238, no. 3, pp. 781–786, 1986.

[11] J. D. Orth, I. Thiele, and B. O. Palsson, "What is flux balance analysis?" *Nature Biotechnology*, vol. 28, no. 3, pp. 245–248, 2010.

[12] N. D. Price, J. L. Reed, and B. O. Palsson, "Genome-scale models of microbial cells: evaluating the consequences of constraints," *Nature Reviews Microbiology*, vol. 2, no. 11, pp. 886–897, 2004.

[13] M. J. Herrgård, S. S. Fong, and B. O. Palsson, "Identification of genome-scale metabolic network models using experimentally measured flux profiles," *PLoS Computational Biology*, vol. 2, no. 7, article e72, 2006.

[14] T. Shlomi, O. Berkman, and E. Ruppin, "Regulatory on/off minimization of metabolic flux changes after genetic perturbations," *Proceedings of the National Academy of Sciences of the United States of America*, vol. 102, no. 21, pp. 7695–7700, 2005.

[15] D. Segrè, D. Vitkup, and G. M. Church, "Analysis of optimality in natural and perturbed metabolic networks," *Proceedings of the National Academy of Sciences of the United States of America*, vol. 99, no. 23, pp. 15112–15117, 2002.

[16] R. Mahadevan and C. H. Schilling, "The effects of alternate optimal solutions in constraint-based genome-scale metabolic models," *Metabolic Engineering*, vol. 5, no. 4, pp. 264–276, 2003.

[17] D. A. Beard, S. D. Liang, and H. Qian, "Energy balance for analysis of complex metabolic networks," *Biophysical Journal*, vol. 83, no. 1, pp. 79–86, 2002.

[18] K. Yizhak, T. Benyamini, W. Liebermeister, E. Ruppin, and T. Shlomi, "Integrating quantitative proteomics and metabolomics with a genome-scale metabolic network model," *Bioinformatics*, vol. 26, no. 12, Article ID btq183, pp. i255–i260, 2010.

[19] M. W. Covert, N. Xiao, T. J. Chen, and J. R. Karr, "Integrating metabolic, transcriptional regulatory and signal transduction models in *Escherichia coli*," *Bioinformatics*, vol. 24, no. 18, pp. 2044–2050, 2008.

[20] A. M. Feist and B. O. Palsson, "The biomass objective function," *Current Opinion in Microbiology*, vol. 13, no. 3, pp. 344–349, 2010.

[21] Y. G. Oh, D. Y. Lee, S. Y. Lee, and S. Park, "Multiobjective flux balancing using the NISE method for metabolic network analysis," *Biotechnology Progress*, vol. 25, no. 4, pp. 999–1008, 2009.

[22] D. Nagrath, M. Avila-Elchiver, F. Berthiaume, A. W. Tilles, A. Messac, and M. L. Yarmush Martin, "Soft constraints-based multiobjective framework for flux balance analysis," *Metabolic Engineering*, vol. 12, no. 5, pp. 429–445, 2010.

[23] S. Kirkpatrick, C. D. Gelatt, and M. P. Vecchi, "Optimization by simulated annealing," *Science*, vol. 220, no. 4598, pp. 671–680, 1983.

[24] N. Bochud-Allemann and A. Schneider, "Mitochondrial substrate level phosphorylation is essential for growth of procyclic *Trypanosoma brucei*," *Journal of Biological Chemistry*, vol. 277, no. 36, pp. 32849–32854, 2002.

[25] V. Coustou, S. Besteiro, M. Biran et al., "ATP generation in the *Trypanosoma brucei* procyclic form: cytosolic substrate level is essential, but not oxidative phosphorylation," *The Journal of biological chemistry*, vol. 278, no. 49, pp. 49625–49635, 2003.

[26] V. Coustou, M. Biran, M. Breton et al., "Glucose-induced remodeling of intermediary and energy metabolism in procyclic *Trypanosoma brucei*," *Journal of Biological Chemistry*, vol. 283, no. 24, pp. 16343–16354, 2008.

[27] S. W. H. Van Weelden, B. Fast, A. Vogt et al., "Procyclic *Trypanosoma brucei* do not use Krebs cycle activity for energy generation," *Journal of Biological Chemistry*, vol. 278, no. 15, pp. 12854–12863, 2003.

[28] N. Lamour, L. Rivière, V. Coustou, G. H. Coombs, M. P. Barrett, and F. Bringaud, "Proline metabolism in procyclic *Trypanosoma brucei* is down-regulated in the presence of glucose," *Journal of Biological Chemistry*, vol. 280, no. 12, pp. 11902–11910, 2005.

[29] M. Heiner, I. Koch, and J. Will, "Model validation of biological pathways using Petri nets—demonstrated for apoptosis," *BioSystems*, vol. 75, no. 1–3, pp. 15–28, 2004.

[30] C. Chaouiya, "Petri net modelling of biological networks," *Briefings in Bioinformatics*, vol. 8, no. 4, pp. 210–219, 2007.

[31] M. A. Marsan, G. Conte, and G. Balbo, "A class of generalized stochastic Petri Nets for the performance evaluation of multiprocessor systems," *ACM Transactions on Computer Systems*, vol. 2, pp. 93–122, 1984.

[32] S. Bandyopadhyay, S. Saha, U. Maulik, and K. Deb, "A simulated annealing-based multiobjective optimization algorithm: AMOSA," *IEEE Transactions on Evolutionary Computation*, vol. 12, no. 3, pp. 269–283, 2008.

[33] M. Galassi, J. Davies, J. Theiler et al., *GNU Scientific Library Reference Manual*, 3rd edition, 2009.

[34] B. M. Bakker, P. A. M. Michels, F. R. Opperdoes, and H. V. Westerhoff, "Glycolysis in bloodstream form *Trypanosoma brucei* can be understood in terms of the kinetics of the glycolytic enzymes," *Journal of Biological Chemistry*, vol. 272, no. 6, pp. 3207–3215, 1997.

[35] B. M. Bakker, P. A. M. Michels, F. R. Opperdoes, and H. V. Westerhoff, "What controls glycolysis in bloodstream form *Trypanosoma brucei*?" *Journal of Biological Chemistry*, vol. 274, no. 21, pp. 14551–14559, 1999.

[36] V. Coustou, M. Biran, S. Besteiro et al., "Fumarate is an essential intermediary metabolite produced by the procyclic *Trypanosoma brucei*," *Journal of Biological Chemistry*, vol. 281, no. 37, pp. 26832–26846, 2006.

[37] E. Grafahrend-Belau, C. Klukas, B. H. Junker, and F. Schreiber, "FBA-SimVis: interactive visualization of constraint-based metabolic models," *Bioinformatics*, vol. 25, no. 20, pp. 2755–2757, 2009.

14

Network Completion for Static Gene Expression Data

Natsu Nakajima and Tatsuya Akutsu

Bioinformatics Center, Institute for Chemical Research, Kyoto University, Gokasho, Uji, Kyoto 611-0011, Japan

Correspondence should be addressed to Tatsuya Akutsu; takutsu@kuicr.kyoto-u.ac.jp

Academic Editor: Yves Van de Peer

We tackle the problem of completing and inferring genetic networks under stationary conditions from static data, where network completion is to make the minimum amount of modifications to an initial network so that the completed network is most consistent with the expression data in which addition of edges and deletion of edges are basic modification operations. For this problem, we present a new method for network completion using dynamic programming and least-squares fitting. This method can find an optimal solution in polynomial time if the maximum indegree of the network is bounded by a constant. We evaluate the effectiveness of our method through computational experiments using synthetic data. Furthermore, we demonstrate that our proposed method can distinguish the differences between two types of genetic networks under stationary conditions from lung cancer and normal gene expression data.

1. Introduction

Estimation of genetic interactions from gene expression microarray data is an interesting and important issue in bioinformatics. There are two kinds of gene expression data: time series data and nontime series data. To estimate the dynamics of gene regulatory networks such as cell cycle and life cycle processes, various mathematical models and methods have been proposed using time series data. Since the number of observed time points in time series data is usually small, these methods suffer from low accuracies. On the other hand, a large number of nontime series data are available, for example, samples from normal people and patients of various types of diseases. Although these data are not necessarily static, we may regard these data as static data because these are averaged over a large amount of cells in rather steady states.

For inference of genetic networks, various reverse engineering methods have been proposed, which include methods based on Boolean networks [1, 2], Bayesian networks [3, 4], differential equations [5–7], and graphical Gaussian models [8–10]. Boolean networks can only be applied to inference of genetic networks from time series data because the Boolean network is intrinsically a dynamic model.

Although Bayesian networks have widely been applied to analysis of static data, they can only output acyclic networks. Many methods have also been proposed using various kinds of differential equation models. However, in many cases, parameter estimation needs a huge amount of computation time. Overall, most methods suffer from inaccuracy and/or computational inefficiency and thus there is not yet an established or standard method for inference of genetic networks using only gene expression data. Therefore, it is reasonable to try to develop another approach for analysis of gene regulatory networks.

In recent years, there have been several studies and attempts for network completion, not necessarily for biological networks but also for social networks and web graphs. Different from network inference, we assume in network completion that a certain type of a prototype network is given, which can be obtained by using existing knowledge. Kim and Leskovec [11] addressed the network completion problem in which an incomplete network including unobserved nodes and edges is given and then the unobserved parts should be inferred. They proposed KronEM, which combined the Expectation Maximization with the Kronecker graphs model to estimate the missing part of the network.

Guimerà and Sales-Pardo [12] presented a mathematical and computational method which can identify both missing and spurious interactions in complex networks by using the stochastic block models to capture the structural features in the network. This method was also applied to a protein interaction network of yeast. Hanneke and Xing [13] defined the network completion as a problem of inferring the rest part of the network, given an observed incomplete network sample and proposed a sampling method to derive confidence intervals from sample networks. As a related work, Saito et al. [14] developed a method to measure the consistency of an inferred network with the measured gene expression data.

Independently, Akutsu et al. [15] proposed another model of network completion in which the objective is to make the minimum amount of modifications to a given network so that the resulting network is most consistent with the observed data. Based on this concept, Nakajima et al. [16] developed a practical method, DPLSQ, for completion of genetic networks from time series data, in which addition and deletion of edges are the basic modification operations and the numbers of added and deleted edges are specified. In addition, if we begin with a network with an empty set of edges, it can be applied to network inference. DPLSQ is based on a combination of least-squares fitting and dynamic programming, where least-squares fitting is used for estimation of parameters in differential equations and dynamic programming is used for minimizing the sum of least-squares errors under the restriction of the number of added and deleted edges. Different from other heuristic or stochastic approaches, DPLSQ is guaranteed to output an optimal solution (in the sense of the minimum least-squares error) in polynomial time if the maximum indegree of nodes is bounded by a constant. Nakajima and Akutsu [17] proposed a method to complete and infer the time varying networks by extending DPLSQ so that additions and deletions of edges can be performed at several time points. However, since DPLSQ is based on a dynamic model, it cannot be applied to inference or completion of genetic networks from static data.

In this study, we propose a novel method, DPLSQ-SS (DPLSQ for Static Samples), for completing and inferring a network using static gene expression data, based on DPLSQ. The purpose of this study is twofold: first, to complete and infer gene networks from static expression profile, instead of time series data and, secondly, to investigate the relationship between different kinds of inferred networks under different conditions (e.g., comparison of normal and cancer networks obtained from samples of normal and cancer cells). Static data typically consist of expression levels of genes, which were measured at single time point but for a large number of samples. As discussed in the beginning part of this section, these types of data can be regarded as the gene expression measurements in a stationary phase. Many of static microarray data are publicly available, in particular for cancer microarray data with a relatively large size of tumor and normal samples. Therefore, it may be possible to estimate and investigate differences between cancer and normal networks. The basic strategy of DPLSQ-SS is the same as that of DPLSQ: least-squares fitting is used for parameter estimation and dynamic programming is used for

minimizing the sum of least-squares errors when adding and deleting edges. In order to cope with static data, we modified the error function to be minimized. Although the idea is simple, it brings wider applicability because a large number of static gene expression data are available. We demonstrate the effectiveness of DPLSQ-SS through computational experiments using synthetic data and gene expression data for lung cancer and normal samples. We also perform computational comparison of DPLSQ-SS as an inference method with some of state-of-the-art tools using synthetic data.

2. Method

The purpose of network completion in this study is to modify a given network by making the minimum number of modifications so that the resulting network is most consistent with the observed data. Here we assume additions and deletions of edges as modification operations (see Figure 1). In the following, graph $G(V, E)$ denotes a given network where V and E are the sets of nodes and directed edges, including loops, respectively. In this graph G, each node corresponds to a gene and each edge represents a direct regulation between two genes. We let n denote the number of genes and let $V = \{v_1, \ldots, v_n\}$. For each node v_i, $e^-(v_i)$ and $\deg^-(v_i)$, respectively, denote the set of incoming edges to v_i and the number of incoming edges to v_i as defined below:

$$e^-(v_i) = \left\{ v_j \mid \left(v_j, v_i \right) \in E \right\},$$
$$\deg^-(v_i) = \left| e^-(v_i) \right|.$$
(1)

We employ least-squares fitting for the parameter estimation and dynamic programming for identifying structure of the network. In the following we explain the algorithm of the proposed method.

2.1. Model of Nonlinear Equation and Estimation of Parameters. Since we consider static data in this paper, we adopt a mathematical model based on nonlinear equations, instead of differential equations in [16]. We assume that the static state of each node v_i is determined by the following equation:

$$x_i = a_0^i + \sum_{j=1}^{h} a_j^i x_{i_j} + \sum_{j \le k} a_{j,k}^i x_{i_j} x_{i_k} + b^i \omega, \quad (2)$$

where $v_{i_1}, \ldots, v_{i_h}$ are incoming nodes to v_i, x_i corresponds to the expression value of the ith gene, and ω denotes a random noise. The second and third terms of the right-hand side of the equation represent linear and nonlinear effects to node v_i, respectively (see Figure 2), where positive a_j^i or $a_{j,k}^i$ corresponds to an activation effect and negative a_j^i or $a_{j,k}^i$ corresponds to an inhibition effect.

We assume that static expression data $\langle y_1(s), y_2(s), \ldots, y_n(s) \rangle$, $s = 1, \ldots, m$, are given, where m is the number of samples and $y_i(s)$ denotes the expression value of node v_i in the sth sample. The parameters (i.e., a_0^i, a_j^i, $a_{j,k}^i$) can be

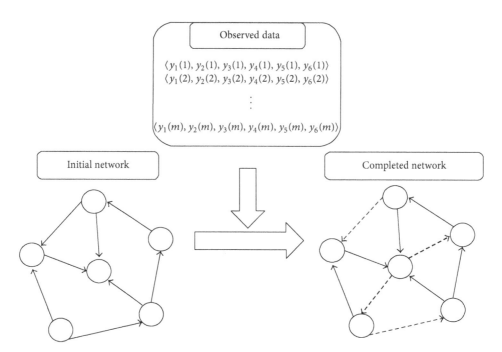

FIGURE 1: Network completion by addition and deletion of edges from m samples. The bold dashed and the thin dashed edges represent added and deleted edges, respectively.

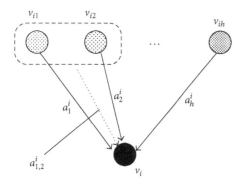

FIGURE 2: Static model of genetic network. The expression level of v_i is determined from those of input nodes. $a^i_{1,2}$ is a coefficient corresponding to cooperative regulation by genes v_{i_1} and v_{i_2} to gene v_i.

estimated by minimizing the following objective function using a standard least-squares fitting method:

$$S^i_{i_1,i_2,\dots,i_h}$$

$$= \sum_{s=1}^{m} \left| y_i(s) - \left(a^i_0 + \sum_{j=1}^{h} a^i_j y_{i_j}(s) + \sum_{j\leq k} a^i_{j,k} y_{i_j}(s) y_{i_k}(s) \right) \right|^2.$$

$$(3)$$

2.2. Completion by Addition of Edges. Once the objective function is determined, the completion procedure is the same as that for DPLSQ [16]. In order to make this paper self-contained, we also present the completion procedure here.

For the simplicity, we begin with network completion by adding k edges in total so that the sum of least-squares errors is minimized.

We let $\sigma^+_{k_j,j}$ denote the minimum least-squares error when adding k_j edges to the jth node and they are defined as

$$\sigma^+_{k_j,j} = \min_{j_1,j_2,\dots,j_{k_j}} S^j_{j_1,j_2,\dots,j_{k_j}},$$

$$(4)$$

where each v_{j_l} must be selected from $V - v_j - e^-(v_j)$. In order to avoid combinatorial explosion, we constrain the maximum k_j to be a small constant K and let $\sigma^+_{k_j,j} = +\infty$ for $k_j > K$ or $k_j + \deg^-(v_j) \geq n$.

Here, we define $D^+[k,i]$ by

$$D^+[k,i] = \min_{k_1+k_2+\cdots+k_i=k} \sum_{j=1}^{i} \sigma^+_{k_j,j}.$$

$$(5)$$

The entries of $D^+[k,i]$ can be computed by the dynamic programming algorithm as follows:

$$D^+[k,1] = \sigma^+_{k,1},$$

$$D^+[k,j+1] = \min_{k'+k''=k} \left\{ D^+[k',j] + \sigma^+_{k'',j+1} \right\}.$$

$$(6)$$

It is to be noted that $D^+[k,n]$ is determined uniquely regardless of the ordering of nodes in the network.

The correctness of this dynamic programming algorithm can be seen by

$$\min_{k_1+k_2+\cdots+k_n=k} \sum_{j=1}^{n} \sigma_{k_j,j}^{+}$$

$$= \min_{k'+k''=k} \left\{ \min_{k_1+k_2+\cdots+k_{n-1}=k'} \sum_{j=1}^{n-1} \sigma_{k_j,j}^{+} + \sigma_{k'',n}^{+} \right\} \quad (7)$$

$$= \min_{k'+k''=k} D^{+}\left[k', n-1\right] + \sigma_{k'',n}^{+}.$$

2.3. Completion by Addition and Deletion of Edges. The above dynamic programming procedure can be modified for addition and deletion of edges.

We let $\sigma_{k_j,h_j,j}$ denote the minimum least-squares error when adding k_j edges to $e^{-}(v_j)$ and deleting h_j edges from $e^{-}(v_j)$, where added and deleted edges must be disjoint. As described in Section 2.2, we also constrain the maximum k_j and h_j to be small constants K and H, respectively. We let $\sigma_{k_j,h_j,j} = +\infty$ if $k_j > K$, $h_j > H$, $k_j - h_j + \deg^{-}(v_j) \geq n$, or $k_j - h_j + \deg^{-}(v_j) < 0$ holds. Then, the problem is stated as

$$\min_{\substack{k_1+k_2+\cdots+k_n=k \\ h_1+h_2+\cdots+h_n=h}} \sum_{j=1}^{n} \sigma_{k_j,h_j,j}. \quad (8)$$

Here, we define $D[k,h,i]$ by

$$D[k,h,i] = \min_{\substack{k_1+k_2+\cdots+k_i=k \\ h_1+h_2+\cdots+h_i=h}} \sum_{j=1}^{i} \sigma_{k_j,h_j,j}. \quad (9)$$

Then, the network completion problem by addition and deletion of edges can be solved by using the dynamic programming algorithm as follows:

$$D[k,h,1] = \sigma_{k,h,1},$$

$$D[k,h,j+1] = \min_{\substack{k'+k''=k \\ h'+h''=h}} \left\{ D\left[k',h',j\right] + \sigma_{k'',h'',j+1} \right\}. \quad (10)$$

We will also discuss the computational complexity of DPLSQ-SS. Since completion by addition of edges is a special case, we only analyze completion by addition and deletion of edges.

It is known that least-squares fitting for a linear system can be done in $O(mp^2 + p^3)$ time where m is the number of samples and p is the number of parameters. In our proposed method, we assume that the maximum indegree in a given network and the number of parameters are bounded by constants. In this case, the time complexity per least-squares fitting can be estimated as $O(m)$.

Next we analyze the time complexity required for $\sigma_{k_j,h_j,j}$ and $D[k,h,i]$. The time complexity required for computation of $\sigma_{k_j,h_j,j}$ is $O(mn^{K+1})$ [16], where the time complexity of computing the minimum least-squares for jth node depends on the upper bounds for the number of adding and deleting

edges per node, K and H. In addition, the time complexity for $D[k,h,i]$s is $O(n^3)$ [16], considering that the size of table $D[k,h,i]$ is $O(n^3)$. Therefore, total time complexity for DPLSQ-SS is

$$O\left(mn^{K+1} + n^3\right). \quad (11)$$

This analysis suggests that DPLSQ-SS can be applicable to large-scale networks if $K \leq 2$ and n is not too large.

If the maximum indegree of the initial network is not bounded by a constant, the time complexity per least-squares fitting increases to $O(mn^4 + n^6)$ and the number of combinations to be examined per node increases to $O(n^{H+K})$, as discussed in [16]. In this case, the total time complexity would be $O(n^{H+K+1} \cdot (mn^4 + n^6))$, which suggests that network completion should not start with dense networks but with sparse networks.

3. Results

To evaluate the effectiveness of DPLSQ-SS, we performed two types of computational experiments using both synthetic data and real expression data. All experiments were performed on a PC with Intel Core 2 Quad CPU (3.0 GHz). We employed the liblsq library (http://www2.nict.go.jp/aeri/sts/stmg/K5/VSSP/install_lsq.html) for a least-squares fitting method.

3.1. Inference Using Synthetic Data. In order to assess the potential effectiveness of DPLSQ-SS, we begin with network inference using two kinds of synthetic data. Recall that network completion beginning with a null network corresponds to network inference.

We employed here nonlinear equations as gene regulation rules between genes. Since it is difficult to generate static data by numerical simulations, we made manually nonlinear equations with obvious solutions as the synthetic network topology and regarded each solution as static data for one sample. For example, if we make n equations with n variables, it is assumed that there exist n genes in the synthetic network. We give an example of nonlinear equations with 3 variables below:

$$x_1 = x_1^2 - 2,$$
$$x_2 = x_2^2 - 6, \quad (12)$$
$$x_3 = x_1 x_2 - 1,$$

where we assume that x_i ($i = 1, \ldots, 3$) corresponds to the expression value of ith gene. Therefore, an example network consists of 3 genes and 4 edges, including self-loops. If we solve this set of equations, we can find four solutions as below:

$$(2, 3, 5), \quad (2, -2, -5), \quad (-1, 3, -4), \quad (-1, -2, 1). \quad (13)$$

Then, we can employ these solutions as synthetic data. Since the use of synthetic static data consisting only of a few solutions easily resulted in numerical calculation error, we generated additional 400 data sets for each of static solutions by adding random numbers uniformly distributed between −0.5 and 0.5.

Under the above model, we examined DPLSQ-SS for network inference, using synthetic data which is generated as described above and letting $E = \emptyset$ in the initial network. It should be noted that we let upper bounds for the number of adding and deleting edges per node to be $K = 2$ and $H = 0$, respectively. Furthermore, in order to examine the CPU time changes with respect to the size of the network, we made synthetic networks with 10 and 20 nodes by making the nonlinear equation with corresponding number of variables.

Since the number of added edges was always equal to the number of edges in the original network, we evaluated the performance of DPLSQ-SS by means of the averaged accuracy, which was defined as the number of correctly inferred edges to the number of edges in the original network (i.e., the number of added edges) and the averaged computational time over 5 modified networks.

We also compared DPLSQ-SS with two well-known existing tools for inference of genetic networks, ARACNE [18, 19] and GeneNet [9, 10]. ARACNE is based on mutual information between genes and GeneNet is based on graphical Gaussian models and partial correlations. Since both tools output only correlation values for genes, we selected the top M from them and regarded $\{v_i, v_j\}$ as a correct edge if either (v_i, v_j) or (v_j, v_i) was included in the edge set of the original network. We employed datasets which were generated by the same way for DPLSQ-SS and default parameter settings for both tools. We evaluated the results by the ratio of correctly inferred edges and averaged CPU time (see Table 1). The CPU time used by ARACNE is user time + sys time and that used by GeneNet is time difference between the start time and end time.

The results on DPLSQ-SS and comparative methods using synthetic data show that the accuracies by DPLSQ-SS are higher than those by ARACNE and GeneNet. Although ARACNE cannot handle networks with self-loops but GeneNet can, both methods showed almost the same performance in the case of $n = 10$. On the whole, three methods have something in common, which perform with low accuracy as the size of the network grows. As for the CPU time, ARACNE was faster than DPLSQ-SS and GeneNet in case of $n = 10$. In addition, the CPU time by DPLSQ-SS increases rapidly as the size of the network grows, in contrast to those by the comparative methods. Since DPLSQ-SS works in polynomial time, if we obtain sufficient computer resource, DPLSQ-SS can handle large-scale networks. Since accuracy is the most important criterion and DPLSQ-SS is more accurate than existing methods, our proposed method might be a useful tool for network inference.

3.2. Inference Using DREAM4 Data.

In this subsection, we try to evaluate the effectiveness of DPLSQ-SS and perform a comparison with other methods in order to perform an unbiased evaluation since the results in Section 3.1 are based on the mathematical model adopted by DPLSQ-SS. We used synthetic datasets generated by GeneNetWeaver (GNW) [20], which provide benchmarks and performance testing

TABLE 1: Results on inference using synthetic data.

		Method		
		DPLSQ-SS	ARACNE	GeneNet
$n = 10$	Accuracy	0.779	0.578	0.571
	CPU time (sec.)	1.784	1.113	4.020
$n = 20$	Accuracy	0.722	0.554	0.390
	CPU time (sec.)	14.482	4.795	4.040

TABLE 2: Results on inference using DREAM4 data, where the accuracy is shown for each case.

	Method		
	DPLSQ-SS	ARACNE	GeneNet
Insilico_size_10_1	0.2666	0.2000	0.0666
Insilico_size_10_2	0.1875	0.2500	0.1250
Insilico_size_10_3	0.1333	0.2000	0.0666
Insilico_size_10_4	0.1538	0.3076	0.0769
Insilico_size_10_5	0.0833	0.1666	0.0833

for network inference methods in the DREAM (Dialogue on Reverse Engineering Assessment and Methods) challenge (http://www.the-dream-project.org/challenges). One aim of the DREAM project is to provide benchmark data on real and simulated expression data for network inference. This challenge includes several editions, where GNW has been developed to generate genetic network motifs and simulated expression data. In this evaluation, we used the DREAM4 challenge which is divided into three subchallenges called InSilico_Size10, InSilico_Size100, and InSilico_Size100_Multifactorial, consisting of five networks.

We validated the performance using InSilico_Size10 subchallenge consisting of gold standard 10 gene networks and simulated expression data generated under different conditions (wild-type, knockouts, knockdowns, multifactorial perturbations, and time series). Since only one set of wild-type data, which corresponds to static data, is provided for each network and it is not enough for inference, we generated 500 static data sets by randomly perturbing each data as in Section 3.1. The result is shown in Table 2, where the accuracy was evaluated as in Section 3.1. It is seen from the table that the performance of any method is not good. It is reasonable because inference was preformed based on one set of expression data (i.e., $m = 1$) although perturbed data were also used. Although ARACNE was better than DPLSQ-SS in four cases, DPLSQ-SS was better than ARACNE in one case. DPLSQ-SS was better than GeneNet in four cases and was comparative to GeneNet in one case. This result suggests that although DPLSQ-SS is not necessarily the best for simulated data in DREAM4, it has reasonable performance when a very few samples are given.

3.3. Completion Using Synthetic Data.

We also examined network completion using synthetic data. In this experiment, we adopted the nonlinear equations described in Section 3.1. In order to examine network completion, we also applied DPLSQ-SS to synthetic networks, which are generated by

TABLE 3: Results on completion with synthetic data on DPLSQ-SS.

	Number of added edges and number of deleted edges	Accuracy	CPU time (sec.)
$n = 10$	$k = 1, h = 1$	1.000	0.720
	$k = 2, h = 2$	1.000	5.810
	$k = 3, h = 3$	1.000	4.610
	$k = 4, h = 4$	1.000	5.000
	$k = 5, h = 5$	0.700	4.410
$n = 20$	$k = 1, h = 1$	1.000	2.760
	$k = 2, h = 2$	1.000	51.870
	$k = 3, h = 3$	0.833	46.220
	$k = 4, h = 4$	1.000	53.880
	$k = 5, h = 5$	0.700	48.910

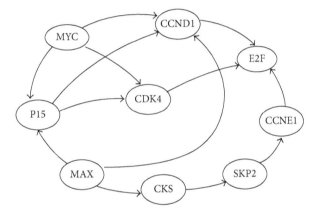

FIGURE 3: A part of small cell lung cancer network, containing RB/E2F pathway.

randomly adding k edges and deleting h edges from an original network.

We assess the DPLSQ-SS performance in terms of the accuracy of modified edges and the computational time for network completion. The accuracy is defined as follows:

$$\frac{h + k + \left| E_{\mathrm{org}} \cap E_{\mathrm{cmp}} \right| - \left| E_{\mathrm{org}} \right|}{h + k}, \tag{14}$$

where E_{org} and E_{cmp} are the set of edges in the original network and the completed network, respectively. This value takes 1 if all added and deleted edges are correct and takes 0 if all added and deleted edges are incorrect. For each (k, h), we took the averaged accuracy and CPU time for completing the network over 5 modifications for 10 and 20 gene networks, where we used the default values of $K = H = 2$. To avoid the numerical calculation error, we also generated additional 400 data sets for each of static solutions by adding random numbers uniformly distributed between -0.5 and 0.5.

The results are shown in Table 3. It is observed that DPLSQ-SS has quite high accuracy regardless of the number of k and h except for $k = h = 5$. It is also seen that the CPU time increases rapidly when applied to networks with

20 genes. In comparison with the CPU time for network inference by DPLSQ-SS, there seems to be a significant difference even if n equals 10. In this study, we used the default values of $K = 2$ and $H = 2$ for network completion, which were $K = 2$ and $H = 0$ for network inference. Moreover, the number of modified edges for network inference is much larger than that for network completion. However, the latter procedure requires more CPU time than the former procedure. This result suggests that the time complexity of DPLSQ-SS depends not so much on the number of modified edges, k and h, but depends much on the number of K and H as indicated in Section 2.3.

3.4. Inference Using Real Data. We also examined DPLSQ-SS for inference of gene networks from static data under multiple conditions. The aim of this experiment is to identify different static gene networks under different conditions and investigate the differences of these network topologies. We focus on the genetic network related to lung cancer and employed a partial network which contains RB/E2F pathway in human small cell lung cancer from the KEGG database [21] shown in Figure 3. RB/E2F pathway is one of two main tumor suppressor pathways and the retinoblastoma gene (RB) plays a key role in cancer [22]. RB is known to control the activity of E2F transcription factor which regulates the cell-cycle progression and E2F is under the control of both CDK4 and CCND1 (CyclinD1). It is also known that the activity of E2F plays an important role in the tumor cell proliferation and that absence of E2F leads to cancer formation. In this way, it is obvious that the gene abnormality of RB/E2F pathway is linked to cancer and there are precise differences between the cancer gene network and the normal gene network. Therefore, inferring the cancer and normal gene networks is quite meaningful. In this study, we demonstrate that DPLSQ-SS can distinguish the difference between cancer and normal networks from static expression data. Based on the KEGG database and Entrez Gene ID, we selected 9 genes shown in Table 4. We referred to RefGene (http://refgene.com/) for gene symbols and annotations and employed the resulting network as the original network.

As for the static expression data, we employed lung cancer microarray data obtained by Beer et al. [23]. They clustered hierarchically the gene expression profiles from lung adenocarcinoma tumor tissues and those from normal lung tissues. This data contains 86 tumor samples and 10 normal samples and is publicly available from the study of Choi and Kendziorski [24]. In order to investigate the relationship between cancer and normal gene network topologies, we performed network inference using these two types of data, where $K = 2$, $H = 0$, and $k = 13$ were used. In order to avoid the numerical calculation error, we also generated additional 5 data sets for each expression value by adding random numbers uniformly distributed between -0.5 and 0.5. The results are shown in Figure 4.

We also compared DPLSQ-SS with ARACNE and GeneNet using these real data. The result is shown in Table 5, where the accuracy (i.e., the ratio of the number of correctly inferred edges to the number of added edges) was calculated

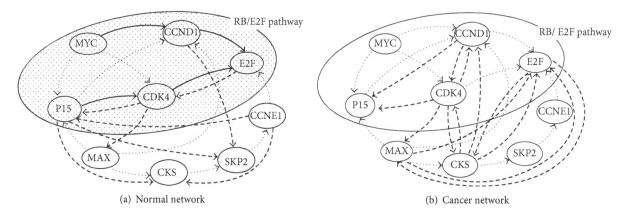

(a) Normal network   (b) Cancer network

FIGURE 4: Results on inference with gene expression data for cancer and normal samples. We could verify the activation of RB/E2F pathway in the normal network and the inactivation of it in the cancer network. The bold dashed arrows denote the incorrectly added edges. The bold solid arrows denote the correctly added edges (i.e., added edges that are included in the original network). Since directions of edges are ignored in comparison with ARACNE and GeneNet, bold dashed arrows connecting to P15 are regarded as correct in the evaluation of accuracy in Table 5.

TABLE 4: List of gene symbols and annotations in human small cell lung cancer network.

Number	Gene symbol	Gene annotation
1	MYC	v-myc myelocytomatosis viral oncogene homolog (avian)
2	P15	Cyclin-dependent kinase inhibitor 2B
3	CDK4/6	Cyclin-dependent kinase 4
4	CCND1	Cyclin D1
5	MAX	MYC associated factor X
6	CKS1	CDC28 protein kinase regulatory subunit 1B
7	SKP2	S-phase kinase-associated protein 2 (p45)
8	CCNE1	Cyclin E1
9	E2F3	E2F transcription factor 3

TABLE 5: Results on inference of real networks, where the accuracy is shown for each case.

	Method		
	DPLSQ-SS	ARACNE	GeneNet
Normal network	0.3846	0.3076	0.0769
Cancer network	0.1538	0.3846	0.0769

as in Section 3.1 and the networks obtained from the KEGG database were regarded as the correct networks. Although DPLSQ-SS was worse than ARACNE for the cancer network, it was better for the normal network. For both networks, DPLSQ-SS was better than GeneNet. This result suggests that the accuracy of DPLSQ-SS for real data is reasonable compared with existing methods.

Although the accuracy of DPLSQ-SS is not high for real data, there are significant differences between cancer and normal networks. The inferred normal network indicated the existence of RB/E2F pathway involved in the regulation of E2F activity. It is observed that the tumor suppressor gene P15 regulated CDK4 activity and E2F was under the regulation of both CDK4 and CCND1. On the other hand, in the inferred tumor network, we found no significant correlations between genes in RB/E2F pathway. Instead, we discovered the

regulation of CCND1 and deregulation of E2F activity. It has been reported that overexpression of CDK4/6 and CCND1 and deregulated E2F could contribute to cancer progression [22, 25]. Therefore, inference of two types of networks could produce the reasonable outcome that matches biological knowledge as mentioned above and could capture the features of each network. Although there is no common edge between the inferred cancer network and the original network, it is reasonable because cancer networks may be very different from normal networks. This result suggests that our proposed method can infer different static networks under the different conditions and can identify the feature of cancer and normal networks.

4. Conclusion

In this study, we addressed the problem of completing and inferring gene networks under the stationary conditions from static gene expression data. In our approach, we defined network completion as making the minimum amount of modifications to an initial network so that the inferred network is most consistent with the gene expression data. The aim of this study is (1) to complete genetic networks using static data and (2) to investigate the differences between two types of gene networks under different conditions. In order to achieve our goal, we proposed a novel method called DPLSQ-SS for network completion and network inference based on dynamic programming and least-squares fitting. This method works in polynomial time if the maximum indegree is bounded by a constant. We demonstrated the effectiveness of DPLSQ-SS through computational experiments using synthetic data and real data. In particular, we tried to infer the normal and lung cancer networks from static gene microarray data. As the results using synthetic data, DPLSQ-SS showed relatively good performance in comparison to other existing methods. As the results using microarray data from normal and lung cancer samples, it is seen that this method allows us to distinguish the differences between gene networks under different conditions.

There is some room for extending DPLSQ-SS. For example, we employed here simple nonlinear equations as gene regulation rules, but it can be replaced by more complex types of nonlinear equations. Although DPLSQ-SS works in polynomial time, the degree of polynomial is not low, which prevents the method from being applied to completion of large networks. However, DPLSQ-SS can be highly parallelizable: $\sigma_{k_j,h_j,j}$ can be computed independently for different $\sigma_{k_j,h_j,j}$s. Therefore, parallel implementation of DPLSQ-SS is also important future work. Although we have focused on completion and inference of gene regulatory networks, completion and inference of large-scale protein-protein or ChIP-chip/seq interaction networks are also important. Since the proposed method is only applicable to gene regulatory networks, extension and application of DPLSQ-SS for these networks should be studied in the future work.

Conflict of Interests

The authors declare that there is no conflict of interests regarding the publication of this paper.

Acknowledgment

This work was partially supported by Grant-in-Aid no. 22240009 from JSPS, Japan.

References

[1] S. Liang, S. Fuhrman, and R. Somogyi, "Reveal, a general reverse engineering algorithm for inference of genetic network architectures," *Pacific Symposium on Biocomputing. Pacific Symposium on Biocomputing*, pp. 18–29, 1998.

[2] T. Akutsu, S. Miyano, and S. Kuhara, "Inferring qualitative relations in genetic networks and metabolic pathways," *Bioinformatics*, vol. 16, no. 8, pp. 727–734, 2000.

[3] N. Friedman, M. Linial, I. Nachman, and D. Pe'er, "Using Bayesian networks to analyze expression data," *Journal of Computational Biology*, vol. 7, no. 3-4, pp. 601–620, 2000.

[4] S. Imoto, S. Kim, T. Goto et al., "Bayesian network and nonparametric heteroscedastic regression for nonlinear modeling of genetic network," *Journal of Bioinformatics and Computational Biology*, vol. 1, no. 2, pp. 231–252, 2003.

[5] P. D'Haeseleer, S. Liang, and R. Somogyi, "Genetic network inference: from co-expression clustering to reverse engineering," *Bioinformatics*, vol. 16, no. 8, pp. 707–726, 2000.

[6] Y. Wang, T. Joshi, X.-S. Zhang, D. Xu, and L. Chen, "Inferring gene regulatory networks from multiple microarray datasets," *Bioinformatics*, vol. 22, no. 19, pp. 2413–2420, 2006.

[7] R.-S. Wang, Y. Wang, X.-S. Zhang, and L. Chen, "Inferring transcriptional regulatory networks from high-throughput data," *Bioinformatics*, vol. 23, no. 22, pp. 3056–3064, 2007.

[8] H. Toh and K. Horimoto, "Inference of a genetic network by a combined approach of cluster analysis and graphical Gaussian modeling," *Bioinformatics*, vol. 18, no. 2, pp. 287–297, 2002.

[9] R. Opgen-Rhein and K. Strimmer, "Inferring gene dependency networks from genomic longitudinal data: a functional data approach," *REVSTAT*, vol. 4, no. 1, pp. 53–65, 2006.

[10] R. Opgen-Rhein and K. Strimmer, "From correlation to causation networks: a simple approximate learning algorithm and its application to high-dimensional plant gene expression data," *BMC Systems Biology*, vol. 1, article 37, 2007.

[11] M. Kim and J. Leskovec, "The network completion problem: inferring missing nodes and edges in networks," in *Proceedings of SIAM International Conference on Data Mining*, pp. 47–58, 2011.

[12] R. Guimerà and M. Sales-Pardo, "Missing and spurious interactions and the reconstruction of complex networks," *Proceedings of the National Academy of Sciences of the United States of America*, vol. 106, no. 52, pp. 22073–22078, 2009.

[13] S. Hanneke and E. P. Xing, "Network completion and survey sampling," *Journal of Machine Learning Research*, vol. 5, pp. 209–215, 2009.

[14] S. Saito, S. Aburatani, and K. Horimoto, "Network evaluation from the consistency of the graph structure with the measured data," *BMC Systems Biology*, vol. 2, article 84, 2008.

[15] T. Akutsu, T. Tamura, and K. Horimoto, "Completing networks using observed data," in *Proceedings of the 20th International Conference on Algorithmic Learning Theory*, pp. 126–140, 2009.

[16] N. Nakajima, T. Tamura, Y. Yamanishi, K. Horimoto, and T. Akutsu, "Network completion using dynamic programming and least-squares fitting," *The Scientific World Journal*, vol. 2012, Article ID 957620, 8 pages, 2012.

[17] N. Nakajima and T. Akutsu, "Exact and heuristic methods for network completion for time-varying genetic networks," *BioMed Research International*, vol. 2014, Article ID 684014, 14 pages, 2014.

[18] A. A. Margolin, K. Wang, W. K. Lim, M. Kustagi, I. Nemenman, and A. Califano, "Reverse engineering cellular networks," *Nature Protocols*, vol. 1, no. 2, pp. 662–671, 2006.

[19] A. A. Margolin, I. Nemenman, K. Basso et al., "ARACNE: an algorithm for the reconstruction of gene regulatory networks in a mammalian cellular context," *BMC Bioinformatics*, vol. 7, no. 1, article S7, 2006.

[20] T. Schaffter, D. Marbach, and D. Floreano, "GeneNetWeaver: in silico benchmark generation and performance profiling of network inference methods," *Bioinformatics*, vol. 27, no. 16, pp. 2263–2270, 2011.

[21] M. Kanehisa, S. Goto, M. Furumichi, M. Tanabe, and M. Hirakawa, "KEGG for representation and analysis of molecular networks involving diseases and drugs," *Nucleic Acids Research*, vol. 38, no. 1, pp. D355–D360, 2009.

[22] J. R. Nevins, "The Rb/E2F pathway and cancer," *Human Molecular Genetics*, vol. 10, no. 7, pp. 699–703, 2001.

[23] D. G. Beer, S. L. R. Kardia, C.-C. Huang et al., "Gene-expression profiles predict survival of patients with lung adenocarcinoma," *Nature Medicine*, vol. 8, no. 8, pp. 816–824, 2002.

[24] Y. Choi and C. Kendziorski, "Statistical methods for gene set co-expression analysis," *Bioinformatics*, vol. 25, no. 21, pp. 2780–2786, 2009.

[25] J. P. Alao, "The regulation of cyclin D1 degradation: roles in cancer development and the potential for therapeutic invention," *Molecular Cancer*, vol. 6, article 24, 2007.

15

Secondary Structure Preferences of Mn^{2+} Binding Sites in Bacterial Proteins

Tatyana Aleksandrovna Khrustaleva

Regulatory Proteins and Peptides Laboratory, Institute of Physiology of the National Academy of Sciences of Belarus, Akademicheskaya 28, 220072 Minsk, Belarus

Correspondence should be addressed to Tatyana Aleksandrovna Khrustaleva; tanissia.lir@gmail.com

Academic Editor: Bhaskar Dasgupta

3D structures of proteins with coordinated Mn^{2+} ions from bacteria with low, average, and high genomic GC-content have been analyzed (149 PDB files were used). Major Mn^{2+} binders are aspartic acid (6.82% of Asp residues), histidine (14.76% of His residues), and glutamic acid (3.51% of Glu residues). We found out that the motif of secondary structure "beta strand-major binder-random coil" is overrepresented around all the three major Mn^{2+} binders. That motif may be followed by either alpha helix or beta strand. Beta strands near Mn^{2+} binding residues should be stable because they are enriched by such beta formers as valine and isoleucine, as well as by specific combinations of hydrophobic and hydrophilic amino acid residues characteristic to beta sheet. In the group of proteins from GC-rich bacteria glutamic acid residues situated in alpha helices frequently coordinate Mn^{2+} ions, probably, because of the decrease of Lys usage under the influence of mutational GC-pressure. On the other hand, the percentage of Mn^{2+} sites with at least one amino acid in the "beta strand-major binder-random coil" motif of secondary structure (77.88%) does not depend on genomic GC-content.

1. Introduction

In general, there are three "major binders" of Mn^{2+} ions: oxygen atoms from carboxyl groups of aspartic and glutamic acids side chains and imidazole nitrogen atom from histidine side chain [1, 2]. Minor binders are oxygen atoms from hydroxyl groups of serine and threonine side chains; amide nitrogen and oxygen atoms from asparagine and glutamine side chains; sulfur atoms from thiol group of cysteine and thioether group of methionine; and oxygen atoms from peptide bonds of all the amino acids including even hydrophobic ones [1, 2].

There is some controversy in the results of *in silico* studies on amino acid preferences for Mn^{2+} binding. According to the work of Zheng et al. [1], there are three amino acid residues most frequently found in Mn^{2+} binding sites: His, Asp, and Glu. Histidine has the highest normalized frequency in binding sites, while glutamic acid has the lowest normalized frequency among those three amino acid residues [1]. According to the work of Brylinski and Skolnick [2],

aspartic acid has much higher preference to bind Mn^{2+} than glutamic acid and histidine.

Information on amino acid preferences and geometry of coordination spheres is used in algorithms for metal binding sites prediction, such as FINDSITE-metal [2], MetalDetector v2.0 [3], Fold-X [4], and FlexX [5]. However, the information on preferable 3D structural motifs is available mostly for Ca^{2+} and Zn^{2+} binding proteins. Well-known EF-hand motif for Ca^{2+} binding consists of two alpha helices and a loop between them [6]. The first helix known as E consists of 10–12 residues, and the second helix known as F also consists of 10–12 residues. The angle between those helices is close to 90°. The loop between the helices approximately 12 residues in length often includes "Asp-Xaa-Asp-Xaa-Asp-Gly" motif which is directly involved in Ca^{2+} coordination [7]. Recently, other proteins, able to bind Ca^{2+} containing the abovementioned motif but lacking one or both helices, have been described [8]. As to Zn^{2+} binding 3D structural motifs, Sri Krishna et al. classified them in eight different groups.

The aim of this study was to find out whether there is a secondary structural motif which is characteristic for relatively short parts of polypeptide chains around Mn^{2+} binding amino acid residues.

In fact, the same kind of secondary structural motif may be found in several 3D structural motifs. For example, four from eight 3D structural motifs for Zn^{2+} binding include such a secondary structural motif as beta hairpin. That is why the knowledge on preferable secondary structural motifs around each of the amino acid residues may be even more helpful for prediction of ion binding sites than the knowledge on the 3D structural motifs for the complete coordination spheres. Amino acid preferences have also been studied in the present work not just for binding residues but also for their neighbors.

It is known that amino acid content is not constant among proteins. The major cause of variations in amino acid content is symmetric mutational pressure [9]. Frequencies of those amino acid residues in proteomes which are encoded by GC-rich codons (Ala, Gly, Pro, and Arg) show direct dependence on GC-content of genomes [10]. The slope of that dependence for alanine is the steepest one [11]. Frequencies of those amino acid residues in proteomes which are encoded by GC-poor codons (Ile, Lys, Asn, Phe, Tyr, and Met) show inverse dependence on GC-content of genomes [10]. Slopes for isoleucine, lysine, and asparagine are steeper than those for phenylalanine, tyrosine, and methionine [12].

It is known that tertiary and secondary structures are more conserved in proteins than their primary sequences. That phenomenon is known as protein structure degeneracy. Different amino acid residues may substitute each other, while secondary and tertiary structures stay almost the same for homologous proteins because of the negative selection [13]. One may predict that secondary structure distribution around the most of residues binding the same cation will be similar for proteins with different amino acid content. However, that statement has to be tested in each particular study.

Even though three amino acids most frequently involved in Mn^{2+} binding (Asp, Glu, and His) are encoded by codons of average GC-content, their binding features and patterns of secondary structure distribution around them may depend on GC-content of genes. There are some interesting consequences of the growth of genomic GC-content which may bring some changes into the structure of Mn^{2+} binding sites. For example, total levels of both strongly hydrophobic and strongly hydrophilic amino acids in proteins show inverse dependence on G+C [11, 13]. The usage of sheet-like pentapeptides grows in alpha helices and in random coil due to mutational GC-pressure [14]. That is why we decided to study Mn^{2+} binding sites in three groups of bacterial proteins: from bacterial species with low, average, and high genomic GC-content. The same kind of methodology may be used in studies on other properties of proteins. Changes in amino acid content that occurred due to symmetric mutational pressure may theoretically result in reorganization of binding sites for certain ligands or even in the availability of potential binding sites.

2. Materials and Methods

Three sets of PDB files containing Mn^{2+} ions coordinated by amino acid residues have been collected from the Protein Data Bank (http://www.pdb.org). The total number of those files was equal to 149. The first set includes 39 PDB files with 3D structures of proteins from bacteria with genomic GC-content lower than 40%. The second set includes 62 PDB files with 3D structures of proteins from bacteria with average genomic GC-content (from 40% to 60%). The third set is composed of 48 PDB files with 3D structures of proteins from bacteria with GC-rich genomes (G + C > 60%). Identical proteins have not been used in this study, as well as close homologues. According to the results of the "decrease redundancy" algorithm (http://web.expasy.org/decrease_redundancy/), there were no sequences with similarity level higher than 60% in each of the three data sets.

GC-poor bacteria used in this study are *Bacillus subtilis* (18 files); *Bacillus anthracis* (4 files); *Bacillus caldovelox* (1 file); *Bacillus cereus* (1 file); *Clostridium cellulolyticum* (1 file); *Haemophilus influenzae* (3 files); *Listeria monocytogenes* (2 files); *Staphylococcus aureus* (5 files); and *Streptococcus pneumoniae* (4 files).

Bacteria with average genomic GC-content are *Escherichia coli* (38 files); *Brucella melitensis* (2 files); *Geobacillus stearothermophilus* (4 files); *Neisseria meningitidis* (3 files); *Paenibacillus polymyxa* (1 file); *Salmonella typhimurium* (1 file); *Synechocystis* sp. (4 files); and *Thermotoga maritima* (9 files).

The list of bacteria with GC-rich genomes is the following: *Mycobacterium tuberculosis* (19 files); *Deinococcus radiodurans* (4 files); *Pseudomonas aeruginosa* (5 files); *Pseudomonas cichorii* (1 file); *Pseudomonas putida* (3 files); *Pseudomonas stutzeri* (2 files); *Streptomyces rubiginosus* (1 file); *Thermus thermophilus* (10 files); and *Xanthomonas campestris* (3 files).

Complete list of PDB identifiers can be found in the supplementary material file "PDB identifiers.xlsx;" (see Supplementary Material available online at http://dx.doi.org/ 10.1155/2014/501841). The data on classification displayed in "Annotations" section of PDB pages were available for almost one half of proteins. About 54% of proteins were classified according to CATH (Class, Architecture, Topology, Homologous superfamily), and 49% were classified according to SCOP (Structural Classification of Proteins). From all proteins classified according to CATH, 77% were alpha and beta proteins, 7% were mostly alpha proteins, and 5% were mostly beta ones, while 11% of them contained several different domains. From all proteins classified by SCOP, 47% were alpha and beta (a/b) proteins, 16% were alpha and beta (a + b) proteins, 10% were *all* alpha proteins, and 4% were *all* beta proteins, while 23% of them were mixed proteins. So, most of the studied proteins contain both alpha helices and beta strands. Percentage of parallel beta strands is higher than that of antiparallel beta strands. It is also important to mention that 85% of proteins used in this study are enzymes. Most of the Mn^{2+} coordinating sites should be involved in enzymatic activity.

We used descriptions of Mn^{2+} binding sites which can be found in PDB files. For each of the amino acid residues involved in Mn^{2+} coordination, the following data have been collected: (i) amino acid residues situated in five positions towards N-terminus (−5/−4/−3/−2/−1) and C-terminus (+1/+2/+3/+4/+5) from the binding residue; (ii) secondary structure of those amino acid residues and of the binding residue itself. In other words, we collected three sets of short amino acid sequences (11 amino acids in length) with the Mn^{2+} binding residue in the center of each of them.

Certain amino acid residues may be included in two binding sites (for different Mn^{2+} ions). To avoid the bias in our data set, we deleted repeated records. Finally, there were 161 amino acids involved in Mn^{2+} binding in proteins from GC-poor bacteria; 248 amino acids in proteins from bacteria with average genomic G + C; and 194 amino acids in proteins from GC-rich bacteria.

There are three amino acid residues (major binders) most frequently coordinating Mn^{2+} ions: aspartic acid, histidine, and glutamic acid. We repeated the procedure of data extraction for Asp, His, and Glu residues which *are not involved* in Mn^{2+} binding in the common set of PDB files. There were 2813 Asp, 1080 His, and 3572 Glu residues in the "control" data set.

Three sets of amino acid sequences containing Mn^{2+} binding residues in their centers are available in supplementary material file "Mn(II) binding sites.xlsx". Three control sets of amino acid sequences with those major binders (Asp, His, and Glu) which did not coordinate Mn^{2+} in their centers can be found in supplementary material file "D, H and E residues non binding Mn(II).xlsx".

Amino acid usage in each of the ten positions around each of the three major binders has been calculated for binding and nonbinding residues. Then, probabilities to be situated around each of the major binders have been calculated as ratios between the usage of a given amino acid in the certain position near the binding residue and the sum of its usages around binding and nonbinding residues. Statistical significance of those probabilities has been acquired from the results of two-tailed t-test. Similar statistical procedure has been performed for secondary structure elements around binding and nonbinding Asp, His, and Glu residues.

For calculation of amino acid frequencies in proteins from three data sets, we deleted their polyhistidine tails. This procedure was important for correct calculation of the percentage of His residues involved in Mn^{2+} binding. We also calculated percentage of Asp and Glu residues involved in Mn^{2+} coordination (relatively to their total usages).

Average usages of Lys and Arg have been calculated near binding and nonbinding glutamic acid residues being in alpha helix, beta strand, and random coil.

To complete analyses of secondary structure motifs involved in Mn^{2+} coordination, we compared by t-test usages of amino acids situated in certain types of secondary and supersecondary structure in the set of binding residues and in the whole set of amino acids. For this *in silico* experiment, we used alpha helices, beta strands, four types of coil regions (BCH: coil between beta strand and alpha helix; HCB: coil between alpha helix and beta strand; BCB: coil between two beta strands; and HCH: coil between two alpha helices), and four types of supersecondary structural motifs (B-BCH-H: beta strand and alpha helix separated by a region of coil; H-HCB-B: alpha helix and beta strand separated by the region of coil; B-BCB-B: two beta strands and coil between them; H-HCH-H: two alpha helices and coil between them).

There are 15 apo forms available in the Protein Data Bank for proteins used in this study. Amino acid sequences of apo and holo forms are 100% identical. All other ligands, except Mn^{2+} cation(s), are identical for apo and holo forms. Secondary structures around Mn^{2+} coordinating residues have been compared for holo and apo forms in subsequent pairs: 1VHA-1VH8; 3F8N-2RGV; 1ONO-1ONN; 1WSE-1WSH; 1XUU-3CM4; 2D0C-2D0A; 2HXG-2AJT; 2NRZ-2NRW; 3GME-3GLL; 3TMY-1TMY; 2E6C-2E69; 2YES-2WE9; 2YF3-2YF4; 2ZXP-2ZXO; 3ITX-3ITY.

Types of pentapeptides composed of hydrophilic and hydrophobic amino acids have been determined for "−5−−1" and "−4−0" positions for Asp, Glu, and His residues. Amino acid residues have been classified into hydrophilic (W) and hydrophobic (O) ones according to the Eisenberg scale [15] in which Asp, Glu, His, Gln, Ser, Thr, Arg, Asn, and Lys are hydrophilic. Percentages of sheet-like pentapeptides [14] in beta strands situated in the N-terminal direction from the binding and nonbinding Asp, Glu, and His residues have been compared by t-test.

3. Results

3.1. Amino Acids Involved in Mn^{2+} Binding. The percentage of aspartic acid residues in Mn^{2+} binding sites is equal to 34.16%. The percentage of histidine residues in those sites is somewhat lower (31.01%), while the difference between them is not significant ($P > 0.05$). The percentage of glutamic acid residues in Mn^{2+} binding sites (21.56%) is significantly lower than those for aspartic acid and histidine ($P < 0.001$). As one can see in Table 1, this situation is characteristic for all the three groups of proteins. There is no dependence between GC-content of genes and the distribution of three major Mn^{2+} binders (aspartic acid, histidine, and glutamic acid) in binding sites.

On the other hand, the difference between the usage of all other amino acid residues (minor binders) in those sites from proteins encoded by GC-rich genes (6.70%) and proteins encoded by genes with average GC-content (17.34%) is significant ($P < 0.001$). The difference between the sum of minor Mn^{2+} binders for proteins encoded by GC-rich and GC-poor genes is also significant (6.70% versus 14.91%; $P < 0.01$). This fact can be explained by the known tendency: total usage of hydrophilic amino acid residues in proteins decreases with the growth of GC-content in genes [11, 13].

It is also important to calculate the percentage of amino acid residues involved in Mn^{2+} binding relative to their average usage in proteins. It is known that histidine is one of the rare amino acids, while glutamic acid is even more abundant than aspartic acid [10, 12]. In the proteins from our data set, amino acid usages of the major Mn^{2+} binders

TABLE 1: The most common interacting residues in Mn^{2+} binding sites.

Amino acid	GC-poor bacteria		Bacteria with average genomic G + C		GC-rich bacteria	
	% among amino acid residues from Mn^{2+} binding sites	% of amino acid residues involved in binding of Mn^{2+} from the total amino acid usage	% among amino acid residues from Mn^{2+} binding sites	% of amino acid residues involved in binding of Mn^{2+} from the total amino acid usage	% among amino acid residues from Mn^{2+} binding sites	% of amino acid residues involved in binding of Mn^{2+} from the total amino acid usage
Asp	32.92	6.68	33.47	6.73	36.08	7.06
Glu	19.25	2.96	22.18	3.47	22.68	4.11
His	32.92	17.10	27.02	13.24	34.54	14.86

are as follows: Glu: $7.59 \pm 0.34\%$; Asp: $6.22 \pm 0.24\%$; His: $2.68 \pm 0.19\%$. One can easily come to the conclusion that histidine is overrepresented in Mn^{2+} binding sites relatively to aspartic and, especially, glutamic acids. Indeed, 14.76% of histidine residues are involved in Mn^{2+} binding. In contrast, 6.82% of aspartic and just 3.51% of glutamic acid residues participate in binding of that ion (ions). GC-content of genes does not significantly influence the percentage of His, Asp, and Glu residues involved in Mn^{2+} binding by proteins (see Table 1).

It is important to mention that 17.69% of glutamic acid residues and 13.59% of aspartic acid residues participated in binding of two Mn^{2+} ions. Histidine residues cannot bind two Mn^{2+} ions simultaneously.

So, the major Mn^{2+} binders are Asp, His, and Glu. His is overrepresented in Mn^{2+} binding sites relatively to Asp, while Glu is underrepresented.

3.2. Secondary Structure of the Region around the Aspartic Acid Involved in Mn^{2+} Binding.

We compared distribution of secondary structure elements around the Asp residues involved in Mn^{2+} binding and those Asp residues which are not involved in that ion coordination. Probabilities for Asp to be Mn^{2+} binding residue are given in Table 2. As one can see in Table 2, beta strand is significantly overrepresented in $-5, -4, -3, -2, -1, 0,$ and $+1$ positions from the Asp residues which bind Mn^{2+} relatively to those which do not bind that ion. It means that there is usually a beta strand near the Asp from Mn^{2+} binding sites. Interestingly, that beta strand can usually be found in the N-terminal direction and not in the C-terminal one. Random coil is significantly overrepresented in $+1, +2, +3, +4,$ and $+5$ positions (see Table 2). So, Asp residues binding Mn^{2+} are usually surrounded by the beta strand in the N-terminal direction and random coil in the C-terminal direction. Alpha helix and helix 3/10 are, in general, underrepresented around Asp residues involved in Mn^{2+} coordination.

Most of the preferences in amino acid distribution near Asp residues binding Mn^{2+} can be explained by their secondary structure formation propensities. Such strong beta strand formers as valine and isoleucine [16] are overrepresented in certain positions in the N-terminal direction from the Asp residues binding Mn^{2+}. Even though leucine

is usually described as strong helix former [16], it is often involved in beta strand formation because of its hydrophobicity [14]. That is why leucine is significantly overrepresented in $-5, -4,$ and -3 positions (see Table 2). Three other strong helix formers (Ala, Glu, and Gln) are underrepresented in certain positions in the N-terminal direction from the Asp involved in Mn^{2+} binding (see Table 2). As to Arg and Lys, which are listed among helix formers too [16], their underrepresentation can be linked with the positive charge of their side chains as well.

It is important to highlight that Asp residues are significantly overrepresented in -2 and $+2$ positions around the Asp residues binding Mn^{2+}. One may think that there should be many Asp-Xaa-Asp-Xaa-Asp-Gly motifs in Mn^{2+} binding sites; see Table 2. However, this type of site characteristic for Ca^{2+} binding regions [17] was found only once in our data set. There are also just two Asp-Xaa-Asp-Xaa-Xaa-Gly and three Xaa-Xaa-Asp-Xaa-Asp-Gly sites which are similar to canonical sites for Ca^{2+} binding. So, relatively short Asp-Xaa-Asp and Asp-Xaa-Xaa-Gly motifs seem to be characteristic for Mn^{2+} binding sites. Histidine residues are also overrepresented around Asp interacting with Mn^{2+} (in $-2, +1, +2, +3,$ and $+4$ positions). Serine which may sometimes provide its –OH group for Mn^{2+} coordination is overrepresented in -1 position, while threonine also possessing that kind of group is overrepresented in $+1$ position. Asparagine with carboxamide group able to participate in Mn^{2+} coordination can frequently be found in $+2$ position (see Table 2). From these data, we can conclude that Mn^{2+} binders can often be found in the same linear sequence. Minor binders (such as Ser, Thr, and Asn) are involved in binding mostly in case if they are close neighbors of the major binders. On the other hand, they can contribute to the total hydrophilicity of the binding area.

Glycine is overrepresented in $-5, -1,$ and $+3$ positions probably contributing into the flexibility of the Asp residue involved in Mn^{2+} binding. Being a strong secondary structure breaker [16], proline is underrepresented in $-3, -1, +1,$ and $+2$ positions, while it is overrepresented in $+4$ position.

In general, Mn^{2+} binding aspartic acid residue is usually surrounded by hydrophobic amino acids (Val, Ile, and Leu) which form beta strand in the N-terminal direction and coil formers (His, Asp, Asn, Pro, and Gly) in the C-terminal direction. Major (His, Asp) and minor (Ser, Thr, and Asn) Mn^{2+} binders are overrepresented near that residue.

TABLE 2: Probabilities of amino acids and secondary structure elements occurrence near the aspartic acid binding Mn^{+2}. Significantly overrepresented amino acids and secondary structure elements are written in **bold** font; significantly underrepresented ones are written in *italic* font.

	Position										
	−5	−4	−3	−2	−1	0	+1	+2	+3	+4	+5
Secondary structure elements											
Alpha helix	*0.1796*	*0.2099*	*0.2427*	*0.2757*	*0.3284*	*0.3450*	*0.3750*	*0.3923*	*0.4062*	*0.4153*	*0.4229*
Helix 3/10	*0.1435*	*0.1510*	*0.1379*	*0.1846*	*0.1902*	*0.3374*	0.3890	0.5680	0.5579	0.5497	0.5340
Beta strand	**0.7168**	**0.7501**	**0.7617**	**0.7797**	**0.7586**	**0.7487**	**0.6100**	0.5517	0.5250	*0.4016*	*0.4096*
Random coil	0.5246	*0.4327*	*0.4106*	*0.4193*	0.4908	0.5285	**0.5748**	**0.5660**	**0.5771**	**0.6264**	**0.6217**
Amino acid residues											
Gly	**0.6370**	0.5558	*0.3270*	0.4731	**0.6460**		0.5860	0.4783	**0.6672**	0.4998	0.5666
Ala	0.4842	*0.3034*	0.4950	*0.3750*	0.4514		0.5373	*0.3277*	0.5514	*0.3597*	0.5503
Arg	*0.2299*	0.3577	*0.1282*	0.4743	*0.1549*		*0.1403*	0.4793	*0.1268*	0.5027	0.5420
Pro	0.5154	0.3658	*0.1608*	0.3739	*0.2431*		0.2746	0.2586	0.4131	**0.6845**	0.5039
Asp	0.5393	0.4436	*0.3350*	**0.6726**	0.5070		0.4226	**0.6602**	0.5108	0.6133	0.5779
Glu	*0.2582*	*0.3646*	*0.1760*	*0.0657*	0.4343		0.4201	*0.3424*	0.4847	0.4610	0.4299
Ser	0.4719	0.5163	0.4048	0.4725	**0.6910**		0.6380	0.5689	0.5003	0.5770	0.6512
Thr	0.3882	*0.1855*	0.4723	0.6461	0.5266		**0.6485**	0.4065	0.5931	0.5352	0.4776
His	0.4805	0.6318	0.6570	**0.7083**	*0.1879*		**0.7599**	**0.7252**	**0.7558**	**0.6928**	0.5135
Gln	0.4885	*0.3112*	*0.3250*	0.4054	0.3304		0.5678	0.3378	0.5758	0.4960	0.5348
Leu	**0.6035**	**0.6947**	**0.6182**	0.4934	0.5553		0.4201	0.5345	0.5134	0.4761	0.4477
Val	**0.6213**	0.5765	**0.7197**	0.4899	**0.6191**		0.5851	0.4018	0.4680	0.4045	0.4777
Cys	0.6184	0.5520	0.5529	0.4680	0.7590		0.4053	0.5605	0.5840	0.3918	0.3335
Trp	*0.0000*	*0.0000*	0.4445	0.4243	0.5059		0.4874	0.7362	*0.0000*	0.2677	0.6925
Phe	*0.2463*	0.4276	0.5089	0.4954	0.6110		0.5702	0.5567	0.4872	0.4516	0.4760
Tyr	0.4526	0.5446	0.5939	0.5095	0.3509		0.3762	0.3193	0.5080	0.4889	0.3463
Met	0.5173	0.3223	0.6056	0.6057	0.4699		0.5728	0.5943	0.2946	0.6626	0.4124
Ile	0.6001	0.6224	**0.7370**	0.5852	0.4886		0.4826	0.4942	0.4968	0.4914	*0.3347*
Asn	0.4551	0.5931	*0.0000*	0.5943	0.3750		0.3671	**0.6858**	0.4067	0.4742	0.4787
Lys	0.3930	0.3637	*0.2196*	*0.2408*	*0.0000*		*0.1701*	0.5178	*0.1870*	*0.2516*	0.4428

In Figure 1, one can see the concrete distribution of secondary structure elements around Asp residues binding Mn^{2+}. More than 60% of amino acid residues in −4 and −3 positions form beta strand (see Figure 1(a)). The percentage of amino acid residues forming beta strand is also high in −5 and −2 positions (see Figure 1(a)). This preference for beta strand from −5 to −2 positions is characteristic for proteins encoded by GC-poor (Figure 1(b)) and GC-rich genes (Figure 1(d)), as well as for proteins encoded by genes with average GC-content (Figure 1(c)).

Random coil is the most frequently observed conformation of amino acid residues near the aspartic acid involved in Mn^{2+} binding in the positions from −1 to +5. This tendency is characteristic for all the three groups of proteins encoded by genes of different GC-content (see Figure 1).

Secondary structure near Asp residues which are not involved in Mn^{2+} binding is quite different from that represented in Figure 1. Alpha helix is the most frequently observed element of secondary structure from −5 to −3 and from +1 to +5 positions (about 35–45%). Random coil is most frequently observed from −2 to 0 positions only (about 40–45%). Beta strand can rarely be found near the Asp residue

which is not involved in Mn^{2+} binding. The highest frequency is characteristic to −5 and +5 positions (above 20%).

There is a clear preference for asymmetric secondary structure distribution around aspartic acid residues providing oxygen atoms from their side chains for Mn^{2+} coordination: beta strand is situated in the N-terminal direction, while random coil is situated in the C-terminal direction.

3.3. Secondary Structure of the Region around the Histidine Involved in Mn^{2+} Binding. Preferable secondary structure around histidine residues binding Mn^{2+} (see Table 3) is similar to that around aspartic acid residues. Beta strand is the preferable type of secondary structure for positions from −5 to 0. Random coil is overrepresented from +2 to +5 positions (see Table 3). Alpha helix is underrepresented around histidine residues binding Mn^{2+}.

Amino acid preferences for ten positions near Mn^{2+} binding histidine residues do not have too much in common with those near aspartic acid residues (see Table 3). The only one overrepresented beta strand former is isoleucine (in −5

TABLE 3: Probabilities of amino acids and secondary structure elements occurrence near the histidine binding Mn^{+2}. Significantly overrepresented amino acids and secondary structure elements are written in **bold** font; significantly underrepresented ones are written in *italic* font.

					Position						
	−5	−4	−3	−2	−1	0	+1	+2	+3	+4	+5
					Secondary structure						
Alpha helix	*0.3529*	*0.3658*	*0.3722*	*0.3875*	*0.3926*	*0.3743*	*0.3520*	*0.4060*	*0.4216*	*0.4283*	*0.4377*
Helix 3/10	*0.1925*	*0.1996*	*0.1087*	0.3760	0.4942	0.6047	0.6233	0.5132	0.5301	0.5028	0.5619
Beta strand	**0.6909**	**0.7072**	**0.6777**	**0.6241**	**0.6109**	**0.6085**	0.5758	0.4659	0.4537	0.4593	0.5050
Random coil	0.4714	*0.4269*	0.4756	0.5203	0.5102	0.5062	0.5415	**0.5858**	**0.5881**	**0.5867**	**0.5562**
					Amino acid residues						
Gly	0.6023	0.5387	**0.6237**	0.4542	0.6047		0.5111	0.5110	0.4700	0.5090	0.5105
Ala	0.4429	0.4286	*0.3014*	0.6146	*0.3698*		**0.6546**	0.3897	0.4648	0.4391	*0.3511*
Arg	0.5318	0.4737	0.4076	*0.2917*	0.4558		*0.3026*	0.4410	0.4804	0.3694	0.5197
Pro	0.4229	0.4390	0.5047	*0.2392*	0.4987		*0.3511*	0.3794	0.5078	0.6874	0.5455
Asp	0.3510	0.6344	0.5209	0.6087	**0.6750**		*0.2911*	0.5713	0.4739	0.4474	0.5105
Glu	0.3804	0.4838	0.5212	0.5326	0.3849		0.4055	0.3864	0.5007	0.4144	**0.6324**
Ser	0.4728	0.5826	0.4980	0.5494	0.5863		**0.7419**	*0.0978*	0.5219	0.5802	0.5573
Thr	0.4240	0.5182	0.5166	0.5641	0.4518		0.5387	**0.6706**	0.4724	0.3971	**0.6449**
His	0.5489	0.5257	0.5404	**0.7368**	0.4190		0.6764	**0.8082**	*0.2810*	0.6637	0.5514
Gln	0.5220	*0.2021*	0.4725	0.3245	*0.1381*		0.3898	0.5475	0.5442	0.4031	0.5182
Leu	0.4046	0.5090	0.5548	0.4323	0.5618		0.4203	0.4750	0.4355	0.4289	0.4841
Val	0.5500	0.4548	0.6161	0.4453	*0.3470*		*0.2674*	*0.3332*	0.3967	*0.2995*	0.4563
Cys	0.8949	0.6196	*0.0000*	0.6837	0.5906		0.2911	0.6570	0.6209	0.6568	0.5891
Trp	0.3405	0.4872	0.2416	0.7546	0.7121		0.7853	0.6885	0.6417	**0.7782**	0.2906
Phe	0.4969	0.3161	0.4387	0.4013	0.3441		0.4560	0.4380	**0.7076**	0.4738	*0.1153*
Tyr	0.6653	0.3878	0.4100	0.5355	0.5442		0.5640	0.6372	0.6323	0.6707	*0.2106*
Met	0.5390	0.5246	**0.7035**	0.5043	0.5459		0.4721	*0.2583*	0.6417	0.3647	0.3892
Ile	**0.6665**	**0.6516**	0.4374	*0.2859*	0.5639		0.5630	0.5199	0.4174	0.4135	0.5182
Asn	0.5579	*0.2262*	0.4300	0.5439	0.6292		0.3194	0.5999	0.4114	**0.7416**	0.4828
Lys	0.3661	0.4821	*0.0886*	*0.1288*	*0.3034*		0.3575	*0.1932*	0.5771	*0.2601*	0.5197

and −4 positions). Interestingly, alanine (strong helix former) has some position specific preferences: it is underrepresented in −3, −1, and +5 positions, but it is overrepresented in +1 position (see Table 3). Glycine is overrepresented in −3 position, while proline is underrepresented in −2 and +1 positions.

Major Mn^{2+} binders are grouped in the following way: His in −2 and +2 positions; Asp in −1 position; Glu in +5 position. As to the minor Mn^{2+} binders, Ser is overrepresented in +1 position; Asn is overrepresented in +4 position, and Thr is overrepresented in +2 and +5 positions.

Positively charged arginine is underrepresented in −2 and +1 positions, while lysine is significantly underrepresented in −3, −2, −1, +2, and +4 positions.

In Figure 2(a), one can see that beta strand is the preferable conformation for amino acid residues from −5 to −3 positions. However, frequencies of amino acid residues in beta strand conformation in those positions are somewhat lower for histidine surroundings (about 45%) than for aspartic acid surroundings. Random coil is the favorable conformation from −2 to +5 positions. There are some variations on this common theme in Figures 2(b)–2(d), while in general GC-content of genes seems to have no influence on the preferable secondary structure around histidine residues binding Mn^{2+}.

Secondary structure elements around histidine residues not involved in Mn^{2+} binding are distributed in the following way: alpha helix is preferable (from 35 to 45%) for all positions, except −1 position with the preference for random coil; the difference between percentage of helix and percentage of coil is low; the percentage of beta strand in all positions is close to 20%.

Manganese (II) ions binding histidine residues are usually surrounded by the same kind of asymmetric secondary structure elements as aspartic acid residues.

3.4. Secondary Structure of the Region around the Glutamic Acid Involved in Mn^{2+} Binding.

There is a clear preference for beta strand situated from −4 to +2 positions for glutamic acid residues involved in Mn^{2+} binding (see Table 4). Random coil is overrepresented in +5 position only (see Table 4). These data confirm that "beta strand-major binder-random coil" secondary structural motif is a characteristic of all the three major Mn^{2+} binders (Asp, His, and Glu).

TABLE 4: Probabilities of amino acids and secondary structure elements occurrence near the glutamic acid binding Mn^{+2}. Significantly overrepresented amino acids and secondary structure elements are written in **bold** font; significantly underrepresented ones are written in *italic* font.

	\-5	\-4	\-3	\-2	\-1	0	+1	+2	+3	+4	+5
						Position					
					Secondary structure						
Alpha helix	*0.4389*	*0.4369*	*0.4184*	*0.4169*	*0.4132*	*0.4239*	*0.4369*	*0.4466*	0.4658	0.4784	0.4824
Helix 3/10	0.3244	*0.1428*	*0.1397*	*0.1206*	*0.2046*	*0.2120*	*0.2941*	0.3227	0.4288	0.4298	0.4209
Beta strand	0.5667	**0.7125**	**0.7486**	**0.7876**	**0.7906**	**0.7422**	**0.6879**	**0.6441**	0.5720	0.5235	0.4387
Random coil	0.5514	*0.4260*	*0.4037*	*0.3634*	*0.3782*	0.4596	0.5024	0.5168	0.5190	0.5276	**0.5635**
					Amino acid residues						
Gly	0.5211	0.6336	0.4237	0.5153	0.4063		0.5083	0.5928	0.5402	0.5435	0.4032
Ala	0.3723	0.4991	0.5324	0.5452	0.4904		0.5185	0.5102	0.5357	0.3980	0.3706
Arg	0.5484	0.3906	*0.1075*	0.6085	*0.1092*		0.4305	0.5382	*0.1652*	0.6204	0.4530
Pro	*0.2502*	0.5342	0.5540	*0.1581*	*0.1908*		0.5971	0.3686	0.5569	*0.1365*	0.5218
Asp	0.5290	0.4307	0.3942	0.6160	0.5934		0.3986	0.6196	0.3634	0.5335	0.5604
Glu	0.4256	0.4299	0.3910	0.3654	0.5080		0.4157	*0.3132*	0.4221	0.4578	0.5145
Ser	0.4331	0.4726	*0.3015*	0.3992	0.5043		0.5340	0.4678	0.5944	0.5238	0.1456
Thr	0.4928	0.6066	0.5354	0.5818	0.5080		0.5094	0.4405	0.4055	0.6249	0.6619
His	0.6939	0.2517	0.5485	0.6433	0.5667		0.6924	0.6965	**0.8356**	0.5716	0.6361
Gln	0.3413	*0.2860*	0.3184	0.5547	0.3351		0.4316	0.4573	0.3449	0.4392	0.6356
Leu	0.4900	*0.3047*	0.5152	0.4727	0.6081		0.4881	*0.3579*	0.4890	0.4532	0.3911
Val	0.4343	0.5487	**0.6632**	*0.3459*	0.5596		**0.6440**	*0.2802*	0.4865	0.5228	0.4701
Cys	*0.0000*	*0.0000*	0.7130	0.4774	0.7331		*0.0000*	0.6770	0.5011	0.4911	0.4146
Trp	0.7566	0.7077	0.3942	*0.0000*	*0.0000*		0.8008	*0.0000*	0.4296	*0.0000*	0.5235
Phe	0.6538	0.6079	**0.7460**	0.6494	0.6041		0.3868	0.5892	0.5105	0.5135	0.5668
Tyr	0.5313	0.5891	0.4059	0.3326	0.4239		0.4810	0.3842	0.6738	0.5359	0.5808
Met	0.7144	0.4412	0.2897	0.6551	0.6262		0.4713	0.4759	0.5786	0.6281	0.6272
Ile	0.5946	0.6594	0.5899	0.4762	**0.6830**		0.4488	0.5580	0.5384	0.5150	0.5065
Asn	*0.1730*	0.5097	0.6126	0.4046	0.3917		0.4976	0.6646	0.4686	0.4375	0.6089
Lys	0.3916	*0.3233*	*0.3320*	0.3510	*0.2028*		*0.1066*	0.5681	*0.2369*	0.4770	0.4492

Hydrophobic amino acids known as strong beta strand formers are overrepresented in the N-terminal direction from the Glu residues binding Mn^{2+} (see Table 4). Valine is overrepresented in −3 and +1 positions; isoleucine is overrepresented in −1 position; phenylalanine is overrepresented in −3 position.

Among major and minor Mn^{2+} binders, only histidine is significantly overrepresented in +3 position (see Table 4). Once again, arginine is underrepresented in three positions, while lysine is underrepresented in five different positions (see Table 4).

In proteins encoded by GC-poor genes and by genes with average G + C, the pattern of secondary structure distribution around Glu residues binding Mn^{2+} (see Figures 3(b) and 3(c)) is in general similar to the patterns found around aspartic acid and histidine. However, in proteins encoded by GC-rich genes, glutamic acid preferably binds Mn^{2+} being included in alpha helix (see Figure 3(d)). The kind of secondary structure elements distribution shown in Figure 3(d) is similar to that for Glu residues which do not bind Mn^{2+} (percentage of alpha helix is about 45–50% in all positions, percentage of coil is equal to approximately 30%, and the rest is left for beta strand

and helix 3/10). However, the traces of the preference for beta strand from −4 to 0 positions still can be seen in Figure 3(d).

Even though the most commonly distributed kind of secondary structural motif (beta strand-major binder-random coil) is characteristic for Glu residues binding Mn^{2+}, in proteins encoded by GC-rich genes glutamic acid residues from alpha helices became able to bind that ion too.

3.5. Secondary Structures in Mn^{2+} Coordinating Spheres without "Beta Strand-Major Binder-Random Coil" Motif. The number of Mn^{2+} coordinating spheres which contain at least one binding residue situated in the "beta strand-major binder-random coil" motif is equal to 77.8%. Coordinating sites without that motif demonstrate some characteristic features. The most frequently used binder in those sites is Glu (51.6%). Two other major binders (Asp, 15.6%, and His, 23.0%) are used less frequently, while the percentage of all other amino acids participating in Mn^{2+} coordination is relatively high (25.4%).

Secondary structure distribution around Glu residues from the described type of Mn^{2+} binding sites is very specific:

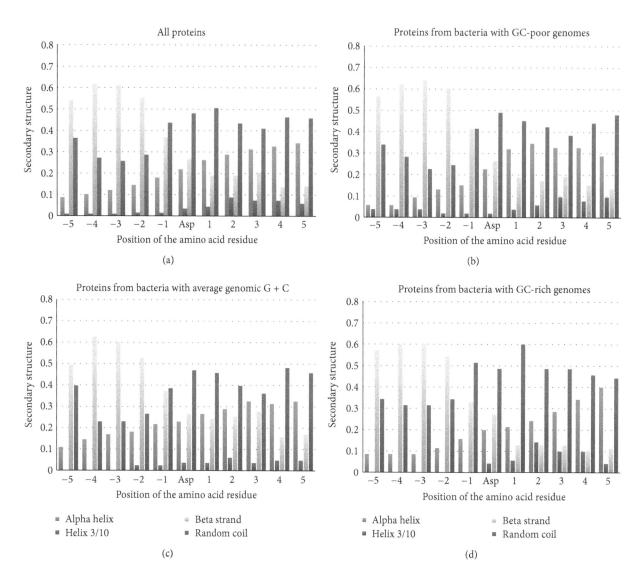

FIGURE 1: Secondary structure distribution around aspartic acid residues binding Mn^{+2} ions in all the proteins (a); in proteins from GC-poor bacteria (b); in proteins from bacteria with average genomic GC-content (c); in proteins from GC-rich bacteria (d).

alpha helix is found in 80–90% of cases in all the positions around glutamic acid. Lysine residues are underrepresented in −4, −3, −2, −1, +1, and +3 positions around Glu, while arginine residues are underrepresented in −3 and +3 positions and overrepresented in −2 and +2 positions. It means that Arg situated on the different surface of alpha helix cannot disturb Mn^{2+} binding by Glu, unlike Arg situated on the same surface. As to Lys, its high frequency in helices seems to be the main cause of their low level of usage around Mn^{2+} coordinating residues. However, those helices (or regions of helices) which have no lysine residues are able to bind Mn^{2+}.

Some parts of coordination spheres which do not have any binder that fit within the dominant pattern (29.2%) contain just a single amino acid residue coordinating Mn^{2+} cation. Other ligands included in coordination spheres together with those single amino acid residues should be responsible for the cation binding.

3.6. Decrease of Lysine Usage as the Most Probable Cause of the GC-Pressure Induced Switch in Structural Types of Mn^{2+} Binding Sites for Glutamic Acid. As one can see in Tables 2–4, lysine is underrepresented around Asp, His, and Glu residues binding Mn^{2+} much more than any other amino acid. Lysine is encoded by GC-poor codons (AAA and AAG). It is known that total level of lysine usage in proteins decreases steeply with the growth of G + C in genes [12]. Indeed, in the set of proteins used in the present work, the usage of lysine is equal to 7.21 ± 0.66% for proteins from GC-poor bacteria; 5.94 ± 0.58% for proteins from bacteria with average genomic G + C; and just 2.92 ± 0.55% for proteins from GC-rich bacteria.

In Figure 4(a), we placed average usage of lysine around Glu residues involved in Mn^{2+} binding and those Glu residues which are not involved in binding. The difference is significant only for Glu residues in alpha helices: the usage of Lys around Glu residues which are not involved in binding is

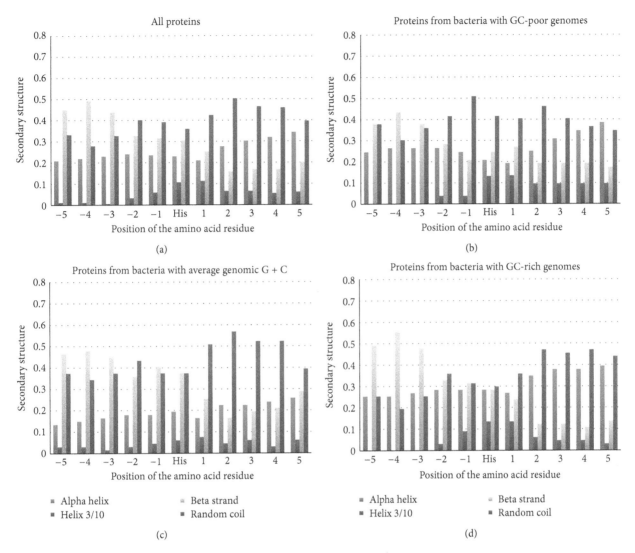

FIGURE 2: Secondary structure distribution around histidine residues binding Mn^{+2} ions in all the proteins (a); in proteins from GC-poor bacteria (b); in proteins from bacteria with average genomic GC-content (c); in proteins from GC-rich bacteria (d).

about 3 times higher than that around Glu residues binding Mn^{2+}. It means that the presence of Lys near Glu residue in alpha helix strongly decreases its ability to participate in Mn^{2+} binding. Once again, we have to highlight that lysine is known to be helix former, as well as glutamic acid [16]. So, they should be situated near each other in helices at a high probability. Some parts of those pairs should be involved in helix stabilization by the way of polar interactions or even salt bridges formation. Probably, those interactions do not allow oxygen atoms from side chains of Glu to participate in Mn^{2+} binding. With the growth of GC-content, the usage of lysine in helices decreases, while the usage of glutamic acid does not decrease (or does not decrease as steeply as the usage of lysine) [11]. That is why some glutamic acid residues from alpha helices become available for Mn^{2+} binding under the influence of mutational GC-pressure.

Arginine is encoded by six codons. Four of those codons are GC-rich (CGX). The usage of arginine in three groups of bacterial proteins used in this study is growing with the increase of genomic G + C (4.12 ± 0.46%; 5.46 ± 0.41%; 7.25 ± 0.54%). Even though both lysine and arginine possess positively charged side chains, arginine is not underrepresented in helices around glutamic acid residues (see Figure 4(b)). That is why the increase of arginine usage with the growth of GC-content does not prevent Mn^{2+} binding by glutamic acid residues situated in helices.

3.7. Mn^{2+} Binding Amino Acid Residues Are Overrepresented in Such Motifs of Supersecondary Structure as B-BCH-H and B-BCB-B. In Figure 5, one can see that the usage of amino acids in beta strands is 1.66 times higher among Mn^{2+} binding residues than among all the residues from the studied proteins (*P* < 0.001). In contrast, the usage of amino acids in alpha helices is 1.66 times lower among Mn^{2+} binding residues than among all the residues (*P* < 0.001).

Regions of coil between beta strand and alpha helix (BCH) contain much more amino acid residues coordinating

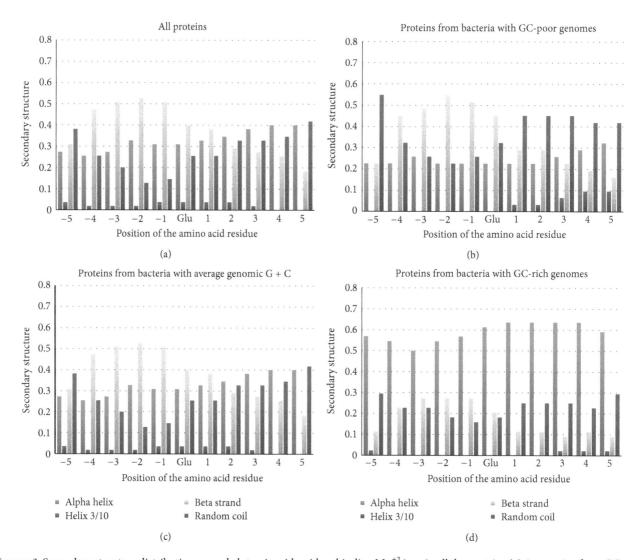

FIGURE 3: Secondary structure distribution around glutamic acid residues binding Mn^{+2} ions in all the proteins (a); in proteins from GC-poor bacteria (b); in proteins from bacteria with average genomic GC-content (c); in proteins from GC-rich bacteria (d).

Mn^{2+} than regions of coil between alpha helix and beta strand (HCB) (see Figure 5). The usage of amino acids situated in the BCH region is 2.3 times higher in the set of residues coordinating manganese cations relatively to the whole set ($P < 0.001$).

Amino acids binding Mn^{2+} ions are significantly overrepresented in regions of coil between two beta strands (BCB) and significantly underrepresented in regions between two alpha helices (HCH) (see Figure 5).

To complete the study, we compared usages of amino acids in the long sequences forming certain supersecondary structure motifs in the set of Mn^{2+} coordinating residues and in the complete set of them. According to our results, Mn^{2+} ions avoid such supersecondary structure motifs as H-HCB-B and H-HCH-H (see Figure 5). Such motifs as B-BCH-H and B-BCB-B are quite suitable for Mn^{2+} coordination (see Figure 5). One may say that both alpha helix and beta strand may be situated after the "beta strand-major binder-random coil" motif.

3.8. Comparison between Apo and Holo Forms of Mn^{2+} Binding Proteins. There were 61 amino acid residues coordinating Mn^{2+} ions in 15 proteins for which apo forms with 100% identical amino acid sequences have been found. Interestingly, 46.7% (7 from 15) of apo forms do not differ from holo forms in secondary structures around Mn^{2+} coordinating amino acids. Moreover, there are no differences in secondary structure elements distribution around 72.1% (44 from 61) of those Mn^{2+} coordinating amino acids.

Around 13.1% (8 from 61) of Mn^{2+} binding amino acids beta strands are shorter in holo forms than in apo forms. The difference between their lengths varies from 1 to 3 residues. It means that sometimes coordination of Mn^{2+} ions may lead to the beta strand to coil transition. On the other hand, there are two cases (3.3%) when beta strand is a little bit longer in holo form than in apo form.

In two cases, the difference between structures of apo and holo forms is associated with the fact that some residues situated around Mn^{2+} coordinating amino acids were not

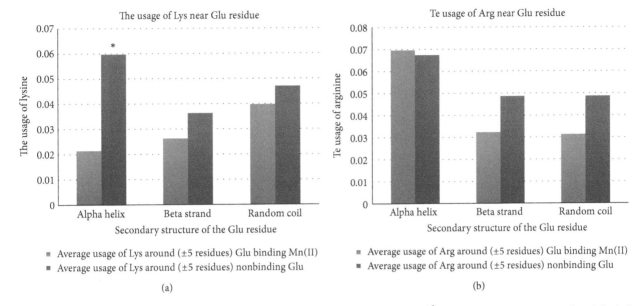

FIGURE 4: The usage of lysine (a) and arginine (b) around glutamic acid residues binding Mn^{+2} and nonbinding ones situated in alpha helices, beta strands, and random coil regions. Significant difference ($P < 0.05$) is shown by asterisk.

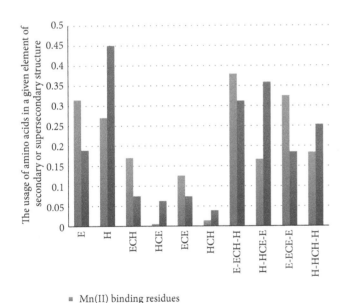

FIGURE 5: The usage of amino acid residues coordinating Mn^{2+} ions in different types of secondary and supersecondary elements in comparison with the usage of all amino acid residues in subsequent elements. All the differences are significant ($P < 0.05$).

located in crystallographic experiment. Other differences are caused by alpha helix to 3/10 helix transition (3.3%), coil to 3/10 helix transition (3.3%), and 3/10 helix to coil transition (1.6%). On one hand, Mn^{2+} ions (as well as other ions) may cause some changes in secondary structures around their binding sites: if atoms from amino acid residues form coordination bonds with cation, they cannot participate anymore in some previously existing interactions stabilizing secondary structure elements. On the other hand, one may find some minor differences between 3D structures of two 100% identical proteins without any ligands or with the same set of ligands. Anyway, differences in secondary structures between apo and holo forms for Mn^{2+} binding proteins are rare and minor.

4. Discussion

In our opinion, such supersecondary structural motif as B-BCH-H is suitable for Mn^{2+} coordination because of some specific amino acid propensities. At first, N-termini of helices are enriched by negatively charged amino acid residues: aspartic and glutamic acids [18]. At second, BCH regions demonstrate decreased usage of positively charged amino acids: lysine and arginine [19]. Because of these reasons, B-BCH-H motifs should frequently carry a total negative charge which should attract positively charged cations, such as Mn^{2+} [19]. In contrast, H-HCB-B motifs should usually carry a total positive charge: both C-termini of helices and HCB regions are enriched by lysine and arginine [19].

There should be certain features of B-BCB-B motifs of supersecondary structure which make them suitable for Mn^{2+} binding. Indeed, BCB regions are enriched by such major Mn^{2+} binder, as Asp [19]. Those regions of coil are flexible because of the enrichment by glycine residues [19]. This feature should play some role in the successful coordination of ions. Moreover, BCB regions are more hydrophilic than HCH ones [19].

It is known that the binding of metal ions may induce changes in secondary structure of proteins. For example, it was shown that Ca^{2+} ions are able to promote intermolecular beta-sheet formation by human prion protein (90-231 fragment) *in vitro* [20]. Aggregation of another amyloidogenic protein (alpha-synuclein involved in Parkinson disease pathogenesis) was shown to be accelerated by Cu^{2+} binding [21]. Alzheimer's beta amyloid peptides in fibril form were shown to be able to bind Cu^{2+} ions [22]. Calcitonin was shown to form aggregates in the presence of Cu^{2+}, Zn^{2+}, and Al^{3+} ions [23]. So, it is important to discuss here the question on causes and consequences.

We showed that there is usually beta strand in the N-terminal direction from the residue binding Mn^{2+}. There are just a few apo structures available for Mn^{2+} coordinating bacterial proteins. Even though changes induced by Mn^{2+} binding are rare and minor in our data set, stability of beta strands found in N-terminal direction of coordinating residues has to be checked bioinformatically. According to the data from Tables 2–4, beta strand formers (Val, Ile, Phe, and Leu) are overrepresented in certain positions in the N-terminal direction from three major binders (Asp, His, and Glu). So, beta strands near Mn^{2+} binding sites should be formed by strong beta formers. It means that most of those beta strands are quite predictable: they should exist in apo forms of the proteins and they should not be destroyed after the binding of Mn^{2+} ion.

According to the propensity scale [14], certain hydrophobic (WOOOO; OWOOO; OOOWO; OOOOW; OOOOO) and amphiphilic (WOWOW; WOWOO; OOWOW; OWOWO) pentapeptides are overrepresented in beta strands. We calculated total usage of those sheet-like pentapeptides in "−5--1" and "−4-0" positions for amino acid residues involved in Mn^{2+} binding in case if there were beta strands in "−3" and "−2" positions, respectively.

As one can see in Figure 6, the percentage of sheet-like pentapeptides in "−5--1" positions from the Asp involved in Mn^{2+} binding is significantly higher than that percentage for Asp which is not involved in metal ion coordination (69.84% versus 55.13%; $P < 0.01$). The difference for "−4-0" pentapeptides is even higher (62.28% versus 37.12%; $P < 0.001$). Beta strands near the aspartic acid residues from Mn^{2+} binding sites are formed from sheet-like pentapeptides even more frequently than beta strands near Asp residues which are not involved in binding. So, the kind of secondary structural site for Mn^{2+} binding described in the present work ("beta strand-major binder-random coil") should be stable. Beta strands from those sites should not be formed or destroyed due to the Mn^{2+} binding.

The same tendency is characteristic for glutamic acid residues binding Mn^{2+}. Pentapeptides in "−5--1" positions are sheet-like in 69.09% beta strands situated near the Glu binding Mn^{2+} and just 48.77% of them are sheet-like in case if Glu is not involved in binding ($P < 0.01$). For "−4-0" pentapeptides, the difference is somewhat higher (56.90% versus 35.68%; $P < 0.01$).

Beta strands situated near histidine residues involved in Mn^{2+} binding contain approximately the same percentage of sheet-like pentapeptides as those situated near histidine residues which are not involved in binding (see Figure 6).

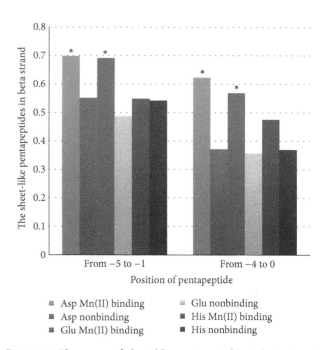

FIGURE 6: The usage of sheet-like pentapeptides in beta strands situated in "−5--1" and "−4-0" positions before Asp, Glu, and His residues involved and not involved in Mn^{+2} binding. Significant differences ($P < 0.05$) are designated by asterisks.

In general, we can state that beta strands in "beta strand-major binder-random coil" secondary structural motifs for Mn^{2+} binding are stable enough since both amino acid residues known as strong beta formers and sheet-like pentapeptides are overrepresented in them.

It is known that the "two-histidines-one-carboxylate" binding motif is a widely represented first coordination sphere motif present in the active site of a variety of metalloenzymes [24]. Since histidine and two amino acid residues with carboxyl groups in their side chains are the major binders of Mn^{2+}, this motif should be present in our data set as well. However, there are just 11 from 215 (5.12%) Mn^{2+} binding sites which consist of two histidines and a single glutamic or aspartic acid. The percentage of sites with three amino acid residues (28.37%) is lower than the percentage of sites with four amino acid residues (36.74%). There also may be five (5.12%), two (17.67%), or even a single amino acid residue (12.09%) in a binding site. Cases when there is only a single atom from the protein participating in Mn^{2+} coordination can be explained by the fact that there are also several atoms from another ligand bound to that protein interacting with Mn^{2+}. Oxygen atoms from water molecules are also frequently described as those participating in Mn^{2+} coordination.

Since there are usually four or three amino acid residues in Mn^{2+} binding site, it is very interesting to estimate the percentage of "type I" sites containing at least one amino acid residue with characteristic beta strand in the N-direction. This percentage is equal to 77.78% for proteins from GC-poor bacteria; 80.00% for proteins from bacteria with average genomic GC-content; and 74.63% for proteins from GC-rich bacteria. The differences between those values are insignificant.

Theoretically, existence of at least one "beta strand-major binder-random coil" secondary structural motif may be important for successful Mn^{2+} binding. In proteins encoded by GC-rich genes, the percentage of binding Glu residues situated in alpha helices increased significantly, while most of those residues bind the ion together with at least one amino acid from characteristic "beta strand-major binder-random coil" motif. It is likely that amino acid residues in that characteristic secondary structural motif are "active" Mn^{2+} binders, while all the other atoms are included in coordination sphere just because they are situated near that "active" binder. On the other hand, 20–25% of Mn^{2+} ions were bound by proteins without involvement of the characteristic "beta strand-major binder-random coil" structural motif. Most of those proteins coordinate Mn^{2+} ions by "type II" sites which are made from Glu residues included in helices with low Lys usage.

5. Conclusions

In this work, we used a new bioinformatical approach to study the preferences in secondary structure motifs for metal coordinating amino acid residues microenvironment. Three sets of PDB files have been collected in respect of GC-content of genes encoding the proteins with determined three-dimensional structures. With the help of this approach, one will be able not only to test whether the data are reproducible in three different sets, but to find out previously unknown consequences of symmetric mutational pressure.

In this particular study, we showed that beta strand is often situated before the amino acid residue participating in Mn2+ ion coordination, region of coil is usually situated after the interacting residue, that region of coil may connect abovementioned beta strand with either another beta strand or alpha helix. This information is useful for future development of an algorithm for Mn(II) binding sites prediction. Moreover, we showed that mutational GC-pressure leads to the more frequent involvement of glutamic acid residues situated in alpha helices into the Mn^{2+} coordination.

Abbreviations

G + C, GC-content:	The usage of guanine and cytosine in a gene or genome
Xaa:	Any amino acid
W:	Any hydrophilic amino acid (Arg; Lys; His; Asp; Glu; Asn; Gln; Ser; Thr)
O:	Any hydrophobic amino acid (Ala; Gly; Pro; Val; Leu; Met; Ile; Tyr; Phe; Cys; Trp)
BCH:	Random coil between beta strand and alpha helix
BCB:	Random coil between two beta strands
HCB:	Random coil between alpha helix and beta strand
HCH:	Random coil between two alpha helices
B-BCH-H:	Supersecondary structural motif which includes beta strand, coil, and alpha helix (from N- to C-terminus)
B-BCB-B:	Supersecondary structural motif which includes beta strand, coil, and beta strand (from N- to C-terminus)
H-HCB-B:	Supersecondary structural motif which includes alpha helix, coil, and beta strand (from N- to C-terminus)
H-HCH-H:	Supersecondary structural motif which includes alpha helix, coil, and alpha helix (from N- to C-terminus).

Conflict of Interests

The author states that there is no conflict of interests regarding the publication of this paper.

References

[1] H. Zheng, M. Chruszcz, P. Lasota, L. Lebioda, and W. Minor, "Data mining of metal ion environments present in protein structures," *Journal of Inorganic Biochemistry*, vol. 102, no. 9, pp. 1765–1776, 2008.

[2] M. Brylinski and J. Skolnick, "FINDSITE-metal: integrating evolutionary information and machine learning for structure-based metal-binding site prediction at the proteome level," *Proteins*, vol. 79, no. 3, pp. 735–751, 2011.

[3] A. Passerini, M. Lippi, and P. Frasconi, "MetalDetector v2.0: predicting the geometry of metal binding sites from protein sequence," *Nucleic Acids Research*, vol. 39, no. 2, pp. W288–W292, 2011.

[4] J. W. H. Schymkowitz, F. Rousseau, I. C. Martins, J. Ferkinghoff-Borg, F. Stricher, and L. Serrano, "Prediction of water and metal binding sites and their affinities by using the Fold-X force field," *Proceedings of the National Academy of Sciences of the United States of America*, vol. 102, no. 29, pp. 10147–10152, 2005.

[5] B. Seebeck, I. Reulecke, A. Kämper, and M. Rarey, "Modeling of metal interaction geometries for protein-ligand docking," *Proteins*, vol. 71, no. 3, pp. 1237–1254, 2008.

[6] M. Kumar, S. Ahmad, E. Ahmad, M. A. Saifi, and R. H. Khan, "In silico prediction and analysis of Caenorhabditis EF-hand containing proteins," *PLoS ONE*, vol. 7, Article ID e36770, 2012.

[7] H.-W. Kim, M. Kataoka, and K. Ishikawa, "Atomic resolution of the crystal structure of the hyperthermophilic family 12 endocellulase and stabilizing role of the DxDxDG calcium-binding motif in Pyrococcus furiosus," *FEBS Letters*, vol. 586, no. 7, pp. 1009–1013, 2012.

[8] D. J. Rigden and M. Y. Galperin, "The DxDxDG motif for calcium binding: multiple structural contexts and implications for evolution," *Journal of Molecular Biology*, vol. 343, no. 4, pp. 971–984, 2004.

[9] N. Sueoka, "Directional mutation pressure and neutral molecular evolution," *Proceedings of the National Academy of Sciences of the United States of America*, vol. 85, no. 8, pp. 2653–2657, 1988.

[10] G. A. C. Singer and D. A. Hickey, "Nucleotide bias causes a genomewide bias in the amino acid composition of proteins,"

Molecular Biology and Evolution, vol. 17, no. 11, pp. 1581–1588, 2000.

[11] V. V. Khrustalev and E. V. Barkovsky, "Percent of highly immunogenic amino acid residues forming B-cell epitopes is higher in homologous proteins encoded by GC-rich genes," *Journal of Theoretical Biology*, vol. 282, no. 1, pp. 71–79, 2011.

[12] V. V. Khrustalev and E. V. Barkovsky, "Study of completed archaeal genomes and proteomes: hypothesis of strong mutational AT pressure existed in Their common Predecessor," *Genomics, Proteomics and Bioinformatics*, vol. 8, no. 1, pp. 22–32, 2010.

[13] T. Banerjee, S. K. Gupta, and T. C. Ghosh, "Role of mutational bias and natural selection on genome-wide nucleotide bias in prokaryotic organisms," *BioSystems*, vol. 81, no. 1, pp. 11–18, 2005.

[14] V. V. Khrustalev and E. V. Barkovsky, "Stabilization of secondary structure elements by specific combinations of hydrophilic and hydrophobic amino acid residues is more important for proteins encoded by GC-poor genes," *Biochimie*, vol. 94, pp. 2706–2715, 2012.

[15] D. Eisenberg, E. Schwarz, M. Komaromy, and R. Wall, "Analysis of membrane and surface protein sequences with the hydrophobic moment plot," *Journal of Molecular Biology*, vol. 179, no. 1, pp. 125–142, 1984.

[16] P. Y. Chou and G. D. Fasman, "Prediction of the secondary structure of proteins from their amino acid sequence," *Advances in Enzymology and Related Areas of Molecular Biology*, vol. 47, pp. 45–148, 1978.

[17] M. Yáñez, J. Gil-Longo, and Campos-Toimil, "Calcium binding proteins," *Advances in Experimental Medicine and Biology*, vol. 740, pp. 461–482, 2012.

[18] R. Aurora and G. D. Rose, "Helix capping," *Protein Science*, vol. 7, no. 1, pp. 21–38, 1998.

[19] V. V. Khrustalev, T. A. Khrustaleva, and E. V. Barkovsky, "Random coil structures in bacterial proteins. Relationships of their amino acid compositions to flanking structures and corresponding genic base compositions," *Biochimie*, vol. 95, pp. 1745–1754, 2013.

[20] S. Sorrentino, T. Bucciarelli, A. Corsaro, A. Tosatto, S. Thellung et al., "Calcium binding promotes prion protein fragment 90–231 conformational change toward a membrane destabilizing and cytotoxic structure," *PLoS ONE*, vol. 7, Article ID e38314, 2012.

[21] F. Rose, M. Hodak, and J. Bernholc, "Mechanism of copper(II)-induced misfolding of Parkinson's disease protein," *Scientific Reports*, vol. 1, article 11, 2011.

[22] S. Parthasarathy, F. Long, Y. Miller et al., "Molecular-level examination of Cu^{2+} binding structure for amyloid fibrils of 40-residue alzheimer's β by solid-state NMR spectroscopy," *Journal of the American Chemical Society*, vol. 133, no. 10, pp. 3390–3400, 2011.

[23] N. Rastogi, K. Mitra, D. Kumar, and R. Roy, "Metal ions as cofactors for aggregation of therapeutic peptide salmon calcitonin," *Inorganic Chemistry*, vol. 5, pp. 5642–5650, 2012.

[24] B. Amrein, M. Schmid, G. Collet et al., "Identification of two-histidines one-carboxylate binding motifs in proteins amenable to facial coordination to metals," *Metallomics*, vol. 4, no. 4, pp. 379–388, 2012.

16

A Parallel Framework for Multipoint Spiral Search in *ab Initio* Protein Structure Prediction

Mahmood A. Rashid,[1,2] **Swakkhar Shatabda,**[1,2] **M. A. Hakim Newton,**[1]
Md Tamjidul Hoque,[3] **and Abdul Sattar**[1,2]

[1] *Institute for Integrated & Intelligent Systems, Science 2 (N34) 1.45, 170 Kessels Road, Nathan, QLD 4111, Australia*
[2] *Queensland Research Lab, National ICT Australia, Level 8, Y Block, 2 George Street, Brisbane, QLD 4000, Australia*
[3] *Computer Science, 2000 Lakeshore Drive, Math 308, New Orleans, LA 70148, USA*

Correspondence should be addressed to Mahmood A. Rashid; mahmood.rashid@gmail.com

Academic Editor: Rita Casadio

Protein structure prediction is computationally a very challenging problem. A large number of existing search algorithms attempt to solve the problem by exploring possible structures and finding the one with the minimum free energy. However, these algorithms perform poorly on large sized proteins due to an astronomically wide search space. In this paper, we present a multipoint spiral search framework that uses parallel processing techniques to expedite exploration by starting from different points. In our approach, a set of random initial solutions are generated and distributed to different threads. We allow each thread to run for a predefined period of time. The improved solutions are stored threadwise. When the threads finish, the solutions are merged together and the duplicates are removed. A selected distinct set of solutions are then split to different threads again. In our *ab initio* protein structure prediction method, we use the three-dimensional face-centred-cubic lattice for structure-backbone mapping. We use both the low resolution hydrophobic-polar energy model and the high-resolution 20 × 20 energy model for search guiding. The experimental results show that our new parallel framework significantly improves the results obtained by the state-of-the-art single-point search approaches for both energy models on three-dimensional face-centred-cubic lattice. We also experimentally show the effectiveness of mixing energy models within parallel threads.

1. Introduction

Proteins are essentially linear chain of amino acids. They adopt specific folded three-dimensional structures to perform specific tasks. The function of a given protein is determined by its *native* structure, which has the lowest possible free energy level. Nevertheless, misfolded proteins cause many critical diseases such as Alzheimer's disease, Parkinson's disease, and cancer [1, 2]. Protein structures are important in drug design and biotechnology.

Protein structure prediction (PSP) is computationally a very hard problem [3]. Given a protein's amino acid sequence, the problem is to find a three-dimensional structure of the protein such that the total interaction energy amongst the amino acids in the sequence is minimised. The protein folding process that leads to such structures involves very complex molecular dynamics [4] and unknown energy factors. To deal with the complexity in a hierarchical fashion, researchers have used discretised lattice-based structures and simplified energy models [5–7] for PSP. However, the complexity of the simplified problem still remains challenging.

There are a large number of existing search algorithms that attempt to solve the PSP problem by exploring feasible structures called *conformations*. For population-based approaches, a genetic algorithm (GA[+] [8]) reportedly produces the state-of-the-art results using hydrophobic-polar (HP) energy model. On the other hand, for local search approaches, spiral search (SS-Tabu) [9], which is a tabu-based local search, produces the best results using HP model. Both algorithms use three-dimensional (3D) face-centred-cubic (FCC) lattice for conformation representation.

The approaches used in [10–13] produced the state-of-the-art results using the high resolution Berrera 20×20 energy matrix (henceforth referred to as BM energy model). Nevertheless, the challenges in PSP largely remain in the fact that the energy function that needs to be minimised in order to obtain the native structure of a given protein is not clearly known. A high resolution 20×20 energy model (such as BM) could better capture the behaviour of the actual energy function than a low resolution energy model (such as HP). However, the fine grained details of the high resolution interaction energy matrix are often not very informative for guiding the search. Pairwise contributions that have low magnitudes could be dominated by the accumulated pairwise contributions having large magnitudes. In contrast, a low resolution energy model could effectively bias the search towards certain promising directions particularly emphasising on the pairwise contributions with large magnitudes.

In a collaborative human team, each member may work individually on his/her own way to solve a problem. They may meet together occasionally to discuss the possible ways they could find and may then refocus only on the more viable options in the next iteration. We envisage this approach to be useful in finding a suitable solution when there are enormously many alternatives that are very close to each other. We therefore try this in the context of conformational search for protein structure prediction.

In this paper, we present a multithreaded search technique that runs SS-Tabu in each thread that is guided by either HP energy or by 20×20 BM energy model. The search starts with a set of random initial solutions by distributing these solutions to different threads. We allow each thread to run for a predefined period of time. The interim improved solutions are stored threadwise and merged together when all threads have finished their execution. After removing the duplicates from the merged solutions, a selected distinct set of solutions is then considered for next iteration. In our approach, multipoint start first helps find some promising results. For the next set of solutions to be distributed, the most promising solutions from the merged list are selected. Therefore, multipoint parallelism reduces the search space by exploring the vicinities of the promising solutions recursively. In our parallel local search, we use both the HP energy model and 20×20 BM energy model on the 3D FCC lattice space. The experimental results show that our new approach significantly improves over the results obtained by the state-of-the-art single-point search approaches for the similar models.

The rest of the paper is organized as follows: Section 2 describes the background of the protein structure; Section 3 presents the related work; Section 4.1 presents the SS-Tabu algorithm used in the parallel search approach; Section 4 describes our parallel framework in detail; Section 5 discusses and analyses the experimental results; and finally, Section 6 presents the conclusions and outlines the future work.

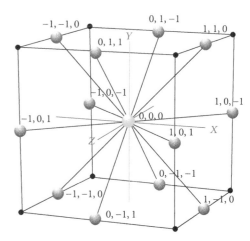

FIGURE 1: A unit 3D FCC lattice with 12 basis vectors on the Cartesian coordinates.

2. Background

There are three computational approaches for protein structure prediction. These are *homology modeling* [14], *protein threading* [15, 16], and *ab initio* methods [17, 18]. Prediction quality of *homology modeling* and *protein threading* depends on the sequential similarity of previously known protein structures. However, our work is based on the *ab initio* approach that only depends on the amino acid sequence of the target protein. Levinthal's paradox [19] and Anfinsen's hypothesis [20] are the basis of *ab initio* methods for PSP. The idea was originated in 1970 when it was demonstrated that all information needed to fold a protein resides in its amino acid sequence. In our simplified protein structure prediction model, we use 3D FCC lattice for conformation mapping, HP and 20×20 BM energy models for conformation evaluation, and the spiral search algorithm [9] (SS-Tabu) in a parallel framework for conformation search. The simplified models (lattice model and energy models) and local search are described below.

2.1. Simplified Model. In this research, we use 3D FCC lattice points for conformation mapping to generate backbone of protein structures. We use the HP and 20×20 BM energy model for conformation evaluation. The 3D FCC lattice, the HP energy model, and BM energy model are briefly described below.

2.1.1. 3D FCC Lattice. The FCC lattice has the highest packing density compared to the other existing lattices [21]. The hexagonal close packed (HCP) lattice, also known as cuboctahedron, was used in [22]. In HCP, each lattice point has 12 neighbours that correspond to 12 basis vertices with real-numbered coordinates, which causes the loss of structural precision for PSP. In FCC, each lattice point has 12 neighbours as shown in Figure 1.

Figure 1 shows the 12 *basis vectors* with respect to the origin. The *basis vectors* are presented below denoting as $\vec{A} \cdots \vec{L}$:

$$
\begin{aligned}
\vec{A} &= (1, 1, 0), & \vec{B} &= (0, 1, 1), \\
\vec{C} &= (1, 0, 1), & \vec{D} &= (-1, 1, 0), \\
\vec{E} &= (0, -1, 1), & \vec{F} &= (-1, 0, 1), \\
\vec{G} &= (1, -1, 0), & \vec{H} &= (0, 1, -1), \\
\vec{I} &= (1, 0, -1), & \vec{J} &= (-1, -1, 0), \\
\vec{K} &= (0, -1, -1), & \vec{L} &= (-1, 0, -1).
\end{aligned} \tag{1}
$$

In simplified PSP, conformations are mapped on the lattice by a sequence of basis vectors or by the *relative vectors* that are relative to the previous basis vectors in the sequence.

2.1.2. HP Energy Model. The 20 amino acid monomers are the building block of protein polymers. These amino acids are broadly divided into two categories based on their hydrophobicity: (a) hydrophobic amino acids (*Gly, Ala, Pro, Val, Leu, Ile, Met, Phe, Tyr, Trp*) denoted by H; and (b) hydrophilic or polar amino acids (*Ser, Thr, Cys, Asn, Gln, Lys, His, Arg, Asp, Glu*) denoted by P. In the HP model [23], when two nonconsecutive hydrophobic amino acids become topologically neighbours, they contribute a certain amount of negative energy, which for simplicity is shown as −1 in Table 1. The total energy (E) of a conformation based on the HP model becomes the sum of the contributions of all pairs of nonconsecutive hydrophobic amino acids as follows:

$$
E = \sum_{i < j-1} c_{ij} \cdot e_{ij}. \tag{2}
$$

Here, $c_{ij} = 1$ if amino acids i and j are nonconsecutive neighbours on the lattice, otherwise 0; and $e_{ij} = -1$ if ith and jth amino acids are hydrophobic, otherwise 0.

2.2. BM Energy Model. By analysing crystallised protein structures, Miyazawa and Jernigan [24] in 1985 statistically deduced a 20 × 20 energy matrix that considers residue contact propensities between the amino acids. By calculating empirical contact energies on the basis of information available from selected protein structures and following the quasichemical approximation Berrera et al. [25] in 2003 deduced another 20 × 20 energy matrix. In this work, we use the latter model and denote it by BM energy model. Table 2 shows the BM energy model with amino acid names at the left-most column and the bottom-most row and the interaction energy values in the cells. The amino acid names that have boldface are hydrophobic. We draw lines in Table 2 to show groupings based on H-H, H-P, and P-P interactions. In the context of this work, it is worth noting that most energy contributions that have large magnitudes are from H-H interactions followed by those from H-P interactions.

The total energy E_{bm} (shown in (3)) of a conformation based on the BM energy model is the sum of the contributions

over all pairs of nonconsecutive amino acids that are one unit lattice distance apart:

$$
E_{bm} = \sum_{i < j-1} c_{ij} \cdot e_{ij}. \tag{3}
$$

Here, $c_{ij} = 1$ if amino acids at positions i and j in the sequence are nonconsecutive neighbours on the lattice, otherwise 0; and e_{ij} is the empirical energy value between the ith and jth amino acid pair specified in the matrix for the BM model.

2.3. Local Search. Starting from an initial solution, local search algorithms move from one solution to another to find a better solution. Local search algorithms are well known for efficiently producing high quality solutions [9, 26, 27], which are difficult for systematic search approaches. However, they are incomplete [28] and suffer from revisitation and stagnation. Restarting the whole or parts of a solution remains the typical approach to deal with such situations.

2.4. Tabu Metaheuristic. Tabu metaheuristic [29, 30] enhances the performance of local search algorithms. It maintains a short-term memory storage to remember the local changes of a solution. Then any further local changes for those stored positions are forbidden for a certain number of subsequent iterations (known as tabu tenure).

3. Related Work

There are a large number of existing search algorithms that attempt to solve the PSP problem by exploring feasible structures on different energy models. In this section we explore the works related to HP and 20 × 20 energy models as below.

3.1. HP Energy-Based Approaches. Different types of metaheuristic have been used in solving the simplified PSP problem. These include Monte Carlo Simulation [31], Simulated Annealing [32], Genetic Algorithms (GA) [33, 34], Tabu Search with GA [35], Tabu Search with Hill Climbing [36], Ant Colony Optimisation [37], Immune Algorithms [38], Tabu-based Stochastic Local Search [26, 27], and Constraint Programming [39].

The Bioinformatics Group, headed by Rolf Backofen, applied Constraint Programming [40–42] using exact and complete algorithms. Their exact and complete algorithms work efficiently if similar hydrophobic core exists in the repository.

Cebrián et al. [26] used tabu-based local search, and Shatabda et al. [27] used memory-based local search with tabu heuristic and achieved the state-of-the-art results. However, Dotu et al. [39] used constraint programming and found promising results but only for smaller sized (length < 100 amino acids) proteins. Besides local search, Unger and Moult [33] applied population-based genetic algorithms to PSP and found their method to be more promising than the Monte Carlo-based methods [31]. They used absolute encodings on the square and cubic lattices for HP energy

TABLE 1: HP energy model [23].

	H	P
H	−1	0
P	0	0

model. Later, Patton [43] used relative encodings to represent conformations and a penalty method to enforce the self-avoiding walk constraint. GAs have been used by Hoque et al. [22] for cubic and 3D HCP lattices. They used DFS-generated pathways [44] in GA crossover for protein structure prediction. They also introduced a twin-removal operator [45] to remove duplicates from the population to prevent the search from stalling. Ullah et al. in [12, 46] combined local search with constraint programming. They used a 20 × 20 energy model [25] on FCC lattice and found promising results. In another hybrid approach [47], tabu metaheuristic was combined with genetic algorithms in two-dimensional HP model to observe crossover and mutation rates over time.

However, for the simplified model (HP energy model and 3D FCC lattice) that is used in this paper, a new genetic algorithm GA$^+$ [8] and a tabu-based local search algorithm Spiral Search [9] currently produce the state-of-the-art results.

3.2. Empirical 20 × 20 Matrix Energy Based Approaches. A constraint programming technique was used in [48] by Dal Palù et al. to predict tertiary structures of real proteins using secondary structure information. They also used constraint programming with different heuristics in [49] and a constraint solver named COLA [50] that is highly optimized for protein structure prediction. In another work [51], a fragment assembly method was utilised with empirical energy potentials to optimise protein structures. Among other successful approaches, a population-based local search [52] and a population-based genetic algorithm [13] were used with empirical energy functions.

In a hybrid approach, Ullah and Steinöfel [12] applied a constraint programming-based large neighbourhood search technique on top of the output of COLA solver. The hybrid approach produced the state-of-the-art results for several small sized (less than 75 amino acids) benchmark proteins.

In another work, Ullah et al. [46] proposed a two stage optimisation approach combining constraint programming and local search. The first stage of the approach produced compact optimal structures by using the CPSP tools based on the HP model. In the second stage, those compact structures were used as the input of a simulated annealing-based local search that is guided by the BM energy model.

In a recent work [10], Shatabda et al. presented a mixed heuristic local search algorithm for PSP and produced the state-of-the-art results using BM energy model on 3D FCC lattice. The mixed heuristic local search in each iteration randomly selects a heuristic from a given number of heuristics designed by the authors. The selected heuristics are then used in evaluating the generated neighbouring solutions of the current solution. Although the heuristics themselves are weaker than the BM energy, their collective use in the random

mixing fashion produces results better than the BM energy itself.

3.3. Parallel Approaches. Vargas and Lopes [53] proposed an Artificial Bee Colony algorithm based on two parallel approaches (master slave and a hybrid hierarchical) for protein structure prediction using the 3D HP model with sidechains. They showed that the parallel methods achieved a good level of efficiency while compared with the sequential version. A comparative study of parallel metaheuristics was conducted by Trantar et al. [54] using a genetic algorithm, a simulated annealing algorithm, and a random search method in grid environments for protein structure prediction. In another work [55], they applied a parallel hybrid genetic algorithm in order to efficiently deal with the PSP problem using the computational grid. They experimentally showed the effectiveness of a computational grid-based approach. All-atom force field-based protein structure prediction using parallel particle swarm optimization approach was proposed by Kandov in [56]. He showed that asynchronous parallelisation speeds up the simulation better than the synchronous one and reduces the effective time for predictions significantly. Among others, Calvo et al. in [57, 58] applied a parallel multiobjective evolutionary approach and found linear speedups in structure prediction for benchmark proteins and Robles et al. in [59] applied parallel approach in local search to predict secondary structure of a protein from its amino acid sequence.

4. Our Approach

The driving force of our parallel search framework is SS-Tabu [9] that has two versions: (i) the existing algorithm, designed for HP model (as shown in Algorithm 1 and described in Section 4.1) and (ii) the customised spiral search algorithm, designed for 20 × 20 BM energy model (as shown in Algorithm 5 and described in Section 4.2). We feed the two versions of spiral search algorithms in different threads in different combinations. The variations are described in the experimental results section.

4.1. SS-Tabu: Spiral Search. SS-Tabu is a hydrophobic core directed local search [9] that works in a spiral fashion. This algorithm (the *pseudocode* in Algorithm 1) is the basis of the proposed parallel local search framework. SS-Tabu is composed of H and P move selections, random-walk [60], and relay-restart [9]. However, this algorithm is further customised for detailed 20 × 20 energy model as described in Section 4.2. Both versions of SS-Tabu are used in parallel threads with different combinations within the parallel framework. The features of existing SS-Tabu are described in Algorithm 1.

4.1.1. Applying Diagonal Move. In a tabu-guided local search (see Algorithm 1), we use the diagonal move operator (shown in Figure 2) to build H-core. A diagonal move displaces *i*th amino acid from its position to another position on the lattice without changing the position of its succeeding (*i* + 1)th and

TABLE 2: The 20 × 20 BM energy model by Berrera et al. [25].

	Cys	Met	Phe	Ile	Leu	Val	Trp	Tyr	Ala	Gly	Thr	Ser	Gln	Asn	Glu	Asp	His	Arg	Lys	Pro
Cys	−3.477																			
Met	−2.24	−1.901																		
Phe	−2.424	−2.304	−2.467																	
Ile	−2.41	−2.286	−2.53	−2.691																
Leu	−2.343	−2.208	−2.491	−2.647	−2.501															
Val	−2.258	−2.079	−2.391	−2.568	−2.447	−2.385														
Trp	−2.08	−2.09	−2.286	−2.303	−2.222	−2.097	−1.867													
Tyr	−1.892	−1.834	−1.963	−1.998	−1.919	−1.79	−1.834	−1.335												
Ala	−1.7	−1.517	−1.75	−1.872	−1.728	−1.731	−1.565	−1.318	−1.119											
Gly	−1.101	−0.897	−1.034	−0.885	−0.767	−0.756	−1.142	−0.818	−0.29	0.219										
Thr	−1.243	−0.999	−1.237	−1.36	−1.202	−1.24	−1.077	−0.892	−0.717	−0.311	−0.617									
Ser	−1.306	−0.893	−1.178	−1.037	−0.959	−0.933	−1.145	−0.859	−0.607	−0.261	−0.548	−0.519								
Gln	−0.835	−0.72	−0.807	−0.778	−0.729	−0.642	−0.997	−0.687	−0.323	0.033	−0.342	−0.26	0.054							
Asn	−0.788	−0.658	−0.79	−0.669	−0.524	−0.673	−0.884	−0.67	−0.371	−0.23	−0.463	−0.423	−0.253	−0.367						
Glu	−0.179	−0.209	−0.419	−0.439	−0.366	−0.335	−0.624	−0.453	−0.039	0.443	−0.192	−0.161	0.179	0.16	0.933					
Asp	−0.616	−0.409	−0.482	−0.402	−0.291	−0.298	−0.613	−0.631	−0.235	−0.097	−0.382	−0.521	0.022	−0.344	0.634	0.179				
His	−1.499	−1.252	−1.33	−1.234	−1.176	−1.118	−1.383	−1.222	−0.646	−0.325	−0.72	−0.639	−0.29	−0.455	−0.324	−0.664	−1.078			
Arg	−0.771	−0.611	−0.805	−0.854	−0.758	−0.664	−0.912	−0.745	−0.327	−0.05	−0.247	−0.264	−0.042	−0.114	−0.374	−0.584	−0.307	0.2		
Lys	−0.112	−0.146	−0.27	−0.253	−0.222	−0.2	−0.391	−0.349	0.196	0.589	0.155	0.223	0.334	0.271	−0.057	−0.176	0.388	0.815	1.339	
Pro	−1.196	−0.788	−1.076	−0.991	−0.771	−0.886	−1.278	−1.067	−0.374	−0.042	−0.222	−0.199	−0.035	−0.018	0.257	0.189	−0.346	−0.023	0.661	0.129
	Cys	**Met**	**Phe**	**Ile**	**Leu**	**Val**	**Trp**	**Tyr**	**Ala**	**Gly**	*Thr*	*Ser*	*Gln*	*Asn*	*Glu*	*Asp*	*His*	*Arg*	*Lys*	**Pro**

```
(1) //H and P are hydrophobic and polar amino acids.
(2) //maxIter terminates the iteration
(3) //maxRetry sets the time of relay-restart
(4) //maxRW sets the time of random-walk
(5) initTabuList()
(6) for (i = 1 to maxIter) do
(7)        mv ⟵ selectMoveForH()
(8)        if (mv != null) then
(9)           applyMove(mv)
(10)           updateTabuList(i)
(11)        else
(12)              mv ⟵ selectMoveForP()
(13)              if (mv != null) then
(14)                   applyMove(mv)
(15)        evaluate(AA) //AA—amino acid array
(16)        if (!improved) then
(17)           retry++
(18)        else
(19)           improvedList ⟵ addTopOfList()
(20)           retry = 0
(21)           rw = 0
(22)        if retry ≥ maxRetry then
(23)           relayRestart(improvedList)
(24)           resetTabuList()
(25)           rw++;
(26)        if rw ≥ maxRW then
(27)           randomWalk(maxPull)
(28)           resetTabuList()
```

ALGORITHM 1: *SpiralSearchHP*(**C**).

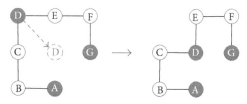

FIGURE 2: Diagonal move operator. For easy understanding, the figures are presented in 2D space.

preceding $(i - 1)$th amino acids in the sequence. The move is just a corner-flip to an unoccupied lattice point.

4.1.2. Forming H-Core.
Protein structures have hydrophobic cores (H-core) that hide the hydrophobic amino acids from water and expose the polar amino acids to the surface to be in contact with the surrounding water molecules [61]. H-core formation is an important objective for HP-based protein structure prediction models. In our work, we repeatedly use the diagonal-move to aid forming the H-core. We maintain a tabu list to control the amino acids from getting involved in the diagonal moves. SS-Tabu performs a series of diagonal moves on a given conformation to build the H-core around the hydrophobic core centre (HCC) as shown in Figure 3. The Cartesian distance between the HCC and the current position or a new position is denoted by d_1 and d_2, respectively. The

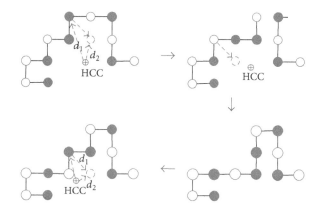

FIGURE 3: Spiral search comprising a series of diagonal moves with tabu metaheuristics. For simplification and easy understanding, the figures are presented in 2D space.

diagonal move squeezes the conformation and quickly forms the H-core in a spiral fashion.

4.1.3. Selecting Moves for HP Model.
In H-move selection algorithm (Algorithm 2), the HCC is calculated (Line 2) by finding arithmetic means of x, y, and z coordinates of all hydrophobic amino acids using (4). The selection is guided by the Cartesian distance d_i (as shown in (5)) between HCC and the hydrophobic amino acids in the sequence. For

```
(1) //H denotes hydrophobic amino acids.
(2) hcc ⟵ findHCoreCentre(S)
(3) for (i = 1 to seqLength) do
(4)        if ((type[i]="H") and (¬tabuList[i])) then
(5)              cfn ⟵ findCommonFreeNeigh(i + 1, i − 1)
(6)              mv_local ⟵ findShortestMove(hcc, cfn)
(7)              moveList·add(mv)
(8)        mv_global ⟵ findShortestMove(moveList)
(9) return mv
```

ALGORITHM 2: The *pseudocode* of H-move selection: selectMoveForH().

the ith hydrophobic amino acid, the common topological neighbours of the $(i − 1)$th and $(i + 1)$th amino acids are computed. The topological neighbours (TN) of a lattice point are the points at unit lattice-distance apart from it. From the common neighbours, the unoccupied points are identified. The Cartesian distance of all unoccupied common neighbours is calculated from the HCC using (5). Then the point with the shortest distance is picked. This point is listed in the possible H-move list for ith hydrophobic amino acid if its current distance from HCC is greater than that of the selected point. When all hydrophobic amino acids are traversed and the feasible shortest distances are listed in H-move list, the amino acid having the shortest distance in H-move list is chosen to apply the diagonal move on it (Algorithm 1 Line 9). A tabu list is maintained for each hydrophobic amino acid to control the selection priority amongst them. For each successful move, the tabu list is updated for the respective amino acid. The process stops when no H-move is found. In this situation, the control is transferred to select and apply P-moves. Consider

$$x_{hcc} = \frac{1}{n_h}\sum_{i=1}^{n_h} x_i, \qquad y_{hcc} = \frac{1}{n_h}\sum_{i=1}^{n_h} y_i, \qquad z_{hcc} = \frac{1}{n_h}\sum_{i=1}^{n_h} z_i,$$

(4)

where n_h is the number of H amino acids in the protein. Consider

$$d_i = \sqrt{(x_i − x_{hcc})^2 + (y_i − y_{hcc})^2 + (z_i − z_{hcc})^2}. \quad (5)$$

However, in P-move selection (Algorithm 1 Line 12), the same kind of diagonal moves is applied as H-move. For each ith polar amino acid, all free lattice points that are common neighbours of lattice points occupied by $(i − 1)$th and $(i + 1)$th amino acids are listed. From the list, a point is selected randomly to complete a diagonal move (Algorithm 1, Line 14) for the respective polar amino acid. No hydrophobic-core-center is calculated, no Cartesian distance is measured, and no tabu list is maintained for P-move. After one try for each polar amino acid the control is returned to select and apply H-moves.

4.1.4. Handling Stagnation. For hard optimisation problems such as protein structure prediction, local search algorithms often face stagnation. In HP model-based conformational

search, stagnation is encountered when a premature H-core is formed. Handling the stagnations is a challenging issue for conformational search algorithms (e.g., GA, LS). Thus, handling such situation intelligently is important to proceed further. To deal with stagnation, in SS-Tabu, random-walk [60] and relay-restart techniques are used on an on-demand basis.

Random-Walk. Premature H-cores are observed at local minima. To escape local minima, a random-walk [60] algorithm (Algorithm 1, Line 27) is applied. This algorithm uses pull moves [62] to break the premature H-cores and to create diversity.

Relay-Restart. When the search stagnation situation arises, a new relay-restart technique (Algorithm 1 Line 23) is applied instead of a fresh restart or restarting from the current best solution [26, 27]. We use relay-restart when random-walk fails to escape from the local minima. The relay-restart starts from an improving solution. We maintain an improving solution list that contains all the improving solutions after the initialisation.

4.1.5. Further Implementation Details. Like other search algorithms, SS-Tabu requires initialisation. It also needs evaluation of the solution in each iteration. It starts with a randomly generated or parameterised initial solution and enhances it in a spiral fashion. Further, it needs to maintain a tabu meta-heuristic to guide the local search.

Tabu Tenure. Intuitively we use different tabu-tenure values based on the number of hydrophobic amino acids (hCount) in the sequence. We calculate tabu-tenure using the following formula:

$$\text{tenure} = \left(10 + \frac{h\text{Count}}{10}\right). \quad (6)$$

The tabu-tenure calculated using (6) is used at Lines 5, 24, and 28 in Algorithm 1 during initialising and resetting tabu-list.

Evaluation. After each iteration, the conformation is evaluated by counting the H-H contacts (topological neighbours) where the two amino acids are nonconsecutive. The *pseudocode* in Algorithm 3 presents the algorithm of calculating the free energy of a given conformation. Note that the energy

```
(1) for (i = 1 to seqLength − 1) do
(2)     for (k = i + 2 to seqLength − 1) do
(3)         if AAType[i] = AAType[k] = H then
(4)             nodeI ⟵ AA[i]
(5)             nodeJ ⟵ AA[k]
(6)             sqrD ⟵ getSqrDist(nodeI, nodeJ)
(7)             if sqrD = 2 then
(8)                 fitness ⟵ fitness − 1
(9) return fitness
```

ALGORITHM 3: *evaluate(**AA**)*.

value is negation of the H-H contact count. For 20×20 BM energy model the pairwise contact potentials are found in matrix presented in Table 2.

Initialisation. Our algorithm starts with a feasible set of conformations known as population. We generate each initial conformation following a randomly generated self-avoiding walk (SAW) on FCC lattice points. The *pseudocode* of the algorithm is presented in Algorithm 4. It places the first amino acid at $(0, 0, 0)$. It then randomly selects a basis vector to place the successive amino acid at a neighbouring free lattice point. The mapping proceeds until a self-avoiding walk is found for the whole protein sequence.

4.2. BM Model Adopted Spiral Search. The basic difference between the HP energy based original spiral search (SS-Tabu [9]) and the BM energy guided adopted spiral search lies on the move selection criteria. In former version of spiral search, the amino acids are divided into two groups (H and P). The moves are selected based on these two properties of the amino acids that are guided by the distance of H amino acid from the HCC. However, to adopt 20×20 BM energy model, all 20 amino acids need to be taken into consideration and the move selection criteria are guided by the distance of any amino acid from the core centre (CC) of the current structure (Algorithm 5). The CC and the distance are calculated using (7) and (8), respectively.

4.2.1. Selecting Moves for BM (20×20) Model. In move selection (Algorithm 5 Line 6), the CC is calculated by finding arithmetic means of x, y, and z coordinates of all amino acids using (7). The selection is guided by the Cartesian distance d_i (as shown in (5)) between CC and the amino acids in the sequence. For the ith amino acid, the common topological neighbours of the $(i − 1)$th and $(i + 1)$th amino acids are computed. The topological neighbours (TN) of a lattice point are the points at unit lattice distance apart from it. From the common neighbours, the unoccupied points are identified. The Cartesian distance of all unoccupied common neighbours is calculated from the CC using (8). Then the point with the shortest distance is picked. This point is listed in the possible move list for ith amino acid if its current distance from CC is greater than that of the selected point. When all amino acids are traversed and the feasible shortest distances are listed in move list, the amino acid having the

TABLE 3: Combination of SS-Tabu variations amongst different threads.

Combinations	HP guide SS-Tabu	BM guide SS-Tabu
1 (PSSB4H0)	0 thread	4 threads
2 (PSSB3H1)	1 thread	3 threads
3 (PSSB2H2)	2 threads	2 threads
4 (PSSB1H3)	3 threads	1 thread
5 (PSSB0H4)	4 threads	0 thread

shortest distance in move list is chosen to apply the diagonal move on it (Algorithm 5, Line 8). A tabu list is maintained for each amino acid to control the selection priority amongst them. For each successful move, the tabu list is updated (Algorithm 5, Line 9) for the respective amino acid:

$$x_{cc} = \frac{1}{n}\sum_{i=1}^{n} x_i, \qquad y_{cc} = \frac{1}{n}\sum_{i=1}^{n} y_i, \qquad z_{cc} = \frac{1}{n}\sum_{i=1}^{n} z_i, \quad (7)$$

where n is the number of amino acids in the protein. Consider

$$d_i = \sqrt{(x_i - x_{cc})^2 + (y_i - y_{cc})^2 + (z_i - z_{cc})^2}. \quad (8)$$

4.3. Parallel Framework. In our implemented prototype, we use four parallel threads. The two versions of SS-Tabu are distributed amongst the four threads as shown in Table 3.

Figure 4 shows the architecture of our parallel search algorithm. In this framework, the search starts with a set of randomly generated initial solutions (Line 2 in Algorithm 6). The solutions are then divided in subsets (Line 4 in Algorithm 6) and are distributed to different threads.

We allow each thread to run for a predefined period of time. The improved solutions are stored threadwise and are merged together (Line 9 in Algorithm 6) when all threads finish. After removing the duplicates (Line 10 in Algorithm 6) from the merged solutions, a selected distinct set of solutions are taken (Line 11 in Algorithm 6) for the next iteration. The iterative process continues until the terminating criteria (Line 3 in Algorithm 6) are satisfied.

5. Experimental Results and Analyses

We conduct our experiments on two different sets of benchmark proteins: HP benchmarks and 20×20 benchmarks. The

```
(1) //AA—amino acid array of the protein
(2) //SAW—Self-avoiding-walk
(3) basisVec[12] ⟵ getTwelveBasisVectors()
(4) AA[0] ⟵ AminoAcid(0, 0, 0)
(5) while (!SAW) do
(6)      for (i = 1 to seqLength − 1) do
(7)          k ⟵ getRandom(12)
(8)          basis ⟵ basisVec[k]
(9)          node ⟵ AA[i − 1] + basis
(10)         if isFree(node) then
(11)             AA[i] ⟵ AminoAcid(node)
(12)         else
(13)             SAW ⟵ false
(14)             break
(15) return  AA[ ]
```

ALGORITHM 4: *initialise()*.

```
(1) //maxIter terminates the iteration
(2) //maxRetry sets the time of relay-restart
(3) //maxRW sets the time of random-walk
(4) initTabuList()
(5) for (i = 1 to maxIter) do
(6)      mv ⟵ selectMove()
(7)      if (mv != null) then
(8)          applyMove(mv)
(9)          updateTabuList(i)
(10)     evalute(AA) //AA—amino acid array
(11)     if (!improved) then
(12)         retry++
(13)     else
(14)         improvedList ⟵ addTopOfList()
(15)         retry = 0
(16)         rw = 0
(17)     if retry ≥ maxRetry then
(18)         relayRestart(improvedList)
(19)         resetTabuList()
(20)         rw++;
(21)     if rw ≥ maxRW then
(22)         randomWalk(maxPull)
(23)         resetTabuList()
```

ALGORITHM 5: *SpiralSearchBM(**C**)*.

```
(1) //thr—Thread
(2) currSet ⟵ initialise()
(3) for (i = 1 to repeat) do
(4)      subSet ⟵ genSubSet(currSet)
(5)      for (i = 1 to thCount) do
(6)          thr[i] = createSSThread(subSet[i], time)
(7)          thr[i]·start()
(8)      if (noAliveThread) then
(9)          mrgLst = mergeImprovedLists()
(10)         distinctLst = removeDuplicate(mrgLst)
(11)         currSet ⟵ genCurrSet(distinctLst)
```

ALGORITHM 6: *SSParallel(**time**, **repeat**)*.

TABLE 4: For 9 medium sized proteins, the three different sets of excremental data—(i) our parallel local search framework (PSS), (ii) the tabu guided spiral search (SS-Tabu), and (iii) the genetic algorithms (GA$^+$). The RI Columns present the relative improvements of parallel local search over the single-thread local search and the genetic algorithm. The RI is calculated on the average energy values.

	Protein Info.		Our approach (Four threads) 0.5 hrs × 4 = 2 hrs PSS		The current state-of-the-art approaches (Single thread) 2 hrs × 1 = 2 hrs SS-Tabu [9]			GA$^+$ [8]		
Seq	Size	LBFE	Best	Avg (E_t)	Best	Avg (E_r)	RI	Best	Avg (E_r)	RI
F90_1	90	−168	**−168**	−166	−168	**−167**	0%	−168	−166	0%
F90_2	90	−168	**−168**	**−166**	−167	−164	50%	−168	−165	33%
F90_3	90	−167	**−167**	**−165**	−167	−165	0%	−167	−164	33%
F90_4	90	−168	**−168**	**−166**	−168	−165	33%	−168	−165	33%
F90_5	90	−167	**−167**	−165	−167	−165	0%	−167	**−166**	0%
S1	135	−357	**−355**	**−350**	−355	−347	30%	−355	−348	22%
S2	151	−360	**−356**	**−351**	−354	−347	31%	−356	−349	18%
S3	162	−367	**−360**	**−354**	−359	−350	26%	−361	−349	28%
S4	164	−370	**−364**	**−358**	−358	−350	40%	−364	−352	**33%**

TABLE 5: For 12 large sized proteins, the three different sets of excremental data—(i) our parallel local search framework (PSS), (ii) the tabu guided spiral search (SS-Tabu), and (iii) the genetic algorithms (GA$^+$). The RI Columns present the relative improvements of parallel local search over the single-thread local search and the genetic algorithm. The RI is calculated on the average energy values.

	Protein Info.		Our approach (Four threads) 1.25 hrs × 4 = 5 hrs PSS		The current state-of-the-art approaches (Single thread) 5 hrs × 1 = 5 hrs SS-Tabu [9]			GA$^+$ [8]		
Seq	Size	LBFE	Best	Avg (E_t)	Best	Avg (E_r)	RI	Best	Avg (E_r)	RI
F180_1	180	−378	**−359**	**−344**	−357	−340	11%	−351	−341	8%
F180_2	180	−381	**−364**	**−352**	−359	−345	19%	−362	−346	17%
F180_3	180	−378	**−368**	**−356**	−362	−353	12%	−361	−350	21%
R1	200	−384	**−366**	**−353**	−359	−345	21%	−355	−346	18%
R2	200	−383	**−368**	**−355**	−358	−346	24%	−360	−346	**24%**
R3	200	−385	**−369**	**−353**	−365	−345	20%	−363	−344	22%
3mse	179	−323	**−296**	**−285**	−289	−280	12%	−290	−279	14%
3mr7	189	−355	**−332**	**−319**	−328	−313	14%	−328	−316	8%
3mqz	215	−474	**−430**	**−414**	−420	−402	17%	−427	−410	6%
3no6	229	−455	**−429**	**−407**	−411	−391	**25%**	−420	−400	13%
3no3	258	−494	**−422**	**−404**	−412	−393	**11%**	−421	−402	**2%**
3on7	279	n/a	**−516**	**−500**	−512	−485	n/a	−515	−485	n/a

rest of this section will present the experimental results in detail.

5.1. Experiment Setup

5.1.1. Implementation.
The parallel spiral search framework has been implemented in Java 6.0 using Java standard APIs. Currently the source code is not available publicly due to the legal bindings. However, an executable version of the application could be requested to the corresponding author.

5.1.2. Execution.
We ran our experiments on the NICTA (NICTA website: http://www.nicta.com.au/) cluster. The cluster consists of a number of identical Dell PowerEdge R415 computers, each equipped with 2 × AMD 6-Core Opteron

4184 processors, 2.8 GHz clock speed, 3M L2/6M L3 Cache, 64 GB memory, and running Rocks OS (a Linux variant for cluster). The experimental results presented in this paper are obtained from 50 different runs of identical settings for each protein when using HP benchmarks and 20 different runs of identical settings for each protein when using 20 × 20 benchmarks.

5.2. Experimental Results on HP Benchmark.
The experimental results on HP benchmarks are presented in Tables 4 and 5. Amongst the sequences, F90, S, F180, and R instances are taken from Peter Clote laboratory website (Peter Clote Lab: http://bioinformatics.bc.edu/clotelab/FCCproteinStructure/). These instances have been used in [8, 9, 26, 27, 39] for evaluating different algorithms. Moreover, we

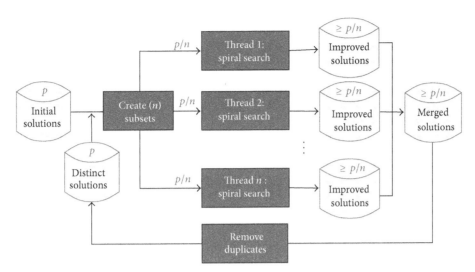

FIGURE 4: Parallel spiral search framework.

use other six larger sequences that are taken from the CASP (CASP website: http://predictioncenter.org/casp9/targetlist .cgi) competition. The corresponding CASP target IDs for proteins *3mse, 3mr7, 3mqz, 3no6, 3no3,* and *3on7* are *T0521, T0520, T0525, T0516, T0570,* and *T0563*. These CASP targets are also used in [27]. To fit in the HP model, the CASP targets are converted to HP sequences based on the hydrophobic properties of the constituent amino acids. The lower bounds of the free energy values (in Column LBFEof Tables 4 and 5) are obtained from [26, 27]; however, there are some unknown values (presented as *n/a*) of lower bounds of free energy for large sequences.

5.2.1. Results on Medium Sized HP Benchmark Proteins.
In Table 4, we present three different sets of result obtained from (i) our parallel local search framework that runs on four parallel threads (30 minutes/run), (ii) a local search (SS-Tabu) that runs on a single thread (2 hours/run), and (iii) a genetic algorithm (GA$^+$) that runs on a single thread (2 hours/run). In the table, the *Size* column presents the number of amino acids in the sequences, and the *LBFE* column shows the known lower bounds of free energy for the corresponding protein sequences in Column *ID*. The best and average free energy values for three different algorithms are presented in the table under the specific column headers (PSS, SS-Tabu, and GA$^+$). The RI Columns present the relative improvements of parallel local search over the single-thread local search and the genetic algorithm. The bold-faced values indicate better performance in comparison to the other algorithms for corresponding proteins.

5.2.2. Results on Large Sized HP Benchmark Proteins.
In Table 5, we present three different sets of result obtained from (i) our parallel local search framework that runs on four parallel threads (1 hour 15 minutes/run), (ii) a local search (SS-Tabu) that runs on a single thread (5 hours/run), and (iii) a genetic algorithm (GA$^+$) that runs on a single thread (5 hours/run). In the table, the *Size* column presents the number

of amino acids in the sequences, and the LBFEcolumn shows the known lower bounds of free energy for the corresponding protein sequences in Column *ID*. However, a lower bound of free energy for protein *3on7* is not known. The best and average free energy values for three different algorithms are presented in the table under the specific column headers (PSS, SS-Tabu, and GA$^+$). The RI Columns present the relative improvements of parallel local search over the single-thread local search and the genetic algorithm. The bold-faced values indicate better performance in comparison to the other algorithms for corresponding proteins.

5.2.3. Relative Improvement on HP Benchmark.
The difficulty of improving energy level is increased as the improved energy level approaches to the lower bound of free energy. For example, if the lower bound of free energy of a protein is −100, the efforts to improve energy level from −80 to −85 are much less than that to improve energy level from −95 to −100 though the change in energy is the same (−5). Relative Improvement (RI) explains how close our predicted results are to the lower bound of free energy with respect to the energy obtained from the state-of-the-art approaches:

$$\text{RI} = \frac{E_t - E_r}{E_l - E_r} * 100\%. \qquad (9)$$

In Tables 4 and 5, we also present a comparison of improvements (%) on average conformation quality (in terms of free energy levels). We compare PSS (target) with SS-Tabu and GA$^+$ (references). For each protein, the RI of the target (*t*) with respect to the reference (*r*) is calculated using the formula in (9), where E_t and E_r denote the average energy values achieved by the target and the reference, respectively, and E_l is the lower bound of free energy for the protein in the HP model. We present the relative improvements only for the proteins having known lower bounds of free energy values. We test our new approach on 16 different proteins of

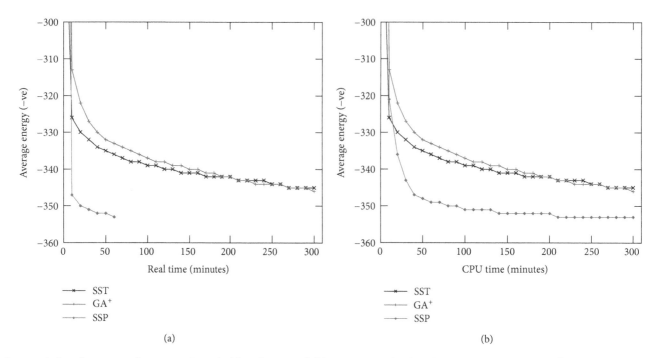

FIGURE 5: Search progress for protein R1 with (a) real time and (b) CPU time of 4 threads (4x real time). SST, GA⁺, and SSP represent tabu-based spiral search [9], genetic algorithms [8], and multipoint parallel spiral search, respectively.

various lengths. The bold-faced values are the minimum and the maximum improvements for the same column.

Improvement with respect to SS-Tabu. The experimental results in Tables 4 and 5, at column RI under SS-Tabu, show that our PSS is able to improve the search quality in terms of minimising the free energy level over all the 16 proteins considered for the test. The relative improvements with respect to SS-Tabu range from 0% to 50%.

Improvement with respect to GA⁺. The experimental results in Tables 4 and 5, at column RI (relative improvement) under GA⁺, show that our PSS is able to improve the search quality in terms of minimising the free energy level over all 16 proteins considered for the test. The relative improvements with respect to GA⁺ range from 0% to 33%.

5.2.4. Search Progress. We compare the search progresses of SS-Tabu, GA⁺, and PSS on the basis of real execution time. Figure 5(a) shows the average energy values obtained with times by the algorithms for protein R1. The graph shows that the progress of PSS stops at 75 minutes (1.25 hours). As we mentioned earlier, we run parallel threads (four threads) in our PSS for 1.25 hours to keep total CPU time equal to five ($1.25 \times 4 = 5$) hours. From the graph, it is clear that multipoint local search with four parallel threads dramatically outperforms the local search and genetic algorithms within (1/4)th of the execution time.

However, in Figure 5(b), we compare the search progresses of SS-Tabu, GA⁺, and PSS over CPU time. The CPU time of PSS is calculated by summing up the individual times of all threads (time per thread × 4) in different instances.

5.2.5. Comments on Our HP-Based Method. In Tables 4 and 5, the Columns LBFE represent the lower bound of free energy. Some of these values are taken from the literatures and others are obtained running exact and complete algorithms based CPSP-tools [42]. However, we do not compare our experimental results with results obtained from CPSP tools because of a fundamental conceptual difference between our approaches and Will and Backofen [63, 64]. Will's HPstruct algorithm [65] proceeds with threading an input HP sequence onto hydrophobic cores from a collection of precomputed and stored H-cores. On the other hand, our algorithms compute H-cores on the fly like Yue-Dill CHCC method [61, 66]. HPstruct requires a precomputed set of H-cores for the number of H amino acids in the given sequence. Therefore, CPSP tools cannot find structure without the availability of a precomputed optimal H-core.

5.3. Experimental Results on 20 × 20 Benchmark. Besides HP energy model, we apply our parallel framework on standard 20 × 20 benchmark proteins. The protein instances used in our experiments are taken from the literature (as shown in Table 6). The first seven proteins *4RXN, 1ENH, 4PTI, 2IGD, 1YPA, 1R69,* and *1CTF* are taken from [12] and the next five proteins *3MX7, 3NBM, CMQO, 3MRO,* and *3PNX* from [10]. In Table 7, we present eight sets of experimental results. The approaches are described below.

(1) *LS-Tabu* is heuristically guided local search based on tabu metaheuristic. The result presented in Table 7 under Column LS-Tabu is the output of 20 different runs of LS-Tabu [10] in an identical setting over 60

TABLE 6: The benchmark proteins used in our experiments.

ID	Length	Sequence
4RXN	54	MKKYTCTVCGYIYNPEDGDPDNGVNPGTDFKDIPDDWVCPLCGVGKDQFEEVEE
1ENH	54	RPRTAFSSEQLARLKREFNENRYLTERRRQQLSSELGLNEAQIKIWFQNKRAKI
4PTI	58	RPDFCLEPPYTGPCKARIIRYFYNAKAGLCQTFVYGGCRAKRNNFKSAEDCMRTCGGA
2IGD	61	MTPAVTTYKLVINGKTLKGETTTKAVDAETAEKAFKQYANDNGVDGVWTYDDATKTFTVTE
1YPA	64	MKTEWPELVGKAVAAAKKVILQDKPEAQIIVLPVGTIVTMEYRIDRVRLFVDKLDNIAQVPRVG
1R69	69	SISSRVKSKRIQLGLNQAELAQKVGTTQQSIEQLENGKTKRPRFLPELASALGVSVDWLLNGTSDSNVR
1CTF	74	AAEEKTEFDVILKAAGANKVAVIKAVRGATGLGLKEAKDLVESAPAALKEGVSKDDAEALKKALEEAGAEVEVK
3MX7	90	MTDLVAVWDVALSDGVHKIEFEHGTTSGKRVVYVDGKEEIRKEWMFKLVGKETFYVGAAKTKATINIDAISGFA YEYTLEINGKSLKKYM
3NBM	108	SNASKELKVLVLCAGSGTSAQLANAINEGANLTEVRVIANSGAYGAHYDIMGVYDLIILAPQVRSYYREMKVDAE RLGIQIVATRGMEYIHLTKSPSKALQFVLEHYQ
3MQO	120	PAIDYKTAFHLAPIGLVLSRDRVIEDCNDELAAIFRCARADLIGRSFEVLYPSSDEFERIGERISPVMIAHGSYADDR IMKRAGGELFWCHVTGRALDRTAPLAAGVWTFEDLSATRRVA
3MRO	142	SNALSASEERFQLAVSGASAGLWDWNPKTGAMYLSPHFKKIMGYEDHELPDEITGHRESIHPDDRARVLAALK AHLEHRDTYDVEYRVRTRSGDFRWIQSRGQALWNSAGEPYRMVGWIMDVTDRKRDEDALRVSREELRRL
3PNX	160	GMENKKMNLLLFSGDYDKALASLIIANAAREMEIEVTIFCAFWGLLLLRDPEKASQEDKSLYEQAFSSLTPREAE ELPLSKMNLGGIGKKMLLEMMKEEKAPKLSDLLSGARKKEVKFYACQLSVEIMGFKKEELFPEVQIMDVKEYLK NALESDLQLFI

minutes duration. The algorithm runs on a single thread using Berrera et al. 20×20 energy model.

(2) *SS-Tabu* is core directed local search based on tabu metaheuristic works in an spiral fashion. The result presented in Table 7 under Column SS-Tabu is the output of 20 different runs of LS-Tabu [9] in an identical setting over 60 minutes duration. The algorithm runs on a single thread using Berrera et al. 20×20 energy model.

(3) *PSSB4H0* is a variant of parallel spiral search running in 4 threads. In this variant of PSS, in all 4 threads, the SS-Tabu is guided by Berrera et al. 20×20 energy model. The parallel threads are terminated after 15 minutes. Therefore, the total CPU time remains ($15 \times$ 4-threads) the same as the SS-Tabu or LS-Tabu.

(4) *PSSB3H1* is a variant of parallel spiral search running in 4 threads. In this variant of PSS, in 3 threads, the SS-Tabu is guided by Berrera et al. 20×20 energy model and in other threads, the SS-Tabu is guided by HP energy model. The parallel threads are terminated after 15 minutes. Therefore, the total CPU time remains (15×4-threads) the same as the SS-Tabu or LS-Tabu.

(5) *PSSB2H2* is a variant of parallel spiral search running in 4 threads. In this variant of PSS, in 3 threads, the SS-Tabu is guided by Berrera et al. 20×20 energy model and in other 2 threads, the SS-Tabu is guided by HP energy model. The parallel threads are terminated after 15 minutes. Therefore, the total CPU time remains (15×4-threads) the same as the SS-Tabu or LS-Tabu.

(6) *PSSB1H3* is a variant of parallel spiral search running in 4 threads. In this variant of PSS, in 3 threads,

the SS-Tabu is guided by Berrera et al. 20×20 energy model and in other 3 threads, the SS-Tabu is guided by HP energy model. The parallel threads are terminated after 15 minutes. Therefore, the total CPU time remains (15×4-threads) the same as the SS-Tabu or LS-Tabu.

(7) *PSSB0H4* is a variant of parallel spiral search running in 4 threads. In this variant of PSS, in all 4 threads, the SS-Tabu is guided by HP energy model. The parallel threads are terminated after 15 minutes. Therefore, the total CPU time remains (15×4-threads) the same as the SS-Tabu or LS-Tabu.

(8) GA^+ is population-based genetic algorithm that uses hydrophobic-core directed macromutation operator and random-walk-based stagnation recovery technique in addition to the regular GA operators. The result presented in Table 7 under Column GA^+ is the output of 20 different runs of GA^+ [11] in an identical setting over 60 minutes duration. The algorithm runs on a single thread using both HP and BM energy models in a mixing manner.

5.4. Energy Values on 20×20 Benchmark. In Table 7, the energy columns show the energy values obtained from different approaches on 12 benchmark proteins (Table 6). Although the searches are guided by both HP and BM energy models, the energy values are calculated by applying Berrera et al. 20×20 energy matrix. The experimental results show that amongst the parallel spiral search variants, PSSB1H3 (6 out of 12 proteins) and PSSB0H4 (6 out of 12 proteins) produce better results in comparison to the other variants in terms of lowest interaction energies. However, the GA^+

TABLE 7: The best and average contact energies obtained from 8 different approaches using Berrera et al. [25] 20 × 20 energy matrix. Rowwise bold-faced values are the winners for the corresponding proteins amongst the variants of spiral search (both single and parallel frameworks) and bold-italic-faced values are the winners for the corresponding proteins amongst all 8 approaches. For both energy and RMSD values, the lower the better.

| Protein details | | | State-of-the-art CPU time 1 hr 1 × br-thread 0 × hp-thread LS-Tabu [10] | | Spiral search CPU time 1 hr 1 × br-thread 0 × hp-thread SS-Tabu | | Comparing all-atomic interaction energy and RMSD values Parallel spiral search (PSS) variants on energy model mixing CPU time 1 hr (4-threads × 15 minutes) | | | | | | | | | | State-of-the-art CPU time 1 hr br and hp based single threaded GA+ [11] | |
| | | | | | | | 4 × br-threads 0 × hp-thread PSSB4H0 | | 3 × br-threads 1 × hp-thread PSSB3H1 | | 2 × br-threads 2 × hp-threads PSSB2H2 | | 1 × br-thread 3 × hp-threads PSSB1H3 | | 0 × br-thread 4 × hp-threads PSSB0H4 | | | |
Seq.	Size	H	Energy	RMSD	Energy	RMSD	Energy	RMSD	Energy	RMSD	Energy	RMSD	Energy	RMSD	Energy	RMSD	Energy	RMSD
4RXN	54	27	-156.32	6.29	-150.11	6.00	-142.22	5.23	-154.47	5.21	-156.94	**5.11**	-157	5.19	**-157.25**	5.17	**-162.72**	5.41
1ENH	54	19	-146.69	6.61	-143.01	5.88	-129.23	5.11	-146.88	5.09	-147.76	5.02	**-148.58**	4.93	-148.39	**4.90**	**-151.65**	5.22
4PTI	58	32	-198.42	7.07	-190.77	6.99	-175.52	6.41	-196.05	6.27	-197.33	6.38	**-198.42**	6.38	-198.3	**6.37**	**-204.56**	6.46
2IGD	61	25	-174.19	9.33	-163.87	8.50	-151.09	**7.26**	-171.74	**7.26**	-172.83	7.28	-173.89	7.33	**-174.02**	7.43	**-176.83**	7.81
1YPA	64	38	-239.98	7.53	-236.10	6.86	-214.60	6.00	-245.19	6.05	-248.43	5.93	-247.35	**5.77**	**-248.54**	5.86	**-253.09**	6.29
1R69	69	30	-204.17	6.47	-191.14	5.65	-175.61	5.14	-203.22	4.92	-204.81	4.85	-205.88	4.88	**-207.06**	**4.78**	**-208.79**	**5.17**
1CTF	74	42	-213.81	7.23	-197.85	5.63	-179.18	5.23	-218.38	5.21	-220.1	5.06	**-222.23**	**5.02**	-221.67	5.06	**-225.42**	5.28
3MX7	90	44	-311.56	8.18	-300.89	8.62	-257.49	7.87	-321.94	8.00	-324.09	7.8	**-326.23**	7.70	-325.55	**7.64**	-325.45	7.94
3NBM	108	56	-401.99	8.58	-380.12	6.95	-329.7	6.88	-409.5	6.12	-406.74	6.06	**-412.96**	6.06	-411.18	**6.00**	**-419.25**	6.46
3MQO	120	68	-455.27	8.86	-422.4	7.52	-336.74	7.39	-461.38	6.98	-465.02	6.83	**-469.27**	6.77	-467.38	**6.67**	**-472.78**	6.84
3MRO	142	63	430.29	10.02	-397.14	9.61	-313.85	8.74	-445.23	8.11	-450.68	7.93	-448.59	7.85	**-452.04**	**7.71**	-447.77	8.72
3PNX	160	84	-571.13	9.38	-502.29	9.55	-383.49	9.05	-586.68	8.73	-593.85	**8.38**	-595.99	8.45	**-600.18**	8.39	-592.25	8.51

performs better in comparison to the parallel spiral search variants for 9 out of 12 proteins.

5.5. RMSD Values on 20 × 20 Benchmark. The RMSD is frequently used to measure the differences between values predicted by a model and the values actually observed. We compare the predicted structures obtained by our approach with the state-of-the-art approaches by measuring the RMSD with respect to the native structures from PDB. For any given structure, the RMSD is calculated using (10). The average distance between two α-Carbons in a native structure is 3.8 Å. To calculate RMSD, the distance between two neighbour lattice points ($\sqrt{2}$ for FCC lattice) is considered as 3.8 Å. Consider

$$\text{RMSD} = \sqrt{\frac{\sum_{i=1}^{n-1} \sum_{j=i+1}^{n} \left(d_{ij}^p - d_{ij}^n\right)^2}{n * (n-1)/2}}, \tag{10}$$

where d_{ij}^p and d_{ij}^n denote the distances between ith and jth amino acids, respectively, in the predicted structure and the native structure of the protein.

In Table 7, the RMSD columns show the root-mean-square deviation (RMSD) values obtained from different approaches on 12 benchmark proteins (Table 6). The experimental results show that amongst the parallel spiral search variants, PSSB1H3 (7 out of 12 proteins) produces better results in comparison to other variants in terms of lowest RMSD values. However, when compared with GA$^+$, the parallel variants perform better for 11 out of 12 proteins.

5.6. Effect of Mixing Energy Models. The best hydrophobic cores do not always correspond to the best structures in terms of RMSD values [67, 68]. These observations inspired us to mix the energy models. The approaches presented in Table 7 are guided by BM, HP, or both energy models. However, the conformations are always evaluated using BM model. The experimental results show that when the variants are guided by HP or both BM and HP models (such as PSSB3H1, PSSB2H2, PSSB1H3, and PSSB0H4) it performs better than the variant guided by BM model (such as PSSB4H0). Therefore, from the observation of RMSD values, it is clear that HP model works as a better guidance heuristic, whereas BM model works as better model for evaluating conformations.

6. Conclusion

In this paper, we present a multipoint parallel local search framework that runs tabu-based local search (spiral search [9]) in parallel threads. In our *ab initio* protein structure prediction method, we develop two versions of SS-Tabu that uses hydrophobic-polar energy model and 20 × 20 Berrera et al. [25] energy model separately on face-centred-cubic lattice. Collaboration and negotiation play vital roles in dealing with real world challenges. In our research, we try to adopt this analogy by considering each thread as a collaborator. We allow each thread to run for a predefined period of time. The threads are met in an assembly point when they finish

their execution and donate or accept better solutions to proceed with. The PSS starts with a set of random initial solutions by distributing a subset of solutions to different threads which are running different combinations of two versions of SS-Tabu. The interim improved solutions are stored threadwise and merged together when the threads finish. After removing the duplicates from the merged solutions, a selected distinct set of solutions is considered for the next iteration. In our approach, multipoint start helps find some promising solutions. For the next working set of solutions from the merged list, the most promising solutions are selected. Therefore, multipoint parallelism reduces the search space by exploring around the promising solutions in every iteration. The experimental results show that our new approach significantly improves over the results obtained by the state-of-the-art single-point search approaches.

Conflict of Interests

The authors declare that there is no conflict of interests regarding the publication of this paper.

Authors' Contribution

Mahmood A. Rashid conceived the idea of applying *Spiral Search* in a parallel framework. M. A. Hakim Newton, Swakkhar Shatabda, Md Tamjidul Hoque, and Abdul Sattar helped Mahmood A. Rashid in modeling, implementing, and testing the approach. All authors equally participated in analysing the test results to improve the approach and were significantly involved in the process of writing and reviewing the paper.

Acknowledgments

The authors would like to express their great appreciation to the people managing the *Cluster Computing Services* at National ICT Australia (NICTA) and Griffith University. Md Tamjidul Hoque acknowledges the Louisiana Board of Regents through the Board of Regents Support Fund, *LEQSF (2013-16)-RD-A-19*. NICTA, the sponsor of the article for publication, is funded by the Australian Government as represented by the Department of Broadband, Communications and the Digital Economy and the Australian Research Council through the ICT Centre of Excellence program.

References

[1] A. Smith, "Protein misfolding," *Nature Reviews Drug Discovery*, vol. 426, no. 6968, p. 78102, 2003.

[2] C. M. Dobson, "Protein folding and misfolding," *Nature*, vol. 426, no. 6968, pp. 884–890, 2003.

[3] "So much more to know," *The Science*, vol. 309, no. 5731, pp. 78–102, 2005.

[4] R. Bonneau and D. Baker, "Ab initio protein structure prediction: progress and prospects," *Annual Review of Biophysics and Biomolecular Structure*, vol. 30, pp. 173–189, 2001.

[5] C. A. Rohl, C. E. M. Strauss, K. M. S. Misura, and D. Baker, "Protein structure prediction using rosetta," *Methods in Enzymology*, vol. 383, pp. 66–93, 2004.

[6] J. Lee, S. Wu, and Y. Zhang, "Ab initio protein structure prediction," in *From Protein Structure to Function with Bioinformatics*, pp. 3–25, 2009.

[7] Y. Xia, E. S. Huang, M. Levitt, and R. Samudrala, "Ab initio construction of protein tertiary structures using a hierarchical approach," *Journal of Molecular Biology*, vol. 300, no. 1, pp. 171–185, 2000.

[8] M. A. Rashid, M. T. Hoque, M. A. H. Newton, D. Pham, and A. Sattar, "A new genetic algorithm for simplified protein structure prediction," in *AI 2012: Advances in Artificial Intelligence*, Lecture Notes in Computer Science, pp. 107–119, Springer, Berlin, Germany, 2012.

[9] M. A. Rashid, M. A. H. Newton, M. T. Hoque, S. Shatabda, D. Pham, and A. Sattar, "Spiral search: a hydrophobic-core directed local search for simplified PSP on 3D FCC lattice," *BMC Bioinformatics*, vol. 14, supplement 2, article S16, 2013.

[10] S. Shatabda and M. A. H. Newton, "Sattar a mixed heuristic local search for protein structure prediction," in *Proceedings of the 27th AAAI Conference on Artificial Intelligence*, AAAI Press, 2013.

[11] M. A. Rashid, M. A. H. Newton, M. T. Hoque, and A. Sattar, "Mixing energy models in genetic algorithms for on-lattice protein structure prediction," *BioMed Research International*, vol. 2013, Article ID 924137, 15 pages, 2013.

[12] A. D. Ullah and K. Steinhöfel, "A hybrid approach to protein folding problem integrating constraint programming with local search," *BMC Bioinformatics*, vol. 11, supplement, article S39, 2010.

[13] S. R. D. Torres, D. C. B. Romero, L. F. N. Vasquez, and Y. J. P. Ardila, "A novel ab-initio genetic-based approach for protein folding prediction," in *Proceedings of the 9th Annual Conference on Genetic and Evolutionary Computation (GECCO '07)*, pp. 393–400, ACM, 2007.

[14] Y. Zhang and J. Skolnick, "The protein structure prediction problem could be solved using the current PDB library," *Proceedings of the National Academy of Sciences of the United States of America*, vol. 102, no. 4, pp. 1029–1034, 2005.

[15] J. U. Bowie, R. Luthy, and D. Eisenberg, "A method to identify protein sequences that fold into a known three-dimensional structure," *Science*, vol. 253, no. 5016, pp. 164–170, 1991.

[16] A. Torda, "Protein threading," in *The Proteomics Protocols Handbook*, pp. 921–938, 2005.

[17] K. T. Simons, R. Bonneau, I. Ruczinski, and D. Baker, "Ab initio protein structure prediction of CASP III targets using ROSETTA," *Proteins*, supplement 3, pp. 171–176, 1999.

[18] D. Baker and A. Sali, "Protein structure prediction and structural genomics," *Science*, vol. 294, no. 5540, pp. 93–96, 2001.

[19] C. Levinthal, "Are there pathways for protein folding?" *Journal of Medical Physics*, vol. 65, pp. 44–45, 1968.

[20] C. B. Anfinsen, "Principles that govern the folding of protein chains," *Science*, vol. 181, no. 4096, pp. 223–230, 1973.

[21] T. C. Hales, "A proof of the Kepler conjecture," *Annals of Mathematics*, vol. 162, no. 3, pp. 1065–1185, 2005.

[22] M. T. Hoque, M. Chetty, and A. Sattar, "Protein folding prediction in 3D FCC HP lattice model using genetic algorithm," in *Proceedings of the IEEE Congress on Evolutionary Computation*, The Annals of Mathematics, pp. 4138–4145, 2007.

[23] K. F. Lau and K. A. Dill, "Lattice statistical mechanics model of the conformational and sequence spaces of proteins," *Macromolecules*, vol. 22, no. 10, pp. 3986–3997, 1989.

[24] S. Miyazawa and R. L. Jernigan, "Estimation of effective interresidue contact energies from protein crystal structures: Quasichemical approximation," *Macromolecules*, vol. 18, no. 3, pp. 534–552, 1985.

[25] M. Berrera, H. Molinari, and F. Fogolari, "Amino acid empirical contact energy definitions for fold recognition in the space of contact maps," *BMC Bioinformatics*, vol. 4, article 8, 2003.

[26] M. Cebrián, I. IDotú, P. V. Hententryck, and P. Clote, "Protein structure prediction on the face centered cubic lattice by local search," in *Proceedings of the 23rd AAAI Conference on Artificial Intelligence*, pp. 241–246, AAAI Press, July 2008.

[27] S. Shatabda, M. A. H. Newton, D. N. Pham, and A. Sattar, "Memory-based local search for simplified protein structure prediction," in *Proceedings of the 3rd ACM Conference on Bioinformatics, Computational Biology and Biomedicine (BCB '12)*, ACM, Orlando, Fla, USA, 2012.

[28] B. Berger and T. Leighton, "Protein folding in the hydrophobic-hydrophilic (HP) model is NP-complete," *Journal of Computational Biology*, vol. 5, no. 1, pp. 27–40, 1998.

[29] F. Glover and M. Laguna, *Tabu Search*, vol. 1, Kluwer Academic, 1998.

[30] F. Glover, "Tabu search. Part I," *ORSA Journal on Computing*, vol. 1, no. 3, pp. 190–206, 1989.

[31] C. Thachuk, A. Shmygelska, and H. H. Hoos, "A replica exchange Monte Carlo algorithm for protein folding in the HP model," *BMC Bioinformatics*, vol. 8, article 342, 2007.

[32] A.-A. Tantar, N. Melab, and E.-G. Talbi, "A grid-based genetic algorithm combined with an adaptive simulated annealing for protein structure prediction," *Soft Computing*, vol. 12, no. 12, pp. 1185–1198, 2008.

[33] R. Unger and J. Moult, "A genetic algorithm for 3D protein folding simulations," in *Proceedings of the 5th International Conference on Genetic Algorithms*, Soft Computing-A Fusion of Foundations, Methodologies and Applications, pp. 581–588, Morgan Kaufmann Publishers, 1993.

[34] M. T. Hoque, *Genetic Algorithm for ab initio protein structure prediction based on low resolution models [Ph.D. thesis]*, Gippsland School of Information Technology, Monash University, Monash, Australia, 2007.

[35] H. J. Bockenhauer, A. Z. M. D. Ullah, L. Kapsokalivas, and K. Steinhofel, "A local move set for protein folding in triangular lattice models," in *Algorithms in Bioinformatics*, K. A. Crandall and J. Lagergren, Eds., vol. 5251 of *Lecture Notes in Computer Science*, pp. 369–381, Springer, 2008.

[36] G. W. Klau, N. Lesh, J. Marks, and M. Mitzenmacher, "Human-guided tabu search," in *Proceedings of the 18th National Conference on Artificial Intelligence (AAAI' 02)*, pp. 41–47, August 2002.

[37] C. Blum, "Ant colony optimization: Introduction and recent trends," *Physics of Life Reviews*, vol. 2, no. 4, pp. 353–373, 2005.

[38] V. Cutello, G. Nicosia, M. Pavone, and J. Timmis, "An immune algorithm for protein structure prediction on lattice models," *IEEE Transactions on Evolutionary Computation*, vol. 11, no. 1, pp. 101–117, 2007.

[39] I. Dotu, M. Cebrián, P. Van Hentenryck, and P. Clote, "On lattice protein structure prediction revisited," *IEEE/ACM Transactions on Computational Biology and Bioinformatics*, vol. 8, no. 6, pp. 1620–1632, 2011.

[40] R. Backofen and S. Will, "A constraint-based approach to fast and exact structure prediction in three-dimensional protein models," *Constraints*, vol. 11, no. 1, pp. 5–30, 2006.

[41] M. Mann, S. Will, and R. Backofen, "CPSP-tools: exact and complete algorithms for high-throughput 3D lattice protein studies," *BMC Bioinformatics*, vol. 9, article 230, 2008.

[42] M. Mann, C. Smith, M. Rabbath, M. Edwards, S. Will, and R. Backofen, "CPSP-web-tools: a server for 3D lattice protein studies," *Bioinformatics*, vol. 25, no. 5, pp. 676–677, 2009.

[43] A. L. Patton, W. F. Punch III, and E. D. Goodman, "A standard GA approach to native protein conformation prediction," in *Proceedings of the 6th International Conference on Genetic Algorithms*.

[44] M. T. Hoque, M. Chetty, A. Lewis, A. Sattar, and V. M. Avery, "DFS-generated pathways in GA crossover for protein structure prediction," *Neurocomputing*, vol. 73, no. 13–15, pp. 2308–2316, 2010.

[45] M. T. Hoque, M. Chetty, A. Lewis, and A. Sattar, "Twin removal in genetic algorithms for protein structure prediction using low-resolution model," *IEEE/ACM Transactions on Computational Biology and Bioinformatics*, vol. 8, no. 1, pp. 234–245, 2011.

[46] A. D. Ullah, L. Kapsokalivas, M. Mann, and K. Steinhöfel, "Protein folding simulation by two-stage optimization," in *Computational Intelligence and Intelligent Systems*, Z. Cai, Z. Li, Z. Kang, and Y. Liu, Eds., vol. 51 of *Communications in Computer and Information Science*, pp. 138–145, Springer, Berlin, Germany, 2009.

[47] T. Jiang, Q. Cui, G. Shi, and S. Ma, "Protein folding simulations of the hydrophobic-hydrophilic model by combining tabu search with genetic algorithms," *Journal of Chemical Physics*, vol. 119, no. 8, pp. 4592–4596, 2003.

[48] A. Dal Palù, A. Dovier, and F. Fogolari, "Constraint logic programming approach to protein structure prediction," *BMC Bioinformatics*, vol. 5, article 186, 2004.

[49] A. Dal Palù, A. Dovier, and E. Pontelli, "Heuristics, optimizations, and parallelism for protein structure prediction in CLP($\mathcal{F}D$)," in *Proceedings of the 7th ACM SIGPLAN Conference on Principles and Practice of Declarative Programming (PPDP '05)*, pp. 230–241, July 2005.

[50] A. Dal Palù, A. Dovier, and E. Pontelli, "A constraint solver for discrete lattices, its parallelization, and application to protein structure prediction," *Software*, vol. 37, no. 13, pp. 1405–1449, 2007.

[51] A. Dal Palu, A. Dovier, F. Fogolari, and E. Pontelli, "Exploring protein fragment assembly using CLP," in *Proceedings of the 22nd International Joint Conference on Artificial Intelligence*, vol. 3, pp. 2590–2595, AAAI Press, 2011.

[52] L. Kapsokalivas, X. Gan, A. A. Albrecht, and K. Steinhöfel, "Population-based local search for protein folding simulation in the MJ energy model and cubic lattices," *Computational Biology and Chemistry*, vol. 33, no. 4, pp. 283–294, 2009.

[53] C. Vargas Benitez and H. Lopes, "Parallel artificial bee colony algorithm approaches for protein structure prediction using the 3DHP-SC model," in *Intelligent Distributed Computing IV*, vol. 315 of *of Studies in Computational Intelligence*, pp. 255–264, Springer, Berlin, Germany, 2010.

[54] A.-A. Tantar, N. Melab, and E.-G. Talbi, "A comparative study of parallel metaheuristics for protein structure prediction on the computational grid," in *Proceedings of the 21st International Parallel and Distributed Processing Symposium (IPDPS '07)*, March 2007.

[55] A.-A. Tantar, N. Melab, E.-G. Talbi, B. Parent, and D. Horvath, "A parallel hybrid genetic algorithm for protein structure prediction on the computational grid," *Future Generation Computer Systems*, vol. 23, no. 3, pp. 398–409, 2007.

[56] I. Kondov, "Protein structure prediction using distributed parallel particle swarm optimization," *Natural Computing*, vol. 12, pp. 29–41, 2013.

[57] J. C. Calvo and J. Ortega, "Parallel protein structure prediction by multiobjective optimization," in *Proceedings of the 17th Euromicro International Conference on Parallel, Distributed and Network-Based Processing (PDP '09)*, pp. 268–275, February 2009.

[58] J. C. Calvo, J. Ortega, and M. Anguita, "Comparison of parallel multi-objective approaches to protein structure prediction," *Journal of Supercomputing*, vol. 58, no. 2, pp. 253–260, 2011.

[59] V. Robles, M. Perez, V. Herves, J. Pena, and P. Larranaga, "Parallel stochastic search for protein secondary structure prediction," in *Parallel Processing and Applied Mathematics*, vol. 3019 of *Lecture Notes in Computer Science*, pp. 1162–1169, Springer, Berlin, Germany, 2004.

[60] M. A. Rashid, S. Shatabda, M. A. H. Newton, M. T. Hoque, D. N. Pham, and A. Sattar, "Random-walk: a stagnation recovery technique for simplified protein structure prediction," in *Proceedings of the ACM Conference on Bioinformatics, Computational Biology and Biomedicine (BCB '12)*, pp. 620–622, ACM, 2012.

[61] K. Yue and K. A. Dill, "Sequence-structure relationships in proteins and copolymers," *Physical Review E*, vol. 48, no. 3, pp. 2267–2278, 1993.

[62] N. Lesh, M. Mitzenmacher, and S. Whitesides, "A complete and effective move set for simplified protein folding," in *Proceedings of the 7th Annual International Conference on Research in Computational Molecular Biology*, pp. 188–195, April 2003.

[63] S. Will, "Constraint-based hydrophobic core construction for protein structure prediction in the face-centered-cubic lattice," *Pacific Symposium on Biocomputing. Pacific Symposium on Biocomputing*, pp. 661–672, 2002.

[64] R. Backofen and S. Will, "A constraint-based approach to structure prediction for simplified protein models that outperforms other existing methods," in *Logic Programming*, pp. 49–71, 2003.

[65] S. Will, *Exact, constraint-based structure prediction in simple protein models [Ph.D. thesis]*, University of Jena, 2005.

[66] K. Yue, K. M. Fiebig, P. D. Thomas, H. S. Chan, E. I. Shakhnovich, and K. A. Dill, "A test of lattice protein folding algorithms," *Proceedings of the National Academy of Sciences of the United States of America*, vol. 92, no. 1, pp. 325–329, 1995.

[67] S. Shatabda, M. H. Newton, M. A. Rashid, D. N. Pham, and A. Sattar, "How good are simplified models for protein structure prediction?," *Advances in Bioinformatics*. In press.

[68] S. Shatabda, M. A. H. Newton, and A. Sattar, "Simplified lattice models for protein structure prediction: how good are they?" in *Proceedings of the 27th AAAI Conference on Artificial Intelligence*, 2013.

17

Elementary Flux Mode Analysis of Acetyl-CoA Pathway in *Carboxydothermus hydrogenoformans* Z-2901

Rajadurai Chinnasamy Perumal, Ashok Selvaraj, and Gopal Ramesh Kumar

Bioinformatics Lab, AU-KBC Research Centre, M.I.T Campus of Anna University, Chromepet, Chennai, Tamil Nadu 600 044, India

Correspondence should be addressed to Gopal Ramesh Kumar; grameshpub@au-kbc.org

Academic Editor: Ming Chen

Carboxydothermus hydrogenoformans is a carboxydotrophic hydrogenogenic bacterium species that produces hydrogen molecule by utilizing carbon monoxide (CO) or pyruvate as a carbon source. To investigate the underlying biochemical mechanism of hydrogen production, an elementary mode analysis of acetyl-CoA pathway was performed to determine the intermediate fluxes by combining linear programming (LP) method available in CellNetAnalyzer software. We hypothesized that addition of enzymes necessary for carbon monoxide fixation and pyruvate dissimilation would enhance the theoretical yield of hydrogen. An *in silico* gene knockout of *pyk*, *pykC*, and *mdh* genes of modeled acetyl-CoA pathway allows the maximum theoretical hydrogen yield of 47.62 mmol/gCDW/h for 1 mole of carbon monoxide (CO) uptake. The obtained hydrogen yield is comparatively two times greater than the previous experimental data. Therefore, it could be concluded that this elementary flux mode analysis is a crucial way to achieve efficient hydrogen production through acetyl-CoA pathway and act as a model for strain improvement.

1. Introduction

Use of fossil fuels causes adverse effect on environment through pollution. Moreover, the availability of fuels such as oils and natural gases is limited and are likely to be depleted soon [1]. Therefore, it is indispensable to search for alternate fuel source and hydrogen is one of the efficient sources of energy that could effectively replace the available fossil fuels. It is also considered as fuel of the future, since it is eco-friendly and emits zero carbon. Besides its application as a fuel, hydrogen can also be used as a potential electron donor for various reactions in biotechnological and chemical industrial processes [2]. Hydrogen is conventionally produced from fossil fuels by steam reforming other industrial methods such as coal gasification and electrolysis [3]. However, these methods uses nonrenewable energy source to produce hydrogen. Therefore, biological hydrogen production by microorganisms especially by hydrogenogens is the most convenient one [4, 5]. Over the past two decades, various researches are going on for enhanced biological hydrogen productivity [6, 7] and improvement of such a product from organisms by optimizing their genetic process is commonly referred to as metabolic engineering [8]. The knowledge of reactions and selection of optimal enzymatic route between the substrate and product is an ultimate task in biological research. Computational based theoretical metabolic yield is a key criterion to study the substrate utilization and product formation of microorganisms [9–11]. *Carboxydothermus hydrogenoformans* Z-2901 is one of the most promising and potential acetogenic hydrogenogenic bacterium produces species which produces hydrogen by utilizing CO and pyruvate as a carbon source [12]. In hydrogenogenic microorganisms, the autotrophic fixation of CO and pyruvate dissimilation have been achieved through acetyl-CoA or Wood-Ljungdahl pathway and hydrogen molecule has been produced as one of the end product. The reactions involved in CO fixation are activated into acetyl group that contains metal ions. The *CooX* cluster of genes is the major component of this pathway that fixes CO and pyruvate dissimilation catalyzed by *pdh* gene during acetyl-CoA pathway, a key biochemical feature that supports hydrogen production [13, 14].

Elementary flux mode (EFM) analysis is one of the powerful tools for metabolic pathway analysis. It allows us to calculate all possible steady-state flux distributions of the network, thereby determining the theoretical molar yield of products and studying their effects of any genetic modifications [15–17]. Such studies would help to design an organism for obtaining the efficient product formation through metabolic engineering. Recently, elementary mode analysis has been used to develop a rational model of methionine production from well-known organisms such as *Escherichia coli* and *Corynebacterium glutamicum* [18], and polyhydroxybutanoate production from *Saccharomyces cerevisiae* [19–21]. The experimental analysis of hydrogen production in wild type *E. coli* resulted in a flux distribution indicating a hydrogen production of 0.17 mol per mole of glucose consumption [22]. The predicted hydrogen production of *E. coli* through metabolic flux analysis by the deletion of *ldh* gene was 0.23 mol per mole of glucose consumed which is slightly higher than the wild type strain. In another case, computational flux analysis studies on hydrogen production in *E. coli* through the formate hydrogen lyase reaction have suggested that the level of hydrogen production matches experimental observations [23]. In this paper, elementary mode based flux analysis has been carried out for the newly modeled acetyl-CoA pathway of *C. hydrogenoformans* that comprises necessary reaction stoichiometry collected from KEGG database [24]. Theoretical capabilities of hydrogen yield limited by the utilization of CO and pyruvate and through *in silico* gene knockout have been studied using metabolic flux analysis tools and software. This elementary mode flux analysis also provides a basis to design a system that has specific phenotypes, metabolic network regulation, and robustness that facilitates the understanding of cell physiology and implementation of metabolic engineering strategies of *C. hydrogenoformans* to improve the hydrogen productivity.

2. Materials and Methods

2.1. Reconstruction and Modeling of Acetyl-CoA Pathway. A simplified model of acetyl-CoA pathway of *C. hydrogenoformans* was constructed based on biochemical features consisting of stoichiometry reactions retrieved from KEGG (Kyoto Encyclopedia of Genes and Genome) database [24]. The KEGG database was used to link annotated genes to protein and to reactions. Gaps in acetyl-CoA pathway were filled based on homology search and context analysis using KEGG-BLAST against orthologs [25, 26]. Initially, the protein ORF sequences (both known and unknown ORFs) of *C. hydrogenoformans* were submitted to KEGG-BLAST tool to find out the reaction information of functionally characterized orthologous gene hits. It was manually checked that the product of orthologous reaction hits should match with reactant of reaction present in the same or any of the pathways of *C. hydrogenoformans*. The metabolite (both substrate and product) of all the unknown reactions has been interconnected to make a subnetwork using Cytoscape software [27]. A cytosolic compartment was applied to ideally depict the influx and efflux rate of substrate, cofactors, and product [28]. This set of modeled reaction equations was further used for elementary flux mode analysis to predict the theoretical yield

of hydrogen and other products. The modeled acetyl-CoA pathway includes both pyruvate dissimilation and methane degradation metabolism [29–31]. For the interconversion of CO to CO_2 during acetyl-CoA pathway, CO dehydrogenase enzyme and pyruvate dehydrogenase activities were initially considered. The precursors such as NADP and ATP necessary for product formation were also included in the reaction stoichiometry. With the use of collected reaction data as discussed above, flux balance-based models of pyruvate and methane metabolism have been built and are known as acetyl-CoA carbon metabolism or Wood-Ljungdahl pathway of *C. hydrogenoformans* [32].

2.2. Elementary Flux Mode Analysis. The elementary flux mode analysis was carried out for studying the biochemical behavior of acetyl-CoA pathway of *C. hydrogenoformans*. The stoichiometric reactions of modeled acetyl-CoA pathway were imported and analyzed using CellNetAnalyzer with MATLAB [32]. The METATOOL program available in CellNetAnalyzer was compiled using MATLAB environment to generate elementary modes having specific reaction sets. The objectives of reactions that maximize the flux rate of products have been calculated using linear programming (LP). For flux optimizations, a GLPK library, GNU based linear programming kit was used through the GLPKMEX interface. The theoretical fluxes were calculated for the substrates pyruvate, CO, and other by-products such as hydrogen, malate, oxaloacetate, and formate.

During metabolic flux analysis, the objective is usually maximizing the flux rate of products or biomass [33]. Here, we considered pyruvate and CO influxes as objective for maximizing the hydrogen and other product formation. The theoretical molar yield of any product is represented by [vp/vs], where vp is flux rate of product and vs is flux rate of substrate. The increase of product yield can be achieved by maximizing the flux vp, constrained by the flux vs of the substrate. The flux balance analysis is described in a mathematical formulation by the following equation:

$$\sum_j s_{ij} v_j = 0, \quad \forall i \in M_i, \tag{1}$$

where S_{ij} is the stoichiometric coefficient of the ith metabolite in the jth reaction and V_j is the flux of the jth reaction. M_i is the internal metabolites. The flux distributions of the metabolic network model in steady state expressed by (1) was solved using METATOOL software [34].

3. Results

3.1. Identification of Essential Reactions for Elementary Flux Mode Studies. To identify the essentiality of ORFs that code for energy producing enzymes and cofactors, an *in silico* gene knockout studies hace been performed [35]. With the use of metabolic stoichiometry data available from KEGG database, a flux balance-based model of pyruvate and methane metabolism of *C. hydrogenoformans* has been built and it is illustrated in Figure 1. This constructed model can be utilized for industrial based hydrogen production.

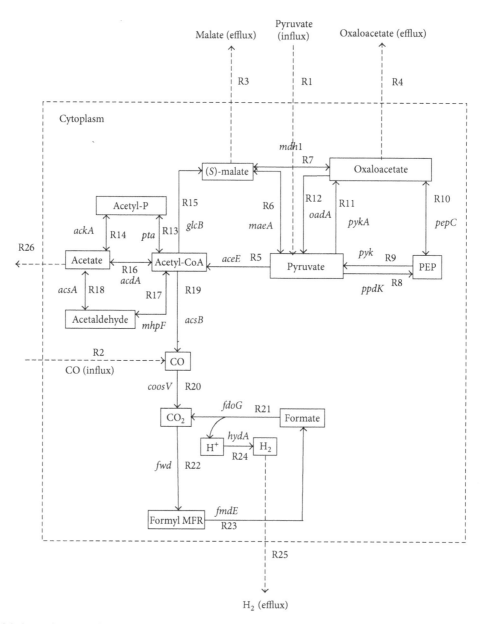

FIGURE 1: The modeled acetyl-CoA pathway of *C. hydrogenoformans* utilizing CO and pyruvate as a carbon source. Black color line shows that the reactions obtained from topology of KEGG orthologous pathway map. The influx and efflux directions of substrates and products were indicated as dotted lines. The Rn indicates the reaction numbers in Table 1.

Totally, twenty- two reactions were collected from KEGG database (excluding influx and efflux reactions) (Table 1) and they were involved in reducing acetyl-CoA during methane metabolism (KEGG Pathway ID: map00680). Here, the flux rate of the newly added enzymes which influence the hydrogen production was identified by *in silico* gene deletion method using CellNetAnalyzer software with MATLAB [32]. The initial uptake of substrate and product formation rates is essential for the enhancement of the growth of *C. hydrogenoformans*.

3.2. Identification of Elementary Modes. Elementary modes (EMs) are the minimal sets of reactions catalyzed by enzymes that allow the network to perform at steady state [36, 37]. They

represent the optimal route of utilizing external substrate and forming external products and thus they are defined in the context of whole-cell metabolism. The modeled acetyl-CoA metabolic pathway was taken for this elementary mode flux analysis studies. In this pathway, carbon monoxide (CO) and pyruvate are the substrate dissimilates to form acetyl-CoA as an important intermediate and yielding malate, acetate, oxaloacetate, and hydrogen as end products. This pathway is also called as Wood-Ljungdahl pathway, since it utilizes CO as a substrate catalyzed by CO dehydrogenase enzyme and converted to acetyl-CoA [38]. In this modeled pathway, the number of metabolites are lesser than number of reactions and therefore satisfies under-deterministic condition [37]. The resulting network comprises totally 26 reactions with 18

TABLE 1: Reactions and enzymes involved in the acetyl-CoA pathway model of *C. hydrogenoformans*.

Reaction number	Reactions	Gene name	EC number	Enzyme
R 1:	pyruvate intake	*	*	Influx
R 2:	$\implies$ CO	*	*	Influx
R 3:	malate $\implies$	#	#	Efflux
R 4:	OAA $\implies$	#	#	Efflux
R 5:	pyr $\implies$ CO2 + ACoA	aceE	1.2.4.1	Pyruvate dehydrogenase E1
R 6:	pyr + CO2 $\Longleftrightarrow$ malate	maeA	1.1.1.38	Malic enzyme
R 7:	OAA + NADH $\Longleftrightarrow$ malate	mdh1	1.1.1.37	Malate dehydrogenase
R 8:	pyr + ATP $\implies$ PEP	ppdK	2.7.9.1	Pyruvate phosphate dikinase
R 9:	PEP $\implies$ pyr + ATP	pyk	2.7.1.40	Pyruvate kinase
R 10:	CO2 + PEP $\Longleftrightarrow$ OAA	pepC	4.1.1.31	PEP carboxylase
R 11:	pyr + CO2 $\implies$ OAA	pykA	6.4.1.1	Pyruvate kinase II
R 12:	OAA $\implies$ pyr + ATP	oadA	4.1.1.3	Pyruvate carboxylase subunit
R 13:	ACoA $\Longleftrightarrow$ acetylP	pta	2.3.1.8	Phosphate acetyltransferase
R 14:	acetylP $\Longleftrightarrow$ ATP + acetate	ackA	2.7.2.1	Acetate kinase
R 15:	ACoA + H2O $\implies$ malate	glcB	2.3.3.9	Malate synthase G
R 16:	ACoA $\Longleftrightarrow$ ATP + acetate	acdA	6.2.1.13	Acetyl-CoA synthase
R 17:	acetaldehyde $\Longleftrightarrow$ ACoA	mhpF	1.2.1.10	Acetaldehyde dehydrogenase
R 18:	NADH + acetate $\Longleftrightarrow$ H2O + acetaldehyde	acsA	6.2.1.1	Acetyl-coenzyme A synthetase
R 19:	ACoA $\implies$ CO	acsB	**2.3.1.169**	CO-methylating acetyl-CoA synthase
R 20:	H2O + CO $\implies$ CO2 + H2	cooSV	1.2.99.2	Carbon-monoxide dehydrogenase
R 21:	Formate + NAD$^+$ $\implies$ CO2 + NADH	fdoG	1.2.1.2	Formate dehydrogenase-O
R 22:	CO2 + MFR $\implies$ H2O + fMFR	fwd	1.2.99.5	Tungsten formylmethanofuran dehydrogenase subunit E
R 23:	fMFR + H2O $\implies$ Formate + MFR	fmdE	1.2.99.5	Formylmethanofuran dehydrogenase
R 24:	2 H$^+$ $\implies$ H2	hydA	1.12.7.2	Ni/Fe hydrogenase large subunit
R 25:	H2 $\implies$	#	#	Efflux
R 26:	Acetate $\implies$	#	#	Efflux

*Substrate influx into the system.
#External product efflux from the system.

metabolites (Table 1). About 8 reactions are reversible and 18 reactions are irreversible. As a result of elementary mode analysis, about 28 elementary modes (EMs) were derived from this pathway totally and among them 18 EMs lead to the formation of hydrogen from pyruvate and CO. Those 18 EMs can be further classified according to their gene catalyzed and product formation. Elementary mode distributions of major metabolites are malate 16 EMs, oxaloacetate 14 EMs, acetate 4 Ems, and hydrogen 18 EMs. The rest of EMs tends to form other compounds such as malate, oxaloacetate, and acetate. Two elementary modes EM 9 and EM 21 are predicted to be having minimal reaction sets for hydrogen production by consumption of pyruvate as a substrate (Figure 2). They attained the steady-state level after allowing the substrate into the system. During acetyl-CoA pathway, utilization of CO by *C. hydrogenoformans* is catalyzed by two major enzymes, CO dehydrogenase and acetyl-CoA synthase [32]. The influx rate of CO and/or pyruvate (substrate) determines the intermediate carbon flux, efflux rate of hydrogen, and other metabolites.

3.3. Gene Participation in EMs. The occurrence of genes involved in hydrogen production during acetyl-CoA pathway was studied through elementary mode analysis. Figure 3 shows that there are seventeen genes that appear in eighteen elementary modes which are the optimal routes responsible for synthesizing hydrogen. Such modes can be characterized by indicating genes sets or enzymes involved in the product formation. The gene sets *ppdK, pepC, mhpF, acsA,* and *CooSV* catalyze reactions with pyruvate and/or CO as carbon sources and they participated in all the eighteen elementary modes (EMs) in acetyl-CoA pathway. The genes *aceA* and *acsB* furthest down the pathway participate in only thirteen EMs. Next to this, genes such as *fdoG, fwd,* and *fmdE* were involved in only ten EMs and genes *maeA, pykA, oadA, hydD, pta, ackA,* and *acdA* participated in less than ten EMs. These findings suggested that the blocking of those gene sets or the reactions does not affect carbon flow during acetyl-CoA pathway. The genes *acs* and *pyk* are involved in many modes, which are predicted to have major role for maintaining the steady-state flux throughout the pathway.

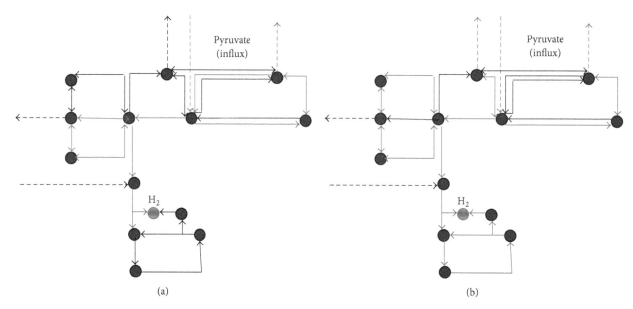

FIGURE 2: Important elementary modes of acetyl-CoA pathway of *C. hydrogenoformans*. (a) Elementary mode 9 consists of minimal reaction sets required for hydrogen production; (b) elementary mode 21 of acetyl-CoA metabolism during which maximum hydrogen was obtained.

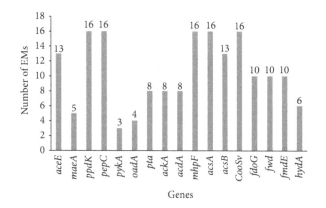

FIGURE 3: Types of gene involved in hydrogen production during acetyl-CoA pathway of *C. hydrogenoformans*. The genes *ppdK, pepC, mhpF, acsA,* and *CooSv* are predicted to be involved in all the eighteen elementary modes.

Malate is one of the important metabolites formed from pyruvate during CO metabolism. Oxaloacetate and acetate are other important metabolites formed by the decarboxylation of pyruvate [39]. Thus, if the genes related to hydrogen will be removed, the formation of malate, oxaloacetate, and acetate will be affected. These discrepancies could cause severe physiological change of the organism.

3.4. Elementary Flux Mode Analysis of Acetyl-CoA Pathway. Elementary flux mode analysis of acetyl-CoA pathway helps to predict the promising gene deletion target necessary for increasing the product rate [40]. This is the first reported elementary flux mode analysis result of *C. hydrogenoformans* for the purpose of augmentation of hydrogen production. By examining the elementary modes (EMs) of acetyl-CoA pathway, the key reaction steps for efficient hydrogen production

have been identified by carrying out flux optimization using METATOOL option available in CellNetAnalyzer software [32]. As a result of flux optimization, the theoretical molar yield of hydrogen has been calculated with different substrate and product combination. It was assumed that the flux rate and concentration of malate, oxaloacetate, acetate, and formate determine the cellular growth of CO oxidizing bacterial species that include carboxydotrophic hydrogenogens [41, 42]. The level of ATP and NADP (co-factors) were also calculated during elementary flux mode analysis.

By generating stoichiometric matrix, the metabolite connections between reactions can be studied to identify the feasible steady-state metabolic flow. These EM studies help to investigate the important subnetworks, their gene participation, and their functionalities for obtaining hydrogen and other important metabolites through acetyl-CoA pathway. This study also help in identifying genes, when deleted through gene knockout would increase hydrogen production. For maintaining the robustness and its sensitivity to perturbation such as new reaction inclusion, gene knockouts were completely analyzed to optimize the modeled acetyl-CoA pathway. The sensitivity of hydrogen yield to the flux values of pyruvate, CO utilization, and acetyl-CoA formation was studied in this work.

3.5. In Silico Gene Knockout Analysis. The gene deletion or knockout studies could have either positive or negative effects on phenotypes of organisms. Essential genes and reactions in the EFM pathways could not be deleted [43]. For the model of acetyl-CoA pathway, elementary mode (EM) has been systematically used to examine gene deletion that influence the hydrogen yield of *C. hydrogenoformans* as well as to identify a set of multiple gene knockout which results in higher product yield. Gene knockouts were carried out by removing the enzymatic reaction corresponding to that gene

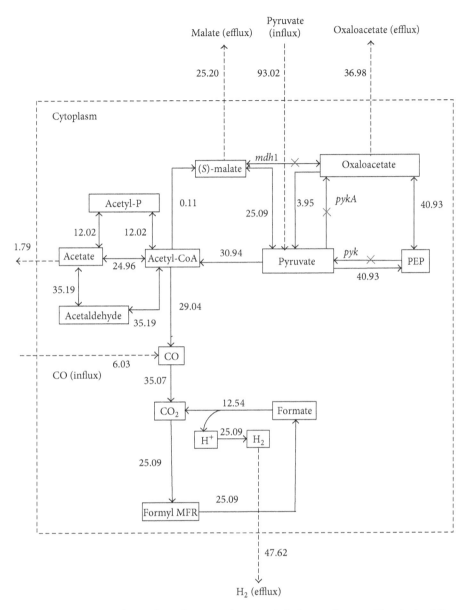

FIGURE 4: Gene knockout on elementary mode 21 of acetyl-CoA pathway in *C. hydrogenoformans*. The obtained fluxes were highlighted in blue color box. Knockout genes *pyk, pykA,* and *mdh* genes were highlighted in red mark (×).

(having zero constraints) from the stoichiometric matrix. Totally, 28 elementary modes were observed and their fluxes were measured. Among them, only two EMs 9 and 21 gene sets or reaction flow have maintained the maximum possible yield of hydrogen and retain a reasonable yield of of of by-products such as acetate, malate, and oxaloacetate while the other possible number of elementary modes with minimal product fluxes was eliminated.

For metabolic flux analysis study, we used the modeled acetyl-CoA pathway (Figure 1) to achieve the enhanced theoretical molar yield of hydrogen. Three genes *pyk, pykA,* and *mdh* were knocked out during flux optimization of EM 21 (Table 2). A cytosolic compartment has been included in network model to measure the external fluxes such as substrate uptake and product formation. As a result,

the influx or consumption rate of pyruvate reaches from 87.11 mmol/gCDW/h to 93.02 mmol/gCDW/h and thereby increases the hydrogen flux from 38.95 mmol/gCDW/h to 47.62 mmol/gCDW/h (Figure 4). The increases in the flux value actually indicate fixation of CO by *CooS* gene and decarboxylation of pyruvate by *pyk* gene [32, 44]. During the gene knockout study on EM 9, malate synthase (*glcB*), malate dehydrogenase (*mdh*), and pyruvate kinase (*pyk*) genes were knocked out (Figure 5, Table 2) and, as a result, the flux rate of hydrogen reached to 46.35 mmol/gCDW/h. The influence of flux rate of other byproducts such as malate, oxaloacetate and acetate on hydrogen production were also examined. The flux distribution of pyruvate, CO, hydrogen, and other major metabolites during normal flux measurement (i.e) without gene knockout is clearly illustrated in Figure 6(A). As

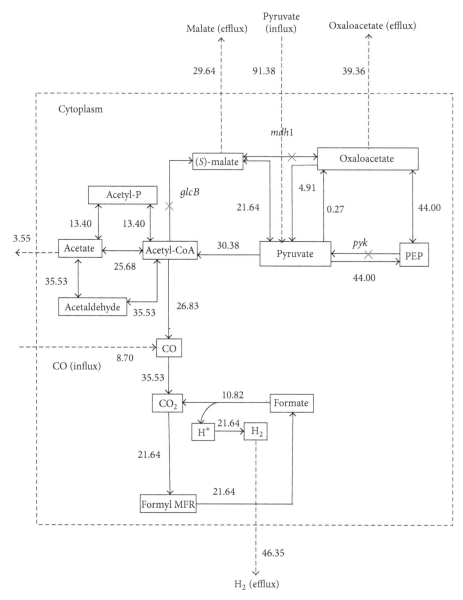

FIGURE 5: Gene knockout on elementary mode 9 of acetyl-CoA pathway in *C. hydrogenoformans*. The knockout genes *glcB*, *mdh*, and *pyk* were highlighted in red mark (×). Here, the reactions connecting the malate and oxaloacetate were blocked and fluxes were maintained in alternate nodes.

TABLE 2: Knockout genes in elementary mode 21 and elementary mode 9.

Reaction number	EC number	Enzyme name	Knockout gene name
		Knockout genes in elementary mode 21	
R 9	2.7.1.40	Pyruvate kinase	*pyk*
R 11	6.4.1.1	Pyruvate carboxylase	*pykA*
R 7	1.1.1.37	Malate dehydrogenase	*mdh*
		Knockout genes in elementary mode 9	
R 15	2.3.3.9	Malate synthase	*glcB*
R 7	1.1.37	Malate dehydrogenase	*mdh*
R 9	2.7.1.40	Pyruvate kinase	*pyk*

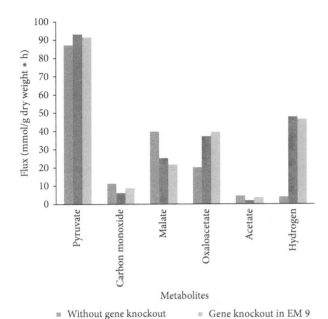

FIGURE 6: The fluxes of hydrogen and other major metabolites during acetyl-CoA pathway of *C. hydrogenoformans*. (A) Blue bar represents the flux rates of metabolites without gene knockout. (B) Red bar shows the maximum fluxes obtained from elementary mode 21 by gene knockout of *pyk*, *pykA*, and *mdh* genes. (C) Green bar represents the flux rates obtained from elementary mode 9 by gene knockout of *glcB*, *mdh*, and *pyk* genes.

a result, flux rate of hydrogen reaches 38.95 mmol/gCDW/h. Maximum flux of 47.62 mmol/gCDW/h of hydrogen was obtained in the twenty-one elementary mode and it is clearly elucidated in Figure 6(B). This flux rate is slightly higher than the normal flux (i.e) flux obtained without gene knockout (Figure 6(A)). During this mode, only pyruvate was influxed forming hydrogen and malate as a product. The enzymes such as pyruvate kinase (pyk), pyruvate carboxylase (pykA), and malate dehydrogenase (mdh) have been knocked out since they are not involved in EM 21 (Table 2). The other major products obtained during EM 21 were malate, oxaloacetate, and acetate. Similarly, the EM 9 has the maximum flux rate of hydrogen formation next to the level of EM 21. The obtained flux rates of hydrogen and other metabolites in EM 9 were illustrated in Figure 6(C).

4. Discussion

In C. hydrogenoformans, pyruvate is initially converted to acetyl-CoA and formate by pyruvate formate lyase (pfl) enzyme and formate are subsequently metabolized into hydrogen and carbon dioxide. In another case, CO can be directly fixed and converted into CO_2 and hydrogen through water gas shift reaction and this reaction is being catalyzed by CO dehydrogenase enzyme complex [45]. Our strategy for improving hydrogen production involved the modification of energy metabolism to direct the flow of major metabolites pyruvate and acetyl-CoA through elementary

flux mode analysis. The biochemical reactions comprised in acetyl-CoA pathway are illustrated in Figure 1 and the functions of corresponding genes are summarized in Table 1. This is the first flux analysis study reported on acetyl-CoA pathway and hydrogen production of *C. hydrogenoformans*. The gene knockouts of selected genes (Table 2) obtained from elementary mode analysis were hypothesized to increase the pyruvate and CO influx rate, thereby increasing the flux rate of hydrogen production. The rate of *pepc* and *pyc* genes encoding phosphoenolpyruvate (PEP) carboxylase and pyruvate kinase was disrupted to increase the pyruvate concentration in cellular system for acetyl-CoA synthesis [39, 46]. A previous metabolic engineering study by gene deletion on model microorganism *Escherichia coli* described that one mole of glucose has maximum hydrogen yields of approximately 14.9 mmols/mg dry cell mass [47]. Similarly, the overexpression studies on transcriptional regulatory genes, *fhl* and *fnr* genes of *E. coli*, resulted in the yield of 34 mmol of H_2/mg of dry cell mass [48]. As a result of elementary mode flux analysis, we obtained a maximum theoretical flux rate of hydrogen yield of 47.62 mmol/gCDW/h for one mole of pyruvate consumption was comparatively comparatively higher than *E. coli* simulation. The elimination of *fdh* and *pyk* genes in *E. coli* strains also results in increase of pyruvate metabolism towards hydrogen [49]. Here, we suggested that gene knockout of *pyk* and *mdh* genes would increase the flux rate of hydrogen during pyruvate dissimilation of acetyl-CoA pathway in *C. hydrogenoformans*. Thus, the analysis of the elementary mode based fluxes showed that the hydrogen yield through acetyl-CoA pathway model proposed here was validated with the experimental data. As acetyl-CoA is one of the precursors of hydrogen formation and the yield depends on the rate of acetyl-CoA and other intermediate produced [50], it was keenly observed that *pyk* and *mdh* genes involved in both EMs 9 and 21 were obtained zero constraints, since their absence does not affect the carbon flux during acetyl-CoA pathway. This *in silico* elementary mode analysis and flux analysis of acetyl-CoA model indicated that the reactions available are feasible for the carbon flow from substrates pyruvate and CO to produce maximum amount of hydrogen. After flux optimization, EMs 21 and 9 (Figures 2(a) and 2(b)) were predicted to be the efficient reaction sets for enhanced hydrogen productivity. As discussed above, to improve the hydrogen yield by *C. hydrogenoformans*, a gene knockout of *mdh*, *pyk*, and *pykA* genes during acetyl-CoA pathway would be a prior consideration. Gene knockout of *pyk* and *pykA* could redistribute the flux of pyruvate into acetyl-CoA synthesis for hydrogen production. It has been reported that knock-out of pyruvate kinase (pyk), pyruvate kinase type-II (pykA), and malate dehydrogenase (mdh) enzymes could increase both the growth rate and yield of hydrogen [11, 39, 50]. The knockout of enzyme pyruvate kinase controls the flux from PEP towards pyruvate, resulting in a relative difference in the rate of carbon flow toward oxaloacetate and other products such as formate and acetate [39]. Our results clearly showed that the disruption of pyruvate kinase enzyme activity maintains the steady-state flux through the combined reactions of oxaloacetate to pyruvate and pyruvate to phosphoenolpyruvate. The results presented in this work illustrate the fixation of CO, dissimilation of pyruvate, and formate related to acetyl-CoA biosynthesis, to achieve the maximum theoretical hydrogen yield. Thus, undercontrolled intake of pyruvate, metabolic perturbations, resulting from pyruvate kinase, and malate dehydrogenase gene knockout led to strongly increase the flux rate of hydrogen formation. proposed *in silico* gene knockout and flux analysis model in this paper will help to improve the strain through metabolic engineering for obtaining the enhanced hydrogen production phenotype.

Conflict of Interests

The authors declare that there is no conflict of interests regarding the publication of this paper.

References

[1] T. Nejat Veziroğlu, "Hydrogen technology for energy needs of human settlements," *International Journal of Hydrogen Energy*, vol. 12, no. 2, pp. 99–129, 1987.

[2] R. T. van Houten, S. Y. Yu, and G. Lettinga, "Thermophilic sulphate and sulphite reduction in lab-scale gas-lift reactors using H_2/CO_2 as energy and carbon source," *Biotechnology and Bioengineering*, vol. 55, pp. 807–814, 1997.

[3] D. Das and T. N. Veziroğlu, "Hydrogen production by biological processes: a survey of literature," *International Journal of Hydrogen Energy*, vol. 26, no. 1, pp. 13–28, 2001.

[4] J. R. Benemann, "Feasibility analysis of photobiological hydrogen production," *International Journal of Hydrogen Energy*, vol. 22, no. 10-11, pp. 979–987, 1997.

[5] S. A. van Ooteghem, S. K. Beer, and P. C. Yue, "H_2 production by the thermophilic bacterium *Thermotoga neapolitana*," *Applied Biochemistry and Biotechnology*, vol. 98–100, pp. 177–189, 2002.

[6] B. Johnston, M. C. Mayo, and A. Khare, "Hydrogen: the energy source for the 21st century," *Technovation*, vol. 25, no. 6, pp. 569–585, 2005.

[7] M. Momirlan and T. N. Veziroglu, "The properties of hydrogen as fuel tomorrow in sustainable energy system for a cleaner planet," *International Journal of Hydrogen Energy*, vol. 30, no. 7, pp. 795–802, 2005.

[8] G. Stephanopoulos, "Metabolic fluxes and metabolic engineering," *Metabolic Engineering*, vol. 1, no. 1, pp. 1–11, 1999.

[9] P. Pharkya, A. P. Burgard, and C. D. Maranas, "OptStrain: a computational framework for redesign of microbial production systems," *Genome Research*, vol. 14, no. 11, pp. 2367–2376, 2004.

[10] C. H. Schilling, J. S. Edwards, D. Letscher, and B. O. Palsson, "Combining pathway analysis with flux balance analysis for the comprehensive study of metabolic systems," *Biotechnology and Bioengineering*, vol. 71, pp. 286–306, 2001.

[11] C. T. Trinh and F. Srienc, "Metabolic engineering of *Escherichia coli* for efficient conversion of glycerol to ethanol," *Applied and Environmental Microbiology*, vol. 75, no. 21, pp. 6696–6705, 2009.

[12] A. M. Henstra and A. J. M. Stams, "Novel physiological features of *Carboxydothermus hydrogenoformans* and *Thermoterrabacterium ferrireducens*," *Applied and Environmental Microbiology*, vol. 70, no. 12, pp. 7236–7240, 2004.

[13] E. Oelgeschläger and M. Rother, "Influence of carbon monoxide on metabolite formation in *Methanosarcina acetivorans*," *FEMS Microbiology Letters*, vol. 292, no. 2, pp. 254–260, 2009.

[14] M. Köpke, C. Held, S. Hujer et al., "*Clostridium ljungdahlii* represents a microbial production platform based on syngas," *Proceedings of the National Academy of Sciences of the United States of America*, vol. 107, no. 29, pp. 13087–13092, 2010.

[15] J. A. Papin, J. Stelling, N. D. Price, S. Klamt, S. Schuster, and B. O. Palsson, "Comparison of network-based pathway analysis methods," *Trends in Biotechnology*, vol. 22, no. 8, pp. 400–405, 2004.

[16] C. H. Schilling, D. Letscher, and B. Ø. Palsson, "Theory for the systemic definition of metabolic pathways and their use in interpreting metabolic function from a pathway-oriented perspective," *Journal of Theoretical Biology*, vol. 203, no. 3, pp. 229–248, 2000.

[17] S. Schuster, T. Dandekar, and D. A. Fell, "Detection of elementary flux modes in biochemical networks: a promising tool for pathway analysis and metabolic engineering," *Trends in Biotechnology*, vol. 17, no. 2, pp. 53–60, 1999.

[18] J. O. Krömer, C. Wittmann, H. Schröder, and E. Heinzle, "Metabolic pathway analysis for rational design of L-methionine production by *Escherichia coli* and *Corynebacterium glutamicum*," *Metabolic Engineering*, vol. 8, no. 4, pp. 353–369, 2006.

[19] R. Carlson, D. Fell, and F. Srienc, "Metabolic pathway analysis of a recombinant yeast for rational strain development," *Biotechnology and Bioengineering*, vol. 79, no. 2, pp. 121–134, 2002.

[20] N. C. Duarte, B. Ø. Palsson, and P. Fu, "Integrated analysis of metabolic phenotypes in *Saccharomyces cerevisiae*," *BMC Genomics*, vol. 5, article 63, 2004.

[21] J. C. Liao and M.-K. Oh, "Toward predicting metabolic fluxes in metabolically engineered strains," *Metabolic Engineering*, vol. 1, no. 3, pp. 214–223, 1999.

[22] M. M. Kabir, M. M. Ho, and K. Shimizu, "Effect of ldhA gene deletion on the metabolism of *Escherichia coli* based on gene expression, enzyme activities, intracellular metabolite concentrations, and metabolic flux distribution," *Biochemical Engineering Journal*, vol. 26, no. 1, pp. 1–11, 2005.

[23] R. Nandi and S. Sengupta, "Involvement of anaerobic reductases in the spontaneous lysis of formate by immobilized cells of *Escherichia coli*," *Enzyme and Microbial Technology*, vol. 19, no. 1, pp. 20–25, 1996.

[24] H. Ogata, S. Goto, K. Sato, W. Fujibuchi, H. Bono, and M. Kanehisa, "KEGG: kyoto encyclopedia of genes and genomes," *Nucleic Acids Research*, vol. 27, no. 1, pp. 29–34, 1999.

[25] K. F. Aoki-Kinoshita and M. Kanehisa, "Gene annotation and pathway mapping in KEGG," *Methods in Molecular Biology*, vol. 396, pp. 71–91, 2007.

[26] X. Mao, T. Cai, J. G. Olyarchuk, and L. Wei, "Automated genome annotation and pathway identification using the KEGG Orthology (KO) as a controlled vocabulary," *Bioinformatics*, vol. 21, no. 19, pp. 3787–3793, 2005.

[27] P. Shannon, A. Markiel, O. Ozier et al., "Cytoscape: a software Environment for integrated models of biomolecular interaction networks," *Genome Research*, vol. 13, no. 11, pp. 2498–2504, 2003.

[28] J. Austin and J. R. Aprille, "Net adenine nucleotide transport in rat liver mitochondria is affected by both the matrix and the external ATP/ADP ratios," *Archives of Biochemistry and Biophysics*, vol. 222, no. 1, pp. 321–325, 1983.

[29] T. Svetlitchnaia, V. Svetlitchnyi, O. Meyer, and H. Dobbek, "Structural insights into methyltransfer reactions of a corrinoid

iron-sulfur protein involved in acetyl-CoA synthesis," *Proceedings of the National Academy of Sciences of the United States of America*, vol. 103, no. 39, pp. 14331–14336, 2006.

[30] G. Fuchs, "CO_2 fixation in acetogenic bacteria: variations on a theme," *FEMS Microbiology Letters*, vol. 39, no. 3, pp. 181–213, 1986.

[31] J. Shieh and W. B. Whitman, "Autotrophic acetyl coenzyme A biosynthesis in *Methanococcus maripaludis*," *Journal of Bacteriology*, vol. 170, no. 7, pp. 3072–3079, 1988.

[32] M. Wu, Q. Ren, A. S. Durkin et al., "Life in hot carbon monoxide: the complete genome sequence of *Carboxydothermus hydrogenoformans* Z-2901," *PLoS Genetics*, vol. 1, no. 5, p. e65, 2005.

[33] S. Klamt, J. Saez-Rodriguez, and E. D. Gilles, "Structural and functional analysis of cellular networks with CellNetAnalyzer," *BMC Systems Biology*, vol. 1, article 2, 2007.

[34] A. Varma and B. O. Palsson, "Stoichiometric flux balance models quantitatively predict growth and metabolic by-product secretion in wild-type *Escherichia coli* W3110," *Applied and Environmental Microbiology*, vol. 60, no. 10, pp. 3724–3731, 1994.

[35] A. von Kamp and S. Schuster, "Metatool 5.0: fast and flexible elementary modes analysis," *Bioinformatics*, vol. 22, no. 15, pp. 1930–1931, 2006.

[36] J. H. Park, K. H. Lee, T. Y. Kim, and S. Y. Lee, "Metabolic engineering of *Escherichia coli* for the production of L-valine based on transcriptome analysis and in silico gene knockout simulation," *Proceedings of the National Academy of Sciences of the United States of America*, vol. 104, no. 19, pp. 7797–7802, 2007.

[37] S. Schuster, C. Hilgetag, J. H. Woods, and P. A. Fell, "Reaction routes in biochemical reaction systems: algebraic properties, validated calculation procedure and example from nucleotide metabolism," *Journal of Mathematical Biology*, vol. 45, no. 2, pp. 153–181, 2002.

[38] J. Stelling, S. Klamt, K. Bettenbrock, S. Schuster, and E. D. Gilles, "Metabolic network structure determines key aspects of functionality and regulation," *Nature*, vol. 420, no. 6912, pp. 190–193, 2002.

[39] H. G. Wood, "Life with CO or CO_2 and H_2 as a source of carbon and energy," *FASEB Journal*, vol. 5, no. 2, pp. 156–163, 1991.

[40] R. R. Gokarn, M. A. Eiteman, and E. Altman, "Metabolic analysis of *Escherichia coli* in the presence and absence of the carboxylating enzymes phosphoenolpyruvate carboxylase and pyruvate carboxylase," *Applied and Environmental Microbiology*, vol. 66, no. 5, pp. 1844–1850, 2000.

[41] G. Melzer, M. E. Esfandabadi, E. Franco-Lara, and C. Wittmann, "Flux design: in silico design of cell factories based on correlation of pathway fluxes to desired properties," *BMC Systems Biology*, vol. 3, article 120, 2009.

[42] C. F. Weber and G. M. King, "Physiological, ecological, and phylogenetic characterization of Stappia, a marine CO-oxidizing bacterial genus," *Applied and Environmental Microbiology*, vol. 73, no. 4, pp. 1266–1276, 2007.

[43] T. V. Slepova, T. G. Sokolova, T. V. Kolganova, T. P. Tourova, and E. A. Bonch-Osmolovskaya, "*Carboxydothermus siderophilus* sp. nov., a thermophilic, hydrogenogenic, carboxydotrophic, dissimilatory Fe(III)-reducing bacterium from a Kamchatka hot spring," *International Journal of Systematic and Evolutionary Microbiology*, vol. 59, no. 2, pp. 213–217, 2009.

[44] N. D. Price, J. L. Reed, and B. Ø. Palsson, "Genome-scale models of microbial cells: evaluating the consequences of constraints," *Nature Reviews Microbiology*, vol. 2, no. 11, pp. 886–897, 2004.

[45] R. L. Kerby, S. S. Hong, S. A. Ensign, L. J. Coppoc, P. W. Ludden, and G. P. Roberts, "Genetic and physiological characterization of the *Rhodospirillum rubrum* carbon monoxide dehydrogenase system," *Journal of Bacteriology*, vol. 174, no. 16, pp. 5284–5294, 1992.

[46] V. Svetlitchnyi, C. Peschel, G. Acker, and O. Meyer, "Two membrane-associated NiFeS-carbon monoxide dehydrogenases from the anaerobic carbon-monoxide-utilizing eubacterium *Carboxydothermus hydrogenoformans*," *Journal of Bacteriology*, vol. 183, no. 17, pp. 5134–5144, 2001.

[47] M. F. Dunn, S. Encarnación, G. Araíza et al., "Pyruvate carboxylase from *Rhizobium etli*: mutant characterization, nucleotide sequence, and physiological role," *Journal of Bacteriology*, vol. 178, no. 20, pp. 5960–5970, 1996.

[48] Z. Fan, L. Yuan, and R. Chatterjee, "Increased hydrogen production by genetic engineering of *Escherichia coli*," *PLoS ONE*, vol. 4, no. 2, Article ID e4432, 2009.

[49] A. Yoshida, T. Nishimura, H. Kawaguchi, M. Inui, and H. Yukawa, "Enhanced hydrogen production from formic acid by formate hydrogen lyase-overexpressing *Escherichia coli* strains," *Applied and Environmental Microbiology*, vol. 71, no. 11, pp. 6762–6768, 2005.

[50] G. Sawers, "The hydrogenases and formate dehydrogenases of *Escherichia coli*," *Antonie van Leeuwenhoek*, vol. 66, no. 1–3, pp. 57–88, 1994.

18

Prediction of B-Cell Epitopes in Listeriolysin O, a Cholesterol Dependent Cytolysin Secreted by *Listeria monocytogenes*

Morris S. Jones and J. Mark Carter

Western Regional Research Center, Agricultural Research Service, U.S. Department of Agriculture, 800 Buchanan Street, Albany, CA 94710, USA

Correspondence should be addressed to Morris S. Jones; morris.s.jones.mil@mail.mil

Academic Editor: Tatsuya Akutsu

Listeria monocytogenes is a gram-positive, foodborne bacterium responsible for disease in humans and animals. Listeriolysin O (LLO) is a required virulence factor for the pathogenic effects of *L. monocytogenes*. Bioinformatics revealed conserved putative epitopes of LLO that could be used to develop monoclonal antibodies against LLO. Continuous and discontinuous epitopes were located by using four different B-cell prediction algorithms. Three-dimensional molecular models were generated to more precisely characterize the predicted antigenicity of LLO. Domain 4 was predicted to contain five of eleven continuous epitopes. A large portion of domain 4 was also predicted to comprise discontinuous immunogenic epitopes. Domain 4 of LLO may serve as an immunogen for eliciting monoclonal antibodies that can be used to study the pathogenesis of *L. monocytogenes* as well as develop an inexpensive assay.

1. Introduction

Listeriosis is a foodborne illness caused by infection with *Listeria monocytogenes*, a gram-positive pathogenic bacterium [1]. *L. monocytogenes* is the only species in the genus *Listeria* that can infect humans [2]. After the bacteria are phagocytosed, listeriolysin O (LLO), an exotoxin, forms a pore in the membrane of the phagosome that allows the bacteria to escape into the cytosol of the phagocyte, where it is adapted to grow [2]. *L. monocytogenes* that is incapable of secreting LLO (Δhly) is not pathogenic [3]. Listeriolysin O is a 529 amino acid protein that is a member of the cholesterol-dependent cytolysin (CDC) family of proteins [4]. LLO is a four-domain poreforming protein that is regulated by pH [5]. LLO also contains a 21 amino acid PEST sequence (Figure 1) in the amino terminus that probably helps to control LLO production in the cytosol [6], as well as an undecapeptide sequence that is important for membrane binding [7] (Figure 1).

Several studies have used bioinformatics to predict the antigenicity of proteins. Frikha-Gargouri et al. used bioinformatics to predict the immunogenicity of the OmcB protein of *Chlamydia trachomatis* [8]. Further experiments confirmed their *in silico* predictions [8]. Jahangiri et al. also used

bioinformatics to find a novel region of ActA, a membrane protein found on the surface of *L. monocytogenes* that they predicted would be immunogenic [9]. Another study used bioinformatic screening as well as three-dimensional modeling to show that several regions in the Bap protein, a surface protein found on the surface of *Acinetobacter baumannii*, had a high probability of eliciting antibodies [10].

Monoclonal antibodies (MAb) have many functions. They can be used to study structure/function of a protein, pathogenesis of an organism, and/or quantitative analysis of a protein [11, 12]. To study the pathogenesis of *L. monocytogenes*, it is necessary to map the function of LLO. Currently, only a few MAbs exist against LLO, none of which are commercially available [11–14]. Site-specific antibodies that are able to neutralize LLO may be useful in the study of toxin membrane binding and pathogenicity. They also have the potential to be used in passive immunization to treat listeriosis.

There are two companies that manufacture ELISAs (BioCompare and MyBioSource) to detect LLO (http://www.biocompare.com/pfu/110627/soids/371711/Assay_Kit/listeriolysin_O and http://www.mybiosource.com/datasheet.php?products_id=705426) [15, 16]. In this study we analyzed

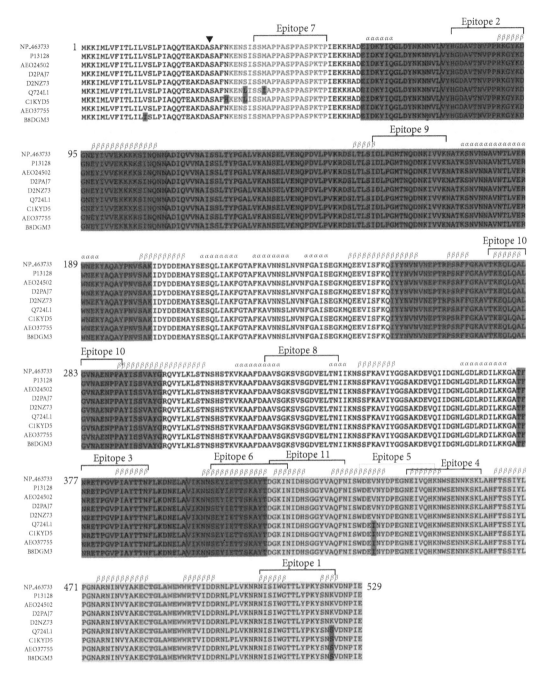

FIGURE 1: ClustalW alignment of antigenic LLO amino acid sequences from GenBank. Red Letters denote the PEST sequence. Amino acids highlighted in red belong to domain 1, amino acids highlighted in blue belong to domain 2, amino acids highlighted in yellow belong to domain 3, and amino acids highlighted in green belong to domain 4. Amino acids highlighted in magenta are polymorphic. Black triangle denotes the location of signal sequence cleavage site. Purple amino acids denote the location of the undecapeptide sequence, required for the formation of the oligomeric pore complex. The purple α and brown β symbols above the alignments denote the locations of alpha helices and beta-pleated sheets, respectively, predicted by the Porter Secondary Structure Prediction method.

LLO using bioinformatics to identify putative immunogenic B-cell epitopes for generating antibodies (Abs) against it. This information will be used to design a recombinant protein that will be used to develop an inexpensive yet sensitive assay for the detection of LLO that will be available for the scientific community at large.

2. Methods

2.1. Sequence Availability and Similarity Search. In this study we used the NCBI GenBank Protein database (http://www .ncbi.nlm.nih.gov/protein/) to acquire the Listeria proteins listeriolysin O (LLO) (NP_463733) and ivanolysin O (P31831)

[17]. The accession numbers for other LLO proteins are listed in Figure 1. To determine the best homologs to listeriolysin O (LLO) we performed a blastp search against the Protein Data Bank database (http://www.rcsb.org) at http://www.ncbi.nlm .nih.gov/blast/Blast.cgi. Suilysin (pdb: 3HVN) [18] had the highest amino acid identity to LLO (compared with the other LLO homologs that were crystallized).

2.2. Alignments. Pairwise sequence alignments of LLO were generated using the ClustalW2 Multiple Sequence Alignment at http://www.ebi.ac.uk/Tools/msa/clustalw2/ [19]. The purpose was to determine the number of polymorphisms amongst LLO proteins (Figure 1). In addition, we also generated alignments of LLO-homologs to determine the epitope conservancy between the LLO and ivanolysin O. Individual percent identities were calculated using the EMBOSS Needle Pairwise Sequence Alignment at http://www.ebi.ac .uk/Tools/services/web/toolform.ebi?tool=emboss_needle& context=protein [20].

2.3. Molecular Modeling. To generate a molecular model of LLO, we used the molecular modeling program I-TASSER http://zhanglab.ccmb.med.umich.edu/I-TASSER/ [21, 22]. We used I-TASSER as the molecular modeling program because it was ranked as the best server for protein structure prediction in recent CASP7, CASP8, and CASP9 experiments [21, 23, 24]. The (Critical Assessment of protein Structure Prediction) CASP is an international competition to assess the best algorithms in the area of 3D protein structure prediction. We chose SLY (pdb: 3HVN) as a template for modeling purposes because it produced a model with the highest C-score. I-TASSER assigns a C-score to each model it generates [21]. The C-score is a confidence score that estimates the quality of each predicted model. A C-score can range from −5 to 2. A C-score closer to 2 indicates a model with high confidence and a model with a C-score closer to −5 signifies low confidence. The C-score for our model was 2. In addition, SLY has the highest amino acid identity to LLO (45.7%) amongst the four crystallized CDCs.

Amino acids 60–525 of LLO were used to predict a three-dimensional model since these residues correspond to amino acids 32–242 and 245–499 in SLY. Molecular models were prepared in different orientations using POLYVIEW 3D (http://polyview.cchmc.org/polyview3d.html) [25].

2.4. Prediction of B-Cell Epitopes. Linear B-cell epitopes were chosen with three different algorithms. ABCPred uses a recurrent neural network to predict B-cell epitopes at http://www.imtech.res.in/raghava/abcpred/ABC_submission .html [26]. ABCPred was created by Saha et al. in 2006 to predict B-cell epitopes in an antigen sequence. Saha et al. used 700 B-cell epitopes and 700 non-B-cell epitopes [26]. Moreover, ABCPred is able to predict epitopes with approximately 66% accuracy using the recurrent neural network [26]. ABCPred assigns scores between 1 and 0 to each epitope it predicts. A score that is closer to 1 indicates a high probability of the epitope existing and a score closer to 0 suggests that the amino acid sequence will not become

an epitope. We set the amino acid length to 16 mer and the scoring threshold to 0.8. These conditions are similar to what was used by a similar study with ActA [9], a membrane protein of *L. monocytogenes*. COBEPro was developed by Sweredoski and Baldi in 2008 to predict continuous B-cell epitopes [27]. Specifically, COBEPro uses a support vector machine to predict 7 mer peptide fragments within the query amino acid sequence and then calculates an epitopic propensity score for individual residues based on the fragment predictions at http://scratch.proteomics.ics.uci.edu [27]. Fourteen epitope annotated proteins, an HIV data set, as well as a data set from BciPep were used to validate COBEPro [27].

Larsen et al. developed BepiPred in 2006 for the purpose of predicting linear B-cell epitopes [28]. Larsen et al. used 14 epitope annotated proteins as well as an HIV data set. BepiPred employs the hidden Markov model and a propensity scale method at http://www.cbs.dtu.dk/services/ BepiPred/ [28]. We used 0.35, because it is the point at which sensitivity/specificity is maximized in BepiPred. BepiPred analyzes each amino acid independently and does not have a minimum or maximum number of amino acids to predict an epitope. Overlapping epitopes chosen by the three B-cell prediction algorithms were chosen as potential B-cell epitopes.

Discontinuous epitopes were predicted using ElliPro Antibody Epitope Prediction at http://tools.immuneepitope .org/tools/ElliPro/iedb_input [29]. ElliPro, when compared to six other software programs that predict discontinuous epitopes, was determined as the best algorithm for predicting discontinuous epitopes inferred from 3D structures [29]. ElliPro predicted three-dimensional discontinuous epitopes on the surface of LLO based on the molecular model described above. ElliPro uses three algorithms to predict discontinuous epitopes. It approximates the protein shape as an ellipsoid, calculates the residue protrusion index (PI), and clusters the neighboring residues based on their PI values. ElliPro generates a PI score (PI) for each predicted epitope. Our cutoff for PI scores was 0.745 (compared to the default value of 0.8), which produced results that generally agreed with BepiPred.

2.5. Immunoinformatic Analysis. Important properties for predicting B-cell epitopes are flexibility, hydrophilicity, and linear epitope predictions. We analyzed the linear epitope predictions, flexibility, and hydrophilicity of LLO using the BepiPred linear epitope prediction [28], Karplus and Schulz flexibility prediction [30], and Parker et al. hydrophilicity prediction [31] algorithms, respectively, at http://tools .immuneepitope.org/tools/bcell/iedb_input. A similar tool that we did not employ here, Bcepred (http://www.imtech.res .in/raghava/bcepred/bcepred_submission.html) also uses physicochemical properties to predict B-cell epitopes similar to BepiPred [32].

3. Results

3.1. Sequence Conservation of LLO. An alignment of all completely sequenced amino acid coding sequences of LLO from

TABLE 1: Potential linear B-cell epitopes in LLO predicted by both ABCpred and BepiPred.

Number	Sequence	Domain	Start position	End position	Score
1	NISIWGTTLYPKYSNK	4	508	523	0.94
2	HGDAVTNVPPRKGYKD	2	79	94	0.93
3	TFNRETPGVPIAYTTN	2	375	390	0.91
4	NEIVQHKNWSENNKSK	4	445	460	0.90
5	WDEVNYDPEGNEIVQH	4	435	450	0.88
6	SEYIETTSKAYTDGKI	4	404	419	0.86
7	SSMAPPASPPASPKTP	PEST	37	52	0.86
8	AAVSGKSVSGDVELTN	3	321	336	0.86
9	IDLPGMTNQDNKIVVK	1	156	171	0.86
10	TKEQLQALGVNAENPP	3	275	290	0.83
11	DGKINIDHSGGYVAQF	4	416	431	0.82

several *Listeria* species revealed that it is highly conserved with only six polymorphic sites (Figure 1). However, only five of those are present in the mature protein (Figure 1). We used NP_463733 as a reference amino acid sequence. A similarity search revealed that the amino acid sequence of LLO was 81.7% and 79.6% identical to LLO (*L. seeligeri*) and ivanolysin O (*L. ivanovii*), respectively. In contrast, NCBI-BLASTn searches against Listeria species *L. grayi, L. innocua, L. marthii* genomes (members of the genus Listeria that have their genomes sequenced) yielded no LLO homologs. The genomes of species *L. fleischmannii* and *L. rocourtiae* have not been sequenced.

3.2. Three-Dimensional Prediction of Listeriolysin O. Since there is no LLO crystal structure, we created a molecular model of LLO to visualize the locations of the predicted B-cell epitopes (Figure 2). The SLY structure was chosen as a template to model LLO, since it has high amino acid identity to LLO (45.7%) amongst crystallized LLO homologs. Comparison of the SLY, perfringolysin O (PFO), intermedilysin (ILY), and alveolysin (ALO) crystal structures in the CDC protein family demonstrated that the aforementioned proteins share a similar 3D structure [4].

3.3. Immunoinformatic Analysis of 3D Listeriolysin O. We used amino acids 60–525 of LLO to predict a three-dimensional model. In contrast, we used amino acids 28–529 to analyze the immunogenicity of LLO since the latter amino acids comprise the full-length mature protein [33]. Three different epitope prediction software programs (ABCPred, BepiPred, and COBEPro) were utilized to predict the most immunogenic linear B-cell epitopes on the surface of LLO (Section 2). ABCPred and BepiPred predicted 24 and 18 different potentially immunogenic regions within LLO, respectively, sixteen of which overlapped (Figure 3). Epitopes that did not overlap were not considered for analysis. COBEPro, a B-cell epitope prediction program that we used in conjunction with ABCPred and BepiPred, only recognized 11 of 16 epitopes that were mutually predicted via ABCPred and BepiPred (Figure 3). Four of 11 epitopes that the three software programs agreed upon were located in domain 4 (Figure 4) and one of them overlapped domains 2 and

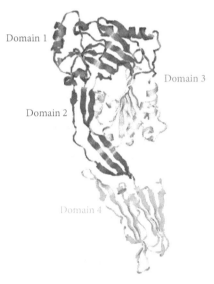

FIGURE 2: Three-dimensional molecular ribbon model of LLO toxin based on the crystal structure of suilysin (SLY). Red ribbons denote amino acids highlighted in domain 1, blue ribbons denote amino acids highlighted in domain 2, yellow ribbons denote amino acids highlighted in domain 3, and green ribbons denote amino acids highlighted in domain 4.

4 (Figure 4(f)). Three, one, and one epitopes were located in domains 1, 2, and 3, respectively (Figures 1, 3, and 4). In addition, one epitope was predicted to be in the PEST sequence (Table 1 and Figure 1).

We also evaluated discontinuous epitopes in the LLO molecular model that we created. ElliPro predicted three discontinuous epitopes with PI scores higher than our cutoff: two in domain 4 and one in domain 1 (Figure 5). Discontinuous epitope number 1, located in domain 4, was predicted to touch several residues (Figure 5(a)).

3.4. Specificity of Predicted Immunogenic Epitopes. In terms of antibody recognition, changing one amino acid in an antibody epitope can dramatically decrease the antigen-antibody interaction [34]. Four of the 11 predicted epitopes have greater than 80% amino acid identity to ivanolysin O (Table 2). Of

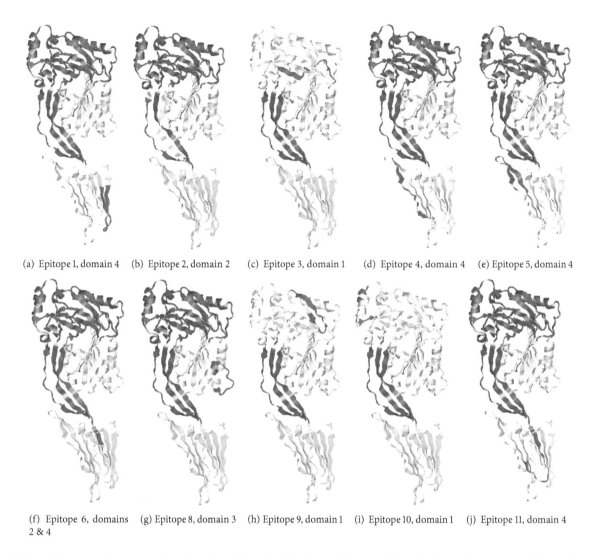

(a) Epitope 1, domain 4   (b) Epitope 2, domain 2   (c) Epitope 3, domain 1   (d) Epitope 4, domain 4   (e) Epitope 5, domain 4

(f) Epitope 6, domains   (g) Epitope 8, domain 3   (h) Epitope 9, domain 1   (i) Epitope 10, domain 1   (j) Epitope 11, domain 4
2 & 4

FIGURE 3: Three-dimensional representation of predicted linear B-cell epitopes. Magenta ribbons designate the position of the predicted linear epitopes. Location of predicted epitope is listed below the epitope number.

the four potentially antigenic B-cell epitopes with high amino acid identity to ivanolysin O, two of them (epitopes 6 and 10) only differ by one amino acid (Table 2). None of the predicted antigenic epitopes were identical to ivanolysin O amino acid sequences, the closest homolog of LLO.

3.5. Epitopes in LLO Exhibit Immunogenic Properties. Immunogenic epitopes are accessible on the protein surface, located in flexible regions, and often overlap [35]. Our predicted linear immunogenic epitopes of LLO are located in protein regions that are predicted to be accessible (Figures 4 and 5) and flexible (Figure 7). In addition, two different sets of epitopes overlap in domain 4 (Figures 1 and 5), implying that domain 4 may be immunodominant.

4. Discussion

In some instances, when a protein has multiple overlapping B-cell epitopes it is referred to as immunodominant [35]. We predicted 11 antibody epitopes in LLO. Specifically, domain 4 had five of the 11 predicted antibody epitopes, in LLO. Two sets of epitopes were predicted to overlap (Figures 1 and 6). These data imply that domain 4 may be immunodominant. Based on the predicted three-dimensional structure of LLO (Figure 2), this is highly plausible as the linear epitopes in domain 4 are predicted to be accessible and hydrophilic (Figures 4 and 8).

Bioinformatics has been used for many purposes, such as vaccine design, characterization of novel genes, and the discovery of novel viruses [36–39]. Recently, Jahangiri et al. used bioinformatics to predict B-cell epitopes in the ActA protein [9]. Jahangiri et al. used bioinformatic methods similar to our study and found unique sequences in ActA that they plan to use as an antigen to elicit antibodies for a diagnostic test [9]. Bioinformatics has also been used successfully to predict antibody-binding sites for known antibodies [40]. Recently a B-cell epitope prediction software successfully predicted 31 of 32 antigenic sites that were known to bind to antibodies,

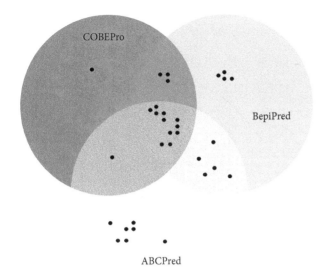

FIGURE 4: Venn diagram of epitopes detected by ABCPred, BepiPred, and COBEPro. Black dots represent epitopes detected by each B-cell prediction algorithm. Epitopes predicted via ABCPred, BepiPred, and COBEPro are in green, purple, and red circles, respectively. The 11 epitopes that were detected by all three algorithms are in the center of the Venn diagram.

TABLE 2: Comparison of epitope conservancy between LLO (*L. monocytogenes*) and ivanolysin O (*L. ivanovii*). All epitopes were 16 amino acids in length.

Number	Epitope sequence	Amino acid identity of LLO and ivanolysin (%)
1	NISIWGTTLYPKYSNK	68.8
2	HGDAVTNVPPRKGYKD	62.5
3	TFNRETPGVPIAYTTN	68.8
4	NEIVQHKNWSENNKSK	68.8
5	WDEVNYDPEGNEIVQH	68.8
6	SEYIETTSKAYTDGKI	93.8
7	SSMAPPASPPASPKTP	87.5
8	AAVSGKSVSGDVELTN	62.5
9	IDLPGMTNQDNKIVVK	75
10	TKEQLQALGVNAENPP	93.8
11	DGKINIDHSGGYVAQF	81.3

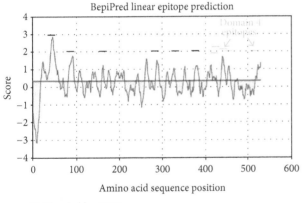

■ Threshold = 0.350

FIGURE 5: Graphical result of BepiPred prediction for linear B-cell epitopes. Yellow color denotes positive score for linear B-cell epitopes. Linear black lines denote the approximate position of the 11 predicted linear epitopes. Linear green lines denote the approximate position of the predicted linear epitopes in domain 4.

Bioinformatics of LLO demonstrates that its closest homologs are the LLO protein of *L. seeligeri* and ivanolysin O expressed by *L. ivanovii*. However, *L. seeligeri* does not infect humans, and *L. ivanovii* is not pathogenic [41]. Therefore, even though there is a low probability that an LLO specific monoclonal antibody may have an affinity to ivanolysin O or LLO from *L. seeligeri,* it is unlikely that the latter toxins would be present in contaminated food products consumed by humans. Thus, even if they readily cross-react with LLO *L. seeligeri* and ivanolysin O, antibodies capable of detecting LLO in an ELISA would not be likely to produce a false positive in food screening or clinical tests. Previous molecular models of LLO used PFO as a template [7, 42]. Our LLO molecular model was based on the crystal structure of SLY. This is because SLY has the highest amino acid identity to LLO (45.7%) amongst SLY, PFO, ILY, and ALO—the homologs of LLO for which crystal structures are available. Interestingly, comparison of the SLY, PFO, ILY, and ALO crystal structures in the CDC protein family demonstrated that they share a similar 3D structure [4]. Taken together this implies that our molecular model may be similar to the actual structure of native LLO.

5. Conclusions

Bioinformatics of LLO predicted that most of the epitopes deemed likely to be immunogenic were located in domain 4. Furthermore, since it is the only domain in LLO that is continuous, we believe that it has a high probability of eliciting antibodies that could be used to study the pathogenesis of *L. monocytogenes* as well as develop a diagnostic test for LLO detection. This analysis is important because it is focusing our antibody development efforts on domain 4 as an immunogen.

Disclosure

The U.S. Department of Agriculture (USDA) prohibits discrimination in all its programs and activities on the basis

for an accuracy of 96.88% [40]. The aforementioned studies demonstrate the usefulness of bioinformatics for epitope prediction.

Several characteristics make domain 4 an attractive immunogenic candidate. Domain 4 is the only continuous domain in LLO (Figure 1). Domain 4 also contains more amino acids predicted to be antigenic than the other domains. Furthermore, domain 4 is predicted to be a stable, soluble fragment that does not make significant contact with domains 1–3. The aforementioned point was illustrated for four other crystallized LLO homologs [4].

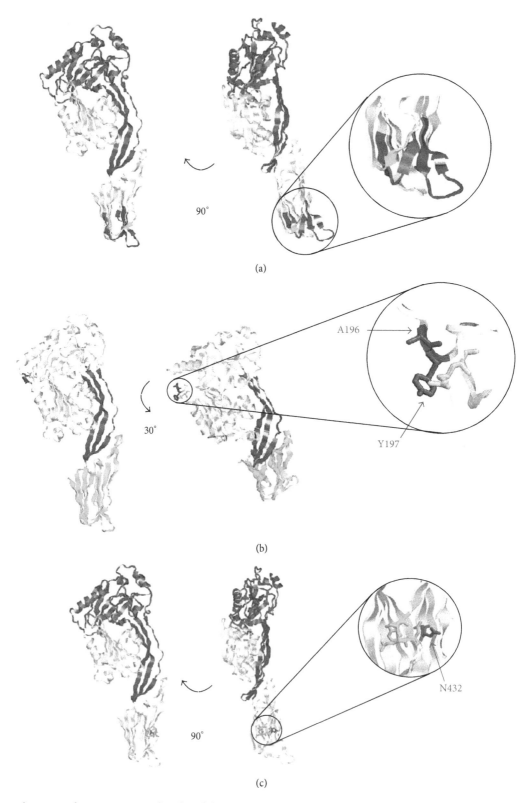

FIGURE 6: Three-dimensional representation of predicted discontinuous B-cell epitopes. (a) LLO with orientation rotated 90° to the left and enlarged to highlight discontinuous epitope in domain 4 representing amino acids 422–431 (red), 458–462 (green), 480–492 (blue), 494–496 (blue), 510-511 (magenta), 513–516 (aqua), and 521 (yellow); (b) LLO with orientation rotated 30° towards the bottom and enlarged to highlight discontinuous epitope in domain 1 representing amino acids A196 (blue), Y197 (red), and R378 (aqua); (C) LLO with orientation rotated 90° to the left and enlarged to highlight discontinuous epitope in domain 4 representing amino acids N432 (in magenta), and 453–456 (green).

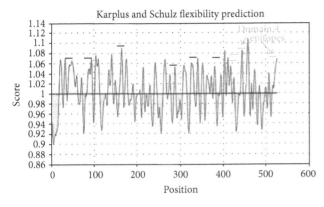

(voice and TDD). To file a complaint of discrimination, write to USDA, Director, Office of Civil Rights, 1400 Independence Avenue, SW, Washington, DC 20250-9410, or call (800) 795-3272 (voice) or (202) 720-6382 (TDD). USDA is an equal opportunity provider and employer.

FIGURE 7: Graphical result of the Karplus and Schulz flexibility prediction for linear B-cell epitopes in LLO. Yellow peaks denote positive score for flexibility throughout the primary amino acid sequence of LLO B-cell epitopes. Linear black lines denote the approximate position of the 11 linear epitopes predicted via BepiPred, ABCPred, and COBEPro. Linear green lines denote the approximate position of the predicted linear epitopes in domain 4.

Conflict of Interests

The authors declare that there is no conflict of interests.

Acknowledgments

The authors would like to thank Drs. Christopher Silva and Lisa Gorski (USDA-ARS, Foodborne Contaminants Research Unit, Albany, CA) for technical advice.

References

[1] J. A. Vázquez-Boland, M. Kuhn, P. Berche et al., "Listeria pathogenesis and molecular virulence determinants," *Clinical Microbiology Reviews*, vol. 14, no. 3, pp. 584–640, 2001.

[2] M. A. Hamon, D. Ribet, F. Stravu, and P. Cossart, "Listeriolysin O: the Swiss Army knife of listeria," *Trends in Microbiology*, vol. 20, no. 8, pp. 360–367, 2012.

[3] M. M. Gedde, D. E. Higgins, L. G. Tilney, and D. A. Portnoy, "Role of listeriolysin O in cell-to-cell spread of *Listeria monocytogenes*," *Infection and Immunity*, vol. 68, no. 2, pp. 999–1003, 2000.

[4] L. Xu, B. Huang, H. Du et al., "Crystal structure of cytotoxin protein suilysin from *Streptococcus suis*," *Protein & Cell*, vol. 1, no. 1, pp. 96–105, 2010.

[5] I. J. Glomski, M. M. Gedde, A. W. Tsang, J. A. Swanson, and D. A. Portnoy, "The *Listeria monocytogenes* hemolysin has an acidic pH optimum to compartmentalize activity and prevent damage to infected host cells," *Journal of Cell Biology*, vol. 156, no. 6, pp. 1029–1038, 2002.

[6] P. Schnupf, D. A. Portnoy, and A. L. Decatur, "Phosphorylation, ubiquitination and degradation of listeriolysin O in mammalian cells: role of the PEST-like sequence," *Cellular Microbiology*, vol. 8, no. 2, pp. 353–364, 2006.

[7] P. Schnupf and D. A. Portnoy, "Listeriolysin O: a phagosome-specific lysin," *Microbes and Infection*, vol. 9, no. 10, pp. 1176–1187, 2007.

[8] O. Frikha-Gargouri, R. Gdoura, A. Znazen et al., "Evaluation of an in silico predicted specific and immunogenic antigen from the OmcB protein for the serodiagnosis of Chlamydia trachomatis infections," *BMC Microbiology*, vol. 8, article 217, 2008.

[9] A. Jahangiri, I. Rasooli, M. Reza Rahbar, S. Khalili, J. Amani, and K. Ahmadi Zanoos, "Precise detection of *L. monocytogenes* hitting its highly conserved region possessing several specific antibody binding sites," *Journal of Theoretical Biology*, vol. 305, pp. 15–23, 2012.

[10] M. R. Rahbar, I. Rasooli, S. L. M. Gargari et al., "A potential in silico antibody-antigen based diagnostic test for precise identification of *Acinetobacter baumannii*," *Journal of Theoretical Biology*, vol. 294, pp. 29–39, 2012.

[11] A. Darji, K. Niebuhr, M. Hense, J. Wehland, T. Chakraborty, and S. Weiss, "Neutralizing monoclonal antibodies against listeriolysin: mapping of epitopes involved in pore formation," *Infection and Immunity*, vol. 64, no. 6, pp. 2356–2358, 1996.

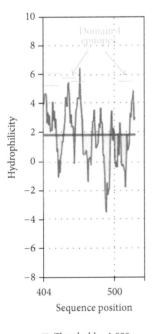

FIGURE 8: Graphical result of Parker hydrophilicity prediction for linear B-cell epitopes in domain 4 of LLO.

of race, color, national origin, age, disability, and, where applicable, sex, marital status, familial status, parental status, religion, sexual orientation, genetic information, political beliefs, reprisal, or because all or part of an individual's income is derived from any public assistance program. (Not all prohibited bases apply to all programs.) Persons with disabilities who require alternative means for communication of program information (Braille, large print, audiotape, etc.) should contact USDA's TARGET Center at (202) 720-2600

[12] B. T. Edelson and E. R. Unanue, "Intracellular antibody neutralizes Listeria growth," *Immunity*, vol. 14, no. 5, pp. 503–512, 2001.

[13] H. Dong, X.-A. Jiao, Y.-L. Yin, Z.-M. Pan, and J.-L. Huang, "Perparation and characterization of the monoclonal antibodies against listeriolysin O," *Xi Bao Yu Fen Zi Mian Yi Xue Za Zhi*, vol. 24, no. 3, pp. 240–242, 2008.

[14] Z. Luo, R. Liu, and S. Zheng, "Prokaryotic expression of Listeria monocytogene (LM) hly and development of monoclonal antibodies against listeriolysin O (LLO)," *Shengwu Gongcheng Xuebao*, vol. 25, no. 11, pp. 1652–1657, 2009.

[15] Biocompare, "Listeriolysin O ELISA kit from antibodies-online", The quantitative determination of human LLO concentrations in serum, plasma, cell culture supernates and tissue homogenate. This ELISA kit is a solid phase ELISA designed for quantitative determination. Atlanta, Ga, USA, 2013.

[16] MyBioSource, "LLO elisa kit", The coated well immunoenzymatic assay for the quantitative measurement of LLO utilizes a multiclonal anti-LLO antibody and an LLO-HRP conjugate, San Diego, Calif, USA, 2013.

[17] D. A. Benson, I. Karsch-Mizrachi, D. J. Lipman, J. Ostell, and E. W. Sayers, "GenBank," *Nucleic Acids Research*, vol. 39, no. 1, pp. D32–D37, 2011.

[18] S. Parasuraman, "Protein data bank," *Journal of Pharmacology & Pharmacotherapeutics*, vol. 3, no. 4, pp. 351–352, 2012.

[19] M. A. Larkin, G. Blackshields, N. P. Brown et al., "Clustal W and Clustal X version 2.0," *Bioinformatics*, vol. 23, no. 21, pp. 2947–2948, 2007.

[20] P. Rice, L. Longden, and A. Bleasby, "EMBOSS: the European molecular biology open software suite," *Trends in Genetics*, vol. 16, no. 6, pp. 276–277, 2000.

[21] A. Roy, A. Kucukural, and Y. Zhang, "I-TASSER: a unified platform for automated protein structure and function prediction," *Nature Protocols*, vol. 5, no. 4, pp. 725–738, 2010.

[22] Y. Zhang, "I-TASSER server for protein 3D structure prediction," *BMC Bioinformatics*, vol. 9, article 40, 2008.

[23] Y. Zhang, "Template-based modeling and free modeling by I-TASSER in CASP7," *Proteins*, vol. 69, no. 8, pp. 108–117, 2007.

[24] Y. Zhang, "I-TASSER: fully automated protein structure prediction in CASP8," *Proteins*, vol. 77, no. 9, pp. 100–113, 2009.

[25] A. Porollo and J. Meller, "Versatile annotation and publication quality visualization of protein complexes using POLYVIEW-3D," *BMC Bioinformatics*, vol. 8, article 316, 2007.

[26] W. Pirovano and J. Heringa, "Protein secondary structure prediction," *Methods in Molecular Biology*, vol. 609, pp. 327–348, 2010.

[27] M. J. Sweredoski and P. Baldi, "COBEpro: a novel system for predicting continuous B-cell epitopes," *Protein Engineering, Design and Selection*, vol. 22, no. 3, pp. 113–120, 2009.

[28] J. E. P. Larsen, O. Lund, and M. Nielsen, "Improved method for predicting linear b-cell epitopes," *Immunome Research*, vol. 2, article 2, 2006.

[29] J. Ponomarenko, H.-H. Bui, W. Li et al., "ElliPro: a new structure-based tool for the prediction of antibody epitopes," *BMC Bioinformatics*, vol. 9, article 514, 2008.

[30] P. A. Karplus and G. E. Schulz, "Prediction of chain flexibility in proteins. A tool for the selection of peptide antigens," *Naturwissenschaften*, vol. 72, no. 4, pp. 212–213, 1985.

[31] J. M. R. Parker, D. Guo, and R. S. Hodges, "New hydrophilicity scale derived from high-performance liquid chromatography peptide retention data: correlation of predicted surface residues with antigenicity and X-ray-derived accessible sites," *Biochemistry*, vol. 25, no. 19, pp. 5425–5432, 1986.

[32] S. Saha and G. P. S. Raghava, "BcePred: prediction of continuous B-cell epitopes in antigenic sequences using physico-chemical properties," *Artificial Immune Systems*, vol. 3239, pp. 197–204, 2004.

[33] M.-A. Lety, C. Frehel, J.-L. Beretti, P. Berche, and A. Charbit, "Modification of the signal sequence cleavage site of listeriolysin O does not affect protein secretion but impairs the virulence of *Listeria monocytogenes*," *Microbiology*, vol. 149, no. 5, pp. 1249–1255, 2003.

[34] G. Zhong, J. Berry, and R. C. Brunham, "Antibody recognition of a neutralization epitope on the major outer membrane protein of Chlamydia trachomatis," *Infection and Immunity*, vol. 62, no. 5, pp. 1576–1583, 1994.

[35] R. A. Goldsby, T. J. Kindt, and B. A. Osborne, *Kuby Immunology*, W. H. Freeman & Company, New York, NY, USA, 2000, J. Kuby.

[36] A. Petrizzo, C. Tornesello, F. M. Buonaguro, and L. Buonaguro, "Immunogenomics approaches for vaccine evaluation," *Journal of Immunotoxicology*, vol. 9, pp. 236–240, 2012.

[37] M. S. Jones II, B. Harrach, R. D. Ganac et al., "New adenovirus species found in a patient presenting with gastroenteritis," *Journal of Virology*, vol. 81, no. 11, pp. 5978–5984, 2007.

[38] E. B. Liu, L. Ferreyra, S. L. Fischer et al., "Genetic analysis of a novel human adenovirus with a serologically unique hexon and a recombinant fiber gene," *PLoS ONE*, vol. 6, no. 9, Article ID e24491, 2011.

[39] E. B. Liu, D. A. Wadford, J. Seto et al., "Computational and serologic analysis of novel and known viruses in species human adenovirus D in which serology and genomics do not correlate," *PLoS ONE*, vol. 7, no. 3, Article ID e33212, 2012.

[40] Y. Wang, W. Wu, N. N. Negre, K. P. White, C. Li, and P. K. Shah, "Determinants of antigenicity and specificity in immune response for protein sequences," *BMC Bioinformatics*, vol. 12, article 251, 2011.

[41] A. Camejo, F. Carvalho, O. Reis, E. Leitão, S. Sousa, and D. Cabanes, "The arsenal of virulence factors deployed by *Listeria monocytogenes* to promote its cell infection cycle," *Virulence*, vol. 2, no. 5, pp. 379–394, 2011.

[42] J. A. Melton-Witt, S. L. McKay, and D. A. Portnoy, "Development of a single-gene, signature-tag-based approach in combination with alanine mutagenesis to identify listeriolysin O residues critical for the in vivo survival of *Listeria monocytogenes*," *Infection and Immunity*, vol. 80, article 2221, 2012.

19

Objective and Comprehensive Evaluation of Bisulfite Short Read Mapping Tools

Hong Tran,[1] Jacob Porter,[1] Ming-an Sun,[2] Hehuang Xie,[2] and Liqing Zhang[1]

[1] *Department of Computer Science, Virginia Tech, Blacksburg, VA 24061, USA*
[2] *Virginia Bioinformatics Institute, Virginia Tech, Blacksburg, VA 24061, USA*

Correspondence should be addressed to Liqing Zhang; lqzhang@cs.vt.edu

Academic Editor: Huixiao Hong

Background. Large-scale bisulfite treatment and short reads sequencing technology allow comprehensive estimation of methylation states of Cs in the genomes of different tissues, cell types, and developmental stages. Accurate characterization of DNA methylation is essential for understanding genotype phenotype association, gene and environment interaction, diseases, and cancer. Aligning bisulfite short reads to a reference genome has been a challenging task. We compared five bisulfite short read mapping tools, BSMAP, Bismark, BS-Seeker, BiSS, and BRAT-BW, representing two classes of mapping algorithms (hash table and suffix/prefix tries). We examined their mapping efficiency (i.e., the percentage of reads that can be mapped to the genomes), usability, running time, and effects of changing default parameter settings using both real and simulated reads. We also investigated how preprocessing data might affect mapping efficiency. *Conclusion.* Among the five programs compared, in terms of mapping efficiency, Bismark performs the best on the real data, followed by BiSS, BSMAP, and finally BRAT-BW and BS-Seeker with very similar performance. If CPU time is not a constraint, Bismark is a good choice of program for mapping bisulfite treated short reads. Data quality impacts a great deal mapping efficiency. Although increasing the number of mismatches allowed can increase mapping efficiency, it not only significantly slows down the program, but also runs the risk of having increased false positives. Therefore, users should carefully set the related parameters depending on the quality of their sequencing data.

1. Introduction

DNA methylation is the addition of a methyl group (CH_3) at the 5th carbon position of the cytosine ring. Most cytosine methylation occurs in the sequence context of $5'CG3'$ (also called CpG dinucleotide) in mammalian DNA but some in CpH dinucleotides (where H = C, T, or A). The human genome is not methylated uniformly, and some small regions called CpG islands are usually unmethylated and GC rich. DNA methylation is responsible for regulation of gene expression, silencing of genes on the inactive X chromosome, imprinted genes, and parasitic DNAs [1]. DNA methylation is also a major contributor to the generation of disease-causing germ-line mutations and somatic mutations that cause cancer [2]. Therefore, accurate genome-wide determination of DNA methylation in different cells, tissues, and developmental stages is crucial for identification of causes for phenotype differences and diseases and cancer.

Large-scale characterization of DNA methylation has been made possible by bisulfite conversion of genomic DNA combined with next generation sequencing. After bisulfite treatment of DNAs, unmethylated Cs are converted to Ts and subsequent mapping of the short reads to a reference genome allows inference of methylated versus unmethylated Cs. Thus, inference on DNA methylation is highly dependable on the mapping of bisulfite treated short reads to a reference genome. Similar to regular next generation sequencing analysis, the great challenge is to be able to map thousands of millions of reads in reasonable time and with high mapping efficiency (i.e., the percentage of reads that are mapped to a reference genome).

Many tools have been developed to tackle this computational challenge such as MAQ [3], Bismark [4], BSMAP [5], PASH [6], RMAP [7], GSNAP [8], Novoalign [9], BFAST [10], BRAT-BW [11], Methylcoder [12], CokusAlignment [13], BS-Seeker [14], BS-Seeker2 [15], Segemehl [16], BiSS [17],

BatMeth [18], and the latest one ERNE-bs5 [19]. The majority of these bisulfite sequencing mappers first conduct some sequence conversions (e.g., Cs to Ts and Gs to As) either on the reads or the reference genomes, or both and then use existing regular aligners such as Bowtie [20], Bowtie2 [21], BLAT [22], SOAP [23], and BWA [24] to map short reads to a reference genome. Fonseca et al. [25] classified the tools according to their indexing techniques and supported features such as mismatches, splicing, indels, gapped alignment, and minimum and maximum of read lengths. Chatterjee et al. [26] compared Bismark, BSMAP, and RMAPBS in terms of uniquely mapped reads percentages, multiple mapping percentages, CPU running time, and reads mapped per second. They also pointed out that trimming the data before aligning could improve mapping efficiency. However, the study did not examine how setting different parameters might impact program performance.

In this paper, we present how modifying default parameters in each program might change the results (i.e., mapping efficiency and CPU time) and the sensitivity of each program to the characteristics of data. Though we examined many software packages, we mainly focused on two mappers: BSMAP and Bismark since they are representatives of two different index algorithms, namely, Burrows-Wheeler Transform in Bismark and hash table in BSMAP. In general, genome indexing based tools performed better than read indexing tools and read indexing does not provide any significant speedup [27]; therefore, we did not include RMAP in our analysis. We also show that trimming data improves mapping efficiency. The paper is organized as follows: first, we briefly describe the bisulfite sequence mapping problem and mapping techniques used by the tools. Then we describe the datasets used in the study and criteria used to evaluate the performance of the tools. Finally we show results on evaluating the tools using both real and simulated data.

2. Overview of the Computational Problem, Algorithms, and Tools

2.1. Computational Challenges of Mapping Bisulfite Short Reads.
Over the decades, bisulfite sequencing has remained the gold standard for DNA methylation analysis. After bisulfite treatment, unmethylated Cs are converted to thymines (T), whereas methylated Cs are unchanged. Several factors make bisulfite short reads more complicated to map than regular reads. Firstly, up to four strands are analyzed from one genomic region. There are two scenarios after PCR amplification. In the first case, if the sequencing library is generated in a directional manner, the strand that the reads are amplified from is known a priori. However, if nondirectional, the Watson and Crick strands of bisulfite treated sequences are no longer complementary to each other due to the conversion, and there are four different strands after PCR amplification: BSW (bisulfite Watson), BSWR (reverse complement of BSW), BSC (bisulfite Crick), and BSCR (reverse complement of BSC), all amplified and sequenced at roughly the same frequency [13]. The search space is, therefore, significantly increased relative to the original reference sequence [5].

Secondly, sequence complexity is reduced as all unmethylated Cs are changed into Ts. In the mammalian genome, because C methylation occurs almost exclusively at CpG dinucleotide, the majority of Cs in BSW and BSC strands will be converted to Ts. Therefore, most reads from the two strands will be C-poor. However, PCR amplification will complement all Gs with Cs in BSWR and BSCR strands, so reads from these two strands are typically G-poor and have a normal C content. As a result, we expect the overall C content of bisulfite reads to be reduced by approximately 50% after the two processes (converting Cs to Ts in bisulfite treatment and transcribing Gs to Cs in PCR amplification) [5]. Lastly, C to T mapping is asymmetric. The T in the bisulfite reads could be mapped to either C or T in the reference genome but not vice versa. This complicates the mapping process.

2.2. Algorithms and Tools for Bisulfite Short Reads Mapping.
For most of the existing programs, alignment process is to build auxiliary data structures called indices for the reference genome, the reads or both. The indices are then used to find matching genomic positions for each read. There are many available methods to build the indices [28]. The two most popular techniques are hash tables and suffix/prefix tries [27] reviewed below together with some representative programs (Figure 1). A comprehensive comparison of detailed functionalities of the programs is shown in Table 1.

Indexing using hash tables can be divided into three strategies: hashing the genome, hashing the reads, or a combination of both. All hash table algorithms essentially follow the seed-and-extend technique. The algorithm keeps the positions of each k-mer fragment of the read/genome in a hash table using k-mer as the key and searches the sequence databases for k-mer matches (called seeds) [28]. After this, seeds can be joined without gaps and refined by local sequence alignment. Tools using this indexing technique include BSMAP (genome hashing) [5], GSNAP (genome hashing) [8], Novalign (genome hashing) [9], BFAST (genome hashing/suffix array) [29], RMAP (read hashing) [7], BiSS (genome hashing) [17], PASH (read hashing) [6], MAQ (read hashing) [3], and ERNE-bs5 (genome hashing) [19].

In particular, BSMAP is implemented based on SOAP (Short Oligonucleotide Alignment Program) [23]. BSMAP indexes the reference genome for all possible k-mers using hash tables. BSMAP masks Ts in bisulfite reads as Cs (i.e., reverse bisulfite conversion) only at C position in the original reference and keeps other Ts in the bisulfite reads unchanged. Then BSMAP maps the masked BS read directly to the reference genome. By combining bitwise masking and hash table seeding in its algorithm, BSMAP offers fast and good performance [5].

BiSS (Bisulfite Sequence Scorer) is based on Smith-Waterman local alignment with a customized alignment scoring function [17]. BiSS uses NextGenMap [30] to align bisulfite reads to a reference genome. NextGenMap involves three steps. In the first step, NextGenMap indexes the reference genome in a hash table. The next step is to identify the genomic region match. NextGenMap only considers

TABLE 1: Detailed comparison of different bisulfite short reads mapping tools.

Programs	Year	Algorithmic Technique used	Language	Aligner	Input	Output	Min./Max. read length	Mismatches	Indels	Gaps	Single/Paired-end	Multi-threaded	Nondirectional
ERNE-bs5	2012	Hash genome indexing uses a 5-letter (Cm, Cu) for storing methylation information and uses a weighted context-aware Hamming distance to identify a T coming from an unmethylated C.	C++	None	gz/bz2/fastq/fasta	BAM/SAM	up to 600 bp	1 every 15 bp (-errors arg)	Yes	Yes	both	Yes	No
BatMeth	2012	FM index integrates mismatch counting, list filtering and mismatch stage filtering and fast mapping onto two indexes.	Perl/C++	None	fasta	NA	NA	up to 5 (-n) in a read	No	No	Yes	Yes	Yes
BiSS	2012	Reference genome hashing, local Smith-Waterman alignment	Perl	None	fasta/fastq/gz/SAM/BAM	SAM/BAM/Next GenMap	up to 4096 bp	(-i from 0 to 1) in a read Default $i = 65\%$	Yes	Yes	Yes	Yes	No
Bismark	2011	FM-Index enumerates all possible T to C conversion	Perl	Bowtie/Bowtie2	fasta/fastq	BAM/SAM	Bowtie: up to 1000 bp Bowtie 2: unlimited	0 or 1 in a seed (-N)	Yes	Yes	both	Yes	Yes
BS-Seeker2	2013	FM-Index enumerates all possible T to C conversion	Python	Bowtie2/Bowtie/SOAP/RMAP	fasta, fastq, qseq, pure sequence	BAM/SAM/BS-Seeker	50–500 bp	up to 4 per read (-m)	Yes	Yes	Single	No	Yes
BS-Seeker	2010	FM-Index, enumerates all possible T to C conversion, converts the genome to 3 letters, and uses Bowtie to align reads	Python	Bowtie	fasta, fastq, qseq, pure sequence	BAM/SAM/BS_Seeker	50–250 bp	up to 3 per read (-m)	Yes	No	Single	No	Yes
BSMAP	2009	hashing of reference genome and bitwise masking tries all possible T to C combinations for reads	Python	SOAP	fasta/fastq/SAM	SAM/txt	up to 144 bp	up to 15 in a read (-v)	Yes	up to 3 bp	both	Yes	Yes
RMAP	2008	Wildcard matching for mapping Ts, incorporates the use of quality scores directly into the mapping process	C++		fastq/fasta	BED	unlimited	up to 10 in a read (-m)	No	No	both	No	No
BRAT-BW	2012	Converts a TA reference and CG reference; two FM indices are built on the positive strand of the reference genome	C++		Text file with input file names in fastq, sequence only	txt	32 bp-unlimited	unlimited	No	No	both	Yes	Yes

TABLE 1: Continued.

Programs	Year	Algorithmic Technique used	Language	Aligner	Input	Output	Min./Max. read length	Mismatches	Indels	Gaps	Single/Paired-end	Multi-threaded	Nondirectional
MAQ	2008	Builds multiple hash tables to index the reads, scans the reference genome against the hash tables to find hits	Perl/C/C++		fastq	maq	Up to 63 bp	up to 3 per read	Yes, - $n = 2$	No	both	No	No
PASH	2010	Implements k-mer level alignment using multipositional hash tables	C		fastq	Txt/SAM	NA	Yes	Yes	No	Single	No	No
Novo-align	2010	Hashing genome	C/C++		fastq	SAM/BAM	up to 8 per read, 16 for paired end reads	Yes	Yes	up to 7 bp on single end reads	Both	No	Yes
Methyl-coder	2011	FM-Index, all Cs converted to Ts	C/C++/Python	GSNAP/bowtie	fastq/fasta	BAM/SAM	Bowtie: up to 1000 bp	Yes	No	Yes	both	No	No
GSNAP	2005	q-mer hashing of reference genome	C/Perl		gzip/fastq, fasta, bzip2	SAM/GSNAP	14–250 bp	Yes	Yes	Yes	both	yes	No
BFAST	2009	Uses multiple indexing strategies: hashing and suffix array of the reference genome	C		fastq/bz2/gzip	SAM	NA	Yes	Yes	Yes	both	Yes	Yes
Segemehl	2008	Enhanced suffix arrays to find exact and inexact matches. Align to read using Myers bitvector algorithm	C/C++		fasta	SAM	unlimited	Yes	(- A^{*1})	Yes	both	Yes	No

* BFAST does not have a direct option for bisulfite mapping, users have to convert Cs to Ts in both a reference genome and reads and then align converted reads to the converted reference genome.
* Parenthesis in mismatches column indicates parameter for mismatches in a program.
*1 A min percentages of matches per read.

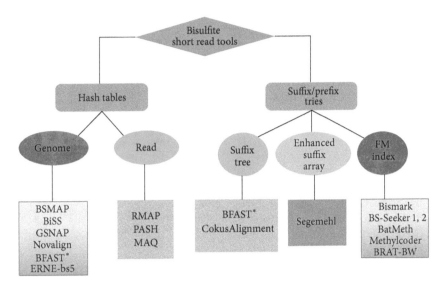

FIGURE 1: Bisulfite mapping tools classification. The tools can be divided into two groups based on indexing strategies: hash tables or suffix/prefix tries. Each of the groups is classified further into subgroups where some example programs are shown. *BFAST uses multiple index strategies: both hashing and suffix tree.

regions where the number of k-mer matches exceeds a certain threshold as a match. Unlike other methods, NextGenMap adaptively chooses the threshold, meaning each read has different threshold rather than one threshold for all reads [30].

Indexing algorithm based on suffix/prefix tries essentially converts the inexact string matching to exact matching problem. The algorithm involves two steps: identifying exact matches and building inexact alignments supported by exact matches. Several representations for searching exact matches in suffix/prefix tries are suffix tree, enhanced suffix array, and FM-index [28]. Therefore, indexing using suffix/prefix tries can be classified into three subgroups: indexing using suffix tree, indexing using enhanced suffix array, and indexing using FM-index based on Burrows-Wheeler Transform. Tools falling into this category include Bismark (FM index), BS-Seeker (and BS-Seeker2, FM index), BatMeth (FM index), Segemehl (enhanced suffix array), Methylcoder (FM index), Cokus Alignment (suffix tree), and BRAT-BW (FM index).

In particular, in Bismark, bisulfite reads are transformed into a C to T and G to A version (equivalent to a C to T conversion on the reverse strand). Then each of them is aligned to equivalently preconverted forms of the reference genome using four parallel instances of Bowtie or Bowtie2 [4]. Bowtie starts by building an FM index for the reference genome and uses the modified FM index [31] to find the matching location. Bowtie2 are designed to support reads longer than 50 bps. The two versions of Bowtie performed quite differently [27]. This read mapping enables Bismark to uniquely determine the strand origin of a bisulfite read.

BS-Seeker is very much similar to Bismark. The only difference is that BS-Seeker only works well for single-end reads, whereas Bismark can work with both single-end and paired-end reads. Also BS-Seeker can explicitly account for tags generated by certain library construction protocols [14]. BS-Seeker records only unique alignments, defined as those

that have no other hits with the same or fewer mismatches in the 3-letter alignment [14].

BRAT-BW is an evolution of BRAT [32]. Two FM indices are built on the positive strand of the reference genome: in the first, Cs are converted to Ts, and, in the second, Gs are converted to As. Original reads with C to T conversion are mapped to the first index and reverse complement reads with all Gs changed to As being mapped to the second index. BRAT-BW uses a multiseed approach similar to Bowtie2 [32].

3. Methods

3.1. Datasets. We evaluated the tools on three types of data, human blood data (GSM791828), human and mouse brain data (GSE47966), and simulated mouse short read data. First, human blood data, including ten datasets (ID: SRR342552, SRR342553, SRR342554, SRR342555, SRR342556, SRR342557, SRR342558, SRR342559, SRR342560, and SRR342561) were downloaded from NCBI's short reads archive [33]. The DNA short read sequences are nondirectional. Each file in SRA format contains about 23 million single-end whole genome shot gun bisulfite sequence reads from human hematopoietic stem/progenitor cells (HSPCs). The BS-Seq reads are conventional base call qualities that are Sanger/Illumina 1.9 encoded Phred values (Phred33) and trimmed to 76 bps. Second, human and mouse brain data, including ten datasets from human brain [33] and eight datasets from mouse brain [33] were downloaded from NCBI's gene expression omnibus [34]. The DNA bisulfite short read sequences are directional. Each file contains around 100 million single-end whole genome shot gun bisulfite sequence reads from human and mouse frontal cortex in SRA format. The BS-Seq reads are conventional base call qualities that are Illumina HiSeq 2000 encoded Phred values (Phred64) and trimmed to 101 bps. Third, simulated bisulfite short reads data were generated from the mouse and human reference genome (versions mm10 and hg19, resp.) using Sherman simulator [35]. Parameters such as sequencing error, bisulfite conversion rate for cytosines in CG-context, and CH-context in Sherman, are determined based on literature for the mouse data [36] and cytosine methylation reports from Bismark for the human data. Reads with different read lengths were generated to mimic the real mouse and human data. In Particular, for examining the effect of sequencing error on mapping efficiency, 24 datasets were generated from the mouse reference genome by varying the sequencing error from 0 to 4.75% (the error rate is a mean error rate per bp). Each dataset contained 1 million short reads with length of 101 bps and CG conversion rate of 10% (10% of all CG-cytosines will be converted into thymines) and CH conversion rate of 98.5% (98.5% of all CH-cytosines will be converted into thymines). For examining the effect of read length on mapping efficiency, 28 datasets were generated by varying the read length from 40 to 160 bps with sequencing error of 0.16%, CG conversion rate of 10%, and CH conversion rate of 98.5% for the mouse data and with sequencing error of 0.16%, CG and CH conversion rate of 19.73% and 98.9%, respectively for the human data. Both human and mouse reference genomes (hg19 and mm10) were downloaded from Ensembl [37].

3.2. Important Parameters in Mapping Tools. Programs often have different default settings for the same parameters that can influence their performance. For example, BiSS sets the default mismatch to be 35% of the read, whereas Bismark sets the equivalent parameter to zero. It is therefore important and fair to compare them on a common ground. Several important parameters that can greatly influence program performance include (1) number of mismatches allowed in the seed (e.g., Bismark); (2) number of mismatches allowed in the read (e.g., BSMAP, BS-Seeker, BiSS, and BRAT-BW); (3) directionality of data library (directional or nondirectional); (4) phred quality score (i.e., whether data have Phred score of 33 or 64). In this study, we examined the effect of these parameters on the performance of the programs and how altering them can influence the final mapping results.

3.3. Evaluation Criteria. The performance of the tools is evaluated mainly by two aspects: the mapping efficiency (i.e., percentage of uniquely mapped reads) and the CPU time. Uniquely mapped reads are reads that are mapped to only one location. Computationally speaking, most reads have multiple matches and from those matches, alignment scores are determined. An alignment is unique when it has much higher score than all other possible alignments, often determined by some statistics or cutoffs. The greater the difference between the best alignment score and the second-best alignment score, the more unique the alignment is, and the higher its mapping quality should be [38]. Mapping quality is a nonnegative integer $Q = -10\log 10\mathbf{p}$, where $\mathbf{p}$ is an estimate of the probability that the alignment does not correspond to the read's true point of origin. Mapping quality is sometimes abbreviated MAPQ. (10 log 10 Pr {mapping position is wrong}).

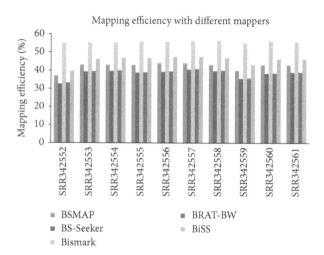

FIGURE 2: Mapping efficiency on ten human blood datasets for BSMAP, Bismark, BS-Seeker, BRAT-BW, and BiSS with zero mismatches allowed between reads and the reference genome.

3.4. Data Preprocessing. The original data were processed so reads have better quality scores and consequently can be mapped to reference genomes. Perl programming language was used to trim the tail of a read with residues quality score less than or equal to 2. After removing the tail, if the read length is shorter than 30, the read is also discarded. We use both trimmed and raw data in the analysis for the purpose of comparison of how mapping efficiency can be improved by preprocessing the data.

4. Results and Discussion

4.1. Performance Comparison of the Programs. Five bisulfite reads mapping tools, BSMAP, Bismark, BS-Seeker, BiSS, and BRAT-BW, were chosen to cover different algorithms discussed in the algorithm overview section (also refer to Table 1). BatMeth, Segmenhl, and ERNE-bs5 were not included as BatMeth failed at last step of the reads alignment, Segmenhl consumed too much computer memory (1 TB) and could not be finished in reasonable time, and ERNE-bs5 produced inaccurate results on small test datasets.

The performance is evaluated by considering two factors: mapping efficiency and CPU running time. Mapping efficiency is determined by the number of uniquely mapped reads divided by the total number of reads. We set the number of mismatches to zero for all the programs and compare mapping efficiency and CPU running time of these programs on ten human blood datasets. Among the five programs, in terms of mapping efficiency (Figure 2), Bismark performs the best, achieving the highest mapping efficiency (average around 56% across the ten human blood samples), followed by BiSS (average around 46%) and BSMAP (average around 42%), and finally BRAT-BW (average around 39%) and BS-Seeker (average around 38%) with similar mapping efficiency across samples.

However, for CPU running time, the trend is almost the opposite (Figure 3), with BRAT-BW taking the shortest time

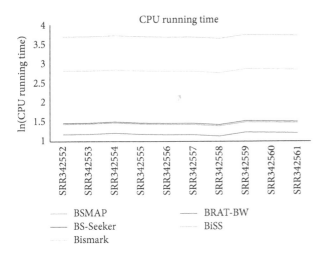

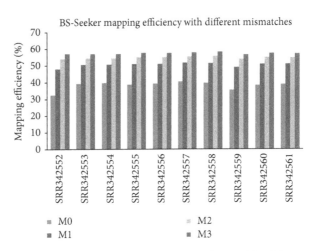

FIGURE 3: CPU running time (on a log scale) on human blood data for BSMAP, Bismark, BS-Seeker, BRAT-BW, and BiSS with zero mismatches allowed between reads and the reference genome.

FIGURE 4: Unique mapping efficiency on ten human blood datasets from BS-Seeker with different numbers of mismatches allowed between reads and the reference genome (0, 1, 2, and 3 mismatches).

(average 16 minutes across samples), followed by BSMAP (average 29 minutes) and BS-Seeker (average 31 minutes). Both BiSS (average 84 hours) and Bismark (average 11 hours) took much longer time than the other three programs, suggesting existence of the tradeoff between mapping efficiency and running time. The observation that BiSS ran the slowest might be because BiSS uses Smith-Waterman local sequence alignment algorithm to align reads to potential genomic locations [17]. Interestingly, although both Bismark (written in Perl) and BS-Seeker (written in Python) use Bowtie (or Bowtie2) for short reads mapping, Bismark ran much slower than BS-Seeker but had much higher mapping efficiency. We then used BSMAP and Bismark to map human fetal brain and mouse brain short reads data (refer to Figure 5). Consistent with the results for human blood data, Bismark has higher mapping efficiency but longer CPU running time than BSMAP. The mapping percentages are very similar across samples (Figure 6). However, mapping efficiency for the human and mouse brain data is higher than those for human blood data, consistent with the original research studies [39], suggesting that mapping efficiency is highly dependent upon the specific experiments producing the data.

Even though tools have similar mapping efficiency, reads that are actually mapped (i.e., mapped reads content) might differ among different programs. To examine how much difference the tools have in mapped reads content, we compared uniquely mapped reads from Bismark and BSMAP. On average, for human blood data, uniquely mapped reads shared by both Bismark and BSMAP account for approximately 97% of the total mapped reads by BSMAP and only 69% by Bismark. The numbers change little with different samples. Therefore, most of the mapped reads identified by BSMAP are also identified by Bismark. The difference in mapped reads content between Bismark and BSMAP can be caused by several factors. First, the two use different string matching strategies. Bismark uses Burrows Wheeler

transform and FM-indexes for searching and BSMAP hashes the reference genome for searching. In particular, Bismark uses aligner Bowtie2, whereas BSMAP uses aligner SOAP (older version of SOAP2) to map bisulfite short reads. As a result, difference in mapping algorithms can contribute to difference in mapped read content. According to Hatem et al. [27], Bowtie maintained the best throughput with higher mapping percentages, which could be why Bismark maps more reads than BSMAP. Second, determining whether a read is uniquely mapped is rather arbitrary and program specific [40]. Depending on how each program defines "uniquely mapped" computationally, uniquely mapped read content can vary as a result. We also examined whether combining multiple tools to analyze bisulfite short reads could improve the overall mapping efficiency. We used BSMAP and BS-Seeker to align the unmapped reads from Bismark to see how much further BSMAP and BS-Seeker can improve the overall mapping efficiency. Table 2 shows that using BSMAP to align the unmapped reads from Bismark improves the overall mapping efficiency slightly better than using BS-Seeker (BSMAP: around 4% improvement; BS-Seeker: only 1%). The lesser improvement from BS-Seeker might be due to the fact that both Bismark and BS-Seeker use Bowtie to align reads although they may have different criteria in postprocessing the mapped reads. Overall, results across different datasets indicate that Bismark was able to identify the most uniquely mapped reads, and addition of more programs does not significantly improve mapping efficiency.

4.2. Effect of Varying Parameters in Different Tools. We mainly focus on how changing numbers of allowed mismatches between reads and the reference genome affects mapping efficiency. Different programs have parameters that serve this purpose but sometimes have different meanings. For example, BSMAP has the option of setting the number of mismatches allowed in each short read using the parameter **v**. If **v** is between 0 and 1, it is interpreted as the mismatch rate with respect to the read length. Otherwise it is interpreted

TABLE 2: Improvement in mapping efficiency after using BSMAP and BS-Seeker to map unmapped reads from Bismark on human blood data.

File name	Total number of reads	Unmapped reads in BISMARK	Overall improvement using BSMAP	Overall improvement using BS-Seeker
SRR342552	23,472,574	10512269	3.72%	0.90%
SRR342553	23,749,583	10610307	4.24%	1.03%
SRR342554	25,232,053	11277407	4.29%	1.07%
SRR342555	23,750,428	10452979	4.23%	1.01%
SRR342556	23,140,352	10204603	4.28%	1.06%
SRR342557	23,089,492	10093756	4.33%	1.05%
SRR342558	21,205,564	9215604	4.26%	1.04%
SRR342560	26,174,056	11491673	4.17%	1.01%
SRR342561	25,457,341	11271400	4.16%	1.02%

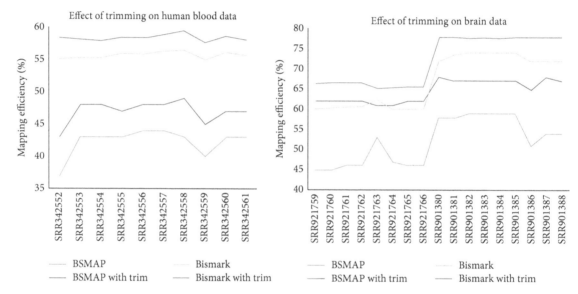

FIGURE 5: The effect of trimming reads on mapping efficiency on ten human blood, ten human brain, and eight mouse brain datasets for BSMAP and Bismark.

as the maximum number of mismatches allowed in a read. The default is 0.08. The maximum number of mismatches allowed is 15 per read. BiSS has the option of setting the number of mismatches allowed in each short read using the parameter **i** (minimum identity between a read and a match) ranging from 0 to 1. The default setting is 0.65, meaning 65% of a read and its corresponding match are identical. All reads mapped with an identity lower than this threshold will be reported as unmapped. Our results on changing these parameters show that, in general, the mapping efficiency increases with the number of mismatches. The results are consistent across datasets and for all the programs tested. For brevity, only the results from BS-Seeker were used to illustrate (Figure 4). BS-Seeker has the option of setting the number of mismatches allowed in each short read using the parameter **m**. The default is 2 and the maximum number allowed is 3. Figure 4 shows that with the number of mismatches allowed increasing from 0 to 3, mapping efficiency increases by 43%–60%. Worth noting is that with mapping efficiency increasing, CPU running time also increases significantly. Therefore, in

real practice, though it is desirable to have high mapping efficiency, CPU time is another important aspect that users need to consider before running the programs. Sometimes cost of having high mapping efficiency becomes inhibitive as it takes too much running time. For example, when we changed Bismark's allowed mismatches from 0 to 1, the time it takes to finish the program doubles (e.g., increased from 657 to 1581 minutes to run on sample SRR342553). Another important aspect to consider is that increasing the number of mismatches allowed also runs the risk of increased false positives, although in real practice it is difficult to determine whether mapped reads having mismatches to the mapped location are actually false positives or real variants from the reference genome.

4.3. Effect of Data Preprocessing. We also preprocessed the reads and used those tools to analyze the trimmed data. Around 2%–4.5% of the blood data and around 1.1%–2.3% were trimmed on the brain data. Figure 5 shows that the mapping efficiency increases by around 5% for BSMAP and

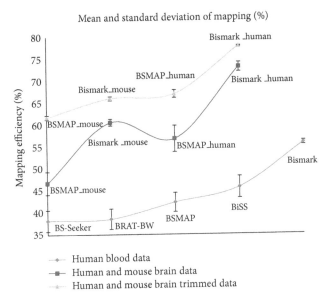

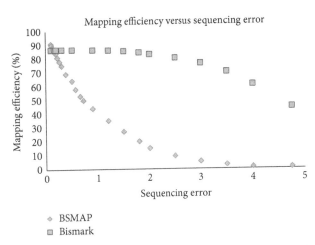

FIGURE 7: The effect of sequencing error on mapping efficiency for BSMAP and Bismark using simulated data generated from Sherman simulator with varying sequencing error from 0.1 to 4.75% (e.g., sequencing error 0.1% means 1 error in every 1000 bases) for read length = 101 bp, CG = 10% (10% of all CG-cytosines will be converted into thymines), and CH = 98.5% (98.5% of all CH-cytosines will be converted into thymines).

FIGURE 6: Mean and standard deviations of mapping percentages across ten human blood, ten human brain, and eight mouse brain datasets.

around 3% for Bismark on the human blood data and by around 10% for BSMAP and around 6% for Bismark on the human fetal brain and mouse brain data. Therefore, preprocessing reads before mapping is an effective approach to improve mapping efficiency.

4.4. Effect of Read Length and Sequencing Error. We used simulated data to see the effect of sequencing error and read length on mapping efficiency. Sequencing error has been found to be an important factor influencing the performance of short reads mapping tools [3]. Consistent with previous finding, our result shows that for both BSMAP and Bismark, as sequencing error increases, mapping efficiency decreases (Figure 7). Comparatively, BSMAP is more sensitive to sequencing error than Bismark as the BSMAP's mapping efficiency decays exponentially with the increase of sequencing error, while Bismark's only gradually.

Read length is another important factor in short reads mapping. Figure 8 shows opposite patterns for BSMAP and Bismark. For BSMAP, as read length increases from 40 to 140 bps, mapping efficiency decreases but with read length above 140 bps, an increase in read length results in an increase in mapping efficiency. On the other hand, unique mapping efficiency from BISMARK increases as read lengths increase consistently. It is unclear what contributes to the pattern exhibited by BSMAP.

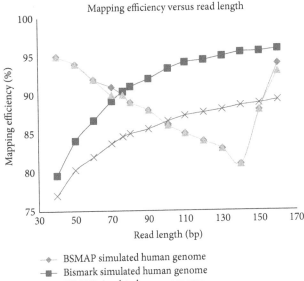

FIGURE 8: The effect of read length on mapping efficiency for BSMAP and Bismark using simulated data generated from Sherman simulator with different read lengths (from 40 to 160 bps) for sequencing error e = 0.16, CG = 10%, and CH = 98.5% for mouse and e = 0.16, CG = 19.73%, and CH = 98.9% for human.

5. Conclusion

Many bisulfite short read mapping tools are available and choosing the best one among them is a difficult task. In our experiments, even though Bismark produced the highest unique mapping efficiency on real data, its CPU running time was not the shortest. BRAT-BW ran the fastest on real data

but with lower mapping efficiency. Also, preprocessing data before mapping can increase mapping efficiency regardless of what tools are used. Changing parameters in the program can affect the mapping results. Overall, as number of mismatches increases, mapping efficiency increases. Short reads length and sequencing error can affect the results. Bismark is more sensitive to read lengths. The longer the read length, the higher the mapping efficiency for Bismark, whereas there is no clear pattern for BSMAP. BSMAP is more sensitive to sequencing error. A small increase in sequencing error can result in significant decrease in mapping efficiency from BSMAP.

Conflict of Interests

The authors declare that there is no conflict of interests regarding the publication of this paper.

References

[1] P. M. Das and R. Singal, "DNA methylation and cancer," *Journal of Clinical Oncology*, vol. 22, no. 22, pp. 4632–4642, 2004.

[2] P. A. Jones and D. Takai, "The role of DNA methylation in mammalian epigenetics," *Science*, vol. 293, no. 5532, pp. 1068–1070, 2001.

[3] H. Li, J. Ruan, and R. Durbin, "Mapping short DNA sequencing reads and calling variants using mapping quality scores," *Genome Research*, vol. 18, no. 11, pp. 1851–1858, 2008.

[4] F. Krueger and S. R. Andrews, "Bismark: a flexible aligner and methylation caller for Bisulfite-Seq applications," *Bioinformatics*, vol. 27, no. 11, pp. 1571–1572, 2011.

[5] Y. Xi and W. Li, "BSMAP: whole genome bisulfite sequence MAPping program," *BMC Bioinformatics*, vol. 10, article 232, 2009.

[6] C. Coarfa, F. Yu, C. A. Miller, Z. Chen, R. A. Harris, and A. Milosavljevic, "Pash 3.0: a versatile software package for read mapping and integrative analysis of genomic and epigenomic variation using massively parallel DNA sequencing," *BMC Bioinformatics*, vol. 11, article 572, 2010.

[7] A. D. Smith, W. Chung, E. Hodges et al., "Updates to the RMAP short-read mapping software," *Bioinformatics*, vol. 25, no. 21, pp. 2841–2842, 2009.

[8] T. D. Wu and S. Nacu, "Fast and SNP-tolerant detection of complex variants and splicing in short reads," *Bioinformatics*, vol. 26, no. 7, pp. 873–881, 2010.

[9] C. Hercus, "Novocraft short read alignment package," 2009, http://www.novocraft.com.

[10] N. Homer, "Bfast: Blat-like fast accurate search tool," 2009.

[11] E. Y. Harris, N. Ponts, A. Levchuk, K. L. Roch, and S. Lonardi, "BRAT: bisulfite-treated reads analysis tool," *Bioinformatics*, vol. 26, no. 4, pp. 572–573, 2010.

[12] B. Pedersen, T. Hsieh, C. Ibarra, and R. L. Fischer, "Methyl-Coder: software pipeline for bisulte-treated sequences," *Bioinformatics*, vol. 27, no. 17, pp. 2435–2436, 2011.

[13] S. J. Cokus, S. Feng, X. Zhang et al., "Shotgun bisulphite sequencing of the Arabidopsis genome reveals DNA methylation patterning," *Nature*, vol. 452, no. 7184, pp. 215–219, 2008.

[14] P. Chen, S. J. Cokus, and M. Pellegrini, "BS Seeker: precise mapping for bisulfite sequencing," *BMC Bioinformatics*, vol. 11, no. 1, article 203, 2010.

[15] W. Guo, P. Fiziev, W. Yan et al., "BS-Seeker2: a versatile aligning pipeline for bisulfite sequencing data," *BMC Genomics*, vol. 14, no. 1, article 774, 2013.

[16] S. Hoffmann, C. Otto, S. Kurtz et al., "Fast mapping of short sequences with mismatches, insertions and deletions using index structures," *PLoS Computational Biology*, vol. 5, no. 9, Article ID e1000502, 2009.

[17] H. Q. Dinh, M. Dubin, F. J. Sedlazeck et al., "Advanced methylome analysis after bisulfite deep sequencing: an example in Arabidopsis," *PLoS ONE*, vol. 7, no. 7, Article ID e41528, 2012.

[18] J. Q. Lim, C. Tennakoon, G. Li et al., "BatMeth: improved mapper for bisulfite sequencing reads on DNA methylation," *Genome Biology*, vol. 13, article R82, 2012.

[19] N. Prezza, C. del Fabbro, F. Vezzi, E. de Paoli, and A. Policriti, "ERNE-BS5: aligning BS-treated sequences by multiple hits on a 5-letters alphabet," in *Proceedings of the ACM Conference on Bioinformatics, Computational Biology and Biomedicine*, ACM, 2012.

[20] B. Langmead, C. Trapnell, M. Pop, and S. L. Salzberg, "Ultrafast and memory-efficient alignment of short DNA sequences to the human genome," *Genome Biology*, vol. 10, no. 3, article R25, 2009.

[21] B. Langmead and S. L. Salzberg, "Fast gapped-read alignment with Bowtie 2," *Nature Methods*, vol. 9, no. 4, pp. 357–359, 2012.

[22] W. J. Kent, "BLAT: the BLAST-like alignment tool," *Genome Research*, vol. 12, no. 4, pp. 656–664, 2002.

[23] R. Li, Y. Li, K. Kristiansen, and J. Wang, "SOAP: short oligonucleotide alignment program," *Bioinformatics*, vol. 24, no. 5, pp. 713–714, 2008.

[24] H. Li and R. Durbin, "Fast and accurate short read alignment with Burrows-Wheeler transform," *Bioinformatics*, vol. 25, no. 14, pp. 1754–1760, 2009.

[25] N. A. Fonseca, J. Rung, A. Brazma, and J. C. Marioni, "Tools for mapping high-throughput sequencing data," *Bioinformatics*, vol. 28, no. 24, pp. 3169–3177, 2012.

[26] A. Chatterjee, P. A. Stockwell, E. J. Rodger, and I. M. Moriso, "Comparison of alignment software for genome-wide bisulphite sequence data," *Nucleic Acids Research*, vol. 40, no. 10, pp. e79–e79, 2012.

[27] A. Hatem, D. Bozdag, A. E. Toland, and U. V. Catalyürek, "Benchmarking short sequence mapping tools," *BMC Bioinformatics*, vol. 14, no. 1, article 184, 2013.

[28] H. Li and N. Homer, "A survey of sequence alignment algorithms for next-generation sequencing," *Briefings in Bioinformatics*, vol. 11, no. 5, pp. 473–483, 2010.

[29] N. Homer, B. Merriman, and S. F. Nelson, "BFAST: an alignment tool for large scale genome resequencing," *PLoS ONE*, vol. 4, no. 11, Article ID e7767, 2009.

[30] F. J. Sedlazeck, P. Rescheneder, and A. von Haeseler, "NextGenMap: fast and accurate read mapping in highly polymorphic genomes," *Bioinformatics*, vol. 29, no. 21, pp. 2790–2791, 2013.

[31] P. Ferragina and G. Manzini, "Opportunistic data structures with applications," in *Proceedings of the 41st Annual Symposium on Foundations of Computer Science (FOCS '00)*, pp. 390–398, November 2000.

[32] E. Y. Harris, N. Ponts, K. G. Le Roch, and S. Lonardi, "BRAT-BW: efficient and accurate mapping of bisulfite-treated reads," *Bioinformatics*, vol. 28, no. 13, pp. 1795–1796, 2012.

[33] http://www.ncbi.nlm.nih.gov/sra.

[34] http://www.ncbi.nlm.nih.gov/geo/.

[35] http://www.bioinformatics.babraham.ac.uk/projects/sherman/.

[36] A. E. Minoche, J. C. Dohm, and H. Himmelbauer, "Evaluation of genomic high-throughput sequencing data generated on Illumina HiSeq and Genome Analyzer systems," *Genome Biology*, vol. 12, no. 11, article R112, 2011.

[37] http://www.ensembl.org/info/data/ftp/index.html.

[38] http://www.biostars.org/p/59281/.

[39] R. Lister, E. A. Mukamel, J. R. Nery et al., "Global epigenomic reconfiguration during mammalian brain development," *Science*, vol. 341, no. 6146, Article ID 1237905, 2013.

[40] C. Trapnell and S. L. Salzberg, "How to map billions of short reads onto genomes," *Nature Biotechnology*, vol. 27, no. 5, pp. 455–457, 2009.

Permissions

The contributors of this book come from diverse backgrounds, making this book a truly international effort. This book will bring forth new frontiers with its revolutionizing research information and detailed analysis of the nascent developments around the world.

We would like to thank all the contributing authors for lending their expertise to make the book truly unique. They have played a crucial role in the development of this book. Without their invaluable contributions this book wouldn't have been possible. They have made vital efforts to compile up to date information on the varied aspects of this subject to make this book a valuable addition to the collection of many professionals and students.

This book was conceptualized with the vision of imparting up-to-date information and advanced data in this field. To ensure the same, a matchless editorial board was set up. Every individual on the board went through rigorous rounds of assessment to prove their worth. After which they invested a large part of their time researching and compiling the most relevant data for our readers. Conferences and sessions were held from time to time between the editorial board and the contributing authors to present the data in the most comprehensible form. The editorial team has worked tirelessly to provide valuable and valid information to help people across the globe.

Every chapter published in this book has been scrutinized by our experts. Their significance has been extensively debated. The topics covered herein carry significant findings which will fuel the growth of the discipline. They may even be implemented as practical applications or may be referred to as a beginning point for another development. Chapters in this book were first published by Hindawi Publishing Corporation; hereby published with permission under the Creative Commons Attribution License or equivalent.

The editorial board has been involved in producing this book since its inception. They have spent rigorous hours researching and exploring the diverse topics which have resulted in the successful publishing of this book. They have passed on their knowledge of decades through this book. To expedite this challenging task, the publisher supported the team at every step. A small team of assistant editors was also appointed to further simplify the editing procedure and attain best results for the readers.

Our editorial team has been hand-picked from every corner of the world. Their multi-ethnicity adds dynamic inputs to the discussions which result in innovative outcomes. These outcomes are then further discussed with the researchers and contributors who give their valuable feedback and opinion regarding the same. The feedback is then collaborated with the researches and they are edited in a comprehensive manner to aid the understanding of the subject.

Apart from the editorial board, the designing team has also invested a significant amount of their time in understanding the subject and creating the most relevant covers. They scrutinized every image to scout for the most suitable representation of the subject and create an appropriate cover for the book.

The publishing team has been involved in this book since its early stages. They were actively engaged in every process, be it collecting the data, connecting with the contributors or procuring relevant information. The team has been an ardent support to the editorial, designing and production team. Their endless efforts to recruit the best for this project, has resulted in the accomplishment of this book. They are a veteran in the field of academics and their pool of knowledge is as vast as their experience in printing. Their expertise and guidance has proved useful at every step. Their uncompromising quality standards have made this book an exceptional effort. Their encouragement from time to time has been an inspiration for everyone.

The publisher and the editorial board hope that this book will prove to be a valuable piece of knowledge for researchers, students, practitioners and scholars across the globe.

List of Contributors

Martin Mann
Bioinformatics, University of Freiburg, Georges-Kohler Allee 106, 79110 Freiburg im Breisgau, Germany
Theoretical Biochemistry, University of Vienna, Wahringerstraße 17, 1090 Vienna, Austria

Cameron Smith and Rolf Backofen
Bioinformatics, University of Freiburg, Georges-Kohler Allee 106, 79110 Freiburg im Breisgau, Germany

Rhodri Saunders and Charlotte M. Deane
Department of Statistics, Oxford University, 1 South Parks Road, Oxford OX1 3TG, UK

Philippe Serhal
Institute for Research in Immunology and Cancer (IRIC), Universite de Montreal, C.P. 6128, Succursale Centre-Ville, Montreal, QC, Canada

Sébastien Lemieux
Institute for Research in Immunology and Cancer (IRIC), Universite de Montreal, C.P. 6128, Succursale Centre-Ville, Montreal, QC, Canada
Department of Computer Science and Operations Research, Universite de Montreal, C.P. 6128, Succursale Centre-Ville, Montreal, QC, Canada

Yunyun Zhou
School of Electrical Engineering and Computer Science, Washington State University, P.O. Box 642752, Pullman, WA 99164-2752, USA

Shira L. Broschat
School of Electrical Engineering and Computer Science, Washington State University, P.O. Box 642752, Pullman, WA 99164-2752, USA
Paul G. Allen School for Global Animal Health, Washington State University, P.O. Box 642752, Pullman, WA 99164-2752, USA
Department of Veterinary Microbiology and Pathology, Washington State University, P.O. Box 642752, Pullman, WA 99164-2752, USA

Douglas R. Call
School of Electrical Engineering and Computer Science, Washington State University, P.O. Box 642752, Pullman, WA 99164-2752, USA
Paul G. Allen School for Global Animal Health, Washington State University, P.O. Box 642752, Pullman, WA 99164-2752, USA

Gaetano Pierro
System Biology, PhD School, University of Salerno, Via Ponte Don Melillo, 84084 Fisciano, Italy

Alain Denise and Claire Herrbach
LRI, UMR 8623 CNRS, Universite Paris-Sud and INRIA Saclay, 91405 Orsay Cedex, France
IGM, CNRS UMR 8621, Universite Paris-Sud, 91405 Orsay Cedex, France

Julien Allali and Pascal Ferraro
LaBRI, UMR 5800 CNRS, Universite Bordeaux, 351, Cours de la Liberation, 33405 Talence Cedex, France
The Pacific Institute for the Mathematical Sciences, University of British Columbia, CNRS UMI 3069, 200-1933 West Mall Vancouver, BC, Canada

Cedric Saule
LRI, UMR 8623 CNRS, Universite Paris-Sud and INRIA Saclay, 91405 Orsay Cedex, France

Cedric Chauve
Department of Mathematics, Simon Fraser University, 8888 University drive, Burnaby, BC, Canada

Claude Thermes and Yves d'Aubenton-Carafa
Centre de Genetique Moleculaire, UPR 3404 CNRS, Avenue de la Terrasse, Bat. 26, 91198 Gif-Sur Yvette, France

Michel Termier, Daniel Gautheret and Christine Drevet
IGM, CNRS UMR 8621, Universite Paris-Sud, 91405 Orsay Cedex, France

Fabrice Leclerc
MAEM, CNRS UMR 7567, Universite Henri Poincare, 1 Boulevard des Aiguillettes, BP 239, 54506 Vandoeuvre-Les-Nancy Cedex, France

Helene Touzet, Aida Ouangraoua and Antoine de Monte
LIFL, CNRS UMR 8022, Universite Lille 1 and INRIA, 59655 Lille Cedex, France

Marie-France Sagot
Inria Rhone-Alpes and LBBE, UMR5558 CNRS, Universite Claude Bernard, Bat. Gregor Mendel, 43 Boulevard du 11Novembre 1918, 69622 Villeurbanne Cedex, France

Tomas Hruz and Christoph Lucas
Institute of Theoretical Computer Science, ETH Zurich, 8092 Zurich, Switzerland

Oliver Laule, Markus Wyss, Peter von Rohr, Philip Zimmermann and Stefan Bleuler
NEBION AG, Hohlstraße 515, 8048 Zurich, Switzerland

Gaston K. Mazandu and Nicola J. Mulder
Computational Biology Group, Department of Clinical Laboratory Sciences, Institute of Infectious Disease and Molecular Medicine, University of Cape Town, Cape Town 7925, South Africa

Amina Noor and Erchin Serpedin
Electrical and Computer Engineering Department, Texas A&M University, College Station, TX 77843-3128, USA

Mohamed Nounou
Chemical Engineering Department, Texas A&M University at Qatar, 253 Texas A&M Engineering Building, Education City, P.O. Box 23874, Doha, Qatar

Hazem Nounou
Electrical Engineering Department, Texas A&M University at Qatar, 253 Texas A&M Engineering Building, Education City, P.O. Box 23874, Doha, Qatar

Nady Mohamed and Lotfi Chouchane
Department of Genetic Medicine, Weill Cornell Medical College in Qatar, P.O. Box 24144, Doha, Qatar

Ning Zhang
Department of Biomedical Engineering, Tianjin University, Tianjin Key Lab of BME Measurement, Tianjin 300072, China

Shan Gao and Jishou Ruan
College of Mathematical Sciences and LPKM, Nankai University, Tianjin 300071, China

Tao Zhang and Lei Zhang
College of Life Sciences, Nankai University, Tianjin 300071, China

J. Paul Brooks
Center for the Study of Biological Complexity, Virginia Commonwealth University, P.O. Box 843083, Richmond, VA 23284, USA
Department of Statistical Sciences and Operations Research, Virginia Commonwealth University, P.O. Box 843083, Richmond, VA 23284, USA

William P. Burns
Center for the Study of Biological Complexity, Virginia Commonwealth University, P.O. Box 843083, Richmond, VA 23284, USA

Stephen S. Fong, Chris M. Gowen and Seth B. Roberts
Center for the Study of Biological Complexity, Virginia Commonwealth University, P.O. Box 843083, Richmond, VA 23284, USA
Department of Chemical and Life Science Engineering, Virginia Commonwealth University, P.O. Box 843083, Richmond, VA 23284, USA

Amina Noor and Erchin Serpedin
Department of Electrical and Computer Engineering, Texas A&M University, College Station, TX 77843-3128, USA

Mohamed Nounou
Chemical Engineering Department, Texas A&M University at Qatar, 253 Texas A&M Engineering Building, Education City, P.O. Box 23874, Doha, Qatar

Hazem Nounou
Electrical Engineering Department, Texas A&M University at Qatar, 253 Texas A&M Engineering Building, Education City, P.O. Box 23874, Doha, Qatar

Kwadwo S. Agyepong, Fang-Han Hsu and Erchin Serpedin
Department of Electrical and Computer Engineering, Texas A&M University, College Station, TX 77843-3128, USA

Edward R. Dougherty
Department of Electrical and Computer Engineering, Texas A&M University, College Station, TX 77843-3128, USA
Computational Biology Division, Translational Genomics Research Institute, Phoenix, AZ 85004-2101, USA

Amine Ghozlane and Patricia Thebault
Laboratoire Bordelais de Recherche en Informatique, UMR CNRS 5800, Universite Bordeaux,
351 Cours de la Liberation, 33405 Talence Cedex, France
Centre de Bioinformatique de Bordeaux, Universite Bordeaux Segalen, 142 Rue Leo Saignat, 33076 Bordeaux Cedex, France

Isabelle Dutour
Laboratoire Bordelais de Recherche en Informatique, UMR CNRS 5800, Universite Bordeaux,
351 Cours de la Liberation, 33405 Talence Cedex, France

Frederic Bringaud
Centre de Resonance Magnetique des Systemes Biologiques, UMR 5536, Universite Bordeaux Segalen, CNRS, 146 rue Leo Saignat, 33076 Bordeaux, France

Hayssam Soueidan
The Netherlands Cancer Institute, Plesmanlaan 121, 1066 CX Amsterdam, The Netherlands

Fabien Jourdan
Institut National de Recherche en Agronomie, UMR 1331 TOXALIM, 180 Chemin de Tournefeuille, 31027 Toulouse, France

Natsu Nakajima and Tatsuya Akutsu
Bioinformatics Center, Institute for Chemical Research, Kyoto University, Gokasho, Uji, Kyoto 611-0011, Japan

Tatyana Aleksandrovna Khrustaleva
Regulatory Proteins and Peptides Laboratory, Institute of Physiology of the National Academy of Sciences of Belarus, Akademicheskaya 28, 220072 Minsk, Belarus

Mahmood A. Rashid, Swakkhar Shatabda and M. A. and Abdul Sattar
Institute for Integrated & Intelligent Systems, Science 2 (N34) 1.45, 170 Kessels Road, Nathan, QLD 4111, Australia
Queensland Research Lab, National ICT Australia, Level 8, Y Block, 2 George Street, Brisbane, QLD 4000, Australia

Md Tamjidul Hoque
Computer Science, 2000 Lakeshore Drive, Math 308, New Orleans, LA 70148, USA

Hakim Newton
Institute for Integrated & Intelligent Systems, Science 2 (N34) 1.45, 170 Kessels Road, Nathan, QLD 4111, Australia

Rajadurai Chinnasamy Perumal, Ashok Selvaraj and Gopal Ramesh Kumar
Bioinformatics Lab, AU-KBC Research Centre, M.I.T Campus of Anna University, Chromepet, Chennai, Tamil Nadu 600 044, India

Morris S. Jones and J. Mark Carter
Western Regional Research Center, Agricultural Research Service, U.S. Department of Agriculture, 800 Buchanan Street, Albany, CA 94710, USA

Hong Tran, Jacob Porter and Liqing Zhang
Department of Computer Science, Virginia Tech, Blacksburg, VA 24061, USA

Ming-an Sun and Hehuang Xie
Virginia Bioinformatics Institute, Virginia Tech, Blacksburg, VA 24061, USA

Printed in the USA
CPSIA information can be obtained
at www.ICGtesting.com
JSHW051439221024
72173JS00006B/1516